SEVEN YEARS THAT CHANGED THE WORLD

Perestroika in Perspective

ARCHIE BROWN

OXFORD

UNIVERSITY PRESS

OXFORD
UNIVERSITY PRESS

Great Clarendon Street, Oxford OX2 6DP

Oxford University Press is a department of the University of Oxford.
It furthers the University's objective of excellence in research, scholarship,
and education by publishing worldwide in

Oxford New York

Auckland   Cape Town Dar es Salaam   Hong Kong   Karachi
Kuala Lumpur Madrid Melbourne Mexico City   Nairobi
New Delhi Shanghai Taipei Toronto
With offices in
Argentina Austria Brazil Chile Czech Republic France Greece
Guatemala Hungary Italy Japan South Korea Poland Portugal
Singapore Switzerland Thailand Turkey Ukraine Vietnam

Oxford is a registered trade mark of Oxford University Press
in the UK and in certain other countries

Published in the United States
by Oxford University Press Inc., New York

ISBN 978-0-19-956245-9

Printed in the United Kingdom by
the MPG Books Group Ltd

To Pat

Contents

Preface

This book is divided into three parts. Parts I and III have been written with the benefit of hindsight and with access to the vast store of new information about the last years of the Soviet Union which has become available since that state disappeared from the political map of the world. Part II consists of analyses written in 'real time'. That is to say, this section of the book contains articles—or in one case, a book chapter—written while the dramatic changes in the Soviet Union during the second half of the 1980s were still underway.

I am very grateful to Dominic Byatt, Chief Editor at Oxford University Press, for his support, advice, and patience. I am indebted both to him and to the four readers who advised the Press, and whose identities are not known to me, for concluding that the articles published some twenty years ago are worth republishing. They also concluded that, taken together with chapters written on the basis of what we know today, they would make up a coherent whole. In the organization of the book, I have taken on board several useful suggestions contained in the anonymous readers' reports.

The only changes I have made to the text of those pieces written in the second half of the 1980s, and now republished, are a very few small cuts to eliminate repetitions. I have, however, put in some additional footnotes and those are printed in italics to avoid any confusion between what is written using the information available today and the text as it was originally published. The new footnotes are either (*a*) to correct a misunderstanding or introduce a clarification or (*b*) to update the story with information which has recently become available, especially from the archives. I have neither added nor subtracted anything in order to pretend to a greater foresight than I possessed when writing in the Soviet era.

This book does not purport to be a comprehensive history of the years between 1985 and 1991 in the Soviet Union. Although quite long, it is still considerably shorter than my earlier volume, *The Gorbachev Factor*, published by Oxford University Press in 1996. It is an interpretation of perestroika, understood as a radical reform or 'revolution from above' (as Aleksandr Yakovlev and others have described it) initiated by Mikhail Gorbachev and a handful of allies in the leadership of the Communist Party of the Soviet Union in the mid-1980s. The views of these leaders on the required scope of the changes evolved greatly in some cases and stayed within narrow limits in others. Perestroika meant not only different things to different people but also different things at different times between its launch and its demise.

That was clear even when the changes were in progress, as I note in Chapters 4 and 5. Part II of the book shows how things appeared to me at the time. As a result of the greater openness of Soviet society after 1985 it was possible to follow what was happening in greater depth and detail than could be done in earlier decades while the events were actually unfolding. Up until at least the mid-1980s a certain amount of detective work and reading between the lines was required. The longer perestroika continued, the less this was needed. Yet, Chapters 2 to 5 are written with access to fewer sources than I had available in the mid-1990s when I completed *The Gorbachev Factor*. By then there was already quite a rich memoir literature and much first-hand material gleaned from interviews.

However, Parts I and III of the present volume benefit from access to still more sources than I had when I was working on *The Gorbachev Factor*. Revealing memoirs have continued to be published and in the present volume I am using archival sources on perestroika which I had not seen when writing the earlier book. These include Politburo transcripts, both the detailed notes of Gorbachev's aides—Anatoliy Chernayev and Georgiy Shakhnazarov as well as Politburo member Vadim Medvedev—and the working record (*rabochaya zapis'*) of Politburo meetings. Many of the latter are to be found in the archive known as Fond 89. That is a selection from the materials located in the Presidential Archive in Moscow. It was made available for perusal on the instructions of President Boris Yeltsin in 1992 and presented to the Constitutional Court of the Russian Federation as part of the attempt to put the Communist Party on trial and to demonstrate that they 'showed a complete disregard for human rights and international law'.[1] Fond 89 contains more than 3,000 documents covering the period from 1919 to the end of the Soviet Union. It is available in Moscow in the Russian State Archive of Contemporary History (RGANI) and also in microfilm in several major Western libraries. I have used it in the National Security Archive in Washington and (especially) in the Hoover Institution Archive at Stanford University. Extracts from the Politburo transcripts are also to be found in the Volkogonov Collection, which I have consulted in the National Security Archive. There is no complete set of transcripts of Politburo meetings for the period 1985–91 currently available to researchers, but I have been able to read a very substantial number.

The provenance of the records of Politburo meetings requires special consideration. Very few scholars, especially those who have written about domestic Soviet politics in the Gorbachev era, have used the Politburo

---

[1] Vladimir P. Kozlov and Charles G. Palm, 'Foreword' to Lora Soroka (ed.), *Fond 89: Communist Party of the Soviet Union on Trial* (Hoover Institution Press, Stanford University, Stanford, CA, 2001), p. ix.

minutes. The main exceptions have been people working in the field of international relations, particularly those concerned with the Cold War and its ending. The minutes have been taken at face value and no one, to my knowledge, has paid attention to the process by which they were compiled and approved. This, as I have discovered, is not a straightforward matter. In the text I use both the 'official' *rabochaya zapis'*—with many of those working records available in Fond 89 and some also in the Volkogonov Collection—and those compiled by associates of Mikhail Gorbachev (in particular, Anatoliy Chernyaev) and kept in the Gorbachev Foundation. I have found no internal evidence of distortion or grounds to doubt the reliability of either. Yet, we should be aware of the possibilities of bias, at least in the *selection* of what is recorded in these transcripts, both in the Gorbachev Foundation archival materials and, especially, in the case of the more 'official' records.[2]

No stenographers were allowed inside Politburo meetings, though the hall in which the Politburo met was large enough to accommodate about eighty people. Those who attended (without the right to speak) included the aides of the General Secretary. Politburo members themselves, as Anatoliy Chernyaev has pointed out, were aware of a strict prohibition, dating from Stalin's time, not only on stenographic records but on any kind of note-taking in sessions of the Politburo.[3] If, as seems probable, Gorbachev was conscious of this un-written rule, he turned a blind eye to it. His aides, Chernyaev and Shakhna-zarov as well as Politburo ally, Vadim Medvedev, were, indeed, the most assiduous note-takers.[4] There is no reason to doubt the integrity of the notes taken and transcribed by those three attendees at Politburo sessions. From my reading of the transcripts, I would say that the only bias is that the note-takers were more interested in capturing as fully as possible what Gorbachev had to say than in recording in similar detail the contributions of every other member of the Politburo. Occasionally, there is just a name of another Politburo member who spoke with no account given of what he said. Since Gorbachev's aides were *not* writing official minutes, but looking for policy pointers and guides to action, the gaps are fully understandable.

---

[2] I put 'official' in inverted commas, for though the Politburo transcripts kept in the Russian state archives would appear thereby to count as official, secrecy surrounded the way in which they were recorded as well as their content, with even Politburo members not given access to the full versions. For help in throwing light on the way in which Politburo transcripts were compiled and approved, I am especially grateful to Anatoliy Chernyaev, Alexey Gromyko, and Olga Zdravomyslova.

[3] Personal communication from Anatoliy Chernayev dated 14 July 2006.

[4] Notes at the meetings were evidently taken also by Politburo member Vitaliy Vorotnikov who incorporates some of them in his diary-based book, *A bylo eto tak... Iz dnevnika chlena Politbyuro TsK KPSS* (Sovet veteranov knigoizdaniya, Moscow, 1995).

Gorbachev's views were more significant in that context than the opinions of any other member of the Politburo, given the hierarchical nature of the system. Chernyaev, Shakhnazarov, and Medvedev were themselves serious reformers who were, and who remained, strongly supportive of Gorbachev. That may, however, have had the effect that their notes underplayed the reservations about Gorbachev's policies expressed by other members of the Politburo, especially since those interventions rarely took the form of outright opposition but were almost invariably couched in diplomatic language. While a variety of opinions certainly emerge in the Gorbachev Foundation transcripts, less space is devoted to the views of the conservative members of the Politburo than is to be found in the 'official' records.[5]

The 'official' working record of the Politburo proceedings was made under the supervision of the head of the General Department of the Central Committee of the CPSU—the department through which all documents (including letters from citizens to the Central Committee or General Secretary)—passed. The departmental head *may*, it seems, have been greatly assisted in this task by the secret recording of the proceedings for stenographers.[6] On one version of the process by which the recordings were made, the stenographers worked in a room below the hall in which the Politburo met and had the proceedings transmitted to them. On another, they worked from a cassette.[7] What seems to be clear is that stenographers worked in a separate room and *recorded verbatim* sessions of the *Central Committee* and also of meetings of the *Presidium of the Supreme Soviet*. This was *not* supposed to happen with meetings of the *Politburo* and if a cassette was, indeed, given to stenographers, that was highly unofficial. Yet, that there were note-takers who were not in the room in which Politburo meetings were held is suggested by the fact that some speakers are identified simply as *Golos* (voice). That lends credibility to the idea that stenographers were involved since, not being present, they are sometimes unable to identify a particular contributor to the discussion. Normally, the task of any note-taker was simplified by the fact

[5] The notes by Chernyaev and his colleagues are undoubtedly a significant source of illumination for students of late Soviet politics. A broader readership will be able to judge their value for themselves, for, just as this book was going to press, about two-thirds of these materials were published in Russian in a book entitled *V Politbyuro TsK KPSS... Po zapisyam A. Chernyaeva, V. Medvedeva i G. Shakhnazarova* (Al'pina Biznes Buks, Moscow, 2006).

[6] Personal communication of 14 July 2006 from Anatoliy Chernyaev. Information I have received independently from Alexey Gromyko suggests that the meetings were, indeed, recorded. However, in another personal communication, Olga Zdravomyslova reports the stenographers telling her that Politburo *protokoly* were dictated to them by the head of the General Department of the Central Committee two days after the Politburo meetings and that they were not listening in to Politburo sessions.

[7] Anatoliy Chernyaev says the stenographers 'transmitted the text from cassette to paper' (ibid.).

that Gorbachev, when chairing the Politburo meetings, would call upon the next person to speak by using his first name and patronymic.

Whether or not stenographers were involved in taking notes of Politburo meetings—and the evidence so far is conflicting—it is clear that it would not be left to them to decide what remained on the record and what did not. In fact, the institutional aspect of this was revealed by Valeriy Boldin in his critical account of his years working with Mikhail Gorbachev published more than a decade ago.[8] Describing the seating plan at Politburo meetings, he wrote: 'To the left of M.S. Gorbachev was a table at which the head and first deputy head of the General Department worked. They kept the working record (*rabochaya zapis'*).'[9]

The fact that it was the head of the General Department who was in charge of the record-keeping is of political significance, for the successive heads of that department during the Gorbachev era were Anatoliy Lukyanov and Valeriy Boldin, with Boldin succeeding Lukyanov in 1987. What they had in common, apart from heading this department, was that they were both parties to the coup against Gorbachev in August 1991 and spent, as a result, some time in prison. In the early part of the perestroika period, it is reasonable to assume that both were loyal to Gorbachev, but with the radicalization of the agenda for change from 1988 onwards their increasing disenchantment brought them closer to more conservative forces within the leadership. Boldin had been an aide to Gorbachev from 1981 until his promotion to head the General Department in 1987, in which capacity he still worked closely with the General Secretary. After Gorbachev became President of the USSR in March 1990, he appointed Boldin as his chief of staff. Not surprisingly, his defection in 1991 was seen by Gorbachev and those close to him as a particularly bitter betrayal.

On Boldin's own account in his part-memoir, part-critical biography of Gorbachev, he was already, some years before the August 1991 showdown, resentful of the style and mistrustful of the decisions of the leader he was supposedly serving. As the person responsible for signing off the working record of the Politburo meetings in the years of most dramatic change and turmoil, it is likely that his selection of which statements to include or

---

[8] V.I. Boldin, *Krushenie p'edestala: Shtrikhi k portretu M.S. Gorbacheva* (Respublika, Moscow, 1995). Boldin's book contains many errors and falsehoods as well as some useful and accurate information. It gives a persistently distorted and negative portrait of both Gorbachev and his wife, Raisa. The book has, therefore, to be used with extreme caution. There seems, though, no reason to doubt the accuracy of Boldin when he is describing the institutional arrangements for maintaining a record of Politburo proceedings.

[9] Ibid., p. 212. The 'official' transcripts of Politburo meetings to be found in Fond 89 and the Volkogonov Collection are headed '*Sov. sekretno. Ekz. edinstvennyy (Rabochaya zapis')*', which means 'Top Secret. One and only copy (working record)'.

exclude from the verbatim reports prepared by stenographers does no favours to Gorbachev, but gives full weight to warnings and criticisms from other members of the Politburo. In that sense, the 'official' record may be seen as complementary to the transcripts produced by Gorbachev's aides. The *rabochaya zapis'* must be regarded, though, as less than a definitive record, given Boldin's growing animosity towards his political master and the strong likelihood that this imparted a bias to his reporting. Not surprisingly, Mikhail Gorbachev himself does not believe in the 'authenticity' of the Politburo records approved by Boldin.[10] In common with the small number of other scholars who have used the 'official' minutes, I have accepted them as a valuable source of data, giving detailed information on some of the things that were said at Politburo meetings. To the extent that they should be used with caution, this is not—so far as I can judge—because of inaccurate reporting but because of possible editorial intervention and probable selection bias, especially in the crisis years of 1990–1.

It is worth noting that there were two sets of minutes of different types produced officially. The *rabochaya zapis'*, or working record, which reproduced verbatim much of what had been said by Politburo members, was not distributed to them—or even, it seems, to the General Secretary, who had a mountain of other papers to contend with. The single copy that was made was kept in the General Department of the Central Committee.[11] In addition to the working records there were, however, *protokoly* (which can also be translated as minutes or as records of the proceedings), distinguished from the *rabochie zapisi* by being guides to action. They consisted of guidelines and decisions that emerged from Politburo meetings. In contrast with the non-circulation of the accounts of what people had actually said, these documents—often in the form of an *extract* from the protocol (*Vypiska iz protokola*)—were sent to the General Secretary and to all or some members of the Politburo, depending on the relevance of the subject matter, by the Secretariat of the Central Committee. Many of these documents are also now available in the Fond 89 archive.

Politburo meetings were held on Thursdays, and Boldin dictated the texts of the *protokoly* to stenographers on Saturdays. Presumably at the same time he finalized the text of the *rabochaya zapis'*. Amid some continuing uncertainty about the methods of compiling the quite detailed accounts of the Politburo discussions to be found in the working record, now kept in RGANI, the one thing that is clear is that the head of the General Department had the last word on what went into these minutes. Thus, for the years in which divisions within the leadership widened, it was Boldin—whose long-festering

10 Personal communication from Anatoliy Chernyaev of 14 July 2006.
11 Boldin, *Krushenie p'edestala*, p. 256.

disagreement with, and resentment of, Gorbachev came into the open in August 1991—who drew the conclusions on who said what and whether it mattered enough to be preserved for posterity.

In the early years of perestroika major debate in the West concerned whether or not this was an attempt at fundamental reform or whether, on the contrary, the policies of Mikhail Gorbachev and his allies amounted to little more than cosmetic change. The question about how far Gorbachev was prepared to go should by now have been settled, but there is still quite a widespread lack of understanding of the extent to which his views evolved. It is all too common for scholars to cite Gorbachev's *Perestroika: New Thinking for Our Country and the World* as if it were the last and only word on Gorbachev's political thinking. Yet that book was published in 1987 and Gorbachev's political ideas became substantially more radical in 1988 and continued to evolve. A hitherto unknown archival source is of interest in that regard. Although the outside world has remained unaware of it, Gorbachev completed another book manuscript in March 1989 which, however, he decided not to publish. In this work his thinking had already moved on significantly from 1987 but it can be seen to be just a stage in the evolution of his political thinking if compared, for example, with the platform he presented to the 28th Congress of the Communist Party of the Soviet Union in 1990 or, still more, the draft party programme he commended to a Central Committee plenum on 25–26 July 1991, which those bodies approved, even though it became evident that many of those present had not the slightest intention of implementing them. Although the unpublished book remains very far from being the last word on the development of Gorbachev's ideas, it is an interesting historical document. I much appreciated being given access to it by the Gorbachev Foundation. The book was to be called *Perestroyka—ispytanie zhizn'yu. Dnevnikovye zapisi* ('Perestroika tested by life. Diary Notes') and it is cited in more than one of the chapters which follow.

During perestroika there were vigorous debates in Western scholarship and in the mass media about its scope and significance, in which I was fully engaged. Many of the issues remain hugely contentious, among them argument over the causes of systemic change in the Soviet Union and of the disintegration of the USSR as well as debate over the end of the Cold War. How important to the Cold War's ending were the hard-line policies attributed to the Reagan administration is an issue of contemporary relevance, from which politicians are still drawing lessons, and not necessarily the right ones. That relates to the even broader issue—also of great consequence today—of how change in a highly authoritarian system can be brought about. These are among the major themes of this volume.

I have a number of debts which it is a pleasure to acknowledge. Some of the earlier travel for research related to this book was supported by the Elliott Fund of the Russian and Eurasian Studies Centre of St Antony's College and recent work benefited from a Small Research Grant awarded by the British Academy. Both sources of funding have been of great help. In gathering material, I have had particularly productive visits to the Gorbachev Foundation in Moscow, the National Security Archive in Washington, DC, and the Hoover Institution Archives at Stanford University. My visit to the last-named institution was courtesy of Stanford University's Centre for Russian, East European and Eurasian Studies and their invitation to me to give the Alexander Dallin Memorial Lecture for 2006.

For permission to study materials, not all of which were on general access (including the Chernyaev, Shakhnazarov, and Medvedev reports of Politburo meetings), at the first of those institutions, I am particularly grateful to Mikhail Gorbachev, Irina Virganskaya-Gorbacheva, and Anatoliy Chernyaev. At the Gorbachev Foundation I am also indebted to Viktor Kuvaldin, Olga Zdravomyslova, Pavel Palazchenko, and Sergey Kuznetsov. My research at the National Security Archive in Washington benefited from the excellent advice and detailed knowledge of Svetlana Savranskaya and I am most grateful to her. In addition to Fond 89 and the Volkogonov papers, I was able to use the National Security Archive's 'End of the Cold War' collection. In California Mary Dakin of Stanford University, and Carol Leadenham and Lora Soroka, Assistant Archivists at the Hoover Institution, were helpful in introducing me to the documentary riches of that institution. As well as making extensive use of Fond 89—with the highly efficient research assistance of Martina Podsklanova, for which I am grateful—I had the opportunity to read the interviews deposited there as part of the 'Hoover Institution and Gorbachev Foundation (Moscow) Collection' on the end of the Cold War.

I am also much indebted to people nearer home. The Secretary of the Russian and Eurasian Studies Centre of St Antony's College, Oxford, Jackie Willcox, very kindly re-entered on the computer the older articles, those which appear in Part II of this book. Jackie somehow manages to combine the posts of Centre Secretary and Librarian and in the latter capacity was also helpful in locating useful books for the Russian and Eurasian Studies Library of St Antony's College. I am indebted, too, to Nina Kozlova for some skilled research assistance in Oxford and to Eugene Mazo for drawing my attention to several very useful articles. I am hugely grateful to my wife, Pat, who compiled the thorough index. She has accompanied me on a majority of the more than forty visits I have made to Russia (between 1966 and 2006) and it is to her that this book is dedicated.

I have found helpful the observations of other scholars on two of the chapters in this volume. Professor Viktor Kuvaldin gave me valuable comments on Chapter 6. That same chapter benefited also from the questions of participants in the VII World Congress of the International Council for

Central and East European Studies (ICCEES), held in Berlin in July 2005, where a preliminary version of the chapter was presented as a paper. Chapter 9—on the end of the Cold War—was read in draft by Alex Pravda and Sam Charap. I am grateful to both of them for their useful comments. Needless to say, those who kindly commented on Chapters 6 and 9 are not to blame for my interpretations or any errors of fact or judgement. Visits to Moscow are always a pleasure because of the number of good and knowledgeable friends I meet there. I cannot name them all, but for their generous hospitality as well as their friendship I would particularly like to thank Rair and Tatiana Simonyan, Sasha Obolonsky and Olya Obolonskaya, and David and Marna Gowan.

I wish to acknowledge, with warm thanks, the permission of various editors and publishers (all of them in the United States) to reproduce material which first appeared under their auspices. Chapter 2 did not require any permission, for the journal in which that piece appeared, *Problems of Communism*, accorded full republication rights to its contributors and, in any event, ceased publication in 1992, a decision unsurprisingly connected with the fact that by then Communist systems in Europe and the Soviet Union no longer existed. Although *Problems of Communism* was funded by the American taxpayer, through a vote in Congress, it had the merit of publishing analyses that were not only highly topical but also written from a variety of different standpoints, by no means necessarily in accord with the predominant view within the American administration of the day.

Where a chapter was first published elsewhere or draws upon my previously published articles, the reference to the original is given in the first footnote to that chapter. For permission to republish, I am very grateful to the following: the publishers of *World Policy Journal* for Chapters 3 and 4; Abraham Brumberg, the editor of *Chronicle of a Revolution* and Pantheon Books for Chapter 5; the editor of *Slavic Review*, Diane Koenker, and the journal's publishers, the American Association for the Advancement of Slavic Studies, for permission to draw extensively in Chapter 7 from an article I published in that AAASS quarterly; and the editor, George Breslauer, and Bellwether Publishing, for allowing me to republish as the basis of Chapter 8 an article which first appeared in *Post-Soviet Affairs*. Since the articles which are the starting points of Chapters seven and eight were written some years after the Soviet Union had come to an end, I was not under the same moral compunction as in Part II of the book to avoid making changes of substance. I have added much new material to them as well as making some cuts. The reference system has also been standardized; in Chapters 5 and 8 I brought it into line with the rest of the book by switching from endnotes in the former case and the Harvard system in the latter to footnotes. Footnoted books are given their full bibliographical reference on first mention in each chapter.

Preface

I have tried to standardize the transliteration scheme used in the volume, adopting the British standard system which, as it happens, was also that employed by *Problems of Communism* and is that used by *Post-Soviet Affairs*. In the text of the chapters, I have, though, simplified 'skiy' endings to 'sky' and 'yy' endings to one 'y'. I have used 'perestroika' rather than 'perestroyka' because the word has become familiar in English with the former spelling. I have also used 'glasnost' without italics, since it, too, was a Russian word which entered the English language in the second half of the 1980s. For similar reasons, names well known to English-speaking readers are presented in the text in their most familiar forms—for example, Yeltsin and Aitmatov—and soft signs are used only in the footnotes (where the titles of books and articles are transliterated strictly). As usual, when transliterating cyrillic into the Latin alphabet (other than in specialist journals), one has to find a compromise between total linguistic consistency, on the one hand, and familiarity and accessibility, on the other.

ARCHIE BROWN
Oxford, 2006

Glossary and Abbreviations

Apparat	apparat (apparatus), bureaucracy
Apparatchik	apparatchik, bureaucrat, full-time official (especially Communist Party official in the Soviet era)
BBC SWB	British Broadcasting Corporation Summary of World Broadcasts
CIA	Central Intelligence Agency (United States)
CPRF	Communist Party of the Russian Federation
CPSU	Communist Party of the Soviet Union
FBIS	Foreign Broadcast Information Service (Washington, DC)
GDR	German Democratic Republic (East Germany)
Glasnost'	glasnost, openness, transparency
Gosplan	[*Gosudarstvennyy planovyy komitet*] State Planning Committee
HIA	Hoover Institution Archives (Stanford University)
IMEMO	[*Institut mirovoy ekonomiki i mezhdunarodnykh otnosheniy*] Institute of World Economy and International Relations
KGB	[*Komitet gosudarstvennoy bezopasnosti*] Committee of State Security (name of Soviet security organs, 1953–91)
Komsomol	[*Kommunisticheskiy soyuz molodezhi*] Young Communist League
Kray	krai, province, region
Kraykom	provincial party committee
Kto kogo	(literally) who-whom, meaning who will dominate or crush whom
MAD	mutually assured destruction
MGB	[*Ministerstvo gosudarstvennoy bezopasnosti*] Ministry of State Security (name of Soviet security organs, 1946–53)
MID	[*Ministerstvo Inostrannykh Del*] Ministry of Foreign Affairs
NEP	[*Novaya ekonomicheskaya politika*] New Economic Policy (of Lenin in the 1920s)
NKVD	[*Narodnyy komisariat vnutrennikh del*] People's Commissariat for Internal Affairs (name of the Soviet security police during the worst of the purges)
Nomenklatura	nomenklatura, Communist system of appointments; also used to refer to the people appointed to high positions by this system as an especially privileged social stratum
NSA	National Security Archive (Washington, DC)

Obkom	obkom, regional party committee
Oblast'	oblast, region
PCI	Italian Communist Party
Perestroyka	perestroika, reconstruction (or restructuring)
Politburo	Political Bureau of the Central Committee of the Communist Party
Politologiya	political science
Pravovoe gosudarstvo	law-governed state; state based on the rule of law
PUWP	Polish United Workers' Party
RSFSR	Russian Socialist Federative Soviet Republic (what is now the Russian Federation)
Samoupravlenie	self-management
SDI	Strategic Defence Initiative
Siloviki	people from the 'power ministries', i.e. the KGB (known by other initials at various times), the Ministry of Internal Affairs, and the Ministry of Defence
USSR	Union of Soviet Socialist Republics
VTsIOM	All-Soviet (subsequently all-Russian) Centre for the Study of Public Opinion
Zakonomernost'	zakonomernost, law (of social development), regularity

Part I

1

Introduction

No one in 1985 expected that within the space of seven years Communist rule would have ended in Europe and the Soviet Union would have ceased to exist. Yet when this happened, there was no shortage of observers who were quick to see such an outcome as little short of inevitable. It is true that a system as inefficient in many (though not in all) respects as that of Communism could not have lasted for ever, but it was also a system that had seen off numerous threats over seventy years and one which had strong political as well as military defences.

Various oversimplifications or misunderstandings concerning perestroika and the end of the Soviet Union have gained more currency than they deserve. Among them have been the idea that the Soviet system was on its last legs and doomed to imminent collapse by the 1980s; the rather different view that the transformation of the Soviet system, the ending of the Cold War, and the breakup of the USSR were mainly brought about by the Reagan Administration; the no less fallacious notion that Boris Yeltsin was primarily responsible for dismantling a Communist system in Russia; as well as the widespread misconception that Yeltsin's rule was a continuation of perestroika but in a more democratic form. Each of these oversimplifications or fallacies will be discussed at various points in this book and, in particular, in the final chapter.[1]

Peaceful change is not easy to bring about in a consolidated, highly authoritarian system. While relative failure on the part of a government in a democracy is liable to lead to that government's replacement, the same does not hold true in conditions of authoritarian rule, especially in as sophisticated

---

[1] Among the numerous authors who have examined the end of the Soviet system and of the USSR are: Alexander Dallin, 'Causes of the Collapse of the USSR', *Post-Soviet Affairs*, Vol. 8, No. 4, October–December 1992, pp. 279–302; Stephen Kotkin, *Armageddon Averted: The Soviet Collapse, 1970–2000* (Oxford University Press, New York, 2001); Martin Malia, *The Soviet Tragedy: A History of Socialism in Russia, 1917–1991* (The Free Press, New York, 1994); Ofira Seliktar, *Politics, Paradigms, and Intelligence Failures: Why So Few Predicted the Collapse of the Soviet Union* (M.E. Sharpe, Armonk, NY, 2004); and Wisła Suraska, *How the Soviet Union Disappeared: An Essay on the Causes of Dissolution* (Duke University Press, Durham, NC, 1998). Dallin's early analysis is notably perspicacious. The best of the above books by quite a wide margin is Kotkin's.

a Communist system as that of the Soviet Union—one, moreover, that had developed indigenously in Russia, rather than being essentially a foreign imposition as were most of the Communist regimes of Eastern Europe. The skill and ruthlessness with which Communist rulers drew on a wide range of rewards and punishments had by the eve of perestroika reduced the never-large dissident movement to groups that were both miniscule and marginalized. It is quite fanciful to imagine that the Soviet state was near breaking point in the mid-1980s and to believe that, no matter what happened within the highest echelons of leadership, it was doomed to imminent collapse.

Political systems change over time and highly authoritarian systems, in particular, do not last for ever. However, even though they may be economically inefficient as well as repressive, that does not necessarily prevent such systems from sustaining themselves far longer than they deserve to survive. The Soviet regime had wide-ranging possibilities for manipulating public opinion through control over the educational system and the mass media, as well as for employing whatever force should be necessary to eliminate organized dissent. When the day after Konstantin Chernenko's death on 10 March 1985, Mikhail Gorbachev was chosen as the new leader of the country, that decision was taken exclusively by the inner leadership of the Communist Party—the Politburo and the Central Committee, with the latter body promptly endorsing the choice of the former. For the average Soviet citizen such events were no more subject to his or her control than the weather.[2]

Although there was no overt pressure from below on the party leadership for departure from previous policies, there were, nevertheless, important stimuli to change for the more thoughtful elements within the political elite. The technological gap between the Soviet Union and Western countries (and, indeed, some of the recently industrialized countries of Asia) was widening rather than narrowing, and there had been a secular decline in the Soviet rate of economic growth from the 1950s to the first half of the1980s. While these, then, were not new phenomena in 1985, and previous Soviet leaderships had generally preferred to avert their gaze from them, a desire to

---

[2] What is perhaps more surprising is that even high officials—at the level of deputy heads of department—in the Central Committee of the Soviet Communist Party not only had no influence on the outcome but also, more than two weeks after Gorbachev had been unanimously chosen by the Politburo to be the Soviet Union's next leader, did not know whether or not his election had been contested within that inner sanctum. Anatoliy Chernyaev in his diary entry of 30 March 1985 reports agnostically 'rumors going around Moscow that the General Secretary election at the PB [Politburo] was "not without a fight"'. See 'The Diary of Anatoly Chernyaev' for the year 1985 (translated by Anna Melyukova, edited by Svetlana Savranskaya), published on the National Security Archive (NSA) website on 25 May 2006: http://gwu.edu/~nsarchiv.

get the country moving again and to tackle serious problems were major impulses to Gorbachev's initial reformism.

Knowing how much the breakup of the Soviet Union is still regretted by Russians,[3] including himself, Gorbachev has at times suggested that there was no alternative to perestroika—that the Soviet Union was in a 'pre-crisis' condition or even in a 'serious crisis'.[4] On other occasions he has, however, said that he could have presided over the system, not changed in its essentials, for many years to come, even though he has invariably added that he would have found such a course morally and politically unacceptable.[5] Both reflections contain their own elements of truth. The Soviet Union—or Russia—could certainly not have flourished in the long run within the confines of an essentially unreformed Communist system. Yet minor reform, combined with a tightening of the screws when there were signs of restlessness within the society, could have kept both the Soviet system and the Soviet Union going into the twenty-first century. In a book which he completed in March 1989, and then decided not to publish because it was already falling behind his own thinking and the pace of political developments, Gorbachev—quite accurately—did not say that there was no alternative to perestroika but, more precisely, that 'perestroika was a necessity' because there was no '*reasonable, constructive* alternative' to it (italics added, AB).[6]

Fundamental reform cumulatively destroyed the pillars of the Soviet regime. It was not so much a case of crisis producing reform as of reform precipitating crisis.[7] As Stephen Kotkin has observed: 'In the 1980s, Soviet society was fully employed and the regime stable. The country had low foreign

---

[3] Russian public opinion, both in the perestroika period and in post-Soviet Russia, favoured the preservation of the Soviet Union. As Matthew Wyman has noted, there was only one brief moment—at the end of 1991—when a majority of Russians went as far as to accept the breakup of the Union. See Wyman, *Public Opinion in Postcommunist Russia* (Macmillan, Houndmills, UK, 1977), pp. 172–3.

[4] For example, writing in 1987, about the impetus to the launch of perestroika, Gorbachev said: 'An unbiased and honest approach led us to the inexorable conclusion that the country was in a pre-crisis state.' See M.S. Gorbachev, *Perestroika i novoe myshlenie dlya nashey strany i vsego mira* (Politizdat, Moscow, 1987), p. 18. In his most recent book, Gorbachev says: 'Bureaucratic supercentralization fettered the country, the people and society. And from that point of view— yes, the Union was experiencing a serious crisis': Mikhail Gorbachev, *Ponyat' perestroyku... pochemu eto vazhno seychas* (Al'pina Biznes Buks, Moscow, 2006), p. 19.

[5] See, for example, the interview with Gorbachev in *Komosomol'skaya Pravda*, 2–9 March 2006, pp. 4–5. Asked if he could not have remained in the Kremlin for 20 years but for the fact that he embarked on perestroika, Gorbachev responded (p. 5): 'Yes, it would have been possible to renovate and patch things up a bit and to sit in the chair of the General Secretary up to now. But to live, as in the past, was unacceptable.'

[6] M.S. Gorbachev, 'Perestroyka—ispytanie zhizn'yu. Dnevnikovye zapisy', unpublished book manuscript, p. 41, The Gorbachev Foundation Archives.

[7] What Gorbachev had, however, from the outset of perestroika called 'pre-crisis phenomena' were clearly visible to the less blinkered minority within the Communist Party hierarchy.

debt and an excellent credit rating. It suffered no serious civil disorders until it began to reform and even then retained the loyalty of its shrinking but still formidable Armed Forces, Ministry of Interior, and KGB.'[8] Similarly, Leon Aron has written:

In 1985, the Soviet Union possessed much the same set of natural and human resources that it had ten years before. Perennial shortages...were nothing new. Indeed, things had been much worse....In any case...in totalitarian regimes the connection between popular deprivation and a change of policies is tenuous at best and often results not in liberalizing reforms but in heavier repression. [Moreover] the Soviet Union was hardly crumbling under external pressures. On the contrary, in 1985 it was at the height of its world power and influence, anchored in a state of strategic nuclear parity with the United States.[9]

At some point in the early decades of this century the system would surely have faced a full-blown crisis. The resultant systemic change *could*, however, have been very different from perestroika. It need not have been in the direction of making the country more liberal or more democratic. Within the Soviet elite there were strong statist and Russian nationalist tendencies as well as reformist and more liberal elements. In the professional apparatus of the Communist Party of the Soviet Union (CPSU), not to mention the large military–industrial complex, the former were more numerous than the latter. Given the multi-national character of the Soviet Union, the coming to power of Russian nationalists would, in all probability, have led to bloodshed and to a more repressive regime than that headed for eighteen years by Leonid Brezhnev. The Brezhnev years were not only an 'era of stagnation', as the period was dubbed during perestroika, but also a period of stalemate between neo-Stalinist and Russian nationalist trends, on the one hand, and reformist and internationalist tendencies, on the other. Perestroika was a victory for the forces representing the latter, but there was nothing preordained about that outcome.

THE UNREFORMED SOVIET SYSTEM

To understand how much was changed by perestroika—even before the process of change slipped out of the control of the reformist wing of the Communist Party leadership, as it had done by 1990–1—some brief attention

[8] Stephen Kotkin, *Armageddon Averted: The Soviet Collapse, 1970–2000* (Oxford University Press, New York, 2001), p. 173.
[9] Leon Aron, 'The "Mystery" of the Soviet Collapse', *Journal of Democracy*, Vol. 17, No. 2, April 2006, pp. 22–3.

to the unreformed Soviet system is necessary. The CPSU had a monopoly of power which was euphemistically known as 'the leading role of the party'. Not only were other political parties banned but so were any independent associations aspiring to influence political events. The highest policymaking body within the party, the Politburo, was also the most authoritative decision-making organ in the state. The General Secretary of the Central Committee of the CPSU was the chief executive within the country, not merely the party leader.

The Communist Party was seen by Vladimir Lenin and his successors as a 'vanguard party'. That is to say, its leaders intended it to be a mass party with an organization in every workplace but at the same time a selective organization which would recruit more from some social groups than from others. In the Soviet case it did not (and was not intended to) embrace more than 10 per cent of the adult population. In the mid-1980s the party included approximately 6.5 per cent of the total population and about one in ten adults. In absolute numbers the party grew from just under 7 million members on the eve of Stalin's death in 1953 to close to 20 million in 1990 before dropping to about 15 million by the summer of 1991, by which time the party was, indeed, in crisis.

In between the five-yearly Party Congresses, which according to the rules of the CPSU constituted its most authoritative forum, the party was run by the Central Committee and, in particular, by its inner bodies—the Politburo and the Secretariat of the Central Committee.[10] The Central Committee as a whole met only a few times a year for a day or two at a time, whereas the Politburo and the Secretariat met as collective bodies in most weeks. When, however, Soviet citizens spoke about the Central Committee deciding this or that, they were not necessarily being naive or ill-informed. They were gener-ally referring *not* to the 'elected' members of the Central Committee (who in reality were co-opted) in plenary session, but to the work of the bureaucracy which went on in the Central Committee buildings. The professional appar-atus of the Central Committee was divided into some twenty departments and a great deal of day-to-day policy was made within them. The system, though, was extremely hierarchical, and Secretaries of the Central Committee had a significantly greater authority than those department heads who did not possess that title. The most powerful of all were the senior secretaries—people who were both members of the Politburo *and* Secretaries of the Central Committee and who had extensive supervisory responsibilities.

---

[10] The congresses themselves were stage-managed by the party leadership, and the docu-ments they approved were prepared over many months in advance under the supervision of Secretaries of the Central Committee.

Mikhail Suslov was one such person of great authority within the CPSU, a conservative Communist who was the overseer of both ideology and foreign policy. He combined membership of the Politburo with a Secretaryship of the Central Committee from 1955 until his death in January 1982.[11]

Although the Communist Party leader, the General Secretary, was the most powerful figure of all within the system, there is a sense in which Communist systems had a dual executive. There was a ministerial network as well as a party hierarchy—indeed, many more ministries and state committees (the latter were the equivalent of ministries or, in the case of the Committee of State Security [KGB], a super-ministry) than departments of the Central Committee. The Chairman of the Council of Ministers was a major figure within the system. The Communist Party and the Council of Ministers were, however, closely intertwined. The Chairman of the latter was invariably a member of the party Politburo and the departments of the Central Committee were overseers of the ministries. In the Brezhnev period decisions taken together by the departments and their corresponding ministries sometimes took the form of decrees issued in the joint names of the Central Committee and the Council of Ministers.

By tradition the Chairman of the Council of Ministers was in charge of the management of the economy with the exception of agriculture, which came within the General Secretary's domain. The General Secretary was primarily responsible for foreign policy and had broad oversight of every other sphere of political activity. Even on economic issues, should there be disagreement between the General Secretary and the Chairman of the Council of Ministers, the former would eventually come out on top. Thus, Aleksey Kosygin, who became Chairman of the Council of Ministers in October 1964, at the same time as Leonid Brezhnev was chosen as party leader, espoused a modest economic reform in 1965 which ended in 1968. Brezhnev responded both to those party officials who were concerned that it was encroaching on their prerogatives and to worried ideologues who linked Kosygin's very modest concession to market forces with the more alarming combination of economic and political reform which had emerged that year in the 'Prague Spring'. Nevertheless, Kosygin retained his post at the head of the ministerial network, and as a senior member of the Politburo, until shortly before his death in 1980.

---

[11] On the CPSU, see Leonard Schapiro, *The Communist Party of the Soviet Union* (Methuen, London, 2nd edn., 1970); Ronald J. Hill and Peter Frank, *The Soviet Communist Party* (Allen & Unwin, London, 3rd edn., 1986); and Graeme Gill, *The Collapse of a Single-Party System: The disintegration of the Communist Party of the Soviet Union* (Cambridge University Press, Cambridge, 1994).

Kosygin's successor, Nikolay Tikhonov, was a long-standing friend and ally of Brezhnev who, however, established a sufficiently strong position that he outlived his patron politically as well as biologically, serving from 1980 until his removal by Gorbachev in 1985. While the Politburo *was* the highest policymaking body within the Soviet state, in practice—and especially during the Brezhnev years—it was frequently approving on the nod decisions that had been taken either in the Central Committee bureaucracy or within the ministries, particularly the State Planning Committee (Gosplan).[12] Speaking on 8 September 1988 in the Politburo,[13] where a number of those present knew at first hand the truth of what he was saying, Gorbachev observed that the pre-perestroika Politburo used to rubber-stamp whatever came up from the Central Committee apparatus. Interestingly, he extended this generalization to include decisions taken in the ministerial network. In a remark which embraced both the party and the ministerial bureaucracy, he said: 'Generally speaking, we rubber-stamped in the Politburo, in the Secretariat, and even in plenums of the Central Committee whatever was proposed to us by the departments (*vedomstva*), starting with Gosplan and below.' Referring to the ministries specifically, he said that if one tried to change anything in the proposals brought to the Politburo by the Council of Ministers, one was 'put in the camp of permanent and eternal enemies by Comrade Tikhonov'.[14]

The General Secretary set the tone in the Politburo. In Brezhnev's Politburo Tikhonov could count on the party leader's backing. The Politburo remained, though, the body whose support was necessary for any important new initiative. That continued to be the case until well into the perestroika period.

---

[12] Aleksandr Yakovlev, noting the existence of three distinct *apparaty* within the Soviet system—the party apparatus, the coercive force apparatus (*apparat nasiliya*, by which he had in mind the KGB and the Ministry of Interior), and the economic apparatus, goes on to observe: 'The party and coercive *apparaty* retained levers sufficient to control an economic planner but not the economic apparatus (*khozapparat*) as a whole' (Yakovlev, *Predislovie. Obval. Posleslovie*, Novosti, Moscow, 1992), pp. 137–8. That stress on the power of the economic apparatus is very much in line with the arguments of Stephen Whitefield who, in his *Industrial Power and the Soviet State* (Clarendon Press, Oxford, 1993), emphasizes more than most scholars the power of the Soviet economic bureaucracy. He stresses the centrality of the ministerial network 'within the old system' and argues that 'radical anti-ministerialism was both difficult and dangerous' for reformist politicians, including Gorbachev (ibid., p. 180). The terminology of the 'leading role' is, I would suggest (though for Whitefield even that might be overstating the case), more appropriate than 'monopoly of power' when the party apparatus's relationship with the ministries is considered in the pre-perestroika context. That is not in contradiction with the view that the Communist Party had a monopoly of power *within Soviet society*, since all the senior officials in the ministries were members of the CPSU, as were army and KGB officers.

[13] The major business of this meeting was to consider Gorbachev's wide-ranging plans for reorganizing and reducing in size the Communist Party apparatus, involving the elimination of more than half of the departments of the Central Committee.

[14] 'Zasedanie Politbyuro TsK KPSS', 8 September 1988, Hoover Institution Archives (HIA), Fond 89, Reel 1.1003, opis 42, file 22, p. 181.

Eventually Gorbachev—following the creation of an executive state presidency in March 1990—at least partially freed himself from the constraints imposed by the Politburo, although, as a result of his radical reforms, he faced a formidable range of new pressures from outside the Communist Party as well as from within it.

In the unreformed Soviet system—and also, though not to the same degree, in the perestroika period—another major force was the coercive power apparatus and, in particular, the KGB. The KGB in the post-Stalin period was subordinated to the top party leadership—and it was, accordingly, a promotion for Yuriy Andropov when he succeeded Suslov in the early months of 1982 as the *second* Secretary of the CPSU (not to speak of his assumption of the General Secretaryship in succession to Brezhnev in November of that year). The head of the KGB could, however, be a dangerous enemy for a party leader. Both in 1964 and in 1991 the Chairman of the KGB turned against, and attempted to oust, the General Secretary—in the earlier year Vladimir Semichastny against Khrushchev and in the latter year Vladimir Kryuchkov against Gorbachev. In neither case, though, did the KGB chief act alone, but in cooperation with other leading party and state officials.

The military–industrial complex cannot be left out of the political equation. It enjoyed a privileged place in the Soviet Union in the years before perestroika. More resources were devoted to military expenditure than made economic sense and an obsession with secrecy meant that there were few spin-offs for civilian industry from military production. In terms of the influence they then wielded and of the promotion of their narrow occupational interests, Soviet military men would look back with nostalgia to the Brezhnev era,[15] although many of the policies actually pursued in those years, such as the armed intervention in Czechoslovakia in August 1968 and the invasion of Afghanistan in December 1979, were longer-term disasters.

The highest organ of state power, according to the 1977 Soviet Constitution, was the Supreme Soviet of the USSR. In reality, that body—the country's nominal legislative assembly—had vastly less power than the institutions already discussed in this chapter. Its constitutional pre-eminence was a legal fiction. Both the legislature and the judiciary were totally dominated by the executive in the pre-perestroika Soviet Union.[16] The Supreme Soviet met for only a few days each year and passed unanimously whatever laws were laid in front of it. Although it was an honour to be a deputy of the Supreme Soviet,

[15] Aleksandr Yakovlev aptly described Brezhnev as a 'lover of the military-industrial complex, for which he did not spare the people's money' (*Predislovie, obval, posleslovie*, p. 101).

[16] These points were recognized, and critically assessed, by Aleksandr Yakovlev in two memoranda he sent to Gorbachev in December 1985. For the texts of the documents, see Yakovlev, *Sumerki* (Materik, Moscow, 2003), pp. 376–83.

such a position was within the gift of the CPSU Central Committee apparatus. In the 'elections' for the Supreme Soviet there was only one candidate for each constituency and that person was duly returned with votes recorded as not less than 99 per cent. The Supreme Soviet was truly a rubber-stamp assembly that could be taken for granted in a way in which no party official (not even the General Secretary) could ever take the Politburo for granted. Oddly, local soviets, although enjoying less prestige than the Supreme Soviet of the USSR (or the Supreme Soviets of the union republics), were in many respects more serious political institutions than the federal legislature, for in the towns and districts the soviets performed not only the tasks which fell to local government in Western countries but also many which were peculiar to a Communist system. Even shops, hairdressers, and laundries were state-owned and so came under the management and control of the local soviet. The local soviet deputies prior to perestroika were, it should be added, chosen in non-competitive, single-candidate elections, which were as manipulated by the party apparatus as were the elections for the Supreme Soviet.[17]

NEED FOR A TRIPLE (OR QUADRUPLE) TRANSFORMATION

If the highly authoritarian Soviet system was to become pluralistic and substantially democratized—and those goals only gradually became central components of Gorbachev's reformist agenda—this required not one transformation but several. A centralized command economy was incompatible with democracy as well as with economic efficiency. That does not mean that, as a corollary, a market economy must inevitably be accompanied by democracy—there has been no shortage of market economies coexisting with right-wing authoritarian regimes. There are, however, numerous market democracies, but *no* example of a state combining a command economy with democratic governance.

The fact that transformative change both of the economic system and of the political system was required made the Soviet transition peculiarly difficult, even in comparison with other Communist states, since a Communist polity and economy had existed for much longer in the USSR than anywhere else.

---

[17] Moreover, the local party organization played a 'leading' (albeit not a monopolistic) role in the decision-making processes at the subnational level, and the regional, city, or district party first secretary enjoyed a higher authority than the chairperson of the local soviet on the same rung of the vertical power structure.

The task was still more demanding than that which faced those engaged in the transition from authoritarian rule in Spain and Portugal more than a decade earlier where the transformation of a dictatorial polity was not matched by a need for root-and-branch transformation of the economic system. Right-wing dictatorships did not require transition from a completely state-owned and state-directed economy to one embracing private ownership and the market.

While in the course of perestroika, part of the Soviet leadership (including Gorbachev) came to realize that prices of commodities would have to be determined by market forces (rather than fixed by the State Committee on Prices), the question of *how* to move to a market was never adequately resolved. Whether, for example, this could be done in an evolutionary process, whether it required a 'big bang', or whether demonopolization should precede price liberalization remained controversial issues. In the last years of the Soviet Union Boris Yeltsin gained popularity by combining support for a market economy (though he avoided saying that he supported 'capitalism') with attacks on existing inequalities and an emphasis on social justice. By implication, the move to a market was going to bring more equality, and much of Yeltsin's support, even among committed democratic activists, rested on his supposed egalitarianism.[18]

Alexander Lukin, who has made by far the most serious study of the belief systems of those who identified themselves as 'democrats' in the final years of the Soviet Union, has shown why there was bound to be tension between marketization and democratization, especially in the light of the specific interpretation given to the latter notion by most self-professed Russian democrats. As Lukin observes:

The understanding of democracy (and of legality as its essential part) *as a means to the introduction of justice* is highly characteristic of Russian 'democrats'. In this line of argument the notions of 'justice' and 'legality' came before the notion of 'democracy' and were more fundamental. Such an understanding contained the possibility of disillusionment with democracy itself in the event that it did not lead to justice. Not surprisingly, many supporters of social justice and legality left 'democratic' groups and some did indeed become disillusioned with democracy when, after the coming to power of Boris Yel'tsin's 'democratic' leadership, it became clear to them that the politics of the new leadership did not lead to the elimination of privileges and the arrival of justice. (italics added, AB)[19]

It was more evident to Gorbachev than it was to Yeltsin that the move to the market, however necessary, was liable to lead to greater inequality than that

---

[18] See on this Alexander Lukin, *The Political Culture of the Russian 'Democrats'* (Oxford University Press, Oxford, 2000).
[19] Ibid., p. 210.

characteristic of the unreformed Soviet economy and, moreover, that living standards would become worse for millions of vulnerable people. Gorbachev's own evolution was in the direction of social democracy, but there was never a consensus about how to move to a social market economy. This was an area in which Gorbachev found himself swayed at different times by conflicting opinions and baulked by entrenched institutional interests, and he did not succeed in finding a consistent strategy for economic transformation.[20]

Nevertheless, there were many obstacles in the way of transforming the Soviet economic system. As Alec Nove observed just two years into perestroika:

It is necessary to stress how inherently complex are the problems of transition from centralized planning to a new alternative. This would be so even if this new alternative already existed in the form of a consistent and agreed model, and even if all concerned were doing their best to implement the desired change.... Soviet citizens at all levels have learned how to live with and within the system.... One of the most significant obstacles to radical reform is that this is a conservative society at all levels.[21]

Similar reflections to those contained in Nove's last sentence were voiced by Aleksandr Yakovlev, writing well after perestroika had passed into history: 'In trying to reform the country we, and here I include myself, underestimated a great deal—above all, the psychological conditions of the society, which turned out to be more inert, indifferent, and dependent than we had imagined.'[22]

The difficulties of changing the political and economic systems were exacerbated by the need for change in another, but closely connected, area in which a third fundamental transformation was required. That was the interrelationship between the multinational composition of the Soviet state and the federal administrative structure of the USSR. Prior to perestroika the Soviet Union was in essence a unitary state, but one with federal forms. With the partial exception of the largest of the fifteen Union Republics, Russia, each republic—whether Armenia, Azerbaijan, Ukraine, or Uzbekistan—had its 'own' republican party organization (with Central Committee and republican First Secretary), Council of Ministers, Supreme Soviet, and Academy of

---

[20] Gorbachev has himself recently observed that perestroika began with great support from the people, but gradually that support was lost: 'The time wasn't used for resolution of the problems of price formation and the market.... It was necessary to balance the consumer market, and more boldly and toughly to turn military industry into providers of good products for the people' (*Ponyat' perestroyku...*), p. 373.

[21] Alec Nove, in his contribution to a symposium, 'What's Happening in the Soviet Union?', *The National Interest*, No. 8, Summer 1987, p. 17.

[22] Alexander N. Yakovlev, *A Century of Violence in Soviet Russia* (Yale University Press, New Haven, CT, 2002), p. 24.

Sciences. Russia was an exception because it contained half the population of the USSR and three-quarters of its territory. It did not, therefore, have its own party organization (or Academy of Sciences, although it had its own Council of Ministers and Supreme Soviet), since that would have meant too much duplication with the all-Union Central Committee and its apparatus. There may also have been a concern that a Russian Central Committee, with its own first secretary, could become a divisive counterweight to the union-wide Central Committee.[23]

The most essential point, however, is that prior to the Gorbachev reforms, the highly centralized nature of the Communist Party meant that there was a strong, top-down vertical organization of the society which cut through and dominated the 'national' institutions that constituted the second echelon of the political hierarchy. The federal forms, however, which appeared to be of comparatively little value other than as a sop to national consciousness during the Stalin, Khrushchev, and Brezhnev eras, turned out to be of huge significance, acquiring real substance under conditions of liberalization and democratization. What happened in this sphere during perestroika testified not only to the mobilizing (and, in this instance, disintegrative) force of national sentiment but also to the latent importance of institutional arrangements which had appeared to most internal and external observers as little more than a meaningless façade throughout the greater part of the Soviet period.[24] It is also of great consequence that there were more than 100 different nationalities in the Soviet Union, many of which below the Union

[23] That, indeed, became the case when late in the perestroika period conservative opponents of Gorbachev succeeded in their demand to have a Russian Communist Party formed. Admittedly, this was after the political system had become *de facto* pluralist and so it was not altogether surprising that the Russian Communist Party organization (with encouragement from like-minded people within the apparatus of the all-Union Central Committee) promptly adopted ideological and policy stances in sharp contrast to those espoused by Gorbachev. On the emergence of the Russian Communist Party, see the detailed account by Gordon M. Hahn, *1985–2000. Russia's Revolution from Above: Reform, Transition, and Revolution in the Fall of the Soviet Communist Regime* (Transaction Publishers, New Brunswick, NJ, 2002), pp. 127–42. The imminent organization of a Russian Communist Party was the subject of lengthy Politburo discussion on 3 May 1990. Yuriy Manaenkov, a Secretary of the Central Committee, pointed to the fact that the members of the Russian Communist Party would make up 58 per cent of the total membership of the CPSU and warned of the danger of two centres within the party and of *dvoevlastie* (dual power). Gorbachev accepted that this threat was a real one, and he had long tried to stave off the establishment of such a party organization, initially creating a Party Buro for the Russian Republic, with himself as the head of it, when demand for a Communist Party organization for the Russian republic (corresponding with those of other republics) first arose. For the Politburo discussion on the eve of the founding Congress of the Russian Communist Party, see HIA, Fond 89, Reel 1.1003, opis 42, file 28.

[24] On the importance of the combination of these institutional arrangements—federal forms based on national territories—see the perceptive works of Ronald Grigor Suny, *The Revenge of the Past: Nationalism, Revolution, and the Collapse of the Soviet Union* (Stanford University Press,

Republican level had territorial units that bore their name, such as the 'autonomous republics' of Bashkortostan and Tatarstan within the Russian republic. Although the Soviet Union eventually broke up into fifteen separate states, which corresponded exactly with the territorial boundaries of the fifteen Union Republics, this did not mean that all national problems had been solved, as some of the nationalities which did *not* achieve independent statehood held that the breakup of the Union had made things worse, not better, for them.[25]

It is arguable that if the Soviet Union were to make a successful transition from a Communist system to one that was pluralist and democratizing, not only a 'triple transformation' but a quadruple change of fundamentals was needed. The fourth challenge was to put an end to the already-noted excessive militarization of the Soviet economy. The size of the military–industrial complex in relation to the rest of the economy gave the military and military industry an overwhelmingly privileged place within the system. It did not grant them autonomy, for the interpenetration of the party and the military was vast.[26] The Communist Party leadership had the last word, and the influence of the military within it depended to a substantial extent on the party standing of its principal representative within the highest echelons of the CPSU. When that person was Dmitriy Ustinov, especially during the eight years between 1976 and 1984 when he was both Minister of Defence and a full member of the Politburo, the voice of the military counted for a great deal— and it was a conservative voice. Discussing the political attitudes of the military during the Brezhnev era, Timothy Colton appositely observed:

Stanford, CA, 1993); Rogers Brubaker, *Nationalism Reframed: Nationhood and the National Question in the New Europe* (Cambridge University Press, Cambridge, 1996); Juan J. Linz and Alfred Stepan, *Problems of Democratic Transition and Consolidation: Southern Europe, South America and Post-Communist Europe* (Johns Hopkins University Press, Baltimore, MD, 1996); Valerie Bunce, *Subversive Institutions: The Design and the Destruction of Socialism and the State* (Cambridge University Press, Cambridge, 1999); and Mark R. Beissinger, *Nationalist Mobilization and the Collapse of the Soviet State* (Cambridge University Press, Cambridge, 2002).

[25] Writing, while the USSR was still in existence, about its need for a 'triple transformation', I noted (with respect to the required third transformation): 'In this area solutions are even less clear-cut than in the other two. It is not enough to support independence for the republics or national self-determination in every case, for the one can conflict with the other. One nation's independent statehood can become a minority nationality's perceived oppression, as the current example of Georgia and its Abkhazian and Ossetian minorities illustrates clearly' (Archie Brown, 'No Role Models for Soviet Transition', *Los Angeles Times*, 2 April 1991).

[26] However, in a Politburo meeting of 30 May 1987, Eduard Shevardnadze said that the army always had 'a certain autonomy' because of its special regime and that 'this served as a barrier for information about the situation in it'. He went on: 'But I consider that we must have full information about the state of affairs in the army' ('Zasedanie Politbyuro TsK KPSS 30 Maya 1987 goda', p. 499, NSA, Volkogonov Papers).

On most basic questions facing Soviet society soldiers are firmly wedded to the status quo. Military leaders can be expected to oppose increased autonomy for national minorities, investment priority for the consumer economy, concessions to intellectuals, and greater openness to the outside world. As for political forms and procedures, the central concern of democratic theory, Soviet officers have displayed indifference to almost every aspect but their own access to national leaders.[27]

These military predispositions did not alter significantly during perestroika and Gorbachev initiated a transformation of Soviet foreign policy not only because of the dangers inherent in the Cold War but also as a prelude to changing the priorities of domestic politics. Radical political and economic reform involved reducing the weight of the military in the decision-making process and of military expenditure as a share of the budget.[28]

Gorbachev and those who shared his view on the need to make the army more responsive to their foreign policy goals, and to deprive the military–industrial complex of its specially privileged position within the Soviet economy, used whatever means they could to combat the institutional inertia which made such a change of priorities an uphill task. The May 1987 unscheduled arrival in Moscow of a young West German, Matthias Rust, who not only flew his light aircraft for hundreds of miles into Soviet air space but landed it just off Red Square, provided Gorbachev with an opportunity which he skilfully exploited. At the Politburo meeting held on 30 May, the day after Rust's arrival, Gorbachev took the chance to berate the top echelon of the military leadership and to replace the Minister of Defence, Marshal Sergey Sokolov, as well as General Aleksandr Koldunov, the Chief of the Air Defences. Responding to the criticism of this scandalous breach of Soviet air defences (albeit one which caused amusement in sections of Soviet society as well as the outside world), General Koldunov admitted that he learned about the aircraft only after it had landed in Moscow. Gorbachev sarcastically asked him if his source of information had been the Moscow traffic police (*'Uznali ot GAI?'*).[29] After a lot of criticism from Gorbachev, backed especially by Shevardnadze, Marshal Sokolov, who was present throughout, said: 'If that is the unanimous opinion of the Politburo, then nothing remains for me but to leave the post of Minister of Defence.'[30] In truth, he had no option. After an interval in the Politburo proceedings Gorbachev proposed to unanimous approval that Dmitriy Yazov be appointed the new Minister of Defence, a decision that had been prepared in advance.

[27] Timothy J. Colton, *Commissars, Commanders, and Civilian Authority: The Structure of Soviet Military Politics* (Harvard University Press, Cambridge, MA, 1979), p. 288.

[28] See Mikhail Gorbachev, *Ponyat' perestroyku*, p. 30.

[29] 'Zasedanie Politbyuro TsK KPSS 30 Maya 1987 goda', op. cit., p. 485.

[30] Ibid., p. 501.

Although Yazov was part of the attempted coup against Gorbachev little more than four years later, initially his appointment weakened military opposition to the foreign policy being pursued by Gorbachev with the active support within the leadership of Shevardnadze and Yakovlev. Anatoly Dobrynin, who attended the Politburo session at which Sokolov's resignation was accepted—and observes that the interval between the resignation and the resumption of the meeting at which Yazov was appointed was only fifteen minutes—wrote that Gorbachev had made 'perfect use of the military's state of confusion and its badly damaged prestige'.[31] Dobrynin adds:

Yazov was far more obedient to Gorbachev than Sokolov, and thus Gorbachev accomplished a quiet coup. The new defense minister knew little about disarmament talks, and had nothing to do with them. With Yazov as defense minister, Shevardnadze felt much more at ease during the talks. Opposition by the military became more moderate. Sokolov was followed into retirement by about one hundred generals and colonels, conservative military leaders who also opposed Gorbachev's reforms and his concessions to the Americans. But the military establishment remained discontented with Gorbachev, and this would show time and again.[32]

It became a cliché of the later perestroika era to assert that Gorbachev was 'indecisive'. That was, to say the least, an oversimplification. There were many occasions when he acted boldly and decisively. This was one of them.

WHAT WAS PERESTROIKA?

As I have already noted in the Preface, and it is a point which will recur in subsequent chapters, perestroika meant different things to different people at different times. However, it should not be used as a synonym for everything that happened in the Soviet Union between March 1985 and December 1991. It refers specifically to a momentous effort by a small minority in the leadership of the Communist Party, backed by a larger minority within the political elite of the country, initially to reform the Soviet system and, subsequently, to transform it. There were tensions from the start within the highest echelons of the Communist Party over the pace and direction of the changes set in motion, and the discord became increasingly overt as the substance and meaning of perestroika became more radical. There were even tensions in the minds of those (including, crucially, Gorbachev) who had

---

[31] Anatoly Dobrynin, *In Confidence: Moscow's Ambassador to America's Six Cold War Presidents (1962–1986)* (Random House, New York, 1995), pp. 625–6.
[32] Ibid., p. 626.

initiated perestroika and who had gone on to embrace its radical variant. While they wished to democratize the Soviet political system, they did not wish to lose all control of that process. However, once the accumulated problems that could previously not even be discussed in public forums were allowed to surface, a step-by-step gradualism became impossible.

Perestroika literally means reconstruction or restructuring. If the term is translated, the former meaning is preferable, for it can carry the connotation of building a new edifice on the same land as well as the alternative and more limited meaning of no more than a modest updating of the existing building. For many of those in the Soviet leadership who went along with what Gorbachev called perestroika, it never denoted more than the latter. For Gorbachev and for a number of his key allies in the launch of this political project, including Aleksandr Yakovlev, perestroika, even at the outset, was more fundamental. It also had a moral dimension.[33] The Russian scholar, Dmitriy Furman, has recently called it 'a sort of *Marxist Protestantism*'.[34] A leading reformer who was an influential aide of Gorbachev, Georgiy Shakhnazarov, had years earlier made the analogy with the Reformation—a concept, he noted, he was consciously using—and evoked the name of Martin Luther.[35] Gorbachev's dilemma, however—and it was remarked upon even during perestroika—was that within the secular religion that was the international Communist movement, complete with Marxist-Leninist scripture, he was *both* Pope and Luther.[36]

The fact that the impetus for change came from above rather than from a broad section of the public was, in many respects, a disadvantage, as perestroika had only a very limited time in which to put down foundations. Elena Bonner has quoted her late husband, Andrey Sakharov, as saying: 'We began to create our new house, not from the basement but from the roof.'[37] That, as Sakharov implied, was far from an ideal manner in which to go about building a new political structure. Yet it was the only way in which change on

---

[33] As Leon Aron correctly observes: 'Yet while economic betterment was their banner, there is little doubt that Gorbachev and his supporters first set out to right political and moral, not just economic, wrongs.' See Aron, 'The "Mystery" of the Soviet Collapse', op. cit., pp. 26–7. In his 1989 unpublished book manuscript, Gorbachev wrote that the underlying idea at the outset of perestroika was the need for 'a revival not only of the economy, but also of the moral health of society' ('Perestroyka—ispitanie zhizn'yu', MS, op. cit., p. 41).

[34] In Andrei Grachev, Chiara Blengino, and Rossella Stievano (eds.), *1985–2005. Twenty Years that Changed the World* (World Political Forum, Editori Laterza, Rome, 2005), p. 54.

[35] Georgiy Shakhnazarov, *Tsena svoboda: Reformatsiya Gorbacheva glazami ego pomoshchnika* (Rossika Zevs, Moscow, 1993), p. 3.

[36] Making, by implication, the analogy between Marxism-Leninism and religion, Aleksandr Yakovlev in a contribution to Politburo discussion on 1 July 1987, spoke of a 'kind of religious conservatism and inertia in the thoughts and actions' of part of the CPSU. See NSA: Volkogonov Papers, R 10862, A.N. Yakovlev, 'Vystuplenie na Politbyuro 1 Iyulya 1987 goda', p. 2.

[37] Grachev, Blengino, and Stievano (eds.), *1985–2005*, p. 175.

the scale produced by perestroika could have begun in the Soviet Union in the last decades of the twentieth century. Neither a mass movement from below for reform nor (still less) a revolution was remotely on the cards. The authorities treated all unauthorized political protests as if they were a danger to the very existence of the state. While this did not exactly exhibit confidence in the legitimacy and popularity of the regime, it was effective enough in nipping embryonic opposition in the bud. As Dmitriy Furman remarked: 'We had one dissident for every 1000 employees of the KGB.... An attempt at revolution would have been immediately stopped at the onset.'[38]

Movements from below in the Soviet Union were a consequence of perestroika, rather than a stimulus to it. By 1990–1 such mass movements were no longer waiting for guidelines from the Kremlin before making hitherto unthinkable demands. As a result, pressures mounted on Gorbachev both from within the mainly conservative apparatus of the Communist Party and from a revitalized society. The attacks from reactionary and conservative forces on Gorbachev's allies within the leadership, especially on Aleksandr Yakovlev and on Eduard Shevardnadze, were until very late in the perestroika period even more severe than those on Gorbachev himself. This was because it was safer to criticize them than to attack Gorbachev in the still hierarchical system, in which he retained a substantial power of appointment and dismissal. It was also because those determined to preserve or recreate the old order wished to separate him from his allies on the radical wing of the Politburo. In this latter respect, they partly succeeded. Shevardnadze, who had been Gorbachev's surprise appointment as Minister of Foreign Affairs in 1985, suddenly resigned from that post in December 1990. Yakovlev, who, entirely on the strength of Gorbachev's patronage, had been given extraordinarily fast promotion into the inner leadership of the CPSU, was dismayed to find Gorbachev turning to him less for advice from 1989 onwards.[39] While Yakovlev remained within the leadership of the country until the summer of 1991, he did not wield the same degree of influence within the system or have the ear of Gorbachev to

---

[38] Ibid., p. 53.

[39] The KGB, with the active engagement of its Chairman, Vladimir Kryuchkov, had been trying to undermine Yakovlev in the eyes of Gorbachev, suggesting that he was an 'agent of influence' of the Central Intelligence Agency (CIA) and thus—to put it at its mildest—someone of whom Gorbachev should be extremely wary. Since Gorbachev kept Yakovlev in high office, it is clear that he did not believe the 'agent of influence' calumny, but he evidently felt it politically prudent to put a greater distance between himself and Yakovlev. Gorbachev's trusted aide and foreign policy adviser, Anatoliy Chernyaev, sent a memorandum to Gorbachev on 11 November 1989 in which he spoke about Yakovlev nursing an 'acute internal grievance' and made it clear that he shared Yakovlev's dissatisfaction that he had been made subordinate to Vadim Medvedev within the Central Committee Secretariat. Chernyaev said that he assumed that Gorbachev had (in effect) downgraded Yakovlev because of 'passing and tactical considerations'. However, arguing that Medevev was 'too cautious'—and, as compared with Yakovlev, 'devoid of political

the extent that he had in the earlier years of perestroika, including the decisive year of 1988 when the fundamentals of the system began to change.

The growing criticism of Gorbachev himself in the last two years of the Soviet Union's existence came from different sources—from radicals who argued for a more thoroughgoing democratization and marketization; from national elites in a number of different republics who sought greater autonomy within, or even complete independence from, the Soviet Union; from ordinary citizens whose expectations had been raised by reform but who were angered by the lack of improvement in the material conditions of their lives (indeed, with the economy in limbo between plan and market, some prices rose and shortages markedly increased); and there was immense pressure also from conservative Soviet forces who feared, not without reason, that a disintegrative process was underway.

Mikhail Gorbachev, who entitled the introduction to one of his own books 'I do not know happy reformers...',[40] could echo the words of Samuel Huntington, written two decades before perestroika:

> The way of the reformer is hard...he necessarily fights a two-front war against both conservative and revolutionary. Indeed, to be successful, he may have to engage in a multi-front war with a multiplicity of participants, in which his enemies on one front are his allies on another. The aim of the revolutionary is to polarize politics, and hence he attempts to simplify, to dramatize, and to amalgamate political issues into a single clear-cut dichotomy between the forces of 'progress' and those of 'reaction'.... The revolutionary promotes rigidity in politics, the reformer fluidity and adaptability.[41]

Perestroika, as it developed, became (as Gorbachev frequently remarked) the pursuit of revolutionary aims by evolutionary means. While from the summer of 1988 onwards what he was seeking was a transformation, rather than mere reform, of the Soviet system, by temperament and character Gorbachev remained a reformer rather than a revolutionary. His esteem for Lenin—but not for Leninism (a point I shall elaborate in Chapter 10)—is based on the idea that the late Lenin saw the error of his earlier ways and wished to reform that which had been created by the Bolsheviks.[42]

---

imagination'—Chernyaev said that 'the interests of our cause' are at stake. See National Security Archive, Alexander Yakovlev and the Role of the Soviet Reforms: http://www.gwu.edu/~nsarchiv for this document (translated by Svetlana Savrankskaya) from the State Archive of the Russian Federation, Fond 10063, Opis 1. See also Yakovlev, *Sumerki*, pp. 532–42.

[40] M.S. Gorbachev, *Gody trudnykh resheniy* (Alfa-Print, Moscow, 1993), pp. 3–25.

[41] Samuel P. Huntington, *Political Order in Changing Societies* (Yale University Press, New Haven, CT, 1968), pp. 344–5.

[42] 'I am a reformer by nature', Gorbachev declared in a book published in 1993 (*Gody trudnykh resheniy...*), p. 25. Gorbachev's career bears that out. It is not, however, something that could be said of Lenin.

OUTLINE OF THE BOOK

The next four chapters, which form Part II of this book, were written between 1985 and 1989 while perestroika was still a work in progress. Chapter 2—commissioned by the American journal, *Problems of Communism*, as the first response to the choice of Gorbachev as General Secretary—was written on the assumption that Gorbachev, as the youngest member of the Politburo, might still be General Secretary of the Soviet Communist Party at the beginning of the new millennium. I adduced reasons for supposing that serious innovation would occur under Gorbachev's leadership, but did not imagine that the Soviet state would no longer exist seven years hence.

This account in Chapter 2 of Gorbachev's career path which took him to the Kremlin is still of relevance to understanding perestroika. Two important documents, used in that April 1985 article for the first time in any scholarly publication, were Gorbachev's speech to a conference on ideology held in Moscow in December 1984, in which the future Soviet leader began to show his reformist colours, and an assessment of Gorbachev produced by his long-standing friend, Zdeněk Mlynář, in the Italian Communist Party (PCI) newspaper, *L'Unità*. Six years before Gorbachev became leader of the Soviet Communist Party, Mlynář, who died in 1997, described Gorbachev to me as 'open-minded, intelligent, and anti-Stalinist'.[43] He did not, however, write—or say a word in public—about his knowledge of the future General Secretary of the CPSU until Gorbachev was installed in the Kremlin as the new Soviet leader. Gorbachev had been Mlynář's best Russian friend when they studied together in the Law Faculty of Moscow University from 1950 to 1955, but Mlynář was very conscious that publicity about the closeness of Gorbachev to a leading 'Prague Spring' reformer, who had been expelled from the Communist Party of Czechoslovakia as a revisionist, would do nothing to assist Gorbachev's chances of reaching the top of the Soviet political hierarchy.[44]

In that same chapter, written at the outset of perestroika, I say that pluralism is not on the political agenda and Gorbachev would be highly unlikely to question the foundations of the system that had permitted him

---

[43] See Archie Brown, 'Introduction', p. xiv, of Mikhail Gorbachev and Zdeněk Mlynář, *Conversations with Gorbachev: On Perestroika, the Prague Spring, and the Crossroads of Socialism* (Columbia University Press, New York, 2002).

[44] For similar reasons, I also wrote nothing about Mlynář's views on Gorbachev, which I had received at first hand in a private conversation in 1979, until Mlynář himself had come out in public—very soon after Gorbachev became General Secretary—with his *L'Unità* article of 9 April 2005 on 'My Fellow Student Mikhail Gorbachev'.

to rise from humble origins to the highest position in the Soviet state. The first statement was true at the time—it was 1987 before pluralism *was* placed on the political agenda, and by Gorbachev himself—and it was also the case that in 1985 Gorbachev (as he has said on countless occasions) did not question the foundations of the system. However, in ruling out a future change in Gorbachev's evaluation of the very essence of the system, I had underestimated the 'open mind' of which Mlynář spoke. As subsequent chapters make clear, Gorbachev came to believe that the Communist system had to be replaced, not merely reformed. Writing soon after the end of perestroika, he said that as Soviet leader he had freed himself from the illusions about reform which he had harboured at the outset and took on to his shoulders 'the burden of transformation in a complex and great country'.[45]

When Chapter 3 was written, in late 1986, perestroika was still in its early stages. It was a time of developing glasnost, of foreign policy initiatives, and some domestic reform, though not yet anything as radical as it was to become. I argued then (and would argue still) that it was entirely wrong to regard the developments of 1985–6 as cosmetic, for important changes had already taken place, and it was evident that a struggle over the pace and direction of innovation had begun. It seemed clear that neither the second secretary of the CPSU, Yegor Ligachev, nor the Chairman of the Council of Ministers, Nikolay Ryzhkov, were prepared for as far-reaching reform as was Gorbachev, and they, after all, were two of the newer members of the Politburo. Some of the old guard were already becoming nostalgic for the past. Even in 1986 what could be published in the Soviet Union was far in advance of what could appear in Brezhnev's time. However, the glasnost of 1986 was still very limited compared with the growing freedom of speech and of publication that was to occur over the next three years.

Chapter 4 considers political developments between 1987 and the middle of 1989. It thus covers the period of radicalization of the reform agenda, including Gorbachev's endorsement of the concepts of pluralism (albeit still qualified) in 1987, of the rule of law, and of checks and balances. It discusses the breakthrough represented by contested elections for a new legislature in the spring of 1989 and the growing attraction of social democracy for the reform wing of the Communist Party leadership. As early as 1985, representatives of Western Communist Parties were complaining to Central Committee officials in Moscow that 'right now the CPSU is on better terms with the socialists and social democrats than it is with fraternal parties'.[46]

---

[45] See Gorbachev, *Gody trudnykh resheniy,* p. 25.
[46] 'The Diary of Anatoly Chernyaev' for 1985, entry of 16 October: http://www.gwu.edu/~nsarchiv.

At that time this tendency reflected mainly the new leadership's assessment that those 'fraternal' parties, with the partial exception of the PCI (although they were among the complainants), were of little political relevance. By 1989 the attraction of Gorbachev and his allies to social democracy had become ideational. It was no longer based simply on a realistic assessment of the comparative strength of Western democratic socialist parties, on the one hand, and Communist Parties, on the other. In general, developments in the political system by June 1989 (when the article which constitutes chapter four was completed) gave rise to much more optimism than what was happening in the economy. Indeed, I noted at that time that it 'remains a moot point' how long the Soviet population 'will give credence to a leadership that does not produce concrete economic results'.

In Chapter 5, completed later in 1989, I discuss briefly the concept of perestroika and go on to suggest that there are four elements of pre-eminent importance in politics (which I discuss in turn): ideas, institutions, interests, and culture. I should have added leadership, and do so now.[47] I note that the outcome of the first competitive national elections—including the overwhelming victory of Boris Yeltsin in Moscow—in the Spring of 1989 was the point at which the balance of forces within the Soviet political system began to be changed from below. Contested elections, even though they were not yet multiparty contests, were a hugely significant step along the road of democratization. Their introduction meant that the highest echelons of the Communist Party (knowingly in some cases, unknowingly in others) had begun a process of sharing power with the people and of making themselves accountable to them. Writing in the second half of 1989, I noted also that the revitalization of national aspirations had brought 'the very survival' of the USSR into question. Given the rise in expectations, a much more meaningful federal system, with perestroika embracing the reality of national diversity, appeared to be the only alternative to a return to a higher level of authoritarianism and the use of naked force if 'the disintegration of the Soviet state' were to be avoided.

Part III of the book—unlike Part II with its contemporaneous assessment of developments under perestroika—is written with the benefit of knowing how it all ended and with the further advantage of access to an abundance of new sources. In Chapter 6 I take up in some detail a theme I had addressed briefly in Soviet times, though not then using the concept of 'institutional

---

[47] However, the attention I devoted to political leadership in my writings of the perestroika period (and, indeed, much earlier) was implicit recognition of the scale of its importance, not least in a system which places great power and authority in the hands of the topmost leader.

amphibiousness'. That useful notion was coined as recently as 1994 by X.L. Ding.[48] The essence of the argument which Ding applies to China and which I apply to the Soviet Union is that it was not the development of civil society but official institutions used for conflicting purposes that paved the way for radical reform. The coming to power of a new leader with different values from his predecessors was of decisive importance, but Gorbachev would have been in no position to effect changes, and his ideas would in all probability not have developed as they did, had he not been able to draw upon the advice of well-educated and unorthodox thinkers who had spent years in the very heart of the Soviet Establishment—in a number of significant instances as senior officials within the International Department of the Central Committee. I discuss also in Chapter 6 the very important advisory role played by a range of policy-oriented research institutes.

The main focus of Chapter 7 is on the last two years of the Soviet Union, in which the dismantling of the Communist system is distinguished from the disintegration of the Soviet state. There was, of course, an interconnection between those two processes, but they should be kept analytically distinct. Moreover, the demise of the system and of the state were not coterminous. The essentials of the system were dismantled before the state disappeared. Gorbachev has recognized that the Soviet Union was a 'party-state' and that, accordingly, weakening the Communist Party weakened the state.[49] Yet, though perestroika had begun from inside the nomenklatura of the Party, the nomenklatura had 'turned into its most utterly reactionary force'.[50] One of Gorbachev's dilemmas was, therefore, that while he was obliged to struggle with, and reduce the importance of, the party apparatus, in doing so he was undermining his vertical chain of command. A way round this would have been for Gorbachev to add strength and legitimacy to the new institution of an executive presidency by standing in a nation-wide election for that office rather than through indirect election by the Congress of People's Deputies. Another would have been to take the risk earlier of splitting the Communist Party, putting himself at the head of its social democratic component.[51]

[48] Ding, 'Institutional Amphibiousness and the Transition from Communism: The Case of China', *British Journal of Political Science*, Vol. 24, No. 3, July 1994, pp. 293–318.

[49] Gorbachev, *Ponyat' perestroyku*..., p. 373.

[50] Ibid.

[51] I made these arguments earlier in Archie Brown, *The Gorbachev Factor* (Oxford University Press, Oxford, 1996), pp. 202–7. Others have made the same points. In his latest book, Gorbachev appears to accept that, with the benefit of hindsight, it would have been worthwhile taking these risks (and he does not, in fact, doubt that in a general election in March 1990 he would have been elected President). See Gorbachev, *Ponyat' perestroyku*..., pp. 373–4.

In Chapter 8 I examine the international dimension of perestroika and look at the transnational influences that were at work in the transition from Communism. One of the arguments is that the changes in the Soviet Union encapsulated by perestroika—ideological change, far-reaching change of the political system, and the dramatic shift in foreign policy (not least towards Eastern Europe)—produced a 'Fourth Wave' of democratization quite distinct from the 'Third Wave' of the 1970s, involving the democratization of Portugal, Spain, and Greece as well as parts of Latin America. This wave began, in other words, in Moscow, but when it led to the rapid overthrow of Communist regimes in Eastern Europe, along with the gain of national independence for the peoples of East-Central Europe, these developments swirled back into the Soviet Union, strengthening both separatist movements in Soviet republics and a growing anti-Communism, even in the Russian heartland of the Soviet Union. There was no direct influence of the earlier Iberian democratization on Soviet reformers, but there was a very real mutual influence between the developments in the Soviet Union and in East-Central Europe in the later 1980s.[52]

In Chapter 9 the issue of explaining the end of the Cold War is tackled. This has kept international relations specialists busy ever since the East–West conflict ended differently and much more suddenly than had been predicted. There has even been debate about *when* the Cold War ended. In Chapter 9 I argue that its ideological base was removed in 1988 and that in a political and military sense it ended no later than 1989, the year in which the Soviet takeover of Eastern Europe which had given rise to the Cold War was reversed. In this penultimate chapter I draw upon archival, memoir, and interview material now available and also consider some of the theoretical debates which the end of the Cold War has spawned.

Chapter 10, the lengthy conclusion of the book, focuses mainly, but not exclusively, on Mikhail Gorbachev. I have been able to use archival material which has not been utilized hitherto either by Western or Russian scholars. In this retrospective examination of Gorbachev, I pay special attention to

---

[52] Most practising politicians would not have heard of the 'Third Wave', a concept which belongs more to the world of political science than the business of politics. Mikhail Gorbachev, however, is one of the exceptions to that generalization, and in his latest book he writes of 'perestroika joining in "the third wave of democratic revolutions"'. Perestroika, he says, caught up with that tradition, and returned to Europe the eastern part of the continent which had 'earlier been hermetically sealed off by the "iron curtain"' (*Ponyat' perestroyku*..., p. 367). While the last statement is correct, Gorbachev is actually understating on this occasion his own role which was that of a prime mover in the 'Fourth Wave', during which most *European* Communist states became democracies, although in a number of the *post-Soviet* states, in particular, the outcome of transition from Communism was either a hybrid regime or an alternative form of authoritarian rule.

a number of controversial issues. These include the relationship of Gorbachev with Lenin and with Leninism; Gorbachev's relationship with the CPSU and his attitude to dismantling the Communist system; his response to the challenge of nationalism and separatism; and the dilemmas the last Soviet leader faced in institution-building. I compare also the mindsets of Gorbachev and Yeltsin, look at some myths concerning the August 1991 coup, and examine public opinion on Gorbachev, both during perestroika and subsequently. I conclude with an assessment of the successes and failures of perestroika and of Gorbachev's place in history.

Part II

2

Gorbachev: New Man in the Kremlin[1]

In the sixty years between the spring of 1922 when Stalin became General Secretary of the Central Committee of the Communist Party and the spring of 1982, the Soviet Union had just three general secretaries—Stalin himself, Nikita Khrushchev, and Leonid Brezhnev. In the last three years, four men have held that office—Brezhnev in the last months of his eighteen-year reign, Yuriy Andropov, Konstantin Chernenko, and now Mikhail Gorbachev. If Gorbachev lives as long as any one of his five predecessors, he can expect to be still at the helm of the Soviet Communist Party and state at the beginning of the next millennium. For that and other reasons, the choice of Gorbachev is of exceptional significance for the Soviet Union and—given the country's role in international affairs—for the rest of the world. There is every possibility that Gorbachev will in time become the most powerful Soviet leader since Khrushchev, though his political style is likely to be very different and his policies more carefully thought through.

Before going on to discuss Gorbachev's path to the top, the speed of his advance, and his attributes, outlook, and priorities, it may be useful to begin by noting those respects in which Gorbachev's election as General Secretary corresponds with Soviet tradition and the respects in which it is a novel succession.

SIMILARITIES TO PREVIOUS SUCCESSIONS

In several ways, the choice of Gorbachev fits the pattern of elevations to the Soviet leadership. Starting with Lenin, there have been only seven undisputed top leaders in Soviet history.[2] All six of Lenin's successors were at the time they

---

[1] *This chapter (apart from several italicized updatings in footnotes) was written in March–April 1985 and published under this title in* Problems of Communism, *Vol. 34, No. 3, May–June 1985.*

[2] I am excluding Georgiy Malenkov, for, though in 1953–4 he was accorded a higher protocol ranking than Khrushchev, it is not clear that even then he wielded greater political power than Khrushchev, and by 1955 Khrushchev had quite evidently established a superior authority to him.

attained the top leadership position already full members of the Politburo and secretaries of the Central Committee.[3] That applies to Stalin who was already *general* secretary at the time of Lenin's death in 1924, though it was only *after* Lenin's death that he was able to consolidate the power of the General Secretaryship to the extent that it became the top job. Chernenko's death on 10 March 1985 left only two Soviet politicians who were full members of the Politburo and secretaries of the Central Committee—Gorbachev himself, who had held such joint membership since 1980, and Grigoriy Romanov, who had combined membership of the Politburo with that of the Central Committee Secretariat only since 1983, even though he had been in the Politburo longer than Gorbachev.

Second, career profile, as well as position at the time the vacancy in the General Secretaryship occurs, is important, and it is of particular relevance that a serious candidate should have experience of party secretaryships at various levels of the hierarchy, including the regional and (as follows from the point made in the previous paragraph) the Central Committee level. The economic experience gained thereby should ideally include acquaintance with agriculture, and some foreign policy experience is an additional asset. Every General Secretary thus far has had his institutional base in the party apparatus and has spent a greater proportion of his career in party work than in any other branch of political activity. Even Andropov is no exception to this rule, though his Ministry of Foreign Affairs and KGB experience made him the nearest thing to one. Gorbachev had a model rise through the party hierarchy, and, like Khrushchev and Brezhnev before him, he had significant knowledge of agriculture—indeed, greater expertise in this realm than any of his predecessors.

Gorbachev's foreign policy experience before coming to the General Secretaryship is not as great as was Brezhnev's, who as chairman of the Presidium of the Supreme Soviet from May 1960 until July 1964 had extensive contacts with foreign statesmen. Nor is his knowledge of the international scene likely initially to be as great as was Andropov's, who from 1951 until 1982 served successively in the Ministry of Foreign Affairs, as head of one of the foreign departments of the Central Committee (Liaison with Communist and Workers' Parties of Socialist Countries), and as chairman of the KGB. Nor, for that matter, has Gorbachev had the opportunity to take part in talks with an

---

[3] I noted this and other prerequisites of a potential General Secretary while Brezhnev was still alive. See Archie Brown, 'Leadership Succession and Policy Innovation', in Archie Brown and Michael Kaser (eds.), *Soviet Policy for the 1980s* (Macmillan, London, and Indiana University Press, Bloomington, 1982), pp. 232–5.

American president as Chernenko had when he participated in the Brezhnev–Carter summit meeting in Vienna in 1979.[4] Yet Gorbachev, too, has had the opportunity to gain some foreign policy experience in addition to that which all Politburo members acquire simply by virtue of regularly attending Politburo meetings at which foreign relations and international issues figure prominently on the agenda.[5] He undertook an eight-day visit as head of a Soviet delegation to Canada in May 1983 in addition to his earlier lower profile visits to various Western countries and to East European ones. When Chernenko became General Secretary, Gorbachev succeeded him as chairman of the Foreign Affairs Commission of the Soviet of the Union of the USSR Supreme Soviet. In that capacity, he made a week-long visit to Britain (cut short by a day because of the death of Marshal Dmitriy Ustinov) in December 1984, which confirmed his grasp of international issues and possession of diplomatic skills.

Third, this latest succession conforms to the general pattern in terms of the nationality of the party leader. Non-Russians in the top leadership team are at a disadvantage in the General Secretaryship stakes. There are still, after all, more Russians in the Soviet Union than all other nationalities put together, and they are disproportionately well represented in the all-Union Central Committee apparatus. Gorbachev, like all of his predecessors except one, is a Russian; Stalin remains the only exception to that rule.

Fourth, and perhaps more surprising, at age 54, Gorbachev is in the age band at which a majority of general secretaries have acceded to the top job. The sight of three aged and infirm Soviet leaders in a row has somewhat obscured the fact that only two of the Soviet Union's seven leaders and six general secretaries have been older than their fifties when they became leaders of the country, and only one (Chernenko) was over 70 when he was elected General Secretary. In so far as it is possible to generalize about what is 'normal' in accession to the General Secretaryship when dealing with only six cases, it can be said that the fifties is the normal age band in which a Soviet leader accedes to the top job.

[4] Not that Chernenko appears to have contributed much. See Zbigniew Brzezinski, *Power and Principle: Memoirs of the National Security Adviser, 1977–81* (Weidenfeld & Nicolson, London, 1983), p. 343; and (for more explicit comment on this) Jimmy Carter, *Keeping Faith: Memoirs of a President* (Bantam Books, New York, 1982), p. 246.

[5] For further elaboration of this point, see Archie Brown, 'The Foreign Policy-Making Process', in Curtis Keeble (ed.), *The Soviet State: The Domestic Roots of Soviet Foreign Policy* (Gower for the Royal Institute of International Affairs, Aldershot, UK, 1985), pp. 191–216, especially pp. 200–3.

DIFFERENCES FROM PREVIOUS SUCCESSIONS

There are, however, three even more important respects in which Gorbachev differs from all previous incumbents of the General Secretaryship. The first is in terms of *relative* age, that is, the General Secretary's age in relation to his or her colleagues. No one before Gorbachev has become top leader as the youngest member of both the Politburo and Central Committee Secretariat. This is of greater potential relevance to the power Gorbachev may yet wield than is absolute age (though Stalin was the only one to become General Secretary at a younger age than Gorbachev).

Stalin, at the time of Lenin's death, was only 44, but he was one of the two oldest members of the Politburo. (The other was Trotsky, also 44.) The average age of the Politburo in 1924 was only 42. Khrushchev was 58 when Stalin died in March 1953 and 59 when he was formally given the title First Secretary of the Central Committee in September of that year. As such, he was a year above the average age of the Politburo. Brezhnev, at 57, was just a little below the average age of the Politburo (59) immediately following the removal of Khrushchev in 1964. Andropov, who was 68 when he succeeded Brezhnev in November 1982, was also fractionally below the Politburo average age, which was 69 at that point.[6] By the time Andropov died on 9 February 1984, the average age of the twelve full members of the Politburo had declined to 67, and so Chernenko, at 72, was significantly above it.

Immediately after Chernenko's death, the Politburo (by this time down to ten voting members as a result of the death also of Marshal Ustinov in December 1984) still had an average age of 67. Of these men, five were over 70, three were in their sixties, and only two were in their fifties. Not only was Gorbachev the youngest member of the Politburo by a full five years, he was thirteen years below the average age of the voting membership. Even more remarkable, he was the youngest member of the entire top leadership team— the twenty-one people who in the immediate post-Chernenko period made up the full and candidate membership of the Politburo and the Secretariat of the Central Committee. This is quite unprecedented and could have important implications for the future.

---

[6] The average age of the Politburo just after Brezhnev's death was 69 if Andrey Kirilenko is counted as a member, which he formally was until released from office at the Central Committee plenary session held on 22 November 1982 (see *Pravda*, 23 November 1982, p. 1). However, Kirilenko had fallen out of favour with Brezhnev and Chernenko and had in practice been dropped from the Politburo while Brezhnev was still alive. If Kirilenko is excluded from consideration, the average age of the Politburo immediately following Brezhnev's demise on 10 November was exactly the same as Andropov's, 68.

Although there has been a strong element of genuine collectivity of the Soviet leadership in the post-Stalin, and especially post-Khrushchev, era, every General Secretary except Chernenko, who came to the leadership too late and was too infirm to make much of an impact on it, has increased his powers during his time in the top post. This is especially true of those who had a lengthy period of office, though in the case of the first three of them— Stalin, Khrushchev, and Brezhnev—each man wielded less power than the previous General Secretary.[7] Although promotions to the Secretariat and to the Politburo require the approval of a majority of members of the Politburo itself, which gives senior members of the Politburo an opportunity to make trade-offs among potential candidates, there is no doubt that the General Secretary is in a better position than anyone else to get his or her nominees promoted to the top leadership team. As the very title General Secretary (or, in Khrushchev's time, First Secretary) suggests, this person's supremacy within the Secretariat is more clearly institutionalized than is his or her position in the Politburo. A General Secretary has sometimes found it easier in the early stages of his leadership to make changes in the composition of the Secretariat than in that of the voting membership of the Politburo. Gorbachev, however, as will be noted in greater detail in the final section, has succeeded in making a dramatic impact on the composition of the Politburo little more than six weeks after becoming party leader. Even when the process of change within the Politburo is a more gradual one, a point tends to be reached at which the General Secretary has a sufficient group of protégés and supporters there to simplify the task of removing those whose presence he has earlier had to tolerate without enthusiasm. For example, there was no love lost between Leonid Brezhnev and Aleksandr Shelepin. But, although

---

[7] This point has been the subject of some misinterpretation. Writing three years before Brezhnev's death, I noted that 'each General Secretary has wielded less individual power over policy than his predecessor, but within his period of office his power vis-à-vis his colleagues has grown' (Archie Brown, 'The Power of the General Secretary of the CPSU', in T.H. Rigby, Archie Brown, and Peter Reddaway (eds.), *Authority, Power and Policy in the USSR* (Macmillan, London, and St Martin's Press, New York, 1980), p. 136). Rather to my dismay, this has been treated by a number of subsequent writers as if it were, or purported to be, a general law of Soviet politics. To take a recent example, Thane Gustafson, reviewing a book by George Breslauer, refers to this generalization as 'Brown's law' (see *Slavic Review* [Urbana, IL], Winter 1984, p. 684). In fact, this was a generalization (which I would still uphold) limited to the only three General Secretaries who had held office up to that time: Stalin, Khrushchev, and Brezhnev. So far as the first point is concerned, there was no suggestion that such a trend towards declining leadership power would continue. Indeed, it seems clear that Andropov was within a year wielding a degree of power that Brezhnev did not possess for at least the first six years of his General Secretaryship. The second part of the statement might, however, be extended into something approaching a law of Soviet politics. It does seem to be a *zakonomernost'* of the Soviet political system that a General Secretary, granted a sufficient span of life, will over a period of time increase his power vis-à-vis his or her colleagues in the Politburo and Secretariat.

Brezhnev was able to have Shelepin removed from the Central Committee Secretariat in 1967, it was not until 1975 (by which time, following other changes in the Politburo composition, the General Secretary's power had greatly increased) that Brezhnev felt strong enough to push for Shelepin's expulsion from the Politburo as well. All the signs are that Gorbachev will continue to move very much faster than Brezhnev did.

If he lives a normal lifespan, Gorbachev may readily become the first Soviet leader to preside over an entire top leadership team that has been appointed under his chairmanship of the Politburo and Secretariat and, accordingly, during a time when he was exercising a greater influence than anyone else on the choice of candidates. At first, the pool from which he can draw people—members of the Central Committee—will be only to a very limited degree of his own choosing, but Gorbachev is fortunate in that respect also. Whereas Andropov and Chernenko had to operate with Brezhnev's Central Committee, which was elected at the 26th Party Congress in 1981 (a factor that was more of an impediment for Andropov than for Chernenko, in view of Andropov's desire for change and of Chernenko's closeness to Brezhnev), Gorbachev has come to power within a year of the next five-yearly party congress and in time to exercise still more influence than he could before on the composition of the Central Committee which will be formally elected at that 27th congress.[8]

Thus, over the long term, Gorbachev has quite remarkable opportunities to promote like-minded people to senior leadership positions. In the shorter term, he will, as previous general secretaries have had to do, preserve alliances with a number of the weightiest members of the Politburo and take care not to tread on too many toes at once. But even in the short and medium term, the age structure of the Politburo and Secretariat is such that a number of changes are inevitable.

A second respect in which Gorbachev is different from all of his predecessors as General Secretary is that he alone has made his professional political career (in the Komsomol and party apparatus) entirely in the post-Stalin period. I shall look at his career in greater detail below, but the main point in the present context is that he is of a different *political generation* with different generational experience from that of all of his predecessors. Unlike them, he

---

[8] At the plenary session of the Central Committee held on 23 April 1985, it was announced that the next party congress would begin on 25 February 1986 (*Pravda*, 25 April 1985, p. 1). Earlier there had been suggestions in the Soviet Union that the date of the 27th congress might be brought forward to late 1985. Thus, for example, in a speech delivered on 7 February 1985, the First Secretary of the Georgian party organization, Eduard Shevardnadze, spoke of 1985 being 'the year of the 27th Party Congress' (British Broadcasting Corporation, *Summary of World Broadcasts: USSR* [hereafter BBC SWB], SU/7877/i, 16 February 1985).

was not involved in any way in Stalin's purges and so is unburdened either by the guilt of having denounced others or by memories of fear of being denounced. He joined the party in 1952 while he was a student at Moscow University, and it is of some consequence that his time there (1950–5) included a period of more than two years after Stalin's death. This was a time of much freer discussion in student circles than had existed for many years. Though there was not yet the explosion of criticism that was to follow the 20th CPSU Congress in 1956, the post-Stalin 'thaw' was already underway in 1954 and 1955, the 'anti-cosmopolitan' campaign[9] was being laid to rest, and the atmosphere at Moscow University had become perceptibly more relaxed.[10] It is certainly worthy of note that Gorbachev's early, and perhaps formative, years in Komsomol and party work were in the Khrushchev era. It was during his first year of full-time professional employment in the Komsomol that the 20th Party Congress took place, and the very first congress that Gorbachev himself attended was the 22nd (in 1961), at which the attack on Stalin was taken further than it had been five years earlier and delivered by Khrushchev in open rather than closed session.[11] It is known, however, that Gorbachev did not regret the fall of Khrushchev, for he was critical of Khrushchev's ill-considered agricultural reorganizations and of his maintenance in reality of the old method of arbitrary interventions from the centre even when he was ostensibly decentralizing.[12]

[9] The 'anti-cosmopolitan' campaign aimed to sow distrust of everything foreign and had strongly anti-Semitic undertones. For a discussion of it, see Adam B. Ulam, *Stalin: The Man and His Era* (Allen Lane, London, 1973), pp. 678–85.

[10] On this, see the testimony of a Czech contemporary of Gorbachev's in the Moscow University Law Faculty: Zdeněk Mlynář, *Nightfrost in Prague* (Hurst, London, 1980), p. 27. A much less convincing account of these years is provided by a Soviet emigrant who graduated from the Moscow University Law Faculty in 1950 but 'fairly frequently' visited the university subsequently. He contrasts what he calls the 'fairly liberal' early postwar atmosphere with the political and academic climate of 1950, but omits to mention the more fundamental atmospheric change produced by the death of Stalin. See Lev Yudovich, 'Gorbachev 2: First Rungs on the Ladder', in *Soviet Analyst* (Richmond, Surrey, London), 19 December 1984, pp. 2–3.

[11] For information on Gorbachev's attendance at party congresses, see, for example, *Pravda*, 12 March 1985, p. 1.

[12] This point is made in an important article published by Zdeněk Mlynář in the daily newspaper of the Italian Communist Party to which I have had access at a late stage in the writing of this chapter. See Zdeněk Mlynář, 'My Fellow Student Mikhail Gorbachev,' *L'Unità* (Rome), 9 April 1985, p. 9. Here Mlynář reveals for the first time in public not only that he and Gorbachev were fellow students throughout Gorbachev's five years in Moscow University, but also that they took the same courses, lived in the same student residence, and were good friends. Gorbachev's views on Khrushchev were expressed in his last meeting with Mlynář which took place in Stavropol in 1967. At that time, Mlynář was a rising personality in the Communist Party of Czechoslovakia, and in 1968 he was to become a Central Committee secretary and Politburo member. In the aftermath of the 'Prague Spring' he was, however, expelled from the party, and since 1977 has lived in emigration. His portrayal of Gorbachev is at once objective, well-informed,

Different members of the same generation may hold very different views, and so there can be no question of automatically assuming in every individual case a certain political outlook on the basis of a particular generational experience. What can fairly be argued is that a Soviet citizen who began his full-time political career in 1955 had a better chance of retaining or acquiring a relatively open mind than one who first set foot on the bottom rung of the ladder twenty years earlier.

A third feature that distinguished Gorbachev from previous general secretaries is his superior level of formal education. Of particular importance is his five years of study in the Law Faculty of the Soviet Union's leading university. As I noted when writing about Gorbachev three years ago, he is remembered by some of his contemporaries as an able and open-minded student.[13] Being in Moscow University brought him into contact with other students of ability, many of whom had had a more privileged pre-university education than geography and circumstances had afforded him (see the section below on his rise from kolkhoz to the Kremlin). There is a vast difference between five years of full-time university education in Moscow and the education picked up, often on a part-time basis, in provincial institutes by many of the older generation of leading party officials. Gorbachev himself later added a second degree by part-time study when he received the qualification of 'agronomist-economist' from the Stavropol Agricultural Institute in 1967.[14] Although academic degrees awarded to established party officials often owe more to their political standing than to their scholarly endeavours, Gorbachev's life-long connection with agriculture and political interest in it, together with his intellectual curiosity, almost surely mean that in this case the degree was earned. At any rate, Canadian agricultural specialists who met with Gorbachev in May 1983 were impressed by his detailed technical knowledge of the subject.

and favourable. Since Mlynář's own hopes for Czech communism were dashed by the Soviet intervention of 1968, he can hardly be accused of a priori bias in favour of a Soviet leader. His sympathetic account of Gorbachev should stand as an important piece of evidence from one who better than anyone else now living in the West knew the younger Gorbachev.

[13] In Brown and Kaser, op. cit., p. 240. Such an assessment has now been confirmed by Mlynář (loc. cit.). Yudovich, who produces a determinedly negative view of Gorbachev as a student on the basis of his own return visits to his alma mater, states, in contrast, that other students regarded Gorbachev as 'dull and badly educated' (loc. cit., p. 3). The assertion that he was 'dull' flies in the face of the recollections of Mlynář and others who, unlike Yudovich, were Law Faculty undergraduates at the same time as Gorbachev, and of the testimony of practically every Western politician, businessman, and official who has met him in more recent years. So far as the assertion that he was 'badly educated' is concerned, it would be surprising if he were academically as well prepared as those students who had had the privilege of an uninterrupted education in city schools. What is evident, and more to the point, is that he had a considerable capacity for learning, which he was to put to good use.

[14] *Pravda*, 12 March 1985, p. 1.

GROMYKO'S NOMINATING SPEECH

Fascinating light on Gorbachev's qualities, as seen by Andrey Gromyko, and insight on Gromyko's view of the attributes to be looked for in a General Secretary were provided by the Foreign Minister's surprisingly informal and genuinely enthusiastic speech of recommendation of Gorbachev to the Central Committee on 11 March 1985.[15] It is of interest to compare it with the nomination speeches of Gorbachev's two immediate predecessors, Andropov and Chernenko, and to consider why Gromyko's speech was accorded a much more restricted circulation than the previous two nomination addresses.

In certain respects, the nomination speech that is the odd one out among the last three is Chernenko's nomination of Andropov at the Central Committee plenary session held on 12 November 1982.[16] Whereas Nikolay Tikhonov's recommendation of Chernenko to the Central Committee on 13 February 1984,[17] and Gromyko's proposal of Gorbachev thirteen months later were clearly the speeches of strong and influential supporters of the prospective General Secretary, Chernenko's speech proposing Andropov was that of a senior and defeated rival. Chernenko devoted by far the greater part of his speech to praise of Brezhnev and his leadership style before informing those present that the Politburo had instructed him to propose Yuriy Andropov as General Secretary. He proceeded to recommend him in terms that exaggerated Andropov's closeness to Brezhnev, emphasizing the similarities between the two men and the prospect of continuity. There was an element both of wishful thinking and of an attempt to constrain Andropov in Chernenko's stress on how well Andropov had grasped 'the Brezhnevist style of leadership, a Brezhnevist concern for the interests of the people, and a Brezhnevist relationship to cadres', and in his emphasis on Andropov's 'respect for the opinion of other comrades' and his 'predilection for collective work'.[18] In describing Andropov as 'the closest comrade-in-arms of Leonid Il'ich [Brezhnev]',[19] Chernenko was according him a proximity to Brezhnev that many in his audience must have known applied more precisely to Chernenko himself. In fact, of course, Andropov lost little time in distancing himself from Brezhnev, quickly adopting his own distinctive style of rule with different priorities and a more demanding personnel policy that involved

---

[15] See *Materialy vneocherednogo plenuma tsentral'nogo komiteta KPSS 11 marta 1985 goda* (Politizdat, Moscow, 1985), pp. 6–8.

[16] *Pravda*, 13 November 1982, pp. 1–2.   [17] Ibid., 14 February 1984, p. 2.

[18] Ibid., 13 November 1982, p. 2.   [19] Ibid.

quite rapid rejuvenation of, and turnover in, the ranks of party and governmental cadres.[20]

When Andropov died some fifteen months later, Tikhonov, in a measured address to the Central Committee, devoted approximately a third of his time to warm praise of Andropov and the second half of his speech to praise of Chernenko. As a close Brezhnev associate from the 1930s, Tikhonov, not surprisingly, brought the name of his former patron back into the public view, praising Chernenko as 'a true comrade-in-arms of such leaders of the Leninist type as were Leonid Il'ich Brezhnev and Yuriy Vladimirovich Andropov'.[21] Tikhonov characterized Chernenko's attitude towards cadres as both 'highly exacting and at the same time benevolent' (by implication a blend of Andropov and Brezhnev), and among Chernenko's special qualifications to which Tikhonov drew attention was the 'prominent part' he had played in 'the elaboration of theoretical problems of the perfecting of a developed socialist society' and in ideological work more generally.[22]

The speeches of Chernenko at the Central Committee plenum that elected Andropov and of Tikhonov at the plenum that endorsed Chernenko were made available in tens of millions of copies through their publication in *Pravda*, in other daily newspapers, and in party journals. One reason why Gromyko's speech of recommendation of Gorbachev to the March 1985 Central Committee plenum was, in contrast, not published in *Pravda* may well be that, for the first time in Soviet history, the Central Committee elected a new General Secretary on the very day (March 11) that the leadership made public the death of the previous General Secretary (though Chernenko had, in fact, died at 7.20 p.m. on the previous day).[23] Thus, whereas on the death of Brezhnev and Andropov, *Pravda* was able to devote entire issues to the departed leader before giving full coverage to the election of a new one, the unprecedented speed with which Gorbachev was elected may have meant that a difficult balancing act had to be preserved in the same issue of the newspaper between due respect to the dead leader and a welcome to his successor.

---

[20] I have elaborated on these points in articles on the last two successions. See Archie Brown, 'Andropov: Discipline *and* Reform?', in *Problems of Communism*, January–February 1983, pp. 18–31; and Brown, 'The Soviet Succession: From Andropov to Chernenko', in *The World Today*, April 1984, pp. 134–41. In the latter article I noted that during Andropov's fifteen months as General Secretary there was a turnover of more than a fifth of the Moscow-based members of the Council of Ministers, more than a fifth of the regional party secretaries, and more than a third of the heads of department of the party's Central Committee. Immediately after Andropov's death, the full and candidate members of the Politburo and secretaries of the Central Committee consisted of twenty-three people. Just over a sixth of them had been brought into that inner circle during Andropov's brief tenure, and as many as a quarter of the full members of the Politburo received their promotions to voting membership during the same period.

[21] *Pravda*, 14 February 1984, p. 2.   [22] Ibid.   [23] *Pravda*, 12 March 1985, p. 2.

As it was, Gorbachev's picture appeared on page one and Chernenko's only on page two. To have included Gromyko's speech as well might have tilted the balance too far away from the appropriate obsequies.

That there may have been some disagreement on how wide a distribution to give to Gromyko's speech was, however, suggested by the fact that, unlike the two previous nomination speeches, it did not appear in the issue of the party journal, *Partiynaya zhizn'*, which carried an account of the March plenum, though it *was* published in full in the Central Committee's journal *Kommunist*, which went to press six days later.[24] It was, however, not published in another Central Committee journal, *Politicheskoe samoobrazovanie*,[25] which went to press two days later than *Kommunist*. There are, perhaps, four reasons for such inconsistency. In the first place, it seems fairly clear that Gromyko was not speaking from a written text.[26] The style of the speech is

[24] The relevant issues are *Partiynaya zhizn'* (Moscow), No. 6, March 1985, which went to press on 14 March, and *Kommunist* (Moscow), No. 5, March 1985, which went to press on 20 March. Although *Partiynaya zhizn'* has a greater circulation (1,030,000) than *Kommunist* (952,000), the difference is hardly substantial enough to be decisive. The fact that Gorbachev's supporters had had a further week in which to establish their and his enhanced authority may well be of great consequence, and one should not totally disregard the possibly divergent wishes of the two editors. The chief editor of *Kommunist*, Richard Kosolapov, is a full member of the Central Committee and was a contemporary of Gorbachev's at Moscow University. For biographies of Kosolapov and of the chief editor of *Partiynaya zhizn'*, Mikhail Khaldeyev, see *Yezhegodnik Bol'shoy Sovetskoy Entsiklopedii 1981* (1981 Yearbook of the Great Soviet Encyclopedia), Moscow, Izdatel'stvo 'Sovetskaya Entsiklopediya', 1981, pp. 584 and 607. [*In fact, as was to become clear in the light of later evidence, Kosolapov was anything but enthusiastic about the elevation of Gorbachev to the party leadership.*]

[25] *Politicheskoe samoobrazovanie*, like the two journals mentioned in n. 24, published the nomination speeches by Chernenko and Tikhonov at the previous two successions. The journal is aimed at party propagandists and other ideological workers and has a circulation of 2,388,000.

[26] Gromyko almost certainly had no time in which to prepare a complete written text. From mid-morning until mid-afternoon of 11 March (including a luncheon at which he made a speech on Soviet–French relations) he was engaged in discussions with the French Minister for External Affairs, Roland Dumas. Thus, between the Politburo meeting that chose Gorbachev and which must have been held either in the late evening of 10 March or, more probably, early in the morning of 11 March, and the Central Committee plenary session in the late afternoon of 11 March, Gromyko was fully occupied. [*We now know that Gorbachev convened a meeting of the Politburo which did, indeed, meet at 11 p.m. on the same evening as Chernenko had died. At that gathering Gorbachev was chosen to chair Chernenko's funeral commission—a clear sign, given recent precedents—that he would be the next General Secretary, but the choice of him as General Secretary was made explicitly only at the Politburo meeting on 11 March which preceded the Central Committee plenum that completed Gorbachev's election. See the transcript of the Politburo meeting, at which every Politburo member (except Vladimir Shcherbitsky who could not get back from the United States in time), candidate member, and Secretary of the Central Committee followed the lead of Andrey Gromyko and spoke in favour of Gorbachev becoming party leader ('Zasedanie Politbyuro TsK KPSS, 11 marta 1985 goda', HIA, Fond 89, Reel 1.1001, opis 36, file 16). The First Secretary of the Moscow Party organization and Politburo member, Viktor Grishin, said at the 11 March Politburo meeting: 'Yesterday evening, when we learned of the death of Konstantin Ustinovich [Chernenko], in some measure we pre-determined this issue, agreeing to approve Mikhail*

very direct (almost a thinking aloud), and the words and phrases are those of everyday discourse. It may be that the almost total absence of official language rendered the speech inappropriate for such wide distribution as its predecessors. Second, the speech is very frank and provides several hitherto undisclosed details about Gorbachev's duties under Chernenko's General Secretaryship. Third, the assessment of Gorbachev is eulogistic and gives every impression of sincerity. To give full publicity in the mass-circulation newspapers to such praise of Gorbachev from the normally low-key Gromyko (who is highly respected in the Soviet Union and whose responsibility for the conduct of Soviet foreign policy keeps him very much in the public eye) might have seemed too much like the launching of a personality cult of the new General Secretary. Fourth (and related to the third point), since the authority and prestige of a General Secretary can be an important political resource, and enhance his or her actual power, the possibility should not be excluded that different parts of the Central Committee apparatus have different views on how fast and how far Gorbachev's authority should be strengthened and that this may reflect varying assessments of what they take to be his policy preferences and priorities. While the exclusion of Gromyko's speech from the newspapers is understandable for the reasons given above, the fact that only one out of three party journals—all of which published the speeches nominating Gorbachev's two predecessors—included it is perhaps revealing of diversity of view within the higher party echelons.

Perhaps because it appeared originally only in booklet form, Gromyko's speech has attracted little or no Western attention up to the present, but it is certainly worth bringing out a number of its salient features. It is noteworthy that Gromyko referred to Chernenko only once—in the context of his absence through illness from the Politburo—choosing instead to devote the whole of his speech to outlining Gorbachev's qualifications for the General Secretaryship. Like Chernenko and Tikhonov, in their speeches nominating Gorbachev's two predecessors, Gromyko observed that he was proposing Gorbachev's election to the Central Committee on the instructions of the Politburo.[27] He suggested by implication that Gorbachev may have been running the Secretariat of the Central Committee for some considerable time. As Gromyko put it: 'He led the Secretariat (*On vel Sekretariat*), as is known.' Gromyko followed that remark with the sentence: 'He also took the

---

Sergeevich [Gorbachev] as the chairman of the funeral commission'(ibid., p. 4). That was doubtless Grishin's way of attempting to ingratiate himself with Gorbachev, reminding everyone, in effect, that he had been the person who had got in first to propose that Gorbachev chair the funeral commission, an initiative on Grishin's part confirmed by Gorbachev in his memoirs. See Mikhail Gorbachev, Zhizn' i reformy, Vol. 1 (Novosti, Moscow, 1995), p. 264.]

27 *Materialy vneocherednogo plenuma tsentral'nogo komiteta...*, p. 6.

chair at sessions of the Politburo in the absence of Konstantin Ustinovich Chernenko.'[28] This was the first definitive confirmation that Gorbachev had indeed been chairing the Politburo when Chernenko was too ill to attend. But the fact that Gromyko did not relate Gorbachev's leading of the Secretariat (as distinct from his chairmanship of the Politburo) specifically to Chernenko's absence through illness in the last months of his leadership suggests that Gorbachev may have been in day-to-day charge of the Secretariat during much of Chernenko's General Secretaryship.

In the first reference, so far as I am aware, by one Soviet leader to another's abilities as a chairman, Gromyko remarked apropos of Gorbachev's chairmanship of the Politburo: 'Without any exaggeration, he conducted himself brilliantly.'[29] Gromyko made no reference to ideology or to the economy or to any other branch of domestic policy, but singled out for praise the degree of flexibility and lack of dogma in Gorbachev's approach to problems. As he put it:

You know, it often happens that problems—both internal and external—are very difficult to consider if you are guided by the law of 'black and white'. There may be intermediate colours, intermediate links, and intermediate decisions. And Mikhail Sergeyevich [Gorbachev] is always able to come up with such decisions that correspond with the party line.[30]

Gromyko also drew attention to one of Gorbachev's attributes that he said was 'perhaps a little clearer to me, in the performance of my duties, than to certain other comrades'—namely, how well and quickly Gorbachev grasped the essence of developments taking place in other countries and in the international arena. Characterizing in general terms Gorbachev's foreign policy orientation, Gromyko said: 'He always defends the point of view that the holy of holies for us all is to struggle for the cause of peace and to maintain our defence at the necessary level.'[31]

To put them with the maximum brevity, these and other attributes of Gorbachev on which Gromyko enlarges can be summarized in 10 points that are revealing both of Gromyko's own desiderata (though not necessarily in this order) for the office of General Secretary and of Gorbachev's qualifications in his eyes for this post: (1) experience of party work at various levels, including the regional level and the Secretariat of the Central Committee; (2) skill in chairmanship (of the Politburo and Secretariat); (3) keen intelligence; (4) grasp of international issues; (5) strong convictions and directness; (6) political sensitivity (not seeing everything in 'black and white' terms); (7) an analytical mind and ability to draw conclusions after dividing a problem into

---

[28] Ibid.   [29] Ibid.   [30] Ibid., p. 7.   [31] Ibid., p. 8.

its component parts; (8) broad erudition; (9) organizational ability; and (10) capacity to establish a rapport, and common language, with others.[32]

FROM KOLKHOZ TO KREMLIN

Assessments of Gorbachev's route to joint membership of the Politburo and Secretariat have previously appeared in academic writing,[33] but it is now possible, while summarizing what was already known, to add some details.[34]

Mikhail Sergeyevich Gorbachev was born on 2 March 1931, in the village of Privolnoe in the Krasnogvardeyskiy district of Stavropol region (*kray*) to the north-west of the city of Stavropol. Both his parents and his grandparents were peasants. His father fought throughout the Second World War and was badly wounded in 1945, and during these years Gorbachev was brought up mainly by his grandparents.[35] If Gorbachev was too young to fight in the Second World War (he was only 10 years old when Hitler's armies invaded the Soviet Union), he was by no means too young to suffer the war's consequences. Not only was he without his father during the war years, but he was in a part of the country that was for several months under German occupation (August 1942–January 1943) and for even longer close to the front.[36]

---

[32] *Materialy vneocherednogo plenuma tsentral'nogo komiteta...*, pp. 6–8.

[33] See my contributions to Brown and Kaser, op. cit., esp. pp. 240–2 and 269–70; Jerry F. Hough, 'Soviet Succession: Issues and Personalities', *Problems of Communism*, September–October 1982, esp. pp. 35–7; and Hough, 'Andropov's First Year', ibid., November–December 1983, esp. pp. 61–3.

[34] I draw upon Soviet published sources, conversations with contemporaries of Gorbachev's in Moscow University, and conversations and interviews with some of those who met Gorbachev in Canada and Britain in 1983 and 1984—especially his British hosts. These conversations were on a non-attributable basis, but where the same points have appeared in the press, I cite such sources. Since not all press comments on Gorbachev's visit to Britain were accurate, I try to cite only those published points that I have been able to verify independently.

[35] *This sentence corrects a factual error in my 1985 article in which I wrote that Gorbachev's father had been killed in the war—information which came to me from one of Gorbachev's interlocutors during his 1984 visit to Britain. Sergeant-Major Sergey Gorbachev was, in fact, wrongly reported to have been killed in action in the summer of 1944. In 1945 he was seriously wounded. However, he not only survived the Second World War, but in the late 1940s received an Order of Lenin for his part in bringing in a record harvest. He died in 1976.*

[36] The impact of this on Gorbachev must have been all the greater because of the extreme brutality of German soldiers at the Russian front where (as is too often forgotten) they behaved incomparably worse than on the Western front. On this brutality, and its ideological underpinnings, see an important study by Omer Bartov, *The Eastern Front, 1941–45, German Troops and the Barbarisation of Warfare* (Macmillan, London, 1985). See also the two major volumes by John Erickson, *The Road to Stalingrad* (Weidenfeld & Nicolson, London, 1975) and *The Road to Berlin* (Weidenfeld & Nicolson, London, 1983). Mlynář writes of Gorbachev having lived

Finally, because of an acute shortage of adult male labour in the Russian countryside during these war years, children, including Gorbachev, had to spend time working in the fields, and thus did not receive regular schooling.

His education in the early post-war years was also, in all probability, disrupted. There is some uncertainty about how much time Gorbachev spent as a manual worker and how much time at school between 1946 and 1950. His official biographies in central newspapers and reference books state that he began work in 1946 at the age of 15 as an assistant to a combine harvester operator in a machine-tractor station.[37] Yet Jerry Hough has drawn attention to a biography in a Stavropol local newspaper that suggests that Gorbachev remained at school until 1950 and worked in the machine-tractor station only during school holidays.[38] Before one accepts the local, rather than the national, version of the biography as the whole story, however, it is worth noting that several of Gorbachev's Moscow University contemporaries have remarked that one of the things that made him unusual was that he had already received, and sometimes wore, the insignia of the Order of Red Banner of Labour.[39] It seems highly unlikely that such an award would have been given to a schoolboy whose working experience was restricted to school holidays.[40]

What needs to be remembered is the appalling devastation of industry and agriculture and disruption of education and much else caused by the war—still very evident in the early post war years—and the fact that ten-year schooling was at that time the exception rather than the rule in the country-side. Although the precise timing and proportions remain a minor mystery, it seems most likely that Gorbachev spent *part* of the period between 1946 and 1950 as a full-time worker and *part* of it at school. Indeed, the recently

---

through the war 'near the Caucasian front' and of the war as 'a fundamental experience for him,' which he had known as a source of suffering for the civilian population (Mlynář, loc. cit.).

[37] See, for example, *Deputaty Verkhovnogo Soveta SSSR: Desyatyy sozyv* (Deputies of the USSR Supreme Soviet: 10th Convocation), Izdatel'stvo 'Izvestiya Sovetov Deputatov Trudyash-chikhsya SSSR', Moscow, 1979, p. 119; *Yezhegodnik Bol'shoy Sovetskoy Entsiklopedii 1981*, p. 573; and *Pravda*, 22 October 1980, p. 1. The brief official outline of Gorbachev's career published since he became General Secretary puts the point in the following terms: 'Soon after the Great Patriotic War of 1941–1945, at the age of 15 he began his working activity. He worked as a machine operator (*mekhanizatorom*) at a machine-tractor station'. See, for example, *Partiynaya zhizn'*, No. 6, March 1985, p. 6.

[38] See Jerry F. Hough, *Soviet Leadership in Transition* (Brookings Institution, Washington, DC, 1980), p. 58; and Hough, 'Soviet Succession: Issues and Personalities', p. 35. Hough's source is *Stavropol'skaya pravda*, 6 February, 1979.

[39] I first drew attention to this in Brown and Kaser, op. cit., pp. 240 and 252–3.

[40] The memories of several Soviet scholars on Gorbachev's Order of Red Banner of Labour find further corroboration in the article by Mlynář, who describes this decoration as 'an extraordinary honour' for a 19-year-old.

published evidence of Zdeněk Mlynář makes it clear that it was the fact that he was an *exemplary worker* (with insignia to prove it) which, together with his obvious intelligence, earned him a place at Moscow University. Mlynář is quite categorical that Gorbachev did not belong to either of the two main groups of students in Moscow University—in terms of background—at that time. That is to say, he was neither an ex-soldier nor someone who had come straight to university from secondary school.[41]

Gorbachev was 19 when he began his studies at Moscow University in September 1950, and he remained there until June 1955 (the normal span of a Soviet first degree course), when he received his law degree. Given the time and place of his pre-university education and the fact that he arrived as a new student in Moscow at the height of the anti-cosmopolitan campaign, it is hardly surprising that he did not have an opportunity to learn foreign languages, and so the myth should not be perpetuated that when he was in Britain he was 'answering even difficult questions *with ease in excellent English*'.[42] He joined the Communist Party in 1952 and was active in the Komsomol. As *komsorg kursa* (the Komsomol leader of his particular student year in the Law Faculty), he served also on the faculty committee of the Komsomol. But Gorbachev's Komsomol duties do not appear to have been on so high and exacting a level as to have prevented him from being a serious, and indeed outstanding, student.[43]

It was, nevertheless, Gorbachev's part-time work in the Komsomol while a student that paved the way for his full-time employment in the Komsomol after graduating. He returned to his native Stavropol region and began a rapid rise in the Komsomol organization. In 1955–6 he was deputy head of the department of propaganda and agitation of the Stavropol regional committee (*kraykom*) of the Komsomol, and from 1956 to 1958 he served as first secretary of the Stavropol city committee of the Komsomol. In 1958 he moved back to the regional apparatus of the Komsomol, serving as second and then first secretary of the Stavropol Komsomol *kraykom*.

---

[41] Mlynář, loc. cit. [*Under wartime conditions in his part of Stavropol kray, there was no functioning school for two years during the war and so Gorbachev's education was massively interrupted. However, he did attend school in the second half of the 1940s, but worked in the fields throughout the summers. It was in 1948 that Gorbachev, at the age of 17, received the Order of Red Banner of Labour (and his father the Order of Lenin) for bringing in a bumper harvest. It was, Gorbachev wrote in his memoirs, of all the Soviet awards he received, the one that was 'most precious' to him. See Gorbachev, Zhizn' i reformy, Vol. 1, p. 56.*]

[42] *International Herald Tribune* (Paris), 12 March 1985, p. 1 (italics added, AB).

[43] Thus, so far as I am aware, Gorbachev did not hold a rank as high as that of 'Komsomol secretary of Moscow University in 1954–55', which Jerry Hough attributes to him ('Soviet Succession: Issues and Personalities', p. 34). Mlynář reports that Gorbachev passed his university examinations with distinction (loc. cit.).

In 1962 Gorbachev moved from Komsomol to party work and began his still more remarkable rise through the party apparatus. The speed of his advance naturally owed something to luck, especially in the form of good connections, but it clearly owed still more to his abilities and performance which impressed those senior party officials who got to know him. From 1960 until 1964 Fedor Kulakov was first secretary of the Stavropol party organization, and he was to become an extremely important patron of Gorbachev. In the early 1960s, when Gorbachev was running the regional Komsomol organization, the two men worked together closely, and it must have been on Kulakov's invitation that Gorbachev moved into the party *kraykom* apparatus. In 1962–3 Gorbachev was party organizer of the Stavropol regional party organization's territorial production administration of collective and state farms, and from 1963 until 1966 he was head of the party organs department of the party *kraykom*.

In 1964 Kulakov had moved to Moscow to head the agriculture department of the Central Committee, and in 1965 he became a secretary of the Central Committee. This was helpful for Gorbachev in more ways than one. Not only did he have a friend at court, he also had one who was well-connected. Kulakov was on good terms with Chernenko (who had been a secretary of the Penza regional party committee from 1945 to 1948 at a time when Kulakov headed the agriculture department of that same *obkom*),[44] and, through Chernenko, with Brezhnev. This was confirmed in 1971 when Kulakov became a voting member of the Politburo while retaining his Central Committee secretaryship. It was also useful for Gorbachev that Kulakov was replaced in Stavropol in 1964 by a high party official on his way down— Leonid Yefremov. Yefremov had become a candidate member of the Politburo under Khrushchev in 1962 and first deputy chairman of the Bureau for Party Work in the Russian Republic (a Khrushchevian creation that was to be abolished by his successors). The Stavropol regional party secretaryship was for Yefremov a clear demotion, and though he held that post until 1970, it was evidently his being out of favour that caused him to lose the post at the age of only 58. With a party congress to be held the following year, the leadership clearly did not want Yefremov on the Central Committee for another five years.[45]

---

[44] On Kulakov, see *Deputaty Verkhovnogo Soveta SSSR: Devyatyy sozyv* (Deputies of the USSR Supreme Soviet: 9th Convocation), Izdatel'stvo 'Izvestiya Sovetov Deputatov Trudyashchikhsya SSSR', Moscow, 1974, p. 243; and on Chernenko's earlier career, *Yezhegodnik Bol'shoy Sovetskoy Entsiklopedii 1981*, p. 608.

[45] That Yefremov had blotted his copybook is indicated by the way he faded out of the reference books. He does not appear in the appropriate volume (Vol. 9) of the *Bol'shaya Sovetskaya Entsiklopediya* published in 1972. For very different reasons Gorbachev does not

Meanwhile Gorbachev had made himself Yefremov's obvious successor. From 1966 to 1968 he was back in city politics as first secretary of the Stavropol *gorkom*. But already in 1968 he was evidently being groomed for the *kraykom* succession, for it was then that he was appointed second secretary of the regional party committee. His acquisition of an agricultural degree a year earlier had strengthened his qualifications for taking over as party chief of this important agricultural region. (Both Kulakov and Yefremov had also acquired such educational qualifications in the agricultural sphere.) Gorbachev's support at the centre ensured that it was indeed he who succeeded Yefremov as first secretary of the Stavropol *kraykom* at the early age of 39. A year later, at the 24th Party Congress, he became a full member of the Central Committee.

Gorbachev was very successful as a regional party secretary, and the Stavropol *kray* under his leadership achieved a particularly good agricultural performance. He evidently approved of the 'link system',[46] which had gone out of fashion under Brezhnev, and supported both in theory and in practice the giving of greater autonomy to agricultural workers to farm a particular piece of land.[47]

These were years in which Gorbachev also broadened his horizons and implemented his wish to see things for himself by taking motoring holidays with his wife through France and Italy[48]—not the vacations of a conventional party secretary. It appears that he also read widely, adding to his knowledge of Russian literature (which emerged in his discussions in Britain) a reading of some of the Western books translated into Russian during the Brezhnev years. Gorbachev told one of the British politicians with whom he had conversation that the first modern English novel he read was C.P. Snow's *Corridors of Power*,

appear in this most recent edition of the major Soviet encyclopedia. Given that the volume in which Gorbachev should have appeared (Vol. 7) was published as recently as 1972 (though sent for typesetting on 22 March 1971), this merely underlines the rapidity of his rise from relative obscurity to the leadership of his party and country. For Yefremov's career, see *Deputaty Verkhovnogo Soveta SSSR: Sedmoy sozyv* (Deputies of the USSR Supreme Soviet: 7th Convocation), Izdatel'stvo 'Izvestiya Sovetov Deputatov Trudyashchikhsya SSSR', Moscow, 1966, p. 157.

[46] For a brief account of the 'link' or 'autonomous work-team' system (*beznaryadnoe zveno*), see Alec Nove's chapter on agriculture in Brown and Kaser, op. cit., pp. 179–80.

[47] See M. Gorbachev, 'The Rural Labour Collective: Paths of Social Development', *Kommunist*, No. 2, January 1976, pp. 29–38. The support in print for the 'link' system became all the more explicit once Gorbachev had become the secretary of the Central Committee responsible for agriculture. On this, see the contributions of Nove and of Brown in Brown and Kaser, op. cit., pp. 179–80, 244–5, 269–70, and 272. See also Sidney I. Ploss, 'Soviet Succession: Signs of Struggle', *Problems of Communism*, September–October 1982, p. 50. It was only under Andropov, however, as will be noted later in this chapter, that Gorbachev was able to expound in some detail his personal support for the autonomous work-team in agriculture.

[48] Laurence Marks, 'Gorbachovs Let the Kremlin Mask Slip', in *The Observer* (London), 23 December 1984, p. 4.

a work that must at least have provided some insight into British-style bureaucratic politics for a Soviet *kraykom* secretary. It became apparent that he had also read *Parkinson's Law* (which was published in Russian by Progress Publishers in the mid-1970s and rapidly sold out). Instantly taking up a reference by the chairman of ICI to 'Parkinson's Law', Gorbachev responded: 'If you're referring to C. Northcote Parkinson, I've got news for you. He lives in Moscow now.'[49] Not the happiest of omens for overstaffed ministerial bureaucracies in the Soviet Union, but entirely consistent with the views of a man who, while still first secretary of the Stavropol *kraykom* but shortly before he became a secretary of the Central Committee, had recorded his support for the controversial Shchekino experiment designed to reward enterprises that release surplus labour.[50]

When Fedor Kulakov died suddenly, at the age of 60, in 1978, it was his protégé, Gorbachev, who was brought to Moscow to succeed him as Central Committee secretary responsible for agriculture. He was then only 47, an unusually early age for anyone to join Brezhnev's top leadership team. Although Kulakov was no longer around to give support, one can be certain that he had in the course of the 1970s drawn Gorbachev's good record in his former *kray* to the attention of his colleagues. Two of them had, moreover, a special interest in the Stavropol region and almost certainly also supported the advancement of Gorbachev's career—Mikhail Suslov, who had been first secretary of the Stavropol *kraykom* from 1939 until 1944 and for whom this was still a regional base, and Yuriy Andropov, who was a native of the Stavropol region and was said to have taken holidays there while chairman of the KGB. If that is correct, Andropov would already have become acquainted with the *kraykom* first secretary even before Gorbachev moved to Moscow. In outlook, Gorbachev was much closer to Andropov than to Suslov, but a combination of political skill and personal charm enabled him to have good relations with Soviet leaders of different views.[51]

Once Gorbachev began to attend Politburo meetings in his capacity as a secretary of the Central Committee, he had an opportunity to impress those Politburo members, such as Gromyko, who had a high regard for real ability and professional competence. Indeed, only on the basis of such wide support

---

[49] Ibid.
[50] See M. Gorbachev, 'Leading Experience—An Important Reserve', *Kommunist*, No. 14, September 1978, p. 82.
[51] It has been noted that at Suslov's funeral, Gorbachev was the only Politburo member to stop and speak with each member of Suslov's family and that when Andropov was lying in state, Gorbachev was the only member of the Politburo shown on Soviet television sitting with Andropov's family. See Hough, 'Soviet Succession: Issues and Personalities', p. 37; and Marc D. Zlotnik, 'Chernenko Succeeds', *Problems of Communism*, March–April 1984, p. 20.

could he, between the ages of 47 and 49, have risen to full membership of the Politburo while retaining his seat in the Secretariat: in November 1978 he became a Central Committee secretary, in November 1979 a candidate member of the Politburo, and in October 1980 a voting member of that body.

When, on the death of Brezhnev, there were two senior members of the Politburo who aspired to the General Secretaryship, Gorbachev was one of several important members of the Politburo (which included Gromyko and Ustinov) who put their weight behind Andropov rather than Chernenko.[52] The twin elements of Andropov's approach—discipline together with struggle against corruption *and* the placing of economic reform on the political agenda in a way that it had not been since the mid-1960s—were fully in line with Gorbachev's own thinking. He not only supported innovation in the organization of agriculture but had also, while still a regional party secretary in Stavropol, attacked indiscipline, corruption, and drunkenness, themes that were to be given an enhanced salience when Gorbachev himself became General Secretary after the Chernenko interregnum.[53]

GORBACHEV IN THE WINGS

In the last year of Brezhnev's life, the importance the leadership attached to agriculture—the sphere of activity that Gorbachev supervised—was underlined by the adoption of the comprehensive 'Food Programme' at the May 1982 plenary session of the Central Committee.[54] Gorbachev no doubt was heavily involved in its preparation and was a strong advocate of some of its main elements, such as the further development of the agro-industrial complexes and the devoting of significantly greater resources to the development of the rural infrastructure, including better roads, transport and storage facilities, and social amenities.[55] What the programme failed to do, however,

[52] For somewhat different accounts that agree, however, on these three names, see Zhores Medvedev, *Andropov* (Blackwell, Oxford, 1983), p. 112; and Brown, 'The Soviet Succession: From Andropov to Chernenko', pp. 136–7.

[53] For an assessment of Andropov's priorities at the outset of his General Secretaryship, see Brown, 'Andropov: Discipline *and* Reform?', and for Gorbachev's renewed emphasis on discipline, and combating corruption and drunkenness and alcoholism, see his speech at the March 1985 plenum of the Central Committee (*Pravda*, 12 March 1985, p. 3) and the reports of the Politburo meetings held on 21 March and 4 April 1985 (ibid., 22 March 1985, p. 1, and 5 April 1985, p. 1).

[54] M. Gorbachev, 'The Food Programme and the Tasks in Bringing It to Fruition', *Kommunist*, No. 10, July 1982, pp. 3–21.

[55] Ibid., p. 6.

was to offer greater autonomy to groups of farmers, and it may be partly because of this and other limitations of this major policy statement that Gorbachev was content not to be one of the speakers at the May plenum[56] and, in a subsequent article, to speak of Brezhnev's 'leading role' in initiating and formulating the programme.[57]

When Andropov succeeded Brezhnev as General Secretary in November 1982, he lost no time in calling for practical measures to 'extend the independence (*samostoyatel'nost'*) of associations (*ob"yedineniya*) and enterprises, [and] of state and collective farms'.[58] Andropov's selection apparently also made it possible for Gorbachev to introduce elements of agricultural reform that he had not been able to include in Brezhnev's 'Food Programme'—in particular, the extension in principle of the 'link' system (but under a new name) to the country as a whole. In a speech to an agricultural conference at Belgorod in March 1983, Gorbachev indicated that the Politburo had recently given its approval to 'the introduction of the collective contract (*kollektivnogo podryada*) in collective and state farm production'.[59] He went on to make clear that this meant that autonomous work teams and brigades should be given the opportunity to make long-term contracts with their collective and state farms, whereby they would have operational independence to organize their own work and distribute among themselves group income that, in turn, would be directly related to production results, though with a necessary minimum guaranteed by the parent farm to take account of years of bad weather. Such teams, said Gorbachev, should be formed voluntarily and be allowed to elect their own leaders.[60]

It would appear that this is one of a number of Soviet partial economic reforms that have not been fully implemented, and the theme of increasing both the independence and responsibility of groups of workers is one to which Gorbachev has reverted more recently.[61] It seems fair to say that nothing short of the powers of the General Secretaryship enables an innovatively inclined Soviet leader to effect radical changes in established organizational and behavioural patterns in agriculture or industry, and even with these powers at one's disposal, it is a far from straightforward task.

Under Andropov, Gorbachev's responsibilities within the Secretariat of the Central Committee were extended from control of agriculture to general oversight of the economy as a whole, and he also became the secretarial

---

[56] *Partiynaya zhizn'*, No. 11, June 1982, p. 3.
[57] Gorbachev, 'The Food Programme and the Tasks in Bringing It to Fruition', p. 6.
[58] *Pravda*, 23 November 1982, p. 1.
[59] Ibid., 20 March 1983, p. 2.   [60] Ibid.
[61] That is a point to which I shall return when discussing Gorbachev's policy orientation in the final section of this chapter.

overlord of the department of the Central Committee responsible for lower-level party appointments.[62] This meant that the two new secretaries of the Central Committee who had been brought in under Andropov— Nikolay Ryzhkov and Yegor Ligachev (who headed, respectively, the Economic Department and the Department of Party Organizational Work)—and who could be presumed to be both sympathetic and responsive to Andropov's and Gorbachev's priorities came under Gorbachev's jurisdiction. (Since Gorbachev became party leader, Ryzhkov and Ligachev have received further highly significant promotion—a point to which I shall return in the concluding section.)

The personnel changes at the top of the Soviet party hierarchy made by Andropov during his fifteen months as General Secretary, taken as a whole, helped to strengthen Gorbachev's power base within the leadership. It is far from evident that Grigoriy Romanov, who became a secretary of the Central Committee in June 1983 while remaining a full member of the Politburo, or even Heidar Aliev, who was advanced to full membership of the Politburo in November 1982, would necessarily have leaned towards Gorbachev rather than Chernenko when it became clear that Andropov was dying. But two others who were promoted to full membership of the Politburo under Andropov—Mikhail Solomentsev and Vitaliy Vorotnikov—were people whose careers had either stagnated or (in Vorotnikov's case) suffered a setback under Brezhnev;[63] given the influence Chernenko was exercising in those years, they would be more than likely to favour Gorbachev who had become the Politburo member closest to Andropov and who was, quite clearly, the man Andropov wished to succeed him.[64] It is also probable that Viktor Chebrikov, who had worked closely with Andropov at the KGB for fifteen years and who was promoted to candidate membership of the Politburo in December 1983, would be favourably disposed towards Gorbachev.

[62] Some of the evidence for this is collected by Jerry Hough in his 'Andropov's First Year', and by Marc Zlotnik in 'Chernenko Succeeds'.

[63] Solomentsev had spent twelve years as a candidate member of the Politburo before being promoted to full membership at the December 1983 Central Committee plenum. Vorotnikov, after serving as first deputy chairman of the RSFSR Council of Ministers from 1975 until 1979, was dispatched to Cuba as Soviet ambassador (a definite demotion) and only brought back to the centre in two stages by Andropov. First, after Andropov became one of the senior secretaries of the Central Committee in May 1982, he recalled Vorotnikov to clean up the Krasnodar *kray* after securing the removal of the corrupt Sergey Medunov. Second, in 1983, when Solomentsev succeeded Arvids Pelše as chairman of the Party Control Committee, Vorotnikov was given Solomentsev's previous job of chairman of the RSFSR Council of Ministers.

[64] That Andropov, even from his sickbed, still had his hands on the levers of power in late 1983 is indicated by the four changes made to the top leadership team at the December plenum and by his remarkably authoritative speech, written in the first person, and read to the plenary session in his absence (see *Pravda*, 27 December 1983, pp. 1–2).

Taken together with the support of Ryzhkov and Ligachev, this undoubt-edly gave Gorbachev a strong position within the top leadership team even while Andropov's health was declining. Yet, Chernenko remained the senior secretary in terms of length of time as joint member of the Politburo and Secretariat, and, during Andropov's absence through illness, he was able to regain some of the influence he was visibly losing in the earlier months of Andropov's General Secretaryship. It was he who chaired Politburo meetings in Andropov's absence, and it was to him that those who were alarmed at the speed of Andropov's departure from Brezhnev's policy of 'stability of cadres'[65] turned for respite when it became evident that Andropov would not recover and that the choice of successor was essentially between the elderly protégé of Brezhnev and the much younger and more vigorous protégé of Andropov. Within the top leadership team and, no doubt, within the Central Committee as a whole, there was a majority ready to settle for a quieter life.

It seems likely that Gorbachev and his supporters recognized that there was a majority for Chernenko and did not push his candidacy too hard. Instead, they used his strong power base as a bargaining position to ensure that his responsibilities would be further extended and that he would become the number two man in the Chernenko Politburo and Chernenko's heir apparent. That is not to say that the succession to Chernenko was definitively settled at the same time as the succession to Andropov, for no Politburo can bind its successors. It could not have been known then how long Chernenko would live, which other members of the Politburo would die or fall into political disfavour in the meantime, and, hence, what would be the composition of the selectorate that would choose Chernenko's successor when the time came. There was at least enough uncertainty to give any waverers within the leader-ship who were not firmly committed either to Chernenko or to Gorbachev, but who might themselves nurture aspirations to the top job, an incentive to support the older man.

That some of those close to Chernenko may not have been wholly recon-ciled to Gorbachev's number two position was suggested by the rather peculiar treatment of his speech to the Central Committee plenum on 13 February 1984, which elected Chernenko to the General Secretaryship. The official communiqué from the plenum, published in *Pravda* and the other daily newspapers the following day, did not so much as mention the fact that Gorbachev had addressed the Central Committee members. It was only when the proceedings of the plenum appeared in booklet form and in the pages of party journals such as *Kommunist*[66] and *Partiynaya zhizn*'[67] several

---

[65] See n. 20.   [66] *Kommunist*, No. 3, February 1984, p. 14.
[67] *Partiynaya zhizn*', No. 5, March 1984, p. 12.

days later that the text of Gorbachev's address was published. His short speech was notable both for its emphasis on the fact that the party would continue on the course worked out by the 26th Party Congress and by the November 1982 and June and December 1983 plenums of the Central Committee (i.e. emphasizing preponderantly the course set in the Andropov period) and for its expression of his conviction that members of the Central Committee would act 'in the spirit of unity and cohesion' that had characterized the February 1984 plenum.

The strength of Gorbachev's position was made still clearer in April 1984 when he proposed Chernenko for the chairmanship of the Presidium of the USSR Supreme Soviet. The main emphasis of Gorbachev's speech was on how the experience of the past few years had shown the necessity of combining the posts of General Secretary and head of state in view of the party's leading role within Soviet society and the part played by the General Secretary in the conduct of foreign policy.[68] When Andropov had become General Secretary, there was just one precedent—that of Brezhnev—for the General Secretary combining the party leadership with the chairmanship of the Presidium of the Supreme Soviet, and it was only for the last five years of his eighteen years as General Secretary that Brezhnev was also the Presidium chairman. That there was still some doubt after Brezhnev's death as to whether this was not too much authority to place in the hands of one man was indicated by the fact that it was not at the first meeting of the Supreme Soviet after Andropov became General Secretary (the one held in late November 1982) but only in June 1983 that he became head of state. The elevation of Chernenko to the chairmanship of the Presidium of the Supreme Soviet within two months of his becoming General Secretary, and the terms in which Gorbachev proposed him, have surely made the combination of these posts a firmly established convention. It is to be expected that at the first meeting of the Supreme Soviet to be held during his General Secretaryship, Gorbachev will become chairman of the Presidium,[69] just as it can be taken for granted that (like Andropov and Chernenko before him) he has been acting as chairman of the Defence Council from the outset of his party leadership.

Apart from his role in proposing Chernenko as head of state, Gorbachev's number two position within the party was evident early on in Chernenko's General Secretaryship from his additional responsibilities—negotiated, no doubt, at the time of the succession. Gorbachev took over from Chernenko

---

[68] *Pravda*, 12 April 1984, p. 1.

[69] *In fact, Gorbachev waited for three years before taking that post, initially giving it to Gromyko both as a reward for supporting him for the General Secretaryship and in order to remove him from the post of Minister of Foreign Affairs which he had occupied since 1957.*

the chairmanship of the Foreign Affairs Commission of the Soviet of the Union of the USSR Supreme Soviet,[70] becoming at the same time the overseer of international affairs within the Central Committee Secretariat. He also became secretarial overlord of ideology and culture.[71] Thus, he was accorded what was, in effect, the old Suslov portfolio but without having to relinquish his responsibilities for the economy and party cadres—a stronger position than even Suslov ever had and which was made possible by the fact that he was one of only two senior secretaries[72] (the General Secretary apart) throughout Chernenko's thirteen months as party leader. The other was Romanov, who appeared to be supervising both the Administrative Organs Department of the Central Committee (which in turn oversees the military and the KGB) and the Defence Industry Department.[73]

One institutional interest with which Gorbachev has had few links hitherto is the military. He was too young to serve in the armed forces during the war, and the time when he reached military age was one in which demobilization was taking precedence over recruitment. This could have been a disadvantage for him as compared with Romanov who served in the Soviet army from 1941 until 1945[74] and whose official duties in the Secretariat preserved his links with the military. But the fact that the military remains under firm party control has been clearer than ever in recent years, and there is no evidence that the army played any part in the elevation to the General Secretaryship of either Chernenko or Gorbachev.[75] One succession earlier, Ustinov had been a strong supporter of Andropov, but Ustinov was essentially a civilian (albeit one with quite exceptional military experience), and in the context of the succession, his party standing was more important than was his office as minister of defence. The fact that there is not the slightest reason to suppose

[70] Gorbachev has had varied experience of Supreme Soviet work. Before taking on the Foreign Affairs Commission chairmanship, he was from 1970 to 1974 a member of the Nature Conservation Commission, from 1974 to 1979 chairman of the Commission for Youth Affairs, and from 1979 to 1984 chairman of the Legislative Proposals Commission of the Soviet of the Union.

[71] The fullest confirmation of this came when Gorbachev made a major speech on 10 December 1984, to the all-Union Conference on 'The Perfecting of Developed Socialism and the Ideological Work of the Party in the Light of the Decisions of the June (1983) Plenum of the Central Committee'.

[72] Or *super-secretaries*—those who combine their secretaryship with full Politburo membership and so qualify to supervise several departments of the Central Committee and one or more of the other secretaries.

[73] It was, for example, Romanov who chaired Marshal Dmitriy Ustinov's funeral commission and who made the principal funeral speech. See *Pravda*, 22 December 1984, p. 1, and 25 December 1984, p. 1.

[74] See *Deputaty Verkhovnogo Soveta SSSR: Desyatyy sozyv*, p. 379.

[75] At Chernenko's funeral, in a break with tradition, the top military men did not appear (presumably because they were not invited) with the party leaders on the Lenin mausoleum.

that his successor, Marshal Sergey Sokolov, played any role in the election of Gorbachev merely underlines this. It may have been helpful for Gorbachev that the assertive Marshal Nikolay Ogarkov was replaced in early September 1984 as chief of the General Staff by Marshal Sergey Akhromeev.[76] Ogarkov's demotion put him out of the running for the succession to Ustinov as minister of defence. Ustinov died on 20 December 1984, and had been seriously ill since October.[77] He was still in the public eye in September and must have played a part, and possibly the leading part, in the removal of Ogarkov as chief of staff. But this merely underlines the fact that the Soviet top brass have been even more firmly subordinated to the civilian party leadership in the post-Brezhnev era than under Brezhnev (who had closer connections with senior officers, dating from the war, than had any of his successors).

When Gorbachev made his December 1984 visit to Britain, his position as number two man within the Soviet leadership was so strong that it was unlikely that his British stay would be of decisive importance to his leadership prospects. Nevertheless, he accepted an element of risk inasmuch as by engaging in discussions with a wide variety of British politicians—including the Prime Minister, Margaret Thatcher—and by bringing himself within focus of the Western mass media, he was guaranteeing that if he made serious mistakes they would be widely publicized. In fact, he so much impressed all who met him both with his ability and personality that the visit could only have strengthened his already strong position in Moscow, not least in the eyes of the Soviet foreign policy establishment.[78] Commentary in the British mass media, while not always on the most serious level, was overwhelmingly favourable. Even Mrs Thatcher delivered an accolade that she has accorded no other Soviet leader: 'I like Mr Gorbachev. We can do business together.'[79] One of the British politicians with the broadest international experience, Denis Healey, former defence minister and chancellor of the exchequer and now shadow foreign secretary, described Gorbachev as 'a man of exceptional charm' who was 'frank and flexible with a composure full of inner strength'.[80]

[76] *Krasnaya zvezda*, 7 September 1984, p. 1.   [77] *Pravda*, 22 December 1984, pp. 1–2.

[78] The Soviet press, radio, and television accorded extensive coverage to Gorbachev's visit to Britain and reported a number of the positive comments of British politicians and businessmen and the British media on the way it was going. See *BBC SWB*, 17–24 December 1984.

[79] *Financial Times*, 22 December 1984, p. 26.

[80] Denis Healey, 'Gorbachev Face to Face', *Newsweek*, 25 March 1985, p. 15. This tallies with the following recollection of Mlynář: 'Gorbachev the student was not only very intelligent and gifted, he was an open man, whose intelligence never carried over to arrogance; he wanted—and was able—to listen to the opinions of all he spoke to. Loyal and personally honest, he won an informal and spontaneous authority. ... He was conscious of himself as a man who knows that everything he has, he possesses thanks to his own powers, his own talent, his own hard work, and that he has gained nothing via protection or social origin' (loc. cit.).

Healey, whose discussions with Soviet leaders stretch back to Khrushchev, added: 'For all who met him in Britain, he left one puzzling question: how can a man who appears so genuinely nice and human run the Soviet system?' The answer, he suggested, might lie in the 'immense authority' that Gorbachev had impressed on those who met him.[81]

Gorbachev's strong position in Moscow was reflected also in the extent to which Chernenko, though accorded constant praise in the Soviet mass media and treated in the speeches of other Soviet politicians as the ultimate authority, was operating with Andropov's agenda. He too had to take up the themes of discipline and reform, and though they were pursued with less vigour and expounded with less urgency than by Andropov, they became more pronounced as Chernenko's health weakened and as Gorbachev's influence grew. This was reflected in some of Chernenko's later speeches and articles,[82] as well as in the further disciplinary action taken against Chernenko's former colleague from Moldavian days, Nikolay Shchelokov, who had been dismissed from his post as minister of internal affairs under Andropov in December 1982 and expelled from the Central Committee in June 1983, and who as far into Chernenko's General Secretaryship as November 1984 was additionally stripped of his rank of army general.[83] Shchelokov died the following month and was rumoured to have committed suicide.[84]

There were numerous other signs during the last months of Chernenko's life of Gorbachev's enhanced authority and of the fact that he had a clearly established lead over any potential party rival. For certain purposes, protocol demanded that Tikhonov, as chairman of the Council of Ministers, should take precedence over Gorbachev. Thus, when the leaders gave speeches to their Russian Socialist Federative Soviet Republic (RSFSR) Supreme Soviet

[81] Ibid. Those British politicians who found it easy to establish a rapport with Gorbachev did not, however, mistake charm for weakness. One who spent a lot of time with Gorbachev in Britain in his capacity as chairman of the British branch of the Inter-Parliamentary Union, the Conservative Member of Parliament Peter Temple-Morris, observed later: 'He is a serious and cultivated man with a great deal of style. Nevertheless, he is as tough as old boots—that's important to remember' (*Newsweek*, 25 March 1985, p. 10).

[82] See, for example, Chernenko's speech to the conference of People's Controllers, *Pravda*, 6 October 1984, pp. 1–2; his article, 'To Meet the Demands of Developed Socialism', in *Kommunist*, No. 18, December 1984, pp. 3–21; and his RSFSR Supreme Soviet election speech, read for him in his absence (through illness) little more than two weeks before his death, in *Pravda*, 23 February 1985, pp. 1–2.

[83] For the dates during which Chernenko and Shchelokov worked together in Moldavia, see *Deputaty Verkhovnogo Soveta: Desyatyy sozyv*, pp. 475 and 494. For the Presidium of the Supreme Soviet decree depriving Shchelokov of his military rank for bring discredit to it and for abuse of office, see *Vedomosti Verkhovnogo Soveta SSSR*, No. 46, 14 November 1984, p. 860.

[84] *The Times*, 19 December 1984, p. 12.

constituents in ascending order of rank, the last three speeches were given by
Gorbachev, Tikhonov, and Chernenko (in absentia),[85] the same order in
which they had made their USSR Supreme Soviet speeches a year earlier.[86]
The leaders' acceptances of their Supreme Soviet nominations were printed in
the same order of importance (with Gorbachev in third place after Tikhonov,
who, at the age of 79 and with a background of ministerial work, was not, of
course, a remotely conceivable candidate for the succession to Chernenko)
and, in terms of number of constituency nominations of leaders as published
by *Pravda*, Gorbachev was actually put on a par with Tikhonov, with only
Chernenko receiving more nominations and all other Politburo members
getting fewer.[87]

When these various esoteric signs are taken in conjunction with Gromyko's
statements, quoted earlier, that Gorbachev had already been 'leading' the
Secretariat and chairing the Politburo during Chernenko's lifetime, it can
be seen that Gorbachev had the succession firmly within his grasp before
Chernenko died. The very fact, furthermore, that the Soviet Union had
had three leaders in a row who were for lengthy periods incapable of
carrying out all of their public functions had turned Gorbachev's relative
youth—considered a handicap during the two previous successions—into a
positive asset. Thus, while there may well be those within the top leadership
team and the Central Committee who are apprehensive lest Gorbachev's new
broom should sweep them aside, or lest he should encourage too much
policy innovation, there is little reason to doubt Gromyko's assertion that
the Politburo members were unanimous in nominating Gorbachev[88] since
it is not the custom for Soviet politicians to oppose directly what is clearly
the winning side.

GORBACHEV AS GENERAL SECRETARY

What is the political climate in which Gorbachev has come to power, and
what can be said of his policy orientations, priorities, leadership style, and
personnel changes, as well as future prospects?

The political climate in the Soviet Union today is more conducive to policy
innovation than it has frequently been in the past. In Soviet terms, there are
both 'objective' and 'subjective' reasons for this. Objectively, there has been
the slowdown in economic growth rate, and this is being openly analysed by

[85] *Pravda*, 21 February 1985, p. 2; 22 February 1985, p. 2; and 23 February 1985, pp. 1–2.
[86] Ibid., 1 March 1984, p. 2; 2 March 1984, p. 2; and 3 March 1984, pp. 1–2.
[87] Ibid., 4 January 1985, pp. 1–2.
[88] *Materialy vneocherednogo plenuma tsentral'nogo komiteta KPSS...*, p. 8.

Soviet scholars.[89] The ordinary Soviet citizen may be unfamiliar with the statistics, but is only too well aware of the problems that remain to be overcome. In the international arena, there is the dilemma posed by the significant increase in American military expenditure, by a general worsening of relations with the United States and with Western Europe dating from the late 1970s, and by relatively static relations with China and Japan, which by the time of Chernenko's death had improved only marginally. Subjectively, there is the fact that Andropov had raised expectations of qualitative improvements in the economy and of a greater sense of purpose in Soviet society, and there was some popular frustration that under Chernenko the country seemed to be marking time again. There is widespread public support for a revival of détente (which the more sophisticated Soviet party intellectuals recognize would have to be accompanied by more clearly defined 'rules of the game') and a readiness to welcome more Soviet diplomatic initiatives as distinct from mere reactions to events.

On the specific issue of economic reform, it is of great importance to recognize that a shift of opinion has taken place within the Soviet party intelligentsia, so that while argument continues, far more people now accept that minor tinkering with the economic mechanism is not enough. There is, however, resistance from powerful sections of the party and state apparatus to reducing the powers of ministries and giving greater autonomy to industrial associations and enterprises and still greater resistance to incorporating market elements within the economic system. But from the very top of the party hierarchy, and not least from Gorbachev himself, there has been encouragement to social scientists to be less slow and timid in tackling 'the resolution of the key theoretical problems of our development'.[90]

The *short-term* changes that actually take place are unlikely to be as far-reaching as some of the proposals that have been published by Soviet scholars. But while Gorbachev was already exercising influence on the broad lines of economic policy under Andropov and Chernenko, encouragement was given to the reform-oriented Institute of Economics and Organization of Industrial Production of the Siberian Division of the Academy of Sciences, based in Novosibirsk, Russia. At the June 1983 plenary session, two economic institutes were singled out for criticism by Chernenko in his speech, and it is difficult to say how much of an influence Gorbachev had over that, though it is very likely that he had some. Chernenko criticized, on the one hand, the

[89] See, notably, M.I. Piskotin, *Sotsializm i gosudarstvennoe upravlenie* (Socialism and State Administration) (Nauka, Moscow, 1984).

[90] M.S. Gorbachev, *Zhivoe tvorchestvo naroda* (Politizdat, Moscow, 1984). This was a speech delivered on 10 December 1984, to the all-Union Conference on 'The Perfecting of Developed Socialism and the Ideological Work of the Party...'.

relatively conservative Institute of Economics of the Academy of Sciences in Moscow and the much more reformist Central Institute of Economics and Mathematics (TsEMI). The common thread in the criticism, however, would appear to be that neither institute was sufficiently closely in touch with real economic life or was offering enough practical guidance to policymakers—a charge that could not be levelled against the Novosibirsk Institute, which works in close cooperation with industry, as can be seen from the pages of its monthly journal, *EKO*. Academician Abel Aganbegyan of Novosibirsk appears to be in good standing with Gorbachev,[91] and it is worth recalling that the frank critique by his Institute colleague Academician Tatyana Zaslavskaya of the obstacles to economic progress in the Soviet Union and of the deficiencies of Soviet social science in producing a 'fully elaborated "model" for the new economic mechanism'[92] was delivered to a closed seminar under the joint auspices of the economic departments of the party's Central Committee, Gosplan, and the Academy of Sciences of the USSR.[93]

Interesting though Zaslavskaya's paper is, it should not distract attention (as it has tended to) from works officially published in the Soviet Union that are no less open-minded and innovative. On the issue of economic reform, these have in the past few years included the works of jurists and political scientists as well as economists.[94] One significant example is a book published in September 1984 (which appears to have been quite overlooked by Western scholars) written by the chief editor of the journal *Sovetskoe gosudarstvo i pravo*, Mikhail Piskotin. Entitled *Socialism and State Administration*,[95] this work records the secular decline in the Soviet economic growth rate from the 1950s to the early 1980s and observes that the decline has 'deeper causes than simple mistakes in the work of particular organs of government, a low level of exactingness, or negligence in moral-educational work'.[96] It is impossible to do justice to Piskotin's quite lengthy and closely argued book in a few lines, but it is worth noting his emphasis on the fact that the Central Committee and the Council of Ministers did not consider their 14 July 1983 joint resolution on the broadening of the rights of production associations and enterprises to be a 'full and final solution of the problem of strengthening the independence of the primary economic unit'.[97] Piskotin criticizes

[91] See his articles in *Pravda*, 14 July 1984, p. 2; and *Trud*, 28 August 1984, p. 2.

[92] 'The Novosibirsk Report', *Survey*, Spring 1984, p. 100.

[93] Philip Hanson, 'The Novosibirsk Report: Comment', ibid., p. 83.

[94] I have drawn attention to some of them in my article, 'Political Science in the Soviet Union: A New Stage of Development?', in *Soviet Studies*, July 1984, pp. 317–44, esp. pp. 334–5.

[95] *Sotzializm i gosudarstvennoe upravlenie*, op. cit.

[96] Ibid., p. 9.   [97] Ibid., p. 147.

'market socialism' but, significantly, is not opposed to every use of the market mechanism. As he puts it: 'Market socialism does not exist wherever there is a market and commodity-production relations, but only where this market becomes the sole or main regulator of the economy.'[98] Accordingly, he is sympathetic to the Hungarian economic reform, though he stresses that this experience is 'impossible to transfer mechanistically to the conditions of the Soviet Union'.[99]

Even more radical calls for economic and, indeed, political reform have come from a sector head in the Institute of State and Law, Boris Kurashvili,[100] who has laid great stress on the need for 'democratization of the state administration', and has noted that many of those working in the state apparatus consider the present ministerial system—a product, essentially, of the 1930s—to be the only system possible. Kurashvili profoundly disagrees with such a view but recognizes that reform will meet with the opposition of 'conservative and inactive elements in the state apparatus'.[101]

Whether Gorbachev will follow the advice of the advocates of more far-reaching economic reform will depend not upon him alone, but upon the strength of the various interest groups involved (above all, in the apparatus), many of whom are opposed to reform. The opposition is to be found not only within the state administration, for at every level of the party apparatus there are departments that work closely with the ministerial network and whose functionaries tend to view issues through the same lenses. Already under Andropov and even under Chernenko, it was clear that within the top party leadership there were those acutely aware of current problems, and who had a more open mind about ways of tackling them than had many lower-level officials. Certainly, Gorbachev himself has given every indication of willingness to listen to constructive proposals for within-system change, and those jurists with ideas for reform should not have too much difficulty of access. It is worth noting in that connection that the director of the Institute of State and Law in Moscow, Academician Vladimir Kudryavtsev (under whose guidance a more sociological approach to the study of law has been encouraged in the

[98] Ibid., p. 157.

[99] Ibid., p. 161. *Gorbachev's* positive evaluation of the Hungarian economic reform may be inferred from an editorial published in *Pravda* less than three weeks after his succession which speaks of Hungary's 'bold, innovative, and at the same time realistic, approach to the working-out of plans for socio-economic development' (*Pravda*, 30 March 1985, p. 1).

[100] See B.P. Kurashvili, 'State Administration of the National Economy: Prospects for Development', *Sovetskoe gosudarstvo i pravo*, No. 6, 1982, pp. 38–48; Kurashvili, 'Objective Laws of State Administration', ibid., No. 10, 1983, pp. 36–44; and Kurashvili, 'The Fates of Branch Management', *EKO*, No. 10, 1983, pp. 34–57.

[101] Kurashvili, 'Objective laws ...'.

Institute over the past decade), was one of the speakers at the RSFSR Supreme Soviet election meeting addressed by Gorbachev on 20 February 1985.[102]

Although Gorbachev's speeches generally repay close study, the one that is most revealing of all those he has made to date in respect of the insight it affords on his policy orientation and priorities is his speech at the conference on ideological work in December 1984. Though what was published from it in the mass media made interesting reading,[103] it was less than half of what Gorbachev actually said. In directing attention to some of the salient points from the speech, I draw in the following paragraphs exclusively from the parts that were not published in *Pravda*. These include some of the most innovative passages and those most revealing of Gorbachev's style—and at the same time the least known because of their more limited circulation.[104]

On the economy, Gorbachev directly referred to the 'slowdown of economic growth at the end of the 1970s and beginning of the 1980s' and said that this was to be explained 'not only by the coincidence of a number of unfavourable factors but also by the fact that the necessity of changes in some aspects of production relationships was not discovered in good time'.[105] This particular argument is very much in line with the views of economic reformers such as Piskotin and Zaslavskaya, as is his attention to the problem of the correspondence of production relations and productive forces.[106] Gorbachev himself insists that the correspondence of production relations to productive forces is not reproduced just by itself, but demands constant, purposeful work in the perfecting of the entire economic system of socialism.[107] While he observes that the dialectical relationship between production relations and productive forces cannot under socialism be an antagonistic one, he also notes that the unwarranted preservation of 'obsolete elements in production

[102] *Pravda*, 21 February 1985, p. 2. One of the scholars whose advice Piskotin acknowledges in the introduction to his recent book is Zaslavskaya. Both he, in that book, and Zaslavskaya in her 1983 report single out for special praise the work of Kurashvili. This is a good example of the kind of opinion grouping or informal group that is of great importance in Soviet politics. These three scholars are, of course, just part of a much wider opinion grouping with broadly similar views on the direction the Soviet economy and Soviet society should be taking. Needless to say, there are informal groups of conservatives and dogmatists as well as of reformers. For a pioneering discussion of the group phenomenon in the USSR by a Soviet scholar, see A.V. Obolonskiy, 'Formal and Informal Groups in the State Administrative Apparatus', *Sovetskoe gosudarstvo i pravo*, No. 5, 1983, pp. 28–35. See also Brown, 'Political Science in the Soviet Union', esp. pp. 332–3 and 335.

[103] See, for example, *Pravda*, 11 December 1984, p. 2.

[104] Gorbachev, *Zhivoe tvorchestvo naroda*. The print run of this Politizdat booklet is 100,000, which is, of course, substantial, but not to be compared with *Pravda*, which has a circulation of over 10 million. The booklet very rapidly sold out.

[105] Ibid., pp. 12–13.

[106] See Piskotin, *Sotsializm i gosudarstvennoye upravleniye*; and 'The Novosibirsk Report'.

[107] Gorbachev, *Zhivoe tvorchestvo naroda*, p. 12.

relations may bring about a deterioration of the economic and social situation'.[108]

Among the practical economic issues touched upon by Gorbachev in his December 1984 speech were those of commodity–monetary relations and the need for 'serious scientific recommendations on the application in contemporary conditions of such economic levers as price, cost, profit, credit, and certain others';[109] the built-in conservatism of much of existing investment policy;[110] and the importance of improving distribution relations, since 'this is a most sensitive sphere that exercises an active influence not only on production but also on the consciousness and the mood of the people'.[111]

In his references to the social sciences, Gorbachev's interest in theoretical issues comes out strongly, and so does his insistence that theory should lead to practical benefit. Thus, he observes:

Not all research institutions work in close connection with practice. Some scholars at times are not able to part company with obsolete conceptions and stereotypes. Their theoretical investigations not infrequently are fitted into preconceived schemes, and they revolve in a circle of scholastic reasoning.[112]

Later in the same speech he referred to the force of inertia and to the attempt 'to squeeze new phenomena into the Procrustean bed of moribund conceptions'.[113] The tone and content of Gorbachev's remarks make clear that he is no friend of dogmatists and that reform-minded social scientists can expect encouragement under his leadership, provided they devote attention to 'the problems of perfecting developed socialism'. This, for Gorbachev, is 'the pressing demand of the times, the basic criterion for evaluating the activity of social scientists'.[114]

It was of greater importance than has generally been recognized that under Andropov there was a shift from Brezhnev's somewhat complacent view of 'developed socialism' to the standpoint that the Soviet Union was only 'at the beginning' of the stage of developed socialism, a shift that emphasized existing shortcomings and how much scope there was for improving (or in Soviet terms, 'perfecting') both the economic and the political systems. In his December speech, Gorbachev did not neglect the political system and made much use of the term, 'self-management' (*samoupravleniye*),[115] urging that the various levels and units within the political system be given more space

---

[108] Ibid., p. 13.   [109] Ibid., p. 14.   [110] Ibid., p. 22.
[111] Ibid., p. 31.   [112] Ibid., p. 11.   [113] Ibid., p. 41.
[114] Ibid., p. 11. *[So long as Chernenko was alive, Gorbachev had to pay lip-service to the notion that the Soviet Union was at the stage of 'developed socialism'. It was one he discarded after becoming General Secretary.]*
[115] See, for example, ibid., pp. 14–15.

(*prostor*) within which to operate. He attacked attempts to regulate all and everything from the centre and stressed the importance of 'every link of the political system' exercising its own functions.[116] In a significant passage, he observed: 'A qualified leadership not only does not limit but, on the contrary, opens up space for initiative of people, of work collectives, and of local organs.'[117]

As General Secretary, Gorbachev has returned to the theme of devolving greater responsibility and financial autonomy to enterprises and to brigades of workers. In a speech to a meeting of economic managers and specialists in April of this year he spoke of the need to release managers from the fetters of superfluous instructions, arguing that economic management was now at a level where accountability to higher organs could be decisively decreased. This would free them from 'the paper chase' and simultaneously contribute to 'the reduction of the managerial apparatus'.[118] On brigades, Gorbachev observed that a considerable number had gone over to 'a progressive method of work', but there were still many that were going over to financial autonomy only slowly and in which labour productivity was rising only slightly.[119]

It is tempting to see Gorbachev's emphasis on devolution of responsibilities and financial autonomy from the centre to industrial associations and enterprises in part as a result of the fact that he has a clearer idea of what life is actually like for a provincial factory manager than some of those who have been in the Central Committee apparatus for far longer. Not only has he evidently paid attention to the findings of Academician Aganbegyan and his colleagues on such matters, but he also has very recent memories of the frustrations of regional life for a highly intelligent official or manager who feels that his abilities are constantly being reined in. (It is the less able officials and managers who feel more comfortable with less responsibility.) It is, indeed, yet another unusual feature of the Gorbachev succession that the present General Secretary should have worked in Moscow for a mere six-and-a-half years. This has its undoubted advantages. It is one reason why there is a breath of real life in Gorbachev's speeches, a sense of how people are living and working far from the confines of the Central Committee building. Like Andropov, Gorbachev stresses discipline—'Ultimately, everything stems from a high degree of exactingness toward people, toward leading cadres, toward all of us, comrades'[120]— although he knows that this cannot be achieved by exhortation or by cadres policy alone, but has to be built into the economic mechanism.

---

[116] See, for example, ibid., p. 16.   [117] Ibid., p. 17.
[118] 'Initiative, Organization, Effectiveness—Speech of M. S. Gorbachev', *Pravda*, 12 April 1985, pp. 1–2.
[119] Ibid.   [120] Ibid.

An important theme for Gorbachev has been that of the need for the party to give people more information. It is of interest in that connection that the length of the published Politburo communiqués has increased since Gorbachev took over. But to change the habits of a lifetime within the party as a whole is not easy. In his December speech, Gorbachev quoted a letter from a party member in Minsk who expresses his satisfaction and that of his colleagues with the publication of information about Politburo meetings (a practice that Andropov began), but who goes on to point out that 'often we members of the party are better informed about the activity of the Politburo of the Central Committee than about the work of the bureau of the primary party organization or of the district committee!'[121] Gorbachev's response was: 'A true observation, and it must be given every attention.'[122]

Gorbachev clearly has political as well as economic changes in mind. But to attempt to foist upon him notions of pluralistic democracy would be wrong and misleading. Pluralism is simply not on the political agenda in the Soviet Union. Economic reform is, and even if the next instalment of it should fall short of the demands of the situation and of Soviet economic reformers (though they, of course, are not all of one mind), the evidence available on Gorbachev suggests that he at least will not be deterred by conservatism or, as his power base grows stronger, by vested interests from taking the reform further. If it be true that the Soviet Union is at present a military but not an economic superpower, Gorbachev's domestic policy can be summarized by saying that he intends to give the highest priority to ensuring that the USSR becomes the second while, in common with other Soviet leaders, remaining determined that it should not cease to be the first. It can, indeed, be argued that for the Soviet Union to maintain its military superpower status, it must increase its economic efficiency and its capacity to generate and diffuse the most advanced technology.

In personnel policy, it is already clear that the Gorbachev period is not going to be marked by the extremely slow pace of change of the Brezhnev years, still less by the immobility at the top that characterized Chernenko's thirteen months as General Secretary. Gorbachev's first six weeks as party leader saw the replacement of many officials at the republican, regional, and city level, and at the first normal Central Committee plenum over which he presided—held on 23 April 1985—no fewer than five promotions within the top leadership team took place.[123] What is more remarkable is that these included three promotions to full membership of the Politburo and all of them people who can be identified as Gorbachev allies. No previous General

---

[121] Gorbachev, *Zhivoe tvorchestvo naroda*, p. 31.   [122] Ibid.
[123] *Pravda*, 24 April 1985, p. 1.

Secretary has ever been able to consolidate his position within the leadership so quickly.

The two most important promotions were those of Yegor Ligachev (aged 64) and Nikolay Ryzhkov (55). Both became full Politburo members without passing through the candidate stage (the first people to perform that feat of upward political mobility since Gromyko did it in 1973) while retaining their secretaryships of the Central Committee. The only other person in that category is Romanov, and it was, of course, because the ranks of senior secretary had become so depleted that Gorbachev had the opportunity to promote further his colleagues who had been brought into the leadership by Andropov. The fact, however, that it was they rather than the 60-year-old Vladimir Dolgikh—to whose secretaryship of the Central Committee candidate membership of the Politburo was added at Brezhnev's last Central Committee plenum in May 1982, suggesting he was destined for senior secretaryship—who received promotion indicates how swiftly and effectively the Andropov–Gorbachev group has overtaken the Brezhnev legatees. In terms of their policy orientation, Ryzhkov and Ligachev are also closely aligned with Gorbachev. Ryzhkov seems to be at least as sympathetic towards innovation in economic policy and organization as the General Secretary himself, and Ligachev has been pursuing with some vigour the policy that Andropov began and Gorbachev favours of crackdown on corruption and ineptitude within the party apparatus as well as replacement of officials who do not meet the more exacting standards now being applied.

The elevation of Viktor Chebrikov (62), the KGB chairman, from candidate to full membership of the Politburo should also strengthen Gorbachev's position within the top leadership. Chebrikov worked closely with Andropov for fifteen years,[124] and it was during Andropov's General Secretaryship that he received both of his previous major promotions—to the chairmanship of the KGB and to Politburo candidate membership.[125] There is every reason to suppose that Chebrikov transferred his loyalty from Andropov to Gorbachev, the man Andropov was grooming for the succession. Chebrikov's full Politburo membership was presumably also well received at KGB headquarters, since it restores to that body the political status it enjoyed between April 1973 and May 1982 when Andropov, as KGB chief, was also a full member of the Politburo.

The promotion of Marshal Sokolov, Ustinov's successor as minister of defence, to candidate membership of the Politburo gives the military an institutional voice once again in the highest counsels of the party. Sokolov

---

[124] See *Yezhegodnik Bol'shoy Sovetskoy Entsiklopedii, 1981*, p. 608.
[125] See *Pravda*, 18 December 1982, p. 2; and 27 December 1983, p. 1.

would appear to be the only one of the five people promoted to be without links to Gorbachev, though given his age (73) that is of no long-term significance. The fifth person to receive advancement at the April plenum was Viktor Nikonov (56), who has become a secretary of the Central Committee. As minister of agriculture for the Russian republic, he was obviously well known to Gorbachev and had been working under his jurisdiction. He has now been elevated by Gorbachev to a position more important than that of the minister of agriculture for the USSR as a whole, since it seems clear that he will be the agricultural overlord within the Secretariat.[126]

All in all, these April plenum changes strengthen, and at the same time somewhat rejuvenate, the top leadership team, though Gorbachev himself remains the youngest member. They confirm that Gorbachev is already wielding great authority within the party and should make it easier for him to put forward and to implement those policies that he believes will meet the needs of the Soviet Union.

In the realm of foreign policy, Gorbachev has already demonstrated in his meetings with Western politicians visiting Moscow that detailed grasp of the issues which had impressed his British hosts last December. The speaker of the United States House of Representatives, Thomas P. (Tip) O'Neill, Jr., is but the latest to assess Gorbachev as formidably accomplished. 'About his ability, his talents, his frankness, his openness, I was tremendously impressed', he said.[127] O'Neill added that he did not perceive any major change in Soviet policy.

Policy change, however, is unlikely to be announced unilaterally,[128] and is more likely to emerge in the course of serious negotiations should these take place. It is not surprising that so far what the outside world has seen is mainly a change of style. But Gorbachev seems determined to improve the Soviet Union's external relations on several fronts. He has accepted invitations to visit France and the Federal Republic of Germany, as well as in principle an invitation to meet with President Ronald Reagan, though the details of time and place have still, at the time of writing, to be decided.[129] He is likely to

[126] For Nikonov's biography, see *Yezhegodnik Bol'shoy Sovetskoy Entsiklopedii, 1981*, p. 592.

[127] *International Herald Tribune*, 11 April 1985, p. 1.

[128] However, Gorbachev did announce a Soviet unilateral moratorium due to last until November 1985 (when the position would be reviewed) on the further deployment of Soviet medium-range missiles in Europe. This announcement came in the course of an interview of Gorbachev by the editor of *Pravda* (see *Pravda*, 8 April 1985, p. 1). In his meeting with Speaker O'Neill and other US congressmen in the Kremlin on 10 April, Gorbachev said that the United States had displayed 'absolutely incomprehensible haste' in declaring its negative attitude to this 'important and constructive gesture of good will'. See *BBC SWB*, SU/7923/I and SU/7923/A11–2, 12 April 1985.

[129] On this, see *International Herald Tribune*, 3 April 1985, pp. 1–2; and *Pravda*, 8 April 1985, p. 1.

make a determined effort to improve relations with China, and the current leaderships in Moscow and Beijing would appear to have better prospects of moving closer together than at any time over the last two decades. Already the two countries had renewed their recognition of each other as 'socialist states', and the editor of *Pravda*, in an interview given in Belgrade, has noted that recently there has been in Chinese statements an improvement 'in tone and in terminology, such as "Comrade Gorbachev", which did not exist before'.[130] Given Gorbachev's acknowledged ability to argue the Soviet case flexibly and reasonably, and without resort either to dogma or to a script, the Soviet Union can well afford to be much more active diplomatically in the coming years than it has been in the recent past.

Gorbachev, who has made the journey from kolkhoz to Kremlin in record time, is about as likely to question the foundations of the system that enabled him to rise from humble origins to the highest office in the land as an American president who rose from log cabin to White House would be to question the wisdom of the Founding Fathers. He is a true believer in the Soviet system who is at the same time far from complacent about it and conscious of many of the ways in which it must be improved. He may yet have a greater opportunity than any individual since the death of Stalin to make an impact on it.

Gromyko said in his nomination speech that Gorbachev was 'a man of strong convictions' who 'states his position frankly, whether or not it is to the liking of his interlocutor'.[131] Mlynář has described Gorbachev as one for whom convictions play a decisive role in politics: 'He has never been a cynic, and he is, in character, a reformer who considers politics as a means to an end, with its objective being to meet the needs of the people.'[132]

Gorbachev is not, however, the kind of 'conviction politician' who does not listen to what others have to say. Because of the extent to which power is shared at the top of the Soviet hierarchy, he *could* not be (especially before he became General Secretary). But it is noteworthy that he listens also to specialist advisers and to his subordinates. British politicians who had extensive dealings with Gorbachev last December observed that he had an easy relationship with the group he led. There was neither bullying from the one side nor obsequiousness from the other. Members of the group with something to say felt free to speak up, though there was never any doubt about Gorbachev's ultimate authority.

---

[130] *BBC SWB*, SU/7920/B/1, 9 April 1985.
[131] *Materialy vneocherednogo plenuma tsentral'nogo komiteta KPSS...*, p. 6.
[132] Mlynář, loc. cit.

Every Soviet leader so far has been different in political style and, to a degree, in political priorities. Already Gorbachev has revealed some of his policy preferences, but these may become clearer as his power increases (as it surely will). His policy aims may also be modified by changing circumstances since he is a man who learns from his experiences and who is open to reason. The responsibilities and burdens placed on Gorbachev's shoulders are immense. But this time round the Soviet selectorate has chosen the man who, of all those in their midst, seems best equipped to carry them.

3

The First Phase of Soviet Reform, 1985–6[1]

The changes now taking place in the Soviet Union are as yet little understood in the West. Often they are dismissed as cosmetic or, at most, as representing a change of style. Indeed, the style of Soviet politics, particularly of the top leader, has changed in certain respects. Mikhail Gorbachev's political manner—more open than that of any previous General Secretary of the Soviet Communist Party apart from Nikita Khrushchev—impresses many thinking Soviet citizens, including those who had little time for a Brezhnev or a Chernenko. This is a fact of no small importance. Nevertheless, style is no substitute for solutions to some of the Soviet Union's pressing problems, as Gorbachev himself well knows.

It is the very seriousness of these problems that will serve to stimulate policy changes. In foreign policy, Gorbachev was the legatee of bad relations with the United States, poor relations with Western Europe and Japan, uneasy relations with Poland's rulers (not to mention with Polish and several other East European *societies*), and only marginally improving relations with China. He inherited a war in Afghanistan and—not the least of his problems—the Reagan administration.

The vast increases in American military expenditure under Ronald Reagan were seen by Moscow not only as imposing an additional strain on the Soviet economy but also—and more importantly—as a threat to Soviet security. Although little credence is given to Reagan's original vision of the Strategic Defence Initiative (SDI) as providing a leak-proof umbrella that could protect the entire United States from nuclear attack, there are very real Soviet worries about the resources being poured into SDI-associated, high-technology weaponry and about the possibility of the United States regaining military superiority and a first-strike capability. Certainly the Soviet Union is conducting research in the same areas; yet its willingness and, indeed, anxiety to restrict research and testing to the laboratory for a ten-year period, as Gorbachev proposed at Reykjavik, indicates its perception of who is ahead and who is likely to make faster progress in new weapons systems.

[1] *This chapter was completed in late 1986 and published in* World Policy Journal, *Vol. IV, No. 1, Winter 1986–7 under the title, 'Soviet Political Developments and Prospects'.*

Domestically, Gorbachev inherited a hidebound bureaucracy and an economy whose growth was in long-term decline from the 1950s to the 1980s. This was true despite the efforts made by Brezhnev's successor, Yuriy Andropov, to shake up and rejuvenate officialdom and to instil both more discipline and greater enthusiasm in the work force—a programme that did achieve a modest improvement in economic performance. Yet, even though Andropov's victory in the 1982 succession struggle had given new hope to Soviet within-system reformers as well as to disciplinarians,[2] much of the momentum on both fronts was lost under Konstantin Chernenko. The very fact that Chernenko was preferred to Gorbachev when Andropov died in February 1984 indicated how worried the party conservatives had been by Andropov's new broom and by the prospect that it might be wielded with still greater vigour by the much younger Gorbachev. He was so obviously superior to Chernenko in ability, knowledge, energy, and potential appeal to public opinion at home and abroad that nothing but the old guard's desire for a return to a quieter life and fear of losing their position and privileges could explain the delay in his accession.

Although the General Secretaryship of the Central Committee of the Communist Party is undoubtedly the post in which more political resources are concentrated than any other within the Soviet system, there is, nevertheless, a sense in which Gorbachev's political struggle was only just beginning when he attained that position.[3] Removing people from their jobs arouses opposition, and overcoming bureaucratic inertia requires immense skill and effort. Gorbachev has made considerable headway in getting his own political agenda adopted as the order of the day. To get agreement on the policies that follow from it—never mind getting them implemented—is, however, an altogether harder task.

There is much greater diversity of opinion within the 19-million strong CPSU (and still more, of course, within Soviet society as a whole) than is generally appreciated in the West. Indeed, Soviet rhetoric that harps on 'the monolithic unity of the party and the people' unwittingly presents a more totalitarian image of the system to the outside world than an objective examination of Soviet politics warrants, thus paradoxically reinforcing the

---

[2] The point is elaborated in Archie Brown, 'Andropov: Discipline *and* Reform?', in *Problems of Communism*, Vol. XXXII, No. 1 (January–February 1983), pp. 18–31.

[3] I have discussed Gorbachev's path to the General Secretaryship and the outlook he brought to that office in 'Gorbachev: New Man in the Kremlin' in *Problems of Communism*, Vol. XXXIV, No. 3 (May–June 1985), pp. 1–23 [*Chapter 2 of this volume*]. For a stimulating discussion of the Gorbachev leadership and its inheritance, see Seweryn Bialer, *The Soviet Paradox: External Expansion, Internal Decline* (Knopf, New York, 1986). For alternative views, see also Christian Schmidt-Hauer, *Gorbachev: The Path to Power* (Tauris, London, 1986) and Zhores Medvedev, *Gorbachev* (Blackwell, Oxford, 1986).

views of the most unthinkingly conservative Western circles. Doubtless, there is a very high degree of determination among Soviet leaders and citizens alike to defend their country against external attack. Given the heroic and successful struggle put up by the great majority of the Soviet population during the Second World War—following the worst years of Stalin's bloodletting and the most extreme internal repression—it would be surprising indeed if that particular kind of unity were not to be even greater now, after a generation of relative tranquillity and (notwithstanding the slowdown in the *rate* of growth) improving living standards. Doubtless, also, there is unity on the goals of improving the performance of the Soviet economy, increasing agricultural output and raising the technological level of Soviet industry. But in the Soviet Union, as elsewhere, this unity vanishes when it comes to making hard policy choices about the particular approaches that may be employed to advance these broadly defined goals.

Within the political establishment, Gorbachev has made new friends and allies among people he has promoted—at the same time, of course, that he has unavoidably made enemies of the numerous officials who have been demoted or pensioned off before they thought their time was up. In the political arena today—among party and state officials, specialists in the research institutes, factory managers, trade union and Komsomol officials, and others—a real political struggle is taking place. To some extent, as in any political system, it is a struggle for position. But it is also a battle of ideas. Genuine differences on where the Soviet Union should be going are being argued out. In some areas, such as economic reform, the debate is relatively open, while in others it is more esoteric.[4] Either way, the current struggle between those who advocate domestic reform and foreign policy innovation and those who favour a conservative approach (sometimes in the guise of 'technocratic modernization') is the most important one to have occurred in Soviet politics for over 20 years. How it will be resolved between now and the early 1990s is of critical significance not only for the Soviet Union but also for the rest of the world.

ECONOMIC REFORM

Beyond dispute, there has been innovation in Soviet economic policy since Gorbachev became General Secretary. Whether serious economic reform will

---

[4] Esoteric debate is, of course, nothing new in Soviet politics. See, for example, Jerry F. Hough, *The Struggle for the Third World: Soviet Debates and American Options* (Brookings Institution, Washington, DC, 1986) and Gilbert Rozman, *A Mirror for Socialism: Soviet Criticisms of China* (Princeton University Press, Princeton, NJ, 1985). What is new is the greater frankness and openness of much of the present discussion.

take place, however, remains debatable. The current catchword is *perestroika*, which means 'restructuring' or 'reconstruction'. This may sound milder than reform, but Gorbachev himself seems well aware that more than tinkering is needed. At the 1986 Party Congress, he spoke not only of restructuring but also of the need for 'radical reform' of the economy, and in a speech last July he said that he would equate the word 'perestroika' with 'revolution'. But by no means do all Soviet officials who pay lip-service to perestroika want anything resembling reform, much less revolution. Indeed, the Soviet press makes clear that there is resistance even to the modest restructuring that has taken place so far. That reconstruction includes, in principle at least, reducing the powers of ministries and granting greater autonomy to factories and farms, while making as many economic enterprises as possible self-financing. In agriculture it involves giving much greater financial autonomy to teams of workers, who are encouraged to draw up a contract with their parent collective or state farm, enabling them to retain and share the profits they earn from the sale of produce above their contractual deliveries.

At the November 1986 session of the Supreme Soviet, improved production and productivity figures were announced. To what extent these were achieved by sacrificing quality for quantity and to what extent by technological innovation and improved work discipline or worker enthusiasm is not immediately clear. Gorbachev, showing his awareness of the possible conflicts between the goals of 'acceleration' and of quality, has observed that increased production at the expense of quality 'is not acceleration, it is from a contemporary point of view the Stone Age'.[5] He has redefined 'acceleration' to mean high-quality work produced by labour saving, resource saving, and new technology. If forced to choose between higher output figures in the short term and higher quality, he has left little doubt that he would give top priority to the latter. Arguing recently that acceleration must come 'above all through technical progress, through going over to new equipment and activization of the human factor', he added: 'The main thing is quality and once again quality.'[6]

One area, though, where higher production figures must have come as a particular relief to Gorbachev is agriculture. In his Bolshevik Revolution anniversary speech in November 1986, the second secretary of the party, Yegor Ligachev, revealed that the grain harvest in 1986 amounted to 210 million tons—30 million tons above the average for the previous five-year period.[7] Throughout that time, in fact, the Soviet Union had ceased publishing the statistics, but later in November—in another move towards greater openness—the year-by-year 1981–5 figures were released. Western estimates

---

[5] *Pravda*, 16 November 1986, p. 1.   [6] Ibid.   [7] *Pravda*, 7 November 1986, p. 2.

had already indicated a poor performance' in those years and the reality was, if anything, even worse.

In superficial Western analyses Gorbachev is usually accorded much of the blame for this, inasmuch as he was the secretary of the Central Committee responsible for agriculture during most of the period. Such a simplistic view completely ignores the constraints upon Gorbachev's powers, which are real enough even now that he is General Secretary but were much stronger before he assumed that office. In fact, it was only when Andropov became General Secretary that Gorbachev gained sufficient authority to campaign directly for the devolution of responsibility to the farms themselves and to groups of workers within them, and it was only in late 1985—once he had established himself as General Secretary—that he succeeded in putting in place administrative machinery designed to implement such a policy.[8] In November of that year five ministries and one state committee were abolished and replaced by a single State Committee for the Agro-Industrial Complex under the chairmanship of a close Gorbachev ally from Stavropol, Vsevolod Murakhovsky. Thus it is from 1986 onward that Gorbachev's agricultural performance must be judged.

While Gorbachev would almost certainly like to streamline much of the non-agricultural sector of the Soviet economy as well, this remains an uphill struggle, the powers of the General Secretaryship notwithstanding. Articles appear in the Soviet press with titles such as 'What is hampering the restructuring?' or in the form of a dialogue between two regional party officials, one for reform and the other against.[9] In his address to the June 1986 plenary session of the Central Committee and again in his speech at Khabarovsk just over a month later, Gorbachev had to complain of foot-dragging in the implementation of restructuring and reform—that is, of the policy adopted in principle at the 27th Party Congress.[10]

Gorbachev observed that 'there are amongst us, of course, people who have difficulty in grasping the word, "perestroika", and sometimes have difficulty

[8] Under Brezhnev, the most he could do was to encourage the publication of articles by others supporting devolution of responsibility to autonomous 'links' or teams within the farms. On this, see Archie Brown and Michael Kaser (eds.), *Soviet Policy for the 1980s* (Macmillan, London, and Indiana University Press, Bloomington, IN, 1982), pp. 241, 244, and 269–70.

[9] V. Kozhemyako, 'Chto meshaet perestroyke?' in *Pravda*, 7 August 1986, p. 2; and Fedor Burlatsky, 'Razgovor nachistotu: Polemicheskiy dialog o perestroyke', in *Literaturnaya gazeta*, 1 October 1986, p. 10. Burlatsky developed his article into a bold play for Soviet television called 'Two Views in One Office'. It raised many sensitive issues and was screened in prime time on 17 December.

[10] *Pravda*, June 17 1986, pp. 1–4; and *Pravda*, 2 August 1986, pp. 1–2. A somewhat fuller report of the latter speech—based on the Soviet radio and television broadcasts of it—is, however, to be found in the BBC Summary of World Broadcasts. See 'Speech to Khabarovsk Kray Party Activists on 31st July', SU/8328/C/7-21, 4 August 1986.

even in pronouncing it'. These people, he went on, 'often see in this process of renewal almost a shaking of our foundations, almost a renunciation of our principles'.[11] These remarks clearly were aimed not only at the party activists of Khabarovsk who formed his audience, but also at people in higher places. It is far from clear that the entire Politburo is as willing to proceed along the road of economic reform as Gorbachev appears to be. He has observed that only the 'first step' of reconstruction has been taken and that there is a danger of its being assumed to have succeeded when in fact there have so far been 'no profound qualitative changes which might consolidate the trend towards accelerated growth'.[12]

Gorbachev frequently stresses the need for the use of 'economic levers'. In question-and-answer sessions during his trips to the countryside, he has argued that prices in peasant markets should not simply be reduced by administrative fiat, since that would merely empty them of produce, but that instead competition should be given greater play. A similar line has been taken by the first secretary of the Moscow party organization, Boris Yeltsin, who, overruling those eager to keep private traders out of Moscow, ordered that new sites be made available where stalls could be set up. As a result, during 1986 people came from far afield in the Soviet Union to sell their produce in Moscow, and the supply of foodstuffs in the markets improved considerably.

A modest but by no means insignificant step towards reform was taken in November 1986 when the Supreme Soviet approved the 'Law on Individual Labour Activity'. Introduced by Ivan Gladkiy, the chairman of the State Committee for Labour and Social Affairs, this legislation permits twenty-nine types of individual or family-based private economic activity such as car repair, television repair, private tuition in foreign languages or other subjects, furniture repair, or running a taxi.[13] While this law, with some exceptions, largely legalizes activity that was taking place anyway on the black or grey market (and is, in its way, a tribute to a more universal law—that of supply and demand), it may stimulate an improvement of services. Although it is currently hedged by restrictions—for instance, confining such activity to 'spare time' labour—it is something of an ideological breakthrough for the contemporary Soviet Union, where such private enterprise has not flourished since the 1920s (though it is commonplace in several of the East European Communist states).

Moreover, there have been hints from two very influential figures in Soviet academic life that more radical change affecting private individual economic

---

[11] BBC SWB SU/8328/C/9, 4 August 1986.   [12] BBC SWB SU/8328/C/8, 4 August 1986.
[13] For Gladkiy's speech, see *Pravda*, 20 November 1986, p. 5.

activity may be on its way. The new director of the Institute of Economics of the Academy of Sciences in Moscow, Leonid Abalkin, has reportedly said that forthcoming legislation, of greater import than the November 1986 law on individual economic activity, will permit groups of individuals to establish new-style cooperatives for the production of consumer goods and foodstuffs. They would be 'largely free to market and price their products without state control' and their activities could make a bigger contribution to meeting the shortfall in certain kinds of consumer goods and foodstuffs than those facilitated by the legislation on individual and family-based economic activity.[14] A December 1986 article in *Pravda* by the director of the Institute of State and Law, Vladimir Kudryavtsev, referred to 'the further development of traders' and consumers' cooperatives', but made two points also of more general significance. Criticizing regulation of the economy on the basis of 'departmental orders and instructions', he called for a general law that would formulate 'the unifying principles of socialist management'. Most tellingly of all—and of considerable potential significance for the economy if carried into practice—Kudryavtsev added: 'Of the two possible principles, "You may do only what is permitted" and "You may do everything that is not forbidden," priority should be given to the latter inasmuch as it unleashes the initiative and activism of people.'[15]

One of the more interesting innovations of recent months in Soviet economic policy has been the extension of rights of foreign trading—and even of joint ventures with foreign firms—to more than twenty industrial ministries and departments and more than seventy major associations and large-scale enterprises.[16] This devolution of some of the powers of the Ministry of Foreign Trade is intended to facilitate more efficient use of imported foreign equipment, to cut down on the bureaucratic delays that have kept foreign technology from reaching Soviet enterprises until it is out of date, to help bring Soviet industry in an increasing number of selected areas up to world level, and to provide both standards and competition for the rest of the Soviet economy. Priority in trade and join ventures will be given to Comecon (The Council for Mutual Economic Assistance—the Soviet-bloc trading group). Yet the fact that Soviet industrial associations and factories have also been granted rights of direct access to companies from capitalist and developing countries further indicates that economic pragmatism is taking precedence over the old ideological rigidities.

---

[14] On this, see the reports of Patrick Cockburn in *The Financial Times*, 27 November 1986, p. 1 and 28 November 1986, p. 2.

[15] V. Kudryavtsev, 'Pravovaya sistema: puti perestroyki', in *Pravda*, 5 December 1986, p. 3.

[16] *Pravda*, 24 September 1986, p. 1.

In other words, *some* economic reform is already taking place within the Soviet Union. To use a Russian term that has become part of the technical vocabulary of Western–Soviet specialists, it is a *khozraschet* reform. *Khozraschet* means self-financing and refers to the principle whereby a factory, farm, publishing house, or theatre, for instance, finances itself from its own revenues without drawing upon central state funds. This system is being extended to more and more sectors of the Soviet economy and may serve to discourage waste and to encourage, up to a point, attention to consumers' wishes. But since the customer (whether for consumer goods or producer goods) very often has no choice but to take what is on offer, the extension of the *khozraschet* principle does not in itself represent a reform with a serious market element.

Moreover, it is still unclear how much latitude the 'self-financing' enterprise will have. Ministries are extremely reluctant to give up any of their powers. And many of the party's economic organs are accustomed to the existing structures and are reluctant to learn new ways, especially if these require them to grant greater autonomy to economic enterprises. A new law on the enterprise is now being prepared in the Soviet Union, with real argument going on both behind the scenes and in print[17] about how much autonomy should be granted to factories and industrial associations. The ministries are likely to bend every effort to safeguarding their position by watering down this legislation in draft. Perhaps because he knows this, Gorbachev asked an audience in Khabarovsk if they would like that draft 'to be published for nationwide discussion'. Getting the answer he expected—yes, they would!—Gorbachev responded: 'I shall report your opinion to the Politburo. I think that it is worthwhile to embark on such a step. This is very important.'[18] Not for the first time, Gorbachev was using a populist touch to steal a march on his opponents in the bureaucracy.

Important though it is to grant the enterprises more autonomy by law, that step alone is not enough. Only if the economy becomes more self-regulating—if, in fact, some significant market element is introduced alongside central strategic economic decision-making—will the reform be a 'radical' or even workable one. If, however, the economy remains an essentially administered economy, and the higher organs are held responsible for the performance of the lower organs, interference from above will continue, and the ministries—as a result of economic stringency—may even become

---

[17] For the views of one of the more radical reformers on what should go into this legislation, see B.P. Kurashvili, 'Osnovnoe zveno khozyaystvennoy sistemy (K kontseptsii zakona o sotsialisticheskom predpriyatii)', in *Sovetskoe gosudarstvo i pravo*, No. 10 (November 1986), pp. 12–21.

[18] BBC SWB SU/8328/C/18, 4 August 1986.

stronger. Thus, as an increasing number of economic reformers are asserting in the broad-ranging debate taking place in Soviet books, journals, and newspapers, a combination of central direction and market is required.

There seems, though, to be very little support in Russia proper for complete market *domination* of the economy, even for a *socialist* market economy (in which most enterprises would remain state-owned or socially owned). There is keen awareness that a market economy would widen existing regional differences and might very well exacerbate national tensions among the Soviet Union's more than 100 different ethnic groups. The Russians themselves would probably lose ground to the more developed Baltic republics and to the Caucasus. Thus *on its own* a market might leave Central Russia even poorer than before and would not necessarily solve the problem of tapping the rich but remote and intractable resources of Siberia.

Yet without a *significant market element* many of the problems of distribution, incentive, waste, and bureaucracy will not be solved. Thus, economic reformers in the ranks of academic specialists, such as Mikhail Piskotin, chief editor of the journal *Sovetskoe gosudarstvo i pravo* (*Soviet State and Law*), argue in favour of a market, while distancing themselves from the view that the market should become the sole determinant of economic relations.[19] It cannot therefore be taken for granted that when Ligachev (the second most powerful man in the party after Gorbachev) attacked the idea of a 'market economy' in the Soviet Union, he was *necessarily* ruling out a 'market element' or even 'market relations'. Still, the tone of his remarks was not encouraging for marketizing reformers, since he opposed the idea of 'socialism' to that of a 'market' and dismissed any movement towards a 'market economy' on the ground that it always and everywhere led to 'injustice and inequality'.[20]

Overall, a reading of the speeches of Ligachev, in particular, and also of the chairman of the Council of Ministers, Nikolay Ryzhkov, suggests that while they share many of Gorbachev's assumptions and policy goals, they are reluctant to countenance as radical an economic reform as he seems prepared for. Thus in the short term a far-reaching reform is unlikely. In the first place, without a clear majority in favour of radical reform within the leadership, half-measures will probably for the time being prevail. As things stand, perestroika appears to mean different things to different members of the Politburo. To Gorbachev it means 'radical reform', and there are a good

[19] See, for example, M.I. Piskotin, *Sotsialism i gosudarstvennoe upravlenie* (Nauka, Moscow, 1984), p. 157. An even more outspokenly pro-reform book written by Piskotin's colleague at the Institute of State and Law in Moscow, B.P. Kurashvili, is due to be published in the first quarter of 1987.

[20] E.K. Ligachev, 'Nam nuzhna polnaya pravda' in *Teatr*, No. 8 (August 1986), pp. 2–7, at p. 3.

many indications that for him this is not just a figure of speech. To some it means technocratic modernization—how much more than that it means for Ligachev and even Ryzhkov is still not clear; and to others it surely means a combination of lip-service to the new ideas and nostalgia for the days of Brezhnev (in this category come the Ukrainian party leader, Vladimir Shcherbitsky, and, still more obviously, Dinmukhamed Kunaev, sacked as the Kazakhstan first secretary on 16 December 1986, and soon to be removed from the Politburo).

Second, without further cadre changes at a level below the Politburo, a serious reform programme is unlikely to be implemented. At present (December 1986), there is no head of the Economic Department of the Central Committee. The fact that this office, a very important one for the fate of reform, has gone unfilled for many months suggests disagreement at the highest level. Yet a further influx of officials who are at least open to ideas of far-reaching economic reform may be a precondition for a reform policy's elaboration and implementation. Perhaps Gorbachev had this in mind when he announced last July that the next plenary session of the Central Committee would be devoted to cadre policy. The fact that this session was not held, as expected, immediately prior to the mid-November meeting of the Supreme Soviet may be another indication of the difficulty of reaching agreement on significant personnel changes.

A third and perhaps even more important factor now inhibiting far-reaching economic reform is the absence of a generally agreed-upon conception of the shape such an integrated reform would take. Since the various institutional interests are divided, and since there is diversity of view within the highest ranks of the party apparatus itself, the chances of a coherent reform policy being adopted and pursued would greatly increase if the experts reached something of a consensus—as Czech economists did in the mid-1960s and as Hungarian economists have done since the late 1960s. While more and more people within the ranks of the Soviet party intelligentsia do seem to have accepted that something new needs to be done, this process still has a long way to go. Even among professional economists, those with considered ideas for far-reaching reform, such as Professor G. Kh. Popov of Moscow University[21] and Academician Tatyana Zaslavskaya of Novosibirsk,[22] seem to be in a minority.

[21] See, for example, Popov's article, 'Razvitie otraslevogo upravleniya promyshlennost'yu', in *Kommunist*, No. 18 (December 1982), pp. 48–59; and his book, *Effektivnoe upravlenie* (Ekonomkia, Moscow, 2nd edn., 1985).

[22] Zaslavskaya is not only an economist. She may be more precisely described as an economist-cum-sociologist. See, for instance, 'The Novosibirsk Report' in *Survey*, Vol. 28, No. 1

Fourth, there appears to be no figure of high political standing who is in charge of the elaboration and pushing through of an economic reform programme. Gorbachev himself comes closest to playing that role, but he is ultimately responsible for everything, including the Soviet Union's relations with the rest of the world. Because of the renewed Soviet diplomatic activism, he spends a great deal of time meeting foreign politicians and cannot realistically be expected also to take charge of economic reform on a day-to-day basis. At the moment, he appears to lack a right-hand man who could do this job for him in the way in which Rezső Nyers assumed responsibility for economic reform in Hungary.[23]

Some change in key personnel responsible for the Soviet economy has, of course, taken place. In 1985, the 80-year-old Nikolay Tikhonov was replaced as chairman of the Council of Ministers by Nikolay Ryzhkov, twenty-four years his junior; and the long-serving and conservative chairman of Gosplan, Nikolay Baybakov, was replaced by the much younger Nikolay Talyzin, who was promptly accorded candidate membership of the Politburo—a political standing that eluded Baybakov during his twenty years as head of state planning. There is a danger that more than the first names of these office-holders may remain the same—that the new men could become the captives of the old institutional interests and pursue much the same policies as their predecessors. Yet, even though they do not appear to be on the most radical reformist wing of the new top leadership team (where Shevardnadze and Yeltsin may be placed alongside Gorbachev), Ryzhkov and Talyzin do seem much more open to new ideas than Tikhonov and Baybakov.

In August 1986 the ultra-conservative chairman of the State Committee on Prices, Nikolay Glushkov, was forced to retire and was replaced by Valentin Pavlov (almost twenty years younger), who only seven months earlier had been appointed first deputy minister of finance. In any far-reaching economic reform, a pricing reform would be essential; and pensioning off Glushkov removes one of the obstacles to it. Several others, however, remain. In a great many instances a price reform would mean price *rises*. Although these would be presented as higher payments for higher-quality goods and services, and might well be accompanied by a rise in the incomes of the most vulnerable sections of Soviet society, a reduction of the large subsidies that at present encourage the wasteful use of many services and products could arouse

---

(Spring 1984), pp. 88–108; T.I. Zaslavskaya, 'Ekonomika skvoz' prizmu sotsiologii' in *EKO*, No. 7 (July 1985); and T. Zaslavskaya, 'Chelovecheskii faktor razvitiya ekonomiki i sotsial'naya spravedlivost'' in *Kommunist*, No. 13 (September 1986), pp. 61–73.

[23] See William F. Robinson, *The Pattern of Reform in Hungary: A Political, Economic and Cultural Analysis* (Praeger, New York and London, 1973).

much popular resentment. Gorbachev seems persuaded of the need for such a change, but making it will draw further on his reserves of authority and will require all of the substantial political skill he can muster.

In this as in other areas of economic policy, Gorbachev faces a double danger: the bureaucracy may hold the first line of defence against his reforms but the workers might well constitute the second. The greatest threat to Gorbachev could lie in an attempt by conservative party officials opposed to such innovation to forge an informal alliance with disgruntled workers, citing principles of social fairness and equality, despite the fact that there is nothing especially fair or egalitarian about the present Soviet economic system, which grants the politically and socially privileged special access to scarce commodities and superior services. (The latter observation, remarkably enough, found its way into *Pravda* in early 1986.)[24]

Thus it seems that radical reform with a serious market element is not an immediate prospect. Nevertheless, in the medium term it should certainly not be ruled out. The fact that the reform process has managed to get underway after years of political stagnation indicates a certain momentum. And many passages in Gorbachev's speeches carry the inference that he sees the advantages of a significant role for markets in the Soviet economy, even if he feels constrained to move gradually. Although his policies are sufficiently bold and innovative that he has already run greater risks than the consensus-seeking Brezhnev ever did, the balance of probability is that he will not only survive as Soviet leader but also, as usually happens with general secretaries, increase his powers vis-à-vis his colleagues over time. It is true that Khrushchev, who also tried to institute reforms, was defeated by the bureaucracy—but then his policies were more impulsive and inconsistent than Gorbachev's, and he was older than the present General Secretary when he came to the top party job.

Many Western commentators, however, dismiss the possibility of far-reaching economic reform taking place in the Soviet Union. One favourite argument proceeds by analogy—not so much with the Khrushchev years as with the second half of the 1960s. Alexey Kosygin, it is recalled, tried to introduce a reform in 1965 and, though not particularly radical, it was nevertheless undermined. This analogy is flawed: in four crucial respects, the current situation is different from the 1960s. Even though a radical economic reform has not happened yet, and may not even be just around the corner, it would be rash indeed to assume that the history of the 1960s is going to repeat itself.

In the first place, objective trends in the still mainly unreformed Soviet economy have become, quite clearly, more unfavourable than they were

---

[24] *Pravda*, 13 February 1986, p. 4.

twenty years ago. The long-term decline in the rate of economic growth, already underway by the mid-1960s, has continued into the 1980s, and over the past few years it has begun to be documented and analysed by Soviet scholars. Although in Brezhnev's time there was much talk about the 'scientific and technological revolution', it was not in the Soviet Union that it was actually taking place; the technological gap between the Soviet economy and the most successful capitalist economies was, in a majority of areas, widening rather than narrowing.

The second difference is in perceptions. Before a political leadership can justify disrupting familiar organizational and behavioural patterns in order to carry through a reform in the fact of entrenched opposition, it has to acknowledge failure for what it is. The lagging growth rate, the inferior quality of many Soviet products, and the technological lag have come to be perceived as deeply serious problems. The difference between Brezhnev, on the one hand, and Gorbachev, on the other, is that the latter has indeed diagnosed the failure as much more significant, and even threatening, than it appeared to Brezhnev.

The third difference from the 1960s is tangentially related to the last and has to do with the impetus for reform. Twenty years ago, this came from the chairman of the Council of Ministers, Kosygin. At the stage of implementing policy, the ministerial network does have considerable power. Most general secretaries have had reason to criticize the lack of responsiveness of ministries to Central Committee directives. Yet the General Secretary possesses more political resources than his governmental counterpart: in a clash over the principles of policy between a General Secretary and a chairman of the Council of Ministers, the odds greatly favour the General Secretary coming out on top. Whether the 'Kosygin reform' would have 'worked' or been taken further had it received Brezhnev's wholehearted backing is an unanswerable question. What is certain is that with, at the very most, Brezhnev's lukewarm support and with his increasing responsiveness to the forces opposed to reform, it had no chance. It was of great importance that when Gorbachev succeeded Chernenko it was the General Secretary who was pushing for reform and the chairman of the Council of Ministers who was more inclined to drag his feet. Not surprisingly, that particular chairman, Tikhonov, was before long replaced by Ryzhkov, whose views seem at least somewhat closer to Gorbachev's than to those of his predecessor.

Finally, though there is in the 1980s, as in the 1960s, an international communist dimension to the issue of economic reform, that context is different now in significant ways from what it was in the earlier period. Gorbachev may have criticized aspects of the Chinese (as well as of the

Yugoslav) reform in at least one forum,[25] but he certainly does not need to worry about being outflanked 'on the left' by the Chinese Communists. The accusations of 'revisionism' that Beijing directed at Brezhnev and Kosygin are a thing of the past; the present Chinese leadership is actually hoping that the Soviet Union will embark on serious economic reform. Even more important is the East European aspect of the change that has occurred over time. Between 1965 and 1968 the country that was setting the pace in economic reform (at least at the level of adoption of its principles) was Czechoslovakia; in 1968, when this economic reform was accompanied by political changes more far-reaching than the Brezhnev Politburo could stomach, Soviet supporters of reform found themselves tarred with the Czech 'revisionist' brush. This became a very useful instrument in the hands of Soviet conservatives: the link forged between economic reform and radical political reform of the Czechoslovak type became the final nail in the coffin of Kosygin's initiative.

In the twenty years since then, however, economic reforms of varying degrees of radicalism have been implemented in Hungary, East Germany, and Bulgaria—without the attempts to institutionalize political pluralism that so alarmed the Soviet leadership in 1968. Thus, far from being a warning of the perils of reform, East Europe is now seen, at least in part, as a source of inspiration. Soviet managers and economic specialists are urged to study 'the experience of the fraternal socialist countries'. While it could be argued that it would embarrass the Soviet Union to follow others, this is not a serious objection. Even Soviet admirers of such alternative models as Hungary or East Germany take pains to stress that a reform could not possibly be a mere copy of what is found in any East European state but would have to be adapted to Soviet conditions. Furthermore, whatever the differences between the Soviet people and the East Europeans, the economic systems being reformed by some of the latter were originally based on the Soviet prototype. Thus the East European reform experiences—the implementation problems and failures as well as the successes—are proving useful to the Soviet Union.

FOREIGN POLICY

Much has been made in the West of Gorbachev's need to reach a broad-ranging arms control agreement and to pursue a more conciliatory foreign policy so that more attention and resources can be devoted to the Soviet

---

[25] See Seweryn Bialer and Joan Afferica, 'The Genesis of Gorbachev's World' in *Foreign Affairs*, Vol. 64, No. 3 ('America and the World 1985', 1986), pp. 605–44, at pp. 612–13.

Union's economic problems. It is undoubtedly true that at present there is more coordination and complementarity between Soviet domestic and foreign policy than has been the case at times in the past. But while domestic economic pressures and priorities play a part in determining current Soviet foreign policy objectives, they are not the whole story. Foreign policy changes are also being made on their own grounds and reflect Soviet security concerns and some new thinking on international politics. One of the most striking signs of this is the extent to which under Gorbachev people with different mindsets and agendas from their predecessors have been assigned to senior foreign policy posts.

Without doubt, it is in the foreign policy establishment that the most dramatic personnel changes have taken place. This has facilitated not only a very different manner of conducting Soviet foreign policy, but also some interesting policy innovation. From the start, Gorbachev was clearly interested in playing a leading foreign policy role despite the demands imposed by domestic problems. It is noteworthy that the four major agencies involved in the determination of Soviet foreign policy have had a change of head in the past two years: the Politburo itself, with Gorbachev succeeding Chernenko in March 1985; the Ministry of Foreign Affairs (MID), where Eduard Shevardnadze succeeded Andrey Gromyko, who was 'promoted' to the formal headship of state, in July 1985;[26] the International Department of the Central Committee, where Anatoliy Dobrynin, after twenty-four years in Washington, succeeded the ideologically conservative Boris Ponomarev in March 1986; and the Socialist Countries Department of the Central Committee,

---

[26] *In his memoirs Gorbachev relates that Gromyko's first reaction when he suggested the name of Shevardnadze as his successor was 'close to shock'. See Mikhail Gorbachev, Zhizn' i reformy, Vol. 1 (Novosti, Moscow, 1995), p. 288. However, Gorbachev allowed Gromyko time to think about it and brought second secretary Yegor Ligachev and KGB Chairman Viktor Chebrikov into their next discussion. Agreement was obtained in this group, each member of whom doubtless realized that Gorbachev had already made up his mind to have someone who had not served Gromyko in the Ministry of Foreign Affairs but who was a personal ally of the new General Secretary from outside MID. Presenting Shevardnadze's name for Politburo approval on 29 June 1985 Gorbachev was careful to associate Gromyko with his recommendation. He said they had discussed a number of names—and mentioned four apart from Shevardnadze—but they had concluded that Shevardnadze was the correct choice. Gromyko, whom Gorbachev had just successfully proposed to the Politburo as the next Chairman of the Presidium of the Supreme Soviet (and hence formal head of state), was the first to offer his support in the choice of his successor. Shevardnadze was at the time a candidate, or non-voting, member of the Politburo who, nevertheless, attended in that capacity all its meetings, including the one at which his move to the Foreign Ministry was being discussed. He was promoted the following day to full membership. Gromyko, who from 1957 until 1973 was Foreign Minister without being even a candidate member of the Politburo, doubtless had his own experience in mind when he pointed to the fact that Shevardnadze already belonged to the 'leading centre' [of the CPSU] and added: 'That is important for the Minister of Foreign Affairs.' See 'Zasedanie Politbyuro TsK KPSS 29 June 1985 goda', Volkogonov Collection, National Security Archive, R 5276, p. 3.*

responsible for relations with other Communist countries,[27] where the trend was likewise in a less conservative direction, with Vadim Medvedev taking over from an old Brezhnev ally, Konstantin Rusakov. The changes also exemplify the rejuvenation of the higher echelons of the Soviet party and state bureaucracy that has been going on since Gorbachev became General Secretary—the new appointees are on average eighteen years younger than their predecessors.

These changes at the top of the foreign policymaking hierarchy have led to a flurry of changes in other senior posts. New Soviet ambassadors have been appointed to most of the more important countries, including the United States, China, Japan, Great Britain, France, and West Germany. One of the most striking changes at home is the influx of men with experience of the West and, in particular, of the United States into the Central Committee's International Department. Next to Dobrynin, the most important such example is Georgiy Kornienko, who was transferred from being first deputy minister of Foreign Affairs to first deputy head of the International Department. Kornienko served in the Soviet Embassy in Washington in the first half of the 1960s and was deputy head and then head of the American Department of the MID from 1965 until 1978. With his and other such high-level appointments the International Department has undoubtedly gained greater influence on policymaking and on East–West relations in general, and on Soviet–American relations in particular, than it enjoyed when Gromyko was running the Ministry and Ponomarev the Department.

It would probably be going too far, however, to suggest that the Ministry has ceded primacy in this area to the Department. The very fact that it is the foreign minister who has most face-to-face meetings with the American and other Western counterparts puts him or her in an advantageous position as conveyer and interpreter of the latest foreign governmental opinion to the Politburo colleagues. And Shevardnadze has more than compensated for his previous lack of foreign policy experience with his undoubted political ability and diplomatic skills, thus helping to ensure that while the Foreign Ministry does not dominate the foreign policymaking process as it did when Gromyko was minister and the hapless Chernenko was General Secretary, it has not been reduced to the role of mere executant of a policy decided elsewhere but instead makes its own substantial input to that process.

In the past, officials in the Ministry of Foreign Affairs have tended to see themselves as the 'doers'—the practical people concerned with the real business of interstate relations—and the International Department as an organization

---

[27] Its official title is the Department of Relations with Communist and Workers' Parties of Socialist Countries.

more interested in liberation and revolutionary movements and in the ideological advance of communism.[28] This had a strong basis in reality as long as
Ponomarev headed the International Department, but under the pragmatic
Dobrynin there has probably been some reordering of priorities. Thus, in so
far as there has been some enhancement of the International Department's
authority in East–West policymaking, the implications are different from what
they would have been before the recent personnel changes.[29] And the influx of
Ministry officials into the Department should make for a relationship of greater
trust between the two organizations than has prevailed in the past, as well as
providing an infusion of more practical experience of the outside world into the
Central Committee apparatus.

In addition to these important personnel shifts, the Gorbachev leadership
has undeniably made innovations in Soviet policy towards Western countries.
The extended unilateral moratorium on nuclear testing is a case in point, as
was the package presented by the Soviet Union at the Reykjavik summit.
Particularly noteworthy is the Soviet acceptance of the 'zero option'—the
elimination of all intermediate-range nuclear weapons in Europe. When this
was first proposed by Reagan in 1981, Moscow dismissed it out of hand, and a
year later the head of the Soviet delegation at the intermediate-range nuclear
forces (INF) talks, Yuliy Kvitsinsky, described it as 'a formula for unilateral
disarmament by our side and, frankly, an insult to our intelligence'.[30] Since
then, of course, the United States has gone ahead with the deployment of
Pershing and cruise missiles, and to that extent was in a stronger bargaining
position in 1986 than it had been earlier; nevertheless, the shift in the Soviet
stance has been spectacular. So also was the decision, enunciated in the
discussions at Reykjavik and confirmed by Gorbachev at his press conference

[28] This view comes out strongly in the memoirs of the former high-ranking official in the
Soviet Ministry of Foreign Affairs and the United Nations, Arkady Shevchenko. See his *Breaking
with Moscow* (Knopf, New York, 1985), especially pp. 188–91.

[29] *To the extent that the above sentence, written in 1986, implies that the International
Department was more conservative than the Ministry, it should be modified. As I show in Chapter
6, senior members of the International Department were sources of much of the 'New Thinking' on
foreign policy of the Gorbachev era. At the same time, as such a notable 'new thinker' as Anatoliy
Chernyaev has noted, it was a department of 'doublethink' (see Chapter 6). Even Chernyaev had to
waste time while he was still a deputy head of the International Department talking to leaders of
unimportant Communist Parties such as the Communist Party of Great Britain, and even chastising
them for their occasional critical comments about the Soviet Union, although his own criticisms of
the Soviet order would soon develop into something more far-reaching than any critique ever
produced by the General Secretary of the CPGB, Gordon McLennan, whom he was scolding. See on
this 'The Diary of Anatoly Chernyaev' for 1985, placed on the website of the NSA on 25 May 2006
(Chernyaev's 85th birthday), translated by Anna Melyakova, edited by Svetlana Savranskaya:
http://www.gwu.edu/~nsarchiv—diary entries of 14 and 16 March 1985.*

[30] Strobe Talbott, *Deadly Gambits: The Reagan Administration and the Stalemate in Nuclear
Arms Control* (Pan, London, 1985), pp. 114–15.

immediately after the breakup of the talks, that the Soviet Union no longer insists on the non-modernization of British and French nuclear missiles as a precondition for an agreement with the United States on medium-range missiles in Europe.[31]

Such policy changes reflect a variety of Soviet concerns about security. Some of these focus on the new generations of weapons that may grow out of SDI, notwithstanding Soviet scepticism of the idea that it could protect the American civilian population. Moscow also worries that the next phase of arms competition could take decisions about peace and war out of the hands of politicians and make them increasingly dependent on the perfect functioning of fallible technology. The Soviet leadership made enough concessions in its efforts towards an agreement that would restrict and slow work on SDI to demonstrate that the latter complex of projects indeed constituted an excellent bargaining chip, had Reagan been prepared to use it as such when his political strength was still at its height. His refusal to do so confirmed Soviet analysts in their belief that his administration's hidden (or not-so-hidden) agenda is to re-establish US military superiority over the Soviet Union and to abandon the idea of approximate parity and stability in the superpower military relationship.

So far as Western Europe is concerned, Moscow has not only made concessions on the modernization of British and French nuclear armouries but has also greatly stepped up its diplomatic activity in Europe. The stock response that this is an attempt to split the alliance is an oversimplification. While the Soviet Union doubtless takes some satisfaction from disagreement within the North Atlantic Treaty Organization (NATO), its main strategic concern is with US military strength and potential; it does not feel particularly threatened by the West European states as such. Moreover, since those countries share with the Soviet Union memories of the horrors of war on their own continent, they are seen as a restraining influence on US administrations as potentially bellicose as Reagan's. Thus the present Soviet leaders envisage the alliance remaining in place for some time, and see this as not entirely to their disadvantage. In fact, many of the Soviet overtures to Western Europe aim indirectly to influence the US administration through European channels rather than to create a fissure in the alliance.

Some innovation in Soviet policy towards the rest of the Communist world has also been emerging. For the East Europeans, not all of this is welcome. The Gorbachev leadership is more demanding than its predecessors of its Comecon partners in terms of the delivery dates and quality of their exports to the USSR; furthermore, the higher degree of integration of the economies of

---

[31] *Pravda*, 14 October 1986, pp. 1–2.

Comecon countries that Moscow is urging is not to the liking of all East Europeans. But along with these changes has come a much less grudging Soviet acceptance of the diversity to be found in the East European economic models and, to some extent, in their political arrangements—indeed, a heightened Soviet interest in learning from them.

The Gorbachev leadership is particularly eager to establish closer ties with China. Even the level of agreement on international issues that exists between the Soviet Union and India would be a considerable step forward in Sino–Soviet relations, and would strengthen the USSR in its international diplomacy. Such an improved relationship would not, Moscow realizes, simply be a return to the position of the 1950s, but would require much greater Soviet respect for Chinese independence and China's right to determine its own major policies. Unlike the period of China's Cultural Revolution, when those on the Soviet side who favoured a Sino–Soviet rapprochement were a rather small minority of neo-Stalinists who felt some affinity with Mao's excesses, today it is the reform wing of the Soviet party intelligentsia that advocates closer relations with China—not only as a measure beneficial to Moscow in international politics but also as a potential stimulus to further Soviet internal reform.

While the policy initiatives towards the rest of the communist world owe much to the shifting balance of forces within the Politburo and to Gorbachev personally, the 1986 personnel changes in the Socialist Countries Department of the Central Committee have also had some effect. The most obvious such change was the transfer and promotion of Vadim Medvedev. Medvedev, who became a secretary of the Central Committee at the 27th Party Congress in March 1986, when he also moved from the headship of the Science and Education Department of the Central Committee to that of the Socialist Countries Department, is a former economist who favoured reform during the debates of the 1960s and a man of more ability and imagination than his predecessor, Rusakov.

One particularly significant change that has taken place under Medvedev is the promotion of Georgiy Shakhnazarov from the position he has held since the 1970s, as one of several deputy heads of the Socialist Countries Department, to first deputy head of the department. At the time of writing, the Socialist Countries Department thus has two first deputy heads, the other being Oleg Rakhmanin, who has held that post since 1968—the year of the Soviet military intervention in Czechoslovakia. But by all indications, Rakhmanin is on the way out, the abilities and approach of Shakhnazarov being preferred by both Gorbachev and Medvedev. Rakhmanin has been a hard-line critic of reform of the Hungarian and Chinese type, and at a time when the Soviet leadership hopes to improve relations with China, he is being accorded some of the blame for the relative lack of progress in that area. (For similar reasons, Mikhail Kapitsa, long in charge of Sino–Soviet relations within the Ministry of Foreign Affairs, was given a sideways move in 1986, which meant that, while he retained his position as one of the deputy ministers, China no longer came within his purview.) Gorbachev himself seems to be giving a high priority to improving Sino–Soviet relations: during his summer 1986 visit to the Soviet Far East he made notably friendly overtures to Beijing in his speech delivered at Vladivostok.[32]

Shakhnazarov's duties within the Socialist Countries Department were extended soon after Gorbachev became General Secretary, but it was only in the late summer of 1986 that he was formally elevated to the number two position in this important branch of the central committee apparatus. The preference for Shakhnazarov over Rakhmanin reflects new policy orientations, not in this case the desire for rejuvenation, since at 62, Shakhnazarov is exactly the same age as Rakhmanin. For many years, Shakhnazarov has been an innovative thinker within the Soviet establishment; had the climate in the Brezhnev era been more hospitable to fresh ideas, his abilities would have ensured an earlier promotion. He has campaigned for more objective study in the social sciences and, along with Fedor Burlatsky, was an early proponent of the development first of sociology and then of political science in the Soviet Union (though in both disciplines this has been an uphill and only partially successful struggle).[33] Shakhnazarov has also been an early advocate of recognizing the existence of different interests within Soviet society, a supporter of greater popular participation in political life, and an exponent of the concept of 'self-management', which for a long time had a revisionist, Yugoslav ring to it but is now acquiring a central place in Soviet ideology.

Moreover, Shakhnazarov has been an innovator in Soviet theory on international relations. In an article published in 1984 entitled 'The Logic of Political Thought in the Nuclear Era', which in those Chernenko days was regarded as remarkably bold even by some Soviet officials and specialists sympathetic to it, Shakhnazarov in effect subordinated a 'class approach' (a traditional 'holy of holies' in Soviet ideology) to a 'humanistic approach' (or 'all-human' considerations) in international politics. Noting that nuclear war clearly would not benefit the working class, he formulated as a maxim for the

[32] *Pravda*, 29 July 1986, pp. 1–3 at p. 2.

[33] See, for example, F. Burlatsky and G. Shakhnazarov, 'Obshchestvennye nauki i zhizn', in *Literaturnaya gazeta*, 24 March 1956, pp. 3–4; and G. Kh. Shakhnazarov and F.M. Burlatsky, 'O razvitii marksistsko-leninskoy politicheskoy nauki', in *Voprosy filosofii*, No. 12, 1980, pp. 10–22. See also Archie Brown, 'Political Science in the USSR', in *International Political Science Review*, Vol. 7, No. 4 (October 1986), pp. 443–81.

nuclear era the proposition that 'political ends do not exist which would justify the use of means liable to lead to nuclear war'.[34]

This kind of thinking, though not unique to Shakhnazarov, had not hitherto been presented so plainly by someone of his political standing. Now it appears even to have become accepted as official Soviet doctrine. A few echoes of it are discernible in Gorbachev's Political Report to the 27th Party Congress,[35] but it emerges particularly clearly in a more recent authoritative Soviet statement—Ligachev's address on the 69th anniversary of the Bolshevik Revolution. While stressing 'the right to social progress' and other 'realities of the modern world' that have not 'retreated into the background', Ligachev asserts that 'the first and most indisputable' of these realities is that *'peace has become the highest value of mankind* and, more than that, an indispensable condition for mankind's survival on the planet'[36] (italics added, AB). To view peace as the highest of all values is, in its way, as great a shift in doctrine as the one that occurred in Khrushchev's time when war was proclaimed to be no longer inevitable.

Shakhnazarov seems to be one of those who have influenced Soviet thinking at the highest level in this area. His range of activities has been astounding. He has written prolifically, even publishing two science fiction novels under the thin disguise of the pseudonym, 'Georgi Shakh'.[37] For many years, he has been president of the Soviet Association of Political Sciences and a vice-president of the International Political Science Association. From its foundation in 1979 to its closing and dispersal in early 1985, he was head of a sector at the Institute of State and Law of the Academy of Sciences in Moscow devoted to the study of 'theory of political systems and political relations'. Shakhnazarov's expanding responsibilities within the Socialist Countries Department of the Central Committee left someone even of his energy with little time for academic administration, especially since he writes his own books and articles (which not every senior Soviet political or, for that matter, academic figure does).

It is, however, Shakhnazarov's work within the Central Committee apparatus that is of greatest political significance. This activity is not in the public domain in the way his writings are. But he can be assumed to be much involved in the attempts to forge closer political and economic links among Communist countries, while advocating, nonetheless, a policy of unity through diversity.

[34] G. Kh. Shakhnazarov, 'Logika politicheskogo myshleniya v yadernuyu eru', in *Voprosy filosofii*, No. 5, 1984, p. 62–74, especially pp. 72–73.

[35] Mikhail Gorbachev, *Political Report of the CPSU Central Committee to the 27th Party Congress* (Novosti, Moscow, 1986), especially pp. 80–1 and 83–4.

[36] *Pravda*, 7 November 1986, pp. 1–3, at p. 3.

[37] The titles are *Net povesti pechal'nee na svete* (Molodaya gvardiya, Moscow, 1984) and *I derev'ya, kak vsadniki* (Molodaya gvardiya, 1986).

He is likely to be more sympathetic to change of the Hungarian and Chinese type than was his former superior, Rakhmanin. Regarding the intractable problem of Poland, it may not be too fanciful to attribute to Shakhnazarov's influence the increased Soviet support for General Jaruzelski and his 'moderate' position, the abandonment of Jaruzelski's harder-line opponents, and Moscow's acquiescence in the release of Polish political prisoners in the fall of 1986.

Overall, the quantitative change in the composition of the Soviet leadership has been substantial. As of late December 1986, only seven of the twelve full members of the Politburo and only two of the seven candidate members were in office when Gorbachev first took over. Of the eleven secretaries of the Central Committee, only four were in the Secretariat at the beginning of the Gorbachev era. These changes at the top have been greater than those at the Central Committee level, where 44 per cent of the members elected at the 27th Party Congress in 1986 were new but a majority had been in Brezhnev's Central Committee elected five years earlier.

What matters even more than these quantitative changes, though, is qualitative change, as represented by policy shifts and by the elevation of reform-minded individuals. Thus the present reality and further possibility of innovation in foreign policy have been considerably enhanced by the promotion of Eduard Shevardnadze, Anatoly Dobrynin, Vadim Medvedev, and Aleksandr Yakovlev. Yakovlev, like Dobrynin and Medvedev, became a secretary of the Central Committee in March 1986 and at the same time added international propaganda to his existing responsibilities for domestic propaganda.[38] Also important are changes just one rung lower, such as the elevation of Shakhnazarov, to which I have paid special attention both because of its potential significance and because it is much less commonly known.

POLITICAL TRENDS: AN OVERVIEW

Personnel shifts,[39] innovations in economic policy, and new approaches in the conduct and content of foreign policy do not comprise the sum total of the

---

[38] The extension of Yakovlev's responsibilities followed the abolition of the International Information Department of the Central Committee and its incorporation in the Propaganda Department. At that time Yakovlev was head of the latter department; now he is the overseer of it within the Secretariat. On Yakovlev, see, for instance, Jerry F. Hough, 'Gorbachev's Strategy', in *Foreign Affairs*, Vol. 64, No. 1 (Fall 1985), pp. 35–55; and Jeremy R. Azrael and Stephen Sestanovich, 'Superpower Balancing Acts', in *Foreign Affairs*, Vol. 64, No. 3 (1985), pp. 479–98.

[39] For further discussion of personnel change, see Archie Brown, 'Change in the Soviet Union', in *Foreign Affairs*, Vol. 64, No. 5 (Summer 1986), pp. 1048–65, especially pp. 1049–53;

political change taking place under Gorbachev. Other phenomena may be observed that underline the point that more movement is now taking place in Soviet society than there has been for well over two decades.

Not all the changes are welcomed. Although the choice of Gorbachev as General Secretary came as a relief to the Soviet people after his three aged and infirm predecessors, the task of retaining the support of public opinion has been far from simple. Some of Gorbachev's social policies have been unpopular with millions of Soviet citizens, particularly the anti-alcohol campaign. This campaign has involved a severe cutback in the production of alcoholic drinks, a radical reduction in the number of retail outlets selling alcohol, and restrictions on the hours at which alcohol can be purchased. Most Soviet women reportedly approve of this policy—alcohol abuse, usually by the male partner, is the most commonly cited cause of divorce in the Soviet Union.[40] But with Soviet men the anti-alcohol programme tends to be less than popular: the Soviet Union, especially the male Slavic part of the population, has hitherto constituted one of the world's most hard-drinking societies. Those with a serious alcohol problem themselves make up a sizeable constituency running into millions, and moderate drinkers are also being greatly inconvenienced by, for example, two- to four-hour waits at liquor stores. Most Soviet citizens are unaware that the strongest driving force behind the new policy is the teetotal and rather puritanical second secretary of the party, Ligachev. Instead, most of the blame (as well as such praise as is going) is directed at Gorbachev; only half-jokingly is he referred to as the *mineral'ny sekretar'* [mineral (water) secretary] rather than the *general'ny secretar'* (general secretary).

As a result of this widespread negative public reaction, even supporters of the present Soviet leadership feel that the anti-alcohol campaign will have to be modified—if only to avoid alienating popular support for Gorbachev and the more reform-oriented wing of the party leadership. The policy of economic 'restructuring' now being pursued threatens the interests of enough powerful groups for the leadership to need all the support it can get. And the radical measures taken to combat alcohol abuse have had divisive social effects and could be used by the enemies of reform to discredit those who advocate change over a broader front.

Yet, so far the leadership has shown few signs of compromise in its struggle against excessive alcohol consumption and can, indeed, point to some

and Thane Gustafson and Dawn Mann, 'Gorbachev's First Year: Building Power and Authority', in *Problems of Communism*, Vol. XXXV, No. 3 (May–June 1986), pp. 1–19.

[40] *Cambridge Encyclopedia of Russia and the Soviet Union* (Cambridge University Press, Cambridge and New York, 1982), pp. 379 and 391–2.

impressive results. In his November 1986 speech commemorating the anniversary of the Bolshevik Revolution, Ligachev claimed that in the year and a half since the radical measures against alcohol abuse were adopted the consumption of wine and vodka had declined by a third, absenteeism had gone down by a similar proportion, crime had declined by a quarter, and the number of road accidents reduced by a fifth. He noted, too, that the economic savings thus obtained were coming close to compensating for the loss of budgetary revenue as a result of sharply reduced alcohol sales, while adding that the benefits in human terms were more important than those that could be measured in rubles. But at a conference held a few days later, mention was made not only of these positive results but also of some negative side effects— a rise in bootlegging and increased concern about drug abuse. While there can be no doubt that alcohol consumption has indeed gone down, Ligachev's reference to 'consumption' being reduced by more than 33 per cent almost certainly refers to official sales and takes no account of the statistically unquantifiable illicit distilling. Both the conference that was addressed by Ligachev and Ligachev's anniversary address reaffirmed, however, that the tough anti-alcohol measures would continue.[41]

Another of the changes that has received great emphasis and that may also be regarded as a double-edged sword is the pursuit of greater openness— glasnost. For the most part, this policy serves a useful purpose for reformers within the Soviet leadership: only by permitting more criticism of the defects of the status quo and by exposing bureaucratic inertia and resistance to reform can they have much hope of overcoming the entrenched forces of conservatism. But increasing the information available to the Soviet population as well as broadening the range of permissible targets for criticism does have its dangers. For example, even though Soviet citizens under Brezhnev took with a grain of salt the abundance of good news and relative absence of bad news in media coverage of internal affairs, the opening up begun under Andropov and continued under Gorbachev runs the risk of associating with misfortune a leader prepared to take such a plunge.

Thus, three major accidents within a period of a few months in the Soviet Union, all of them beyond the control of the General Secretary, were somewhat damaging for Gorbachev's authority if only to the extent that he became associated with a run of bad luck. The first, and by far the most important in terms of the alarm it caused and its impact on public consciousness, was the Chernobyl nuclear power station disaster in April 1986, the causes and

---

[41] *Pravda*, 7 November 1986, p. 2; and 'Conference on Discipline, Alcoholism and Non-Labour Incomes', Moscow home service, 10 November 1986, reported in BBC SWB: SU/8417/B/2-4, 15 November 1986.

after-effects of which were, after a dreadfully slow start in relaying information, widely reported over a period of months in the Soviet mass media. The loss of approximately 400 lives when the Soviet liner *Admiral Nakhimov* sank in the Black Sea on the last day of August, followed by the loss of a Soviet nuclear submarine in October (events that were promptly reported, as they would not have been in the Brezhnev era) did nothing to relieve the gloom.[42]

If the only criteria used for measuring change in the Soviet Union are the treatment of overt dissent or the issue of emigration, it may appear that, thus far, it is mainly continuity rather than change that deserves emphasis. But the Soviet Union neither is nor purports to be a pluralistic political system. To disregard all change short of the institutionalization of rights of dissent and protest—in effect, acceptance of political pluralism—is to guarantee in advance a failure to comprehend those changes that *are* taking place within the system and society. These are not only important to Soviet citizens but also worthy of Western policymakers' consideration.

One thing that began to happen under Andropov and has continued under Gorbachev is a broadening of the limits of the possible within the system. This is taking several forms, some a result of conscious attempts from above to widen opportunities for criticism and debate, and others a consequence of efforts from below to push back limits and throw light on dark areas, including some kept deliberately shrouded for more than twenty years.

A number of the clearest illustrations of this broadening of the limits are to be found in Soviet cultural life. For better or worse, Soviet culture is intimately linked with the world of politics and serves as a significant barometer of the political climate. Under Gorbachev, important changes are taking place in the cultural arena at a speed that has surprised many observers.

Some of these developments are connected with personnel change at the top. Although Gorbachev himself is much more preoccupied with foreign and economic policy than with cultural policy, and though the ideological overlord within the Central Committee Secretariat, Ligachev, has warned that literature and art should not concentrate exclusively on 'the negative' features of Soviet society ('We need *not a one-sided* truth; we need the *full* truth'),[43] they are both more inclined to allow greater innovation in the arts than were

---

[42] *As late as 26 April 1989, however, Eduard Shevardnadze noted, in a memorandum to the Secretariat of the Central Committee (which was eventually included in the papers for a later Politburo meeting), that although the information given out about accidents had improved, it was still far from satisfactory. Particular agencies were putting their interests above those of the state and this cast a shadow over glasnost and damaged the image of the USSR internationally. In other words, the costs of partial concealment outweighed the costs of greater honesty in conveying bad news. ('Vypiska iz protokola No. 164 zazedaniya Politbyuro TsK KPSS ot 25 avgusta 1989 goda', Hoover Institution Archives: Fond 89, Reel 1.1991, opis 9, file 24.)*

[43] E.K. Ligachev, 'Nam nuzhna polnaya pravda', in *Teatr*, No. 8 (August 1986), pp. 2–7, at p. 3.

Brezhnev and Suslov, their past counterparts. Another factor in the equation is added by the cultural interests of the General Secretary's wife, Raisa Gorbacheva. Those who have had serious conversation with her have been left in no doubt about her intelligence and intellectual predisposition; confirmation of her active interest in literature and the arts came in November 1986, when it was announced that she had been elected to the presidium of the board of the Culture Fund, a new Soviet body with responsibilities for safeguarding the country's cultural heritage. Also in 1986, there was a change both of the Minister of Culture and of the head of the Culture Department of the Central Committee—the officials most directly responsible for what happens in Soviet cultural life.

Though the personnel shifts at the top have undoubtedly had a beneficial effect on the conditions and atmosphere in which writers, artists, and film and theatre directors work, by no means all of the changes are a result of greater enlightenment in high places. There has also been a vigorous movement from below: creative artists have taken the offensive against the conservative hacks dominant in the artistic unions, who had tended to be even more cautious of innovation and suspicious of social criticism than their political masters, since their main goal in life was not to jeopardize their comfortable positions and privileges by offending the party hierarchy. At the May 1986 congress of the Cinema Workers' Union, a rank-and-file revolt swept the old guard off the board of the union; in its place, film-makers chosen from the floor by the congress delegates were elected.[44] Normally, elections at such meetings are carefully prearranged events; this outbreak of democracy took the old-style cinema bureaucrats by surprise. The comparatively young Elem Klimov, whose own films had suffered severely from censorship and delayed distribution, was elected the new first secretary of the union in place of Lev Kulidzhanov (whose obsequiousness at the 27th Party Congress had earned him a reproving interruption from Gorbachev).[45]

Since the May Congress, films on a wide range of topics that for years had been considered too sensitive to permit distribution, including the crimes of the Stalin era and the catastrophic aftermath of nuclear war, have been released. Because good films on socially and politically significant topics had been gathering dust on the shelves, the change of leadership in the Cinema Workers' Union, together with the changes further up the cultural hierarchy, meant that the Soviet public did not have to wait long for the positive effects of the Cinema Workers' Congress. It was mainly a matter of

[44] Among the young film directors elected to the board was the son of Georgiy Shakhnazarov, the party official and political writer whose work has been discussed here.
[45] *Pravda*, 2 March 1986, p. 5.

dusting down and releasing for the first time films that had already been made.

The conservative defences were better prepared by the time the Writers' Union Congress took place in June 1986 and the changes at the top of the union, while considerable, were not on the scale of those at the Cinema Workers' Union Congress. The most significant move was to ease the time-serving first secretary of the Union, Georgiy Markov, into a largely honorific post and to replace him with Vladimir Karpov, the distinctly less conservative editor of the literary journal *Novy mir*, whose reputation with talented writers of integrity was much higher than that of his predecessor. The speeches at the Congress, even as reported in abbreviated form in the weekly Writers' Union newspaper, *Literaturnaya gazeta*, represented a breakthrough in frankness. More importantly, both before and especially since the Congress, a much wider range of views and of criticism has been getting into print. Classical twentieth-century writers who had previously been either ignored or excoriated, such as the poet Nikolay Gumilev, have been partially rehabilitated; and there have been demands for the full rehabilitation of outstanding writers of the Soviet period who have hitherto been given only partial and grudging official recognition (most notably, Boris Pasternak), and for the publication of their complete works (including *Doctor Zhivago*). The extremely touchy and divisive issue of the Stalin era, 'out of bounds' to Soviet writers for the past twenty years, has been raised again—for example, in a published criticism of forced collectivization by the novelist Vasiliy Bykov[46]—and is likely to be further explored in 1987 with the publication of a novel about 1937, the year when Stalin's purges reached their height. Among the literary events of 1986 was the publication, over several issues of *Novy mir*, of a bold novel by the Kirgiz writer, Chingiz Aitmatov, who had recently been elected first secretary of the Kirgiz Writers' Union. One of this work's many notable features was its acknowledgement of drug addiction in the Soviet Union.[47]

Social scientists have, on the whole, been slower than creative artists to break with the past. In fact, party and social science journals are having to be pushed *by the leadership* to accommodate a wider range of constructive critical views than they were prepared to publish if left to their own devices. Thus the main theoretical journal of the Communist Party, *Kommunist*, has been criticized for its conservatism, and its chief editor since 1976, Richard Kosolapov, was dismissed in the summer of 1986. In August, under its new editor, Ivan Frolov, it published the Central Committee's detailed account of

---

[46] *Literaturnaya gazeta*, 14 May 1986, p. 2.   [47] See *Novy mir*, Nos. 6, 8, and 9, 1986.

its shortcomings; in the next issue, it printed articles by two well-known economic reformers, Tatyana Zaslavskaya of the Institute of Economics of Industrial Production at Novosibirsk and Otto Latsis of the Institute of Economics of Socialist Countries in Moscow.[48]

Gorbachev himself has tried to enlist social scientists on the side of change during this period of struggle within the Soviet system. In an October 1986 speech to the heads of social science departments, he spoke of the need to overcome the deeply entrenched forces of conservatism:

It is clear that in the course of the restructuring of our life, the issue of renewal becomes sharper and there is a not always open, but uncompromising struggle of ideas, of psychological positions, and of styles of thinking and behaviour. The old ways will not give in without a fight; they will find new forms of adaptation to the dynamics of life in various scholastic stratagems. Moreover, there are attempts already to include even the very concepts of *uskorenie* [acceleration] and perestroika in the framework of obsolete dogmas and stereotypes, emptying them of their novelty and revolutionary substance.[49]

Stressing that 'the search for truth must be through the comparison of various points of view, discussion and the breaking of the former stereotypes', Gorbachev attacked the existing way of teaching the social sciences, which he said 'promotes to a large extent what we call dogmatism and scholasticism', giving 'mechanical rote learning' precedence over 'creative thinking'. Greater attention needed to be paid to inculcating 'the capacity for independent judgment', and academic programmes, lectures, and textbooks should be rewritten from scratch.[50] All this was music to the ears of reformers in Gorbachev's audience; the many conservatives who still occupy important places in the universities and the research institutes were undoubtedly put on the defensive. In general, the university social science departments—precisely because they are responsible for the teaching of young people—have hitherto been more cautious and conservative than their counterparts in the institutes of the Academy of Sciences. This has had such deleterious effects on students that some Soviet scholars now question the entire division between universities, where undergraduate teaching is confined, and the Academy of Sciences, where much of the most innovative research is conducted.

---

[48] See *Kommunist*, No. 12 (August 1986), 'O zhurnale "Kommunist" ', pp. 3–10; and No. 13 (September 1986), especially O. Latsis, 'Po-novomu vzglyanut',' pp. 32–41, and T. Zaslavskaya, 'Chelovecheskiy faktor razvitiya ekonomiki i sotsial'naya spravedlivost',' pp. 61–73.
[49] *Pravda*, 2 October 1986, p. 1.   [50] Ibid.

HOW MUCH REFORM?

There is, then, a good deal of restructuring and new thinking going on in the contemporary Soviet Union. What is happening in cultural as well as economic life must be embraced under the broad rubric of political change. There have, of course, been 'thaws' in the past that were followed not by a Moscow Spring but by harsh winter again. And there is no reason to suppose that the changes taking place in the Soviet Union will soon go as far as those of the Prague Spring of 1968, since the political and cultural contexts of the Soviet Union and Czechoslovakia are very different. Yet many of Gorbachev's speeches are closer in tone to those of moderate reformers within the Czechoslovak Communist Party in the 1960s than to those of the spokesmen of the counter-reformation who took their places in 1969 and remain there to this day.

Some experienced Western observers have argued that the Soviet leadership faces a fundamental dilemma: namely, that 'radical reform' of the economy cannot work without political reform, and that since the party leadership is afraid of political reform it is not likely, in the end, to adopt radical economic reform. This is an interpretation that cannot be lightly dismissed.

It is far from self-evident, however, that Gorbachev is as afraid of political reform as Brezhnev was. The very concept of reform, often anathematized in the history of the communist movement, has regained respectability, thanks partly to the imprimatur given it by the General Secretary himself. Gorbachev does not see the problem precisely in terms of the dilemma outlined above; rather he knows—indeed, *emphasizes*—that economic restructuring will not work without a great psychological change on the part of officials, managers, and workers, and that this change of consciousness cannot be brought about if political institutions function in the old way and political relations remain the same.

Thus Gorbachev is in fact likely to favour some measures of political reform. These will probably include competitive elections to soviets, at least at the local level, and some strengthening of the soviets vis-à-vis the ministries and their subordinate enterprises. Such electoral competition would not, of course, amount to pluralist democracy, for the different candidates will, in effect, still need the approval of the Communist Party to get on the ballot. But it would be a significant step. A leading expert on soviets, V.I. Vasilev, recently pointed out that existing Soviet law does not forbid several candidates rather than one per constituency, but that in practice there had, in fact, been only one. Vasilev suggested that it was time to change the practice, since doing so would contribute to the development of the political consciousness of millions of people, making them 'real participants in socialist self-government'.[51]

It seems unlikely that in the near future electoral reform will go as far in the Soviet Union as it has in Hungary, where a majority of elected positions—even in parliament—involve an element of choice on the part of the voter. Some Soviet analysts favour choice in elections all the way up to the Supreme Soviet of the USSR; others oppose any electoral competition whatsoever, since this might seem a tacit admission of defects in the existing practice of 'socialist democracy', and since they do not wish to reduce the powers of the small 'selectorate', which by choosing a *candidate* actually chooses a *deputy*. These issues are being debated by the specialist groups that are considering new legislation on the deputies to the soviets—just one of many pieces of forthcoming legislation that may serve as a yardstick by which to measure the success of reformers within the Soviet system. In the case of elections to soviets, it would not be surprising if choice were to be introduced but at first confined to elections no higher than the district level.

The extent to which the soviets themselves will be given enhanced powers is not yet known, but this is another area worth observing closely. Experimental reform has taken place in Soviet Georgia, where particular local soviets were given much greater control over economic enterprises within their locality at the expense of the factories' ministerial overlords. This innovation had the blessing of the former Georgian party first secretary, Eduard Shevardnadze, who, as minister of foreign affairs, is now a full member of the Politburo, and was also praised by both Gorbachev and Ryzhkov before they assumed their present positions as General Secretary and chairman of the Council of Ministers respectively. How concerted an effort is made to universalize such a redrawing of the boundaries between, on the one hand, ministerial control and industrial branch management and, on the other, territorial government will be another test of the relative success of the forces favouring reform within the Soviet system.[52]

Radical economic reform would have still broader implications. In so far as the economy becomes more self-regulating and the role of the market is expanded, there will be a decline in the powers, functions, and numbers not only of the ministries and other state institutions but also of certain party agencies. In itself, this would amount to a significant political reform; indeed,

---

[51] V. Vasil'ev, 'Vlast' otkrytaya dlya vsekh', in *Literaturnaya gazeta*, 17 September 1986, p. 10.

[52] For a good account of the Georgian reform and its possible implications, see Darrell Slider, 'More Power to the Soviets? Reform and Local Government in the Soviet Union', in *British Journal of Political Science*, Vol. 16, Part 4 (October 1986), pp. 495–511.

it is one of the reasons for the hesitations and divisions within the party on the issue of economic reform.[53]

Such hesitations do not, however, completely rule out the possibility of far-reaching economic reform in the Soviet Union. Those who hold that it does usually argue that the party would never willingly give up its 'leading role'. But the fact is that this role can mean different things to different Communists in different countries. In a very important sense the party retains its leading role in contemporary China and Hungary, even though the way its powers are exercised in those two societies differs markedly, especially in relation to economic management, from the situation in the Soviet Union. Of course, there will be fierce conservative opposition to any curtailing of ministerial and especially party functions, but it is by no means a foregone conclusion that the conservatives will win, especially if the General Secretary puts the political resources of his office to skilful use on the side of reform.

How far such a reform process may go in the Soviet Union remains to be seen. Without question, it involves political risks: these include the dangers of stimulating 'localism' and more intense ethnic nationalism as some loss of central control whets appetites for a greater devolution of power. But to argue that reform will be eschewed because it entails dangers is to assume that doing nothing new is a viable alternative, a no-risk or lesser-risk strategy. By now, a fair amount of evidence suggests that Gorbachev personally believes that this is false, that attempting to muddle through, only tinkering slightly with the system, would be even riskier than 'radical reform'. Foremost among the dangers of the do-nothing approach would be the relative decline of the Soviet Union vis-à-vis much of the developed world and a significant part of the developing world. Non-reform poses fewer risks only in a short-term perspective, which is why it appealed to Brezhnev, who had no personal need to look as far ahead as the year 2000. Gorbachev, in contrast, has a real prospect of seeing in the new millennium from the Kremlin. In a very simple sense, therefore, he has a greater need than Brezhnev ever had to take a long-term view of Soviet prospects.

Nothing I have said should be taken to suggest that the Soviet Union is about to embrace a form of democracy that would be recognized as such in Western Europe or the United States. But to rule out of court or to dismiss as trivial change over time from quasi-totalitarianism to authoritarianism to the beginnings of a more enlightened authoritarian regime is an abdication of responsibility on the part of scholars and policymakers. Western observers

---

[53] For an interesting discussion of related issues, see Ronald Amann, 'Searching for an Appropriate Concept of Soviet Politics: The Politics of Hesitant Modernization?', *British Journal of Political Science*, Vol. 16, No. 4, October 1986, pp. 475–94.

who respond in this manner to change in the Soviet Union tend to be carrying more ideological ballast than is to be found these days in the arguments of some of the better Soviet scholars and political analysts.

Further evidence that something new is afoot in the Soviet Union came in one remarkable week that ended on 19 December 1986—the 80th anniversary of the birth of Leonid Brezhnev. That day saw not only the first direct criticism by name of Brezhnev—in an authoritative *Pravda* article—but also the announcement by the Soviet deputy foreign minister, Vladimir Petrovsky, that the internal exile of Academician Andrey Sakharov to the closed city of Gorky was over and that he was free to return with his wife, Elena Bonner, to Moscow. A few days earlier, the archetypal Brezhnev client, Kunaev, had been removed from the leadership of the Kazakhstan republican party organization. While the stepping up of the attack on Brezhnev clients and on their former patron himself may be interpreted in normal power-politics terms as Gorbachev consolidating his personal position, it is also of policy significance inasmuch as it weakens at least a substantial section of the conservative opposition to the change that is taking place.

Moreover, the way in which the aftermath of Kunaev's dismissal was reported to the world at large and Sakharov's release was intimated to the Soviet Union's leading dissident showed that Gorbachev is not lacking in either political courage or imagination. The riots in Kazakhstan that followed the replacement of Kunaev (a Kazakh) by Gennadiy Kolbin (a Russian) were reported by the Soviet news agency, Tass, before any Western journalist was aware of them. That they were broadcast by the Soviet mass media, in spite of their sensitive ethnic nationalist component, was one of the more remarkable manifestations of the new 'openness'.

More dramatic was the way in which the news of his release from exile was conveyed to Sakharov—in a lengthy telephone call from Gorbachev himself. This symbolic act can too easily be dismissed as nothing but a sop to international public opinion. Although the expectation that it would make a favourable impact in the West was undoubtedly an important factor influencing the decision, it is legitimate to ask—if the issue were as simple as that— why no other General Secretary made the call at some time earlier during the seven years the Sakharovs have spent in Gorky. The action has a domestic as well as an international context. It should, perhaps, be seen as an attempt to bring Sakharov back 'within the system' and as a signal to other talented and independent-minded Soviet intellectuals—who respect Sakharov's scientific achievements and moral authority—that the times have changed and that they should work wholeheartedly for the cause of perestroika.

There should no longer be any dispute over the fact that interesting political developments are taking place in the Soviet Union—in the political climate, in foreign policy, in the economy, in culture, and in the legislative arena. Their real significance and eventual extent do, of course, remain legitimate subjects for argument. Even such positive features as have emerged in the personnel and policy changes made under Gorbachev are not necessarily irreversible. But the shifts that have occurred, and seem likely to continue, do need to be reckoned with.

There are strict limits, it must be said, on what Western policy may do to influence internal political developments in the Soviet Union in ways that will not have unintended consequences, and the beginning of political wisdom is to recognize this. But policies based on knowledge at least have a better chance of identifying areas of mutual interest, or even of exercising beneficent influence, than do those based on stereotypes. To ignore many important changes and to dismiss others on the grounds that they are 'within the system' or 'do not challenge basic Soviet values' is to be guilty of a dangerous ethnocentrism.[54] It would be ironic if, at a time when many in the Soviet Union are discovering or rediscovering the virtues of reform and evolutionary change—concepts that have such an honourable place in the Western political tradition—nothing short of instant systemic change, revolution, or destabilization should satisfy Western critics.

[54] For a typical dismissal of 'within-system' reform, see Paul Lendvai, 'Who is Afraid of Mikhail Gorbachev?', in *Survey*, Vol. 29, No. 2, 1985, pp. 202–17, especially p. 204. That large sections of the American mass media ignore or discount Soviet policy innovation or internal criticism that is not obviously rejective of the Soviet system is confirmed by a recent New York University study. See Robert Karl Manoff, 'The Media's Moscow', in *Newsletter of the American Association for the Advancement of Slavic Studies*, Vol. 26, No. 5 (November 1986), pp. 1 and 3. It is hardly surprising, therefore, that the level of public knowledge of the Soviet Union remains disturbingly low. Manoff reports that as of late 1986 only half the American citizens could identify Mikhail Gorbachev as the leader of the Soviet Union and that 36 per cent believe that China and India are parts of the USSR. (Two summit meetings in successive years between Mikhail Gorbachev and Ronald Reagan have, however, made a difference. On the eve of the 1985 summit, as many as 76 per cent of Americans were unable to name Gorbachev when asked who was the top Soviet leader. See the *New York Times Magazine*, 10 November 1985, p. 48.)

4

Fundamental Political Change, 1987–9[1]

A new Soviet political system is being created from day to day. At the moment, the new sits uneasily alongside the old, and the old is not giving way without a fight. The changes call into question a great deal that has been taken for granted throughout much of Soviet history, and it has become more difficult than ever before to predict what the system will look like a decade from now. But even those who as recently as 1987 were arguing—wrongly— that nothing of consequence had changed in the Soviet Union must now recognize that dramatic and fundamentally important change is taking place.[2]

Political reform is, of course, proceeding much faster and more successfully than economic reform. So long as material shortages get worse rather than better and there is no improvement in the standard of living of the average Soviet citizen, the continuation of political reform cannot be taken for granted. But many Western commentators, even once they belatedly accepted that Gorbachev was serious about radical reform, have underestimated his staying power and the prospects for perestroika moving forward. It has been argued, for example, that the opposition of the Party and state apparatus

[1] This chapter was completed in June 1989 and published under the title, 'Political Change in the Soviet Union', in World Policy Journal, Vol. VI, No. 3, Summer 1989, pp. 468–501.

[2] I have, from the outset of Mikhail Gorbachev's General Secretaryship, suggested that he was a reformer by disposition and that he would be an agent of significant change. See, for example, my article, 'Can Gorbachev Make a Difference?' Détente, No. 3 (May 1985). By 1987, change, especially in the political climate and reform agenda, was proceeding faster than anyone had foretold, though it has gone still further in the two years since the June Central Committee plenum of that year. Yet in 1987 there was still a blinkered inability on the part of many observers to understand what was happening in the Soviet Union. A review article of mine on Soviet politics, 'Change and Challenge', published in the Times Literary Supplement (27 March 1987), that should have been criticized, with the benefit of hindsight, for its excess of caution, was vehemently attacked for its excessive optimism in a series of readers' letters published between 15 May and 10 July. One of the letter-writers (and by no means the most virulent), Françoise Thom, was the co-author with Alain Besançon of a rather extreme contribution to a symposium entitled 'What's Happening in Moscow?' published in The National Interest, No. 8 (Summer 1987). The symposium embraced a wide spectrum of views, including my own, but in their almost total misunderstanding of Soviet developments, Besançon and Thom were in a class apart. Gorbachev's policy, these authors tell us, 'consists of an all-out attack on civil society' (p. 27), and the Soviet Union remains 'a uniform, atomized and voiceless society' (p. 29).

represents an insurmountable obstacle, or that conservative forces are able to draw strength from popular grievances and disappointed expectations.[3]

The combination of freedom to criticize and lack of economic progress is undoubtedly an important factor in the Soviet political equation. But so far, while it has reduced Gorbachev's *popularity* at home as compared with the early days of his leadership in 1985, it has not undermined his *power*.[4] On the contrary, Gorbachev has skilfully used both old and new institutions—on the one hand, the powers of the Party General Secretaryship and, on the other, the outcome of the elections to the Congress of People's Deputies and the first meeting of that legislative body—to reduce the numerical weight and political influence of conservative Communists in the highest echelons of the Party and state apparatus.

The energetic part being played by radically reformist journalists, social scientists, and writers has helped to create a political climate in which it is far from easy for conservative Party and state bureaucrats to exploit domestic economic and social problems to their advantage. There are many differences between the present period of Soviet history and Khrushchev's time of attempted reform. One, of course, is the greater political insight and subtlety of Gorbachev, but no less important is the far greater sophistication of the political analyses appearing now in many (though not all) Soviet journals and newspapers and on some radio and television programmes. There has been a dramatic increase in the circulation of the most liberal and forward-looking weeklies and monthlies, and the enhanced political education of their readers is now a factor to be reckoned with. (The most spectacular example of this trend is the weekly *Ogonek* which, since Vitaliy Korotich became its editor in 1986, has increased its circulation from a few hundred thousand to almost three-and-a-half million. The monthly journal *Znamya*, now under the editorial direction of Georgiy Baklanov and Vladimir Lakshin, has a circulation

---

[3] In the above-mentioned symposium in *The National Interest*, Peter Reddaway did not make the mistake of thinking that Soviet change was merely cosmetic, but he was pessimistic about the prospects for Gorbachev and for glasnost: 'If Gorbachev is trying to square the circle by embarking on the democratization of the Soviet system, as he shows every sign of doing, then, in my view, he is unlikely to remain in power for many more years. Sooner or later, the *nomenklatura* will surely remove him. And in that case *glasnost* would be bound to suffer in the inevitable conservative reaction' (p. 26).

[4] I have discussed Gorbachev's consolidation of his power at some length in my contributions to Archie Brown (ed.), *Political Leadership in the Soviet Union* (Indiana University Press, Bloomington, IN, 1989). See also Seweryn Bialer (ed.), *Politics, Society and Nationality Inside Gorbachev's Russia* (Westview Press, Boulder, CO, 1989), especially Bialer's final chapter; the symposium, 'Gorbachev and Gorbachevism', in *The Journal of Communist Studies*, Vol. 4, No. 4 (December 1988), especially the contributions of Ronald J. Hill, Alex Pravda, and Stephen White; and Patrick Cockburn, 'Gorbachev and Soviet Conservatism', *World Policy Journal*, Vol. 6, No. 1 (Winter 1988–9).

of 980,000 copies today [*1989*] as compared with 175,000 in 1985; and *Novy mir* currently has a print run of 1,573,000 copies monthly as compared with approximately 496,000 as recently as late 1987. *Novy mir*'s announcement that it would serialize George Orwell's *Nineteen Eighty-Four* in 1989—which it has, indeed, now published—was one reason for the substantial rise in the number of subscriptions taken out for the present year.)

New ways of thinking and speaking about Soviet politics as well as new ways of behaving have emerged in Gorbachev's Soviet Union, especially since 1987. In an article written at the end of 1986, I emphasized the significance of the political developments already underway but described the change (in itself far from insignificant) in the post-war Soviet Union as one 'from quasi-totalitarianism to authoritarianism to the beginnings of a more enlightened authoritarian regime'.[5] In the last two-and-a-half years, the Soviet system has developed beyond that. It is now indeed a more enlightened authoritarian regime and one, furthermore, that already contains some significant elements of political pluralism and of democratization.

In this chapter, after first putting these changes in context, I focus on two interconnected aspects of Soviet political developments—conceptual change and institutional change. Some attention will be paid also to the resistance that is manifesting itself both to the new thinking and to the institutional developments. This resistance takes many forms and, although (or perhaps because) the Gorbachev era has thus far been one of unprecedented progress on the part of Soviet reformers, there is still an intense political struggle taking place. On the one hand, new actors have emerged on the political stage who have adopted positions more radical than that of Gorbachev. On the other hand, Gorbachev remains significantly more of a political reformer than a majority of the Party Central Committee. This remains the case even after his spectacular success, in late April, in engineering the removal of more veteran members of the Central Committee than had ever before left that body between the quinquennial Party congresses.[6]

MODELS OF SOCIALISM

So far as *political* change is concerned, what is happening now in the Soviet Union is the most comprehensive reform effort since the Bolshevik

---

[5] Archie Brown, 'Soviet Political Developments and Prospects', *World Policy Journal*, Vol. 4, No. 1 (Winter 1986–7) *which constitutes Chapter 3 of this volume.*

[6] *Pravda*, 26 April 1989, p. 1.

Revolution, not excluding Lenin's New Economic Policy (NEP) launched in 1921. One of the most important elements of that change is in the realm of language and ideas. Given the explicit role accorded to theory and ideology in Communist states, and the vast resources traditionally devoted in the Soviet Union to bolstering the position of a specific political doctrine, here, even more than elsewhere, 'conceptual change must be understood politically, and political change conceptually'.[7]

Some of the new ideas that are now being proclaimed in the Soviet Union were cautiously anticipated in Brezhnev's time, but as one of the most innovative thinkers then and now, Yevgeniy Ambartsumov, has put it, in those days—so far as the social sciences at least were concerned—'creative search and bold scientific endeavour were reprehensible and even risky'.[8] As Ambartsumov notes:

The tone was set by hallelujah-singers who eulogized the status quo, by dogmatists and scholastics who studied speculative, far-fetched, unrepresentative categories and properties and not real processes. Given the atmosphere of ostentation and social apologetics, this was an intellectually fruitless, but paying occupation. That is why many young and some mature scientists took the line of least resistance, adjusting themselves to the situation. Even if they dared to pose a burning question, they tended to mask it with verbosity, seeking safety behind platitudes and commonplace statements.[9]

In contrast with Brezhnev's time, when it was firmly held that, though there could be different *roads* to socialism, there were no different *models* of it (socialism was what was to be found in the Soviet Union and in other orthodox Communist states at any given time), there is now a cautious espousal by the top Party leadership—and a more wholehearted embracing by many Party intellectuals—of the idea that different models of socialism can and do exist. There is, in addition, a much greater willingness to learn from the experience of others.[10]

Developments in Communist countries as diverse as China, Hungary, Poland, East Germany, Czechoslovakia, and Yugoslavia have been closely scrutinized, with different Soviet leaders drawing upon different models.

---

[7] Terence Ball, James Farr, and Russell L. Hanson (eds.), *Political Innovation and Conceptual Change* (Cambridge University Press, Cambridge, 1989), p. x.

[8] Foreword by Ye. A. Ambartsumov to A.N. Yakovlev et al., *Soviet Society: Philosophy and Development* (Progress, Moscow, 1988), p. 6.

[9] Ibid., p. 7.

[10] See, for instance, Vadim Medvedev in *Pravda*, 5 October 1988, p. 4; Georgiy Shakhnazarov, *Pravda*, 26 September 1988, p. 6; the press conference given by Oleg Bogomolov, reported in BBC Summary of World Broadcasts, SU/0381 C2/3-C2/4, 10 February 1989; and Yevgeniy Ambartsumov in A.N. Yakovlev et al., *Soviet Society* (n. 7), p. 9.

Thus, aspects of the Hungarian and Chinese economic reforms, especially in agriculture, appeal to those of more radical reformist orientation, while Yegor Ligachev, the overlord of Soviet agriculture within the Central Committee Secretariat, prefers to look to the more conservative Communist states of East Germany and Czechoslovakia to justify his faith in the essentials of the state and collective farm structure.

Of course, attention is being paid to the negative as well as the positive aspects of the experience of other Communist countries. In the case of China, with which the Soviet Union has re-established interparty as well as interstate relations following Gorbachev's visit in May (itself an important event, although overshadowed by the collapse in the authority of the Chinese leadership that was, coincidentally, taking place), it has for some time been agreed by social scientists in the Soviet Union and China with knowledge of the other country that while Deng Xiaoping's China was ahead of the Soviet Union in the radicalism of its economic reform, the Soviet Union was well ahead of China in political reform and in relative freedom of expression.[11]

The mass student protests of May and early June and the eventual brutal military suppression of peaceful and popular demonstrations in Beijing are doubtless being interpreted in different ways by different opinion groupings within the Soviet Communist Party. For some, it is confirmation of the dangers of allowing spontaneous political movements to get out of hand and of the need for an early restoration of firmer 'discipline' within the Soviet Union itself. For reformers, however, it is one more proof of the correctness of creating political institutions (the freest Soviet elections in seventy years and the nearest thing to a parliament the Soviet Union has ever had) that provide a mechanism for a higher degree than hitherto of accountability on the part of political office-holders as well as a forum for criticism and debate. The present period of remarkable ferment and innovation in a significant part of the Communist world (notably, in Hungary and Poland as well as the Soviet Union and China) is one in which events in one country can have a dramatic impact on another, and not always in predictable ways.

It is not only, however, what is happening in other Communist states that is now influencing the top Soviet leadership. The sources of learning have been extended to include certain aspects of the political systems of

---

[11] On a study visit to China in September 1988, I encountered massive support among Chinese social scientists, including those with expert knowledge of the Soviet Union, for the political reform process underway and for the great expansion in cultural freedom and of the possibilities of the mass media in the Soviet Union. One of their main hopes was that the re-establishment of harmonious relations with the Soviet Union would be a stimulus to political reform in China. Gorbachev was held in enormously high esteem and there was a yearning (and, as later events were to show, with good reason) for a 'Chinese Gorbachev'.

'bourgeois democratic' countries and not merely, as in the past, technical or managerial features of their economic systems. Both Gorbachev and Vadim Medvedev, a Politburo member and the secretary of the Central Committee with responsibility for ideology, have stressed the necessity of learning from the non-socialist world as well as from other socialist countries.[12] Medvedev has appeared to call for a reinterpretation of the achievements of European social democracy, a shift of which there have been numerous other signs in Soviet publications (and on Soviet television), including sympathetic discussion of Sweden and other Scandinavian countries.[13] Indeed, on the reform wing of the Soviet Communist Party the long-standing barrier between communism, on the one hand, and social democracy or democratic socialism, on the other, is crumbling. In a dramatic break with the past, it is not uncommon now to hear prominent Soviet Party intellectuals and some of the more enlightened officials say that they regard Sweden not only as an example of socialism but as the best model currently on view.

At the inaugural meeting of the Congress of People's Deputies, held at the end of May and beginning of June, the prominent Soviet writer Chingiz Aitmatov went further. Aitmatov made two major speeches to the congress. In the first, he proposed Mikhail Gorbachev for the post of Chairman of the Supreme Soviet.[14] The very fact that Aitmatov was pre-selected to do this by the overwhelming majority of deputies who are members of the Communist Party and that he was, furthermore, one of the 100 deputies chosen by the Party to represent it at the congress is evidence enough that he is in good standing with the Party leadership and in the mainstream of reformist thinking rather than on its radical fringes. Yet Aitmatov, in his second speech to the congress, stretched the meaning of socialism in ways unimaginable a few years ago. His address was a long way from traditional socialist theory, in almost any of its variants, but a good example of the importance of understanding the changing meanings of concepts politically and not merely from a theoretical or doctrinal standpoint.

Instead, said Aitmatov, of making an idol of socialism as 'the holy of holies of our theoretical doctrine', and instead of laying down the law on what did and what did not constitute socialism, it was necessary to reach an

---

[12] Gorbachev's speech to the United Nations in December 1988 was notable for its insistence that the time of 'closed societies' was over. See *Pravda*, 8 December 1988, pp. 1–2. See also Vadim Medvedev, *Pravda*, 5 October 1988, p. 4.

[13] Medvedev (n. 11). For a variety of interesting views on the contemporary meaning of socialism, including some that do away with the distinction between socialism of a 'Marxist-Leninist' type and 'democratic socialism', see the symposium on the concept of socialism in *Voprosy filosofii*, No. 11 (November 1988).

[14] *Pravda*, 26 May 1989, p. 3.

understanding whereby it was judged by its fruits—that is, by its contribution to people's creativity and prosperity. He suggested that the Soviet Union could learn from other countries for whom the Soviet example had performed the service of demonstrating how *not* to go about constructing socialism:

I have in mind the flourishing law-governed societies of Sweden, Austria, Finland, Norway, the Netherlands, Spain and, finally, Canada across the ocean. About Switzerland I don't even speak—it's a model. The working person in those countries earns on average four to five times more than our workers. The social protection and the level of welfare of those societies are something we can only dream about. This is real and, if you like, worker trade-union socialism, although these countries do not call themselves socialist, but are none the worse for that.[15]

The comparisons important Soviet reformers now make both with the Soviet past and with Western countries are remarkable. Aleksandr Yakovlev, Gorbachev's closest ally on the Politburo, said in response to the questions of a Soviet television journalist on 27 May: 'For the first time in the history of our country we have a platform of conscience, a platform of morality.'[16] When he was asked whether the Congress of People's Deputies could be compared with parliaments abroad, Yakovlev did not argue for the superiority of the new Soviet legislature, though until very recently Soviet officials routinely suggested that even the unreformed Supreme Soviet was vastly more democratic than Western parliaments. Instead, he emphasized the comparative underdevelopment of Soviet parliamentary theory and practice:

Parliaments in other countries have existed for decades and they have entirely different traditions. They have written many volumes about procedural matters there. We do not have that. Of course, we must learn professionalism in the economy and politics; above all we must learn democratic professionalism. We must learn democracy, tolerance of others' opinions and thoughts. That's not easy. I believe that the work of the Soviet parliament will demonstrate where we are right and where we are wrong; what we must continue and what must be corrected.[17]

NEW CONCEPTS

As James Farr has noted in a recent essay, 'Where there are different concepts, there are different beliefs, and so different actions and practices', even though

---

[15] *Izvestiya*, 4 June 1989, p. 2. In a somewhat similar vein, the director of the Institute of Economics of the World Socialist System, Oleg Bogomolov, is quoted, in answer to a question about what he hoped the Soviet Union would look like twenty years from now, as replying, 'Sweden... Sweden or perhaps Austria'. See Richard Parker, 'Assessing Perestroika', *World Policy Journal*, Vol. 6, No. 2 (Spring 1989), p. 294.

[16] BBC SWB, SU/0473 C/1, 3 June 1989.   [17] Ibid.

political practice is only partly constituted by concepts.[18] But while acting politically 'for strategic and partisan purposes', people do so 'in and through language' and 'language is an arena of political action'. Accordingly, 'political change and conceptual change must be understood as one complex and interrelated process'.[19]

In the Soviet context, three new concepts in particular deserve special emphasis, as they help to open up space for new political activity and provide a theoretical underpinning for some of the concrete reforms that the more radical interpreters of perestroika are attempting to implement. It is worth noting that within a period of eighteen months—between the summer of 1987 and the end of 1988—all three received the endorsement of Gorbachev.

The first of these concepts is that of 'socialist pluralism', and its adoption represents a radical break with past Soviet doctrine. It is of interest that, whereas many reformist concepts are to be encountered first in the writings of scholarly specialists and only later in the speeches of Party leaders, in this instance it was Gorbachev who took the bold step of embracing the concept of 'pluralism' in public before anyone else had done so.[20] Indeed, the notion of pluralism had been the subject of so many attacks by Soviet leaders and ideologists since it was adopted by 'Prague Spring' intellectuals in the late 1960s and by 'Eurocommunists' in the 1970s that it would have been difficult for anyone other than the top leader to break the taboo on endorsing it.

But Gorbachev took the lead on this because he was persuaded that to continue to attack 'pluralism' was to play into the hands of those in the Soviet Union who wished to stifle debate and innovative thought, and to assist the enemies, rather than the proponents, of perestroika. Only one year separated Gorbachev's first use of the term 'socialist pluralism', in the limited context of opening up the columns of Soviet newspapers to a wider range of writers in order that 'the whole of socialist pluralism, so to speak, is present',[21] to his use of the concept in a broader sense, and the endorsement of that use in a most authoritative Party forum, the Nineteenth Conference of the Soviet Communist Party in the summer of 1988.[22]

Thus, what had seemed to some to be no more than a throwaway remark when first used by Gorbachev in conversation with Soviet writers in July 1987 had a year later been elevated into new Party doctrine, the traditional 'monist'

---

[18] James Farr, 'Understanding Conceptual Change Politically', in Ball, Farr, and Hanson (n. 6), p. 29.

[19] Ibid., pp. 30 and 32.

[20] On Gorbachev's expanding use of the notion of 'socialist pluralism', see also Archie Brown, 'The Soviet Leadership and the Struggle for Political Reform', *The Harriman Institute Forum*, Vol. 1, No. 4 (April 1988).

[21] *Pravda*, 15 July 1987, p. 2.　　　　[22] *Pravda*, 5 July 1988, p. 3.

theory of the Soviet state and oft-repeated claim of the 'monolithic unity' of the Party and the people notwithstanding. Gorbachev's adoption of the concept of 'socialist pluralism' and the positive reference made to a 'socialist pluralism of opinions' in the resolution on glasnost adopted by the Party Conference represented a considerable boost for the more radical Soviet political reformers. These endorsements provided a legitimacy previously lacking for political debate and diversity of opinion on political and social issues in Soviet publications, even though the fact that 'pluralism' was qualified by the adjective 'socialist' indicated that there were still limits on what was deemed fit to print.

Whereas in Poland and Hungary, following fierce struggles, the top Party leadership now speak approvingly of 'political pluralism' (though there remains room for argument concerning its scope in practice), Gorbachev and even the reform wing of the Soviet leadership continue to make a distinction between 'socialist pluralism'—desirable—and 'political pluralism', which is still suspect because of its free-for-all connotations and implication that under such a banner the 'leading role' of the Communist Party might cease to be guaranteed. In practice, a 'socialist pluralism of opinion' makes ample room for publications by Roy Medvedev, previously regarded as a dissident but now a member of the new Supreme Soviet and also readmitted to the Communist Party, but has not so far accommodated Aleksandr Solzhenitsyn, who made increasingly clear after the publication of his works in Russia ceased in the mid-1960s that his rejection of the Soviet system was a root-and-branch one that embraced Lenin and Leninism as well as Stalin and Stalinism. (Even in Solzhenitsyn's case, however, some recent movement has taken place. TASS, the Soviet news service, reported on 6 June *[1989]* that the publishing house Sovetskaya Rossiya would be bringing out Solzhenitsyn's *Cancer Ward*, written in the Soviet Union but never published there, as well as *One Day in the Life of Ivan Denisovich* and *Matryona's Home*.)[23]

The boundaries of 'socialist pluralism' are not fixed. On the one hand, many Soviet commentators now use the term 'pluralism' positively—and with reference to political, cultural, and intellectual life—in the mass media, without finding it necessary to qualify it either with 'socialist' or 'political'. On the other hand, all this is being accompanied by a debate on, and constant redefinition of, socialism itself. If that process continues, the shackles imposed by the word 'socialist' may be far removed from the constraints it implied in the Soviet past.[24]

[23] BBC SWB, SU/0480 i, 12 June 1989.
[24] For Soviet discussions of 'socialist pluralism', see 'Sotsialisticheskiy plyuralizm' (the proceedings of a round table), *Sotsiologicheskie issledovaniya*, No. 5 (September–October 1988); and N.N. Deev and N.F. Sharafetdinov, 'Sotsialisticheskiy plyuralizm v politike', *Sovetskoe gosudarstvo i pravo*, No. 4 (April 1989).

The second concept adopted in recent times that is of great importance for the advancement of the cause of political and legal reform is that of the *pravovoe gosudarstvo* (state based on the rule of law). While there is nothing new about an emphasis on 'socialist legality', the idea of the law-governed state goes beyond that. The 'socialist legality' introduced under Khrushchev meant an end to the excesses and extremes of arbitrariness of Stalin's time, but lawyers and the legal system remained firmly subordinated to the Party leadership. The aim of the serious proponents of the *pravovoe gosudarstvo* is a system in which all institutions and individuals are subordinate to the law as administered by impartial and independent courts. What is more, while it is generally assumed in Soviet writings that a 'socialist legality' has prevailed in the Soviet Union throughout the post-Stalin era, the state based upon the rule of law is seen as a goal to which Soviet society should aspire, rather than as one that has already been attained.

The idea of the law-governed state is part of a much more profound analysis of arbitrary rule and the abuse of power than took place in Khrushchev's time. It reflects a consciousness of the extent to which powerful individuals and institutions have been able to bend the law to their own purposes, as well as a concern with the inadequacy of the rights of attorneys and of the independence of judges in cases where the interests and views of well-connected officials are involved. A prominent Soviet scholar of notably reformist disposition, Mikhail Piskotin, who was from 1978 until 1987 chief editor of the major legal journal *Sovetskoe gosudarstvo i pravo*, and who now heads the Centre of Political Science Research established in Moscow in the summer of 1988, has written in the newspaper *Sovetskaya kul'tura* that even today 'it is far from possible to regard our state as one fully based on the rule of law', adding that the attainment of the *pravovoe gosudarstvo* requires reform of the political system.[25]

The concept of the state based upon the rule of law has not only been embraced by Gorbachev but was also included in the resolution on legal reform adopted by the Nineteenth Party Conference in early July 1988.[26] It leaves open many questions, including, not least, the issue of whether in practice courts will have any independence vis-à-vis the very highest Party and state authorities, as distinct from the competence to check abuses of power at local levels. As with other innovative concepts that have been accepted by the Soviet leadership, different leaders and theorists can interpret the idea of the law-governed state in different ways. But adoption of the concept marks a considerable step forward in the advancement of the *role* of law—even if there does not yet exist in practice a full-fledged *rule* of law—in Soviet society.

---

[25] *Sovetskaya kul'tura*, 14 July 1988, p. 3.   [26] *Pravda*, 5 July 1988.

The third concept that is quite new in the Soviet context is that of 'checks and balances'. Its adoption is a remarkable departure from previous patterns of Soviet thought and it, too, is part of the breakthrough in thinking about the Soviet political system that took place in 1987 and 1988. In the past, the notion of checks and balances, in so far as it was referred to at all, was viewed as part of the deceptive screen behind which the ruling class exercised untrammelled power in bourgeois states. But the more serious Soviet study of foreign political systems in recent years, as well as the contemplation of some of the horrendous results of unchecked power within the Soviet Union (especially in the Stalin period), have led to a re-evaluation of the theory and practice of checks and balances. The idea that the concept might have something to offer reformers of the Soviet political system was first broached in print in Moscow as short a time ago as July 1987,[27] and it was adopted by Gorbachev even more recently, at the end of November 1988, in his speech commending the first phase of political reform to the Supreme Soviet.[28]

This is one instance where the influence on Gorbachev's thinking can be traced with some confidence. It was at a meeting of the Soviet Association of Political Sciences presided over by Georgiy Shakhnazarov in February 1987 (reported in the monthly journal *Sovetskoe gosudarstvo i pravo* in July of that year) that the call for the development of a 'socialist theory of checks and balances' was first heard.[29] To assist in the elaboration of this, it was advocated that the development of bourgeois states should be studied from the stand-point of the creation within them of checks and balances and that relevant Western theoretical writings should also be examined. All this was linked to the necessity of 'preventing the concentration in the hands of one organ (or individual) of all political power'.[30]

Shakhnazarov was already at that time—while still First Deputy Head of the Socialist Countries Department of the Central Committee—an informal adviser of Gorbachev, but in early 1988 he became one of his four *pomoshchniki*, or full-time personal assistants. He is now an influential figure whose judgement Gorbachev clearly respects. Accordingly, when Gorbachev concluded a discussion of the proposed Committee for Supervision of the Constitution by commenting, 'Thus, one may say, comrades, that our own socialist system of "checks and balances" is taking shape in this country, designed to protect society against any violation of socialist legality at the highest state level',[31] it was not difficult to detect the influence of Shakhnazarov

---

[27] S.E. Deytsev and I.G. Shablinsky, 'Rol' politicheskikh institutov v uskorenii sotsial'no-ekonomicheskogo razvitiya', *Sovetskoe gosudarstvo i pravo*, No. 17 (July 1987), p. 120.
[28] *Pravda*, 30 November 1988, p. 2.   [29] Deytsev and Shablinsky (n. 27), pp. 118–20.
[30] Ibid., p. 120.   [31] *Pravda*, 30 November 1988, p. 2.

and of scholars in the reform-minded Soviet Association of Political Sciences, whose presidency Shakhnazarov still combines with his senior political advisory functions. For the leader of the Soviet Communist Party and head of the Soviet state to accept the need for checks and balances, albeit *socialist* checks and balances, is a significant illustration of the 'new thinking' that has emerged on Soviet political institutions as well as on foreign policy.

THE PROCESS OF INSTITUTIONAL CHANGE

The most important point about reform of the Soviet political system is that it is not an event but a *process* and, in all probability, a *long-term* process if the reform wing of the Communist Party continues to prevail, as it has increasingly done since Gorbachev became General Secretary (and especially since 1987). Gorbachev himself has emphasized that the reforms adopted by the old Supreme Soviet at the end of November 1988 represent only the first phase of reform of the political system. It is impossible to say where they will end, for Soviet reformers themselves do not know. There was much less serious thinking about reform of the political system than about reform of the economy (inadequate though that was) prior to perestroika, and ideas on institutional change are being elaborated all the time. It is entirely possible that reform of the Soviet political system will go very much further than it has already if the balance of influence continues to shift in favour of 'new thinkers', as it has over the past few years.

The institutional change that has already taken place is far from inconsequential. On the one hand, some major existing institutions are functioning in a significantly different way from before. This is true of the Communist Party as a whole and of some of its constituent institutions. On the other hand, a number of essentially new political institutions have been created. Thus, for example, Soviet elections in 1989 were so different from what were called 'elections' in the Soviet Union in the past that they have little in common except the name. Similarly, the new Supreme Soviet is likely to be a much more serious legislature than the body that carried that name previously, and it has been elected by a novel (and already important) institution, the Congress of People's Deputies. There is a new-style presidency, and there is to be a Committee for Supervision of the Constitution. Although it is not possible to provide here an exhaustive survey of the changes in Soviet political institutions, three aspects of this process particularly merit closer examination: electoral reform, the evolving legislature, and the changing structure and role of the Party.

Elections

As early as 1987, by way of 'experiment', Soviet voters were offered a choice of candidates in elections to local soviets in approximately 5 per cent of the constituencies.[32] But the big breakthrough in the Soviet electoral system came with the elections to the new Congress of People's Deputies in late March of this year [*1989*]. Of the 2,250 members of the Congress, 1,500 are drawn from territorial constituencies, with 750 seats distributed among the various parts of the country on the basis of population density and 750 divided equally among the national-territorial units from union republics to autonomous regions (thus giving disproportionate representation to the smaller nationalities, since tiny Estonia and the enormous Russian republic return the same number of deputies on this 'nationality slate'). Approximately three-quarters of the territorial elections to the Congress were competitive ones,[33] but even running in a single-candidate district was no guarantee against defeat, as a number of Party officials discovered to their dismay when they failed to secure 50 per cent support from those who voted.

A negative vote could be cast by crossing out the names of the candidate or candidates a voter wished to reject. However, all voters had to mark their ballots, even if they wished to support the prospective deputy in a single-candidate election. This was an important change from previous Soviet electoral practice, whereby voters were not obliged to enter the voting booth at all. To drop an unmarked ballot in the ballot box counted as support for the candidate and was the normal way of voting. To make any mark at all on the ballot was, up until the most recent elections, to draw attention to oneself as a probable negative voter. Thus, the 1989 national elections were the first in Soviet history to combine universal adult suffrage with secrecy of the ballot and the competitive principle in at least a majority of seats.

The electoral process varied widely from one part of the country to another and had many imperfections. The Party apparatus was, for example, much more successful in Soviet Central Asia than in the major European cities in getting its favoured candidates elected. But elsewhere the attempt of Party officials to foist themselves or their nominees on the electorate provoked, in many cases, an effective backlash. Thus, with the entire Moscow Party apparatus opposed to the election of the maverick populist Boris Yeltsin and putting its resources behind his factory manager opponent, Yeltsin won

---

[32] For an interesting account of these elections and of some of the surrounding discussion, see Jeffrey Hahn, 'An Experiment in Competition: The 1987 Elections to the Local Soviet', *Slavic Review*, Vol. 47, No. 2 (Fall 1988).

[33] See G. Barabashev and V. Vasilev, 'Etapy reformy', *Pravda*, 7 May 1989, p. 3.

a landslide victory with approximately 90 per cent of the votes in a constituency comprising the entire city of Moscow. In fact, the three major Soviet cities—Moscow, Leningrad, and Kiev—all returned deputies who were chosen by the electorate in defiance of their city Party bureaucracies. In Moscow, they included not only Roy Medvedev but also the radically reformist director of the Moscow Historical-Archival Institute, Yuriy Afanasev, who was elected in a working-class district of Moscow where the overt hostility to him of the local Party machine evidently counted in his favour with the electorate. In Moscow, Leningrad, and Kiev, there was an easily detectable 'anti-apparatus' vote, of which the most highly placed victim was Yuriy Solovev, the First Secretary of the Leningrad regional Party organization and a candidate member of the Politburo.

Not surprisingly, the election results (even though they included a comfortable majority of successful candidates who could be relied upon to follow the top Party leadership at the Congress of People's Deputies) sent shock waves of alarm and anger through the Party apparatus. At a Central Committee plenary session held on 25 April, many of the regional Party secretaries who spoke blamed shortages, the mass media, insufficient Party unity, and the central Party leadership for their lack of electoral success. The First Secretary of the Krasnodar regional Party committee, Ivan Polozkov, said it was getting harder to answer people's questions as to why there was no butter, children's shoes, baby carriages, or bicycles for sale. He added sarcastically: 'They listen, but they do not understand very well. And as for the absence of soap, they do not wish even to listen.'[34] Aleksandr Melnikov, a former Central Committee department head and now a regional Party secretary, complained that ordinary people had been led astray by 'a massive onslaught from the mass media'.[35]

The defeated Leningrad Party chief, Yuriy Solovev, noted that 'not one of the six leaders of the Party and soviet in Leningrad and its region assembled the necessary number of votes'.[36] This, he pointed out, was not unique to Leningrad, and the only pattern he detected in such votes against the local official establishments was that they had been cast in 'major industrial, scientific and cultural centres'.[37] That was hardly an encouraging post-mortem for the Central Committee.

The 750 deputies who were chosen by public organizations—ranging in size and political weight from the Communist Party itself to the Soviet Culture Foundation and the Soviet Peace Foundation, and including such important bodies as the Academy of Sciences, the Komsomol, and the creative unions (writers, artists, etc.)—produced a still clearer majority of people who

---

[34] *Pravda*, 27 April 1989, p. 5.   [35] Ibid., p. 6.   [36] Ibid., p. 4.   [37] Ibid.

could be relied upon not to rock the boat too much.[38] At the same time, though, these organizations provided a minority who were among the most radical people to attend the inaugural session of the Congress of People's Deputies. This was especially true of the Academy of Sciences, whose Presidium produced a list of only twenty-three candidates, out of which the membership was to choose twenty representatives—and left off the list some of the country's most talented and politically outspoken scientists and scholars, including Academician Andrey Sakharov, who had been nominated by some sixty scientific institutes. In response, the Academy voters struck out fifteen of the names presented to them, giving the required 50 per cent support to only eight of the candidates. These results necessitated a second round of voting, this time for a list that included the names of some of the Soviet Union's most prominent reformers (the Presidium had learned its lesson). In the end, practically every deputy elected from the Academy was close to the liberal or radical reformist end of the Soviet political spectrum. In the second round, Sakharov was elected comfortably and one of the boldest of economic reformers, Nikolay Shmelev, topped the poll.[39]

The move from elections without choice, in which the social composition as well as the political conformity of the deputies could be determined in advance, to competitive elections and opportunities for citizens to nominate candidates from below (though still within the framework of a one-party system) had a number of consequences probably unintended by the top Party leadership. One was that in certain republics, especially the Baltic ones, only those candidates—whether Party or non-Party—who were prepared to take a strongly national line and defend the interests of the titular nationality of their republic could hope to be elected. Another was the radical shift in the occupational and class composition of the Congress of People's Deputies as compared with that of its predecessor, the unreformed Supreme Soviet 'elected' in 1984. The proportion of industrial and farm workers, for example, went down from 49.5 to 23.1 per cent. The representation of employees with higher education and of intellectuals went up. Heads of higher educational institutions, who were entirely unrepresented in the 1984 Supreme Soviet, made up 4.1 per cent (eighty-three deputies) of the 1989 Congress of People's Deputies. The representation of senior KGB officials went down between 1984 and 1989 from 1.1 to 0.5 per cent, while entirely new categories of occupations

---

[38] For a list of the public organizations designated to elect deputies, their quota of representatives, and the number of candidates who competed to represent each organization in the elections to the Congress of People's Deputies (and for a useful brief discussion of the elections themselves), see Dawn Mann, 'Elections to the Congress of People's Deputies Nearly Over', *Radio Liberty Report on the USSR*, Vol. 1, No. 15 (14 April 1989).

[39] *Izvestiya*, 21 April 1989, p. 3.

to be represented in the list of deputies included those of scientific workers (sixty-one deputies: 3 per cent), journalists (twenty-eight deputies: 1.4 per cent), attorneys (two deputies: 0.1 per cent) and clergymen (five deputies: 0.2 per cent).[40]

In practice, these changes meant a strengthened representation of highly articulate deputies; not surprisingly, though, the decline in worker representation was strongly attacked by opponents of reform. The growing importance of initiative from below, as opposed to control from above, also led to a sharp fall in the proportion of women deputies as compared with the old Supreme Soviet. This may be a backhanded tribute to the vastly greater significance of the new legislature, given the generally weak position of women in Soviet political life; there has for many years been an inverse relationship between the power of an institution in the Soviet political system and the percentage of women to be found in that body.

Taking the elections as a whole, they must be seen as a remarkable landmark in the process of the democratization of the Soviet political system. The fact that they were still held within the framework of a one-party system did not, as many Soviet citizens feared, mean that there was nothing to choose from among different candidates in terms of their policies and principles. The political reality that the Soviet Communist Party itself (a 20-million-strong body comprising approximately 10 per cent of adult citizens) is a coalition of very diverse viewpoints and interests became clearer than ever. In a number of the major cities, there was a lively clash of opinions in the course of the election campaign. This was notwithstanding the fact that 85.3 per cent of candidates nominated and 87.6 per cent of those actually elected to the Congress of People's Deputies were Party members.[41] Short of a 'counter-revolutionary' reversal of the entire process of perestroika, it is difficult to see any return to the sham elections of the past. In view of the evident dissatisfaction of many of the electorates presented with only a single candidate in the 1989 elections, it is much more likely that movement will be in the direction of electoral choice in *all* constituencies.

One issue that remains unresolved thus far is whether Party First Secretaries who were defeated in the elections for the Congress of People's Deputies should resign their Party office (or be forced to resign by their Party committee). There have been hints from Gorbachev that this should indeed happen; the line taken by the top Party leadership as a whole has been that a case-by-case approach to this question should be adopted by the various Party committees concerned. It would be even more difficult for First Secretaries at the republican, region, city, and district level to keep their Party posts

---

[40] *Izvestiya*, 6 May 1989, p. 7.   [41] Ibid.

if they were defeated in elections to soviets at those levels (as distinct from the all-Union Congress of People's Deputies). This is no doubt one reason (though the need to improve the electoral law is given as the main one) why local elections have been postponed from late 1989 to the spring of 1990.

Given that the breakthrough towards heterodox voting has already been made, and given the decline in the authority of the Party apparatus that was acknowledged both at the April plenary session of the Central Committee and at the Congress of People's Deputies, defeat for many local Party bosses in the elections for local soviets is a real possibility. In such cases, the Party, if it wishes to retain authority at the local level, will come under pressure from its rank-and-file membership (and probably from Gorbachev and the reformers now consolidating their ascendancy at the top of the Party hierarchy) to elect a new First Secretary for the locality. This will then constitute an important and unforeseen element in the democratization of the Soviet political system. It will, in effect, give the non-Party majority of the local electorate a veto over the Party's choice for First Secretary in their locality (a choice that in the past often owed more to the preferences of the apparatus one rung higher in the Party hierarchy than to the local Party committee itself). While that change would still occur within the confines of a single-party system, it would be a dramatic departure from what the 'leading role' of the Communist Party has meant hitherto. Indeed, the Party would be following rather than leading.

This electoral dilemma should be seen in a broader context. A revitalized and politicized Soviet society—no longer 'the most silent majority in the world'[42]—poses entirely new challenges to the Party. No one recognizes this more clearly than Gorbachev. In his closing address to the First Congress of People's Deputies on 9 June, he argued that Soviet society still needed a vanguard party, but added that if it is going to be such a vanguard, then 'the Party must reconstruct itself faster than society'.[43]

The New Legislature

Just one of many unique features of the First Congress of People's Deputies was that no one (not even Gorbachev) knew how long it was going to last.

---

[42] The phrase is that of Alexander Kabakov. In context, it reads: 'For decades we have been the most silent majority in the world. Really interesting points were discussed only in kitchens, with the closest friends, in the compartments of trains, and with unknown people who do not know your name and address and, therefore, are safe. Today we are probably the most vocal nation. Everything left unsaid accumulated over a long time, and it is impossible to talk about all points at the same time'. See *Moscow News*, No. 24 (11 June 1989), p. 14.

[43] *Pravda*, 10 June 1989, p. 14.

As originally conceived, it appeared that the main task of the 2,250 deputies was to elect the inner body, the bi-cameral, 543-member Supreme Soviet. It is the Supreme Soviet that is to be the more or less permanently functioning part of parliament, meeting for more than half of the year (unlike the old Supreme Soviet, which met for only a few days annually). But the First Congress of People's Deputies itself was in session for far longer than was the pattern with the unreformed Supreme Soviet; it began its deliberations on 25 May, and ended them on 9 June. If the elections that brought the deputies to the Palace of Congresses in Moscow were a milestone on the road to a form of democracy in the Soviet Union, the congress itself broke new frontiers in public freedom of speech. And it was quite a public. What made the impassioned debate and the breaking of one taboo after another of far greater political consequence than would otherwise have been the case was the live broadcasting on Soviet television and radio of the congress proceedings. The speeches were heard by an estimated audience of between 90 and 100 million people.[44] Some of the addresses, if they had been distributed even in 90 or 100 copies five years ago, would undoubtedly have earned their authors a spell in a labour camp.

A public opinion poll conducted on the eve of the convening of the Congress of People's Deputies showed that there were relatively high hopes for the congress, as well as a new popular willingness to distinguish between the role to be played by the hierarchy of elected soviets and the activity of the Party.[45] Asked with which institutions people linked their hopes for an improvement in the state of affairs in the country, respondents mentioned the Congress of People's Deputies more often than any other institution. The soviets at all levels came next, and the General Secretary, as a source of hope, was in third place (but, significantly, enjoying a higher level of support than all other Party institutions, such as the Politburo, the Central Committee, and Party congresses).[46]

The atmosphere at the First Congress of People's Deputies was characterized by one Soviet commentator, Vitaliy Tretyakov, as 'glasnost galore'. Even more important, the congress had, in Tretyakov's words, 'reduced to

---

[44] Telephone polls of respondents in major Soviet cities suggested that, in fact, the overwhelming majority of these urban dwellers were watching or listening to the congress proceedings all or most of the time, whether at home or at work. Thus, for example, a poll conducted on 29 May found 80 per cent of Muscovites following the proceedings constantly or almost constantly, a figure that had dropped only to 78 per cent by early June. The other cities included in these polls were Leningrad, Kiev, Tallin, Tbilisi, and Alma-Ata, and other questions put to the respondents brought out wide differences in the reaction of the inhabitants to some of the major issues discussed at the congress. See *Izvestiya*, 31 May 1989, p. 7; and *Izvestiya*, 4 June 1989, p. 1.

[45] *Izvestiya*, 24 May 1989, p. 6.   [46] Ibid.

a minimum the distance between the canonized glasnost and freedom of speech'.[47] And this was, said the same author, a 'selfless glasnost' because 'as is very well known, the legal and political guarantees of any glasnost are pretty weak in our country still'.[48]

One speaker Tretyakov probably had in mind was Yuriy Vlasov, a writer and former champion weightlifter who devoted most of his speech (relayed, like the others, live on Soviet television and radio) to an attack on the KGB. Vlasov described that organization as 'not a service, but a real underground empire' that was 'subordinate only to the apparatus' and not 'under the control of the people'. He called for the KGB to be moved out of its Dzerzhinsky Square headquarters in central Moscow to 'a modest building in the suburbs' and insisted that it must be held accountable for its activities to the new Supreme Soviet.[49] Vlasov's speech, *Izvestiya* noted, was greeted with 'prolonged applause'.[50]

One of the most important outcomes of the First Congress of People's Deputies and of the initial sessions of the new Supreme Soviet was the setting up of a whole series of commissions (both permanent and ad hoc) and committees, which include a new permanent committee of the Supreme Soviet on defence and state security.[51] It seems likely that at least a minority of deputies on that committee and in the Supreme Soviet as a whole will be prepared to ask awkward questions and to demand that steps be taken towards making the defence establishment and the state security organs accountable to the legislature. Previously, the military and the KGB were politically accountable only to the Party leadership, but if the Congress of People's Deputies and the Supreme Soviet continue as they have begun, these bodies may be subjected to a more detailed scrutiny than that to which they have become accustomed.

The Committee on Defence and State Security is just one of fifteen committees set up by the Supreme Soviet as a whole. In addition, each of the two chambers of the Supreme Soviet (the Soviet of the Union and the Soviet of Nationalities) has set up standing commissions of its own. Thus, for example, the Soviet of Nationalities has set up a commission on national policy and interethnic relations within the Soviet Union.[52] The Congress of People's Deputies, in response to pressure from many of the deputies who addressed it, has also set up commissions of its own to investigate particularly sensitive issues. These include a commission 'to investigate the circumstances

---

[47] Vitaliy Tretyakov, 'Congress of People's Deputies: Whose Hopes will it Justify?', *Moscow News*, No. 24 (11 June 1989), p. 7.
[48] Ibid.   [49] *Izvestiya*, 2 June 1989, pp. 4–5.   [50] Ibid., p. 5.
[51] *Izvestiya*, 8 June 1989, p. 1.   [52] Ibid.

connected with events in Tbilisi on 9th April 1989'[53] (the killing and wounding of a number of Georgian demonstrators by soldiers, an event that outraged public opinion in Georgia and became a major bone of contention at the Congress, with deputies from the Baltic republics and from Moscow giving support to their Georgian colleagues), and a commission to make a 'political and legal appraisal of the Soviet-German non-aggression pact of 1939'.[54] The latter commission was formed after deputies from the three Baltic republics had insistently brought up the issue of a secret protocol to the Molotov–Ribbentrop pact sanctioning the forcible incorporation of Estonia, Latvia, and Lithuania into the Soviet Union.

It is noteworthy that the composition of the various commissions was the subject of discussion both in front of the cameras and behind the scenes, and that enough deputies of independent mind and, in some cases, of radically libertarian views were included to give the commissions authority in the eyes of the aggrieved parties. Thus, for example, the twenty-three-person commission on the events in Tbilisi includes the greatly respected literary scholar, Academician Dmitriy Likhachev; the equally respected scientist and outspoken reformer, Academician Roald Sagdeev; the radical young Moscow deputy and historian, Sergey Stankevich; and the prominent and liberal specialist on criminal law at the Institute of State and Law in Moscow, Aleksandr Yakovlev—not to be confused with his Politburo namesake.[55]

The Politburo's Aleksandr Yakovlev (himself very much on the 'new thinking' wing of the Politburo) was named chairman of the twenty-six-member commission on the Soviet–German pact. The Baltic republics themselves are strongly represented on the commission, which also includes liberal or radical non-Balts such as the historian, Yuriy Afanasev; the Armenian sociologist, Lyudmila Arutyunyan; and the editor of *Ogonek*, Vitaliy Korotich. Other members include the writer, Chingiz Aitmatov; the director of the Institute of the USA and Canada, Georgiy Arbatov; and the head of the International Department of the Party Central Committee, Valentin Falin.[56]

A particularly important body created by the Congress of People's Deputies towards the end of its deliberations is the Constitutional Commission. (This is a different body from the Committee for Supervision of the Constitution that has yet to be set up and that will provide quasi-judicial review of the constitutionality of governmental acts.) It has now been decided that the Soviet Union needs a new constitution to replace the current one, which was adopted in 1977 under Brezhnev, and the main task of the Constitutional Commission is to draft that new fundamental law.[57] This provides opportunities to develop

---

[53] *Pravda*, 1 June 1989, p. 1.   [54] *Pravda*, 3 June 1989, p. 6.
[55] *Pravda*, 1 June 1989, p. 1.   [56] *Pravda*, 3 June 1989, p. 6.
[57] For a list of members of the Constitutional Commission, see *Pravda*, 10 June 1989, pp. 1–2.

further the reform of the Soviet political system and to institutionalize and solidify some of the changes for the better—such as the great strides towards freedom of expression—that have already manifested themselves, but that are still excessively dependent on the enlightened intervention or benign non-intervention of Gorbachev and the reform wing of the Party leadership.

The chairman of the Constitutional Commission is Gorbachev, who was duly elected to the new-style state presidency at the beginning of the First Congress of People's Deputies. Its deputy chairman is his close colleague Anatoliy Lukyanov, who was elected to the vice-presidency of the Supreme Soviet at the congress. Lukyanov, a fellow student of Gorbachev's at the law faculty of Moscow University in the early 1950s, has maintained particularly close links with academic lawyers, especially at Moscow's Institute of State and Law. Lawyers are in fact well represented on the 107-person commission, and they include quite a wide spectrum of opinion from within their professional ranks—for example, from the relatively conservative Dzhangir Kerimov to the cautiously reformist Vladimir Kudryavtsev (the former director of the Institute of State and Law, now vice-president of the Academy of Sciences with responsibility for law and the social sciences) to the long-standing proponent of electoral reform and reform of the soviets, Moscow University law professor Georgiy Barabashev.[58]

While *radical* reformers may not—and that is hardly surprising—constitute a majority of the members, the Constitutional Commission includes enough people who both fit that description and possess intellectual weight for them to exercise a more than proportionate influence on the elaboration of a new constitution. The most remarkable name on the list, in the context of recent Soviet history, is that of Andrey Sakharov. Bold reformers such as Oleg Bogomolov, Gavril Popov, and Tatyana Zaslavskaya are also members of the commission, as is the radicalized and unpredictable Boris Yeltsin. Two members likely to be important are Fedor Burlatsky and Georgiy Shakhnazarov. Both of them have long records as significant within-system reformers whose whole lives have, in a sense, been a preparation for the opportunities open to them now. Burlatsky—now a member of the Supreme Soviet as well as political commentator for the Writers' Union newspaper *Literaturnaya gazeta*—has never been short of ideas for political reform, and Shakhnazarov, one of Gorbachev's full-time aides and, therefore, especially well placed to make an impact on the content of the new constitution, has, like Burlatsky, been in the forefront of 'new thinking' on both foreign and domestic policy.

[58] Ibid.

The tone of the Congress of People's Deputies was set on the first day, shortly after Gorbachev was proposed as Chairman of the Supreme Soviet (the new and more powerful state presidency). One of the very first speakers to be called to the rostrum by Gorbachev was Sakharov, who protested against the fact that only Gorbachev was being nominated for the presidency and argued for the necessity of a competitive election. Sakharov said that he did 'not see anyone else who could lead our country', but he stressed that his support for Gorbachev was 'of a conditional nature'.[59] Although many conservative voices were heard as well at the Congress of People's Deputies, and the speeches embraced a very wide spectrum of political opinion, the radicals from Moscow (who were soon being dubbed the 'Moscow group' or even the 'Moscow faction'), the Baltic republics, and elsewhere were given a greater share of time to speak than their minority representation within the total body of deputies strictly merited. This was partly a tribute to their determination and articulateness, but it could not have happened without Gorbachev's guidance and support and his uphill struggle to create a spirit of tolerance in an atmosphere that was often highly charged.

In the event, Gorbachev did have a challenger in the election for the presidency—a self-proposed, previously unknown but nevertheless impressive 46-year-old engineer/designer from the Leningrad region, Aleksandr Obolensky. A non-Party member, Obolensky attacked the privileges attached to the *nomenklatura*, which, he said, corrupted its beneficiaries by giving them a material interest in the maintenance of the existing system and also provided a convenient lever for controlling them.[60] Obolensky who, like Sakharov, was concerned to establish a precedent of competition for all high political offices, was able to make his case at length, but in a vote as to whether his name should appear on the ballot, a majority of deputies (1,415) voted against, though a very sizeable minority (689) (there were 33 abstentions) voted in favour. In the secret ballot for or against Gorbachev that followed, the General Secretary was supported by 95.6 per cent of those who voted, with 87 votes cast against him.[61]

One of the most controversial, as well as important, parts of the work of the Congress of People's Deputies was its election of the Supreme Soviet. After the election had taken place, Yuriy Afanasev made a combative speech in which he accused the deputies of having chosen an inner body that was no better than the Supreme Soviet of Stalin's and Brezhnev's time.[62] That was a considerable exaggeration. Many of the republics and regions put forward no more candidates than was their entitlement for the Soviet of the Union and

---

[59] *Izvestiya*, 26 May 1989, p. 4.   [60] *Izvestiya*, 27 May 1989, p. 4.
[61] Ibid.   [62] *Izvestiya*, 29 May 1989, p. 1.

the Soviet of Nationalities, and so the conservative majority in the Congress of People's Deputies had no choice but to endorse them. This ensured that a significant minority of outspoken critics—for example, from the Baltic republics, Georgia, and Armenia—made their way into the Supreme Soviet. The cause of the dissatisfaction of Afanasev and that of other radicals was the fate of the Moscow slate of candidates. Endorsing the principle of competitive elections, the Moscow group of deputies put up 55 candidates for its allotted 29 places in the Soviet of the Union and 12 candidates for 11 places in the Soviet of Nationalities. This gave the regional Party secretaries and their like-minded colleagues who formed a majority in the Congress an opportunity to take their revenge on the most outspoken Moscow intellectuals and cross out the names of Popov, Stankevich, Zaslavskaya, and others from the list. Even so, Roy Medvedev and Fedor Burlatsky were among the 29 from Moscow who made their way into the Soviet of the Union.

The cause of greatest outrage was Boris Yeltsin's finish in twelfth place in the election for the Soviet of Nationalities, so that he became the *only* Moscow nominee for that body to fail to be elected, notwithstanding the fact that he had been supported in the elections to the Congress of People's Deputies by more Muscovites than anyone else. For Gorbachev and the reformers within the leadership, this was an embarrassment, even though Yeltsin has become one of their critics (while saving his harshest remarks for Yegor Ligachev). When another elected deputy resigned to make way for Yeltsin, Gorbachev lost little time in guiding the congress to accept that proposal.[63] Yeltsin is likely to be a thorn in the flesh of the leadership from within the Supreme Soviet, but he would be of more danger to them—and, in particular, to the authority of the new legislature—if he were excluded from that body, given the level of popular support he commands. It may well be that helping to make the Supreme Soviet a critic of the executive and holding ministers and Party leaders to account will be the most useful function Yeltsin can perform. Every parliament needs its Yeltsins, whereas it would be an illusion to think that he could lead the Communist Party or head the Soviet state with the imagination and skill of a Gorbachev.

Intra-Party Change

The Communist Party is undergoing significant change as a result of the reform of its internal structure, the personnel changes that have reduced the decision-making power of conservative Communists, and the creation of new

---

[63] Soviet television, 29 May 1989, as reported in BBC SWB, SU/0475 C/3-C/6, 6 June 1989.

state institutions. In particular, the introduction of competitive elections and the formation of a new legislative assembly have helped to bring to life dormant political forces within the Soviet Union and have compelled the Party to become more responsive to that society as a whole, if it is to retain authority and, perhaps, even its power.

In a memorandum to the Politburo dated 24 August 1988 (but published in a new Soviet journal only in 1989),[64] Gorbachev put forward concrete proposals for the restructuring of the Central Committee apparatus. By authorizing its subsequent publication, he revealed publicly for the first time the precise size of that body immediately prior to its radical reorganization, which was implemented in October. 'Today', Gorbachev wrote in the memorandum, 'the apparatus of the Central Committee numbers 1,940 responsible workers and 1,275 technical staff'.[65] Western estimates of the number of officials working in the Central Committee apparatus have generally varied between 1,000 and 1,500, whereas the actual figure was close to 2,000, excluding support staff. By the beginning of 1989, the numbers were closer to what Western observers had imagined they were earlier. Gorbachev was aiming at a 50 per cent cut in the size of the central apparatus, and by the end of 1988 approximately 40 per cent of Central Committee officials had moved either into retirement or to other posts.

The most important feature of this Party restructuring was the reduction of the number of Central Committee departments from twenty to nine[66] and the creation of six new Central Committee commissions, the latter giving senior Party members outside the apparatus a greater opportunity to exercise influence on policy. The commissions, approved at the Central Committee plenary session at the end of September 1988, concern Party construction and cadres policy (chaired by Georgiy Razumovsky), ideology (headed by Vadim Medvedev), social and economic policy (chaired by Nikolay Slyunkov), agriculture (headed by Yegor Ligachev), international policy (chaired by Aleksandr Yakovlev), and legal policy (chaired by Viktor Chebrikov).[67] Three of the six commission chairmen—Razumovsky, Yakovlev, and Medvedev—are close to Gorbachev and can be regarded as serious reformers. Ligachev and Chebrikov are on the more conservative wing of the Politburo, while Slyunkov stands somewhere in between. Taken in conjunction with the leadership changes at the same September plenum of the Central Committee—the retirement of Andrey Gromyko and Mikhail Solomentsev from full membership of the Politburo, and the removal of three candidate members (Vladimir Dolgikh,

---

[64] *Izvestiya TsK KPSS*, Vol. 1, No. 1 (January 1989), pp. 81–6.   [65] Ibid., p. 85.
[66] For a list of the new departments and their heads, see ibid., p. 86.
[67] *Kommunist*, No. 15 (October 1988), p. 4.

Petr Demichev, and Anatoliy Dobrynin, of whom the first two were far from enthusiastic about the Soviet Union's dramatic turn towards reform)—the creation of the new commissions represented a considerable strengthening of Gorbachev's personal position and of the commitment to perestroika within the leadership.[68]

It involved, however, some compromises on Gorbachev's part. The price he paid for moving Chebrikov out of the chairmanship of the KGB was, in effect, to promote him, for Chebrikov became a secretary of the Central Committee alongside the full membership of the Politburo he already enjoyed. Moreover, his twenty-one years in a senior position in the KGB did not make him the most obvious person to head a commission with responsibility for advancing the cause of the state based on the rule of law. Similarly, by cutting back on Ligachev's supervisory responsibilities within the Secretariat—which had previously included agriculture, but also much more—and confining him to agriculture, Gorbachev forced Ligachev to concentrate his attention on an area crucial to the success of reform, and one that might have benefited from being in the hands of someone less suspicious of marketization. Given, however, Gorbachev's knowledge of, and personal interest in, agriculture and his degree of commitment to the introduction of a leasehold system granting greater autonomy to groups of farmers (including family groups), Ligachev's new post gave him fewer possibilities to apply a brake to the process of reform than he had previously enjoyed.

Gorbachev's skill and determination in using both his authority and power to the full to advance the cause of reform were shown again in April 1989, when the first Central Committee plenum after the elections for the Congress of People's Deputies took place. While many of the current members of the Central Committee took the opportunity to voice their discontent about the new insecurity of their positions generated by the elections and the changed political climate, the plenum accepted the resignation of seventy-four full members of the Central Committee, twenty-four candidate members, and twelve members of the Central Auditing Commission.[69] At the same time, it promoted twenty-four candidate members of the Central Committee to full membership. Taking into account both the resignations and the promotions, the number of voting Central Committee members was reduced from 303 to 251.[70]

This was an unprecedented degree of turnover to occur between Party congresses. Since it is only at these congresses, held every five years, that

---

[68] For a full list of the leadership personnel changes made at the 30 September 1988 plenary session of the Central Committee, see ibid., p. 3.

[69] *Izvestiya TsK KPSS*, Vol. 1, No. 5 (May 1989), pp. 45–6.   [70] Ibid., p. 47.

regular elections for the Central Committee take place, Gorbachev's chances of achieving a Central Committee more attuned to the spirit of the times (that of 1989 rather than 1986, when the present Central Committee was elected) seemed slim. But by *persuading* those Central Committee members who had lost the jobs that justified their membership in that body in the first place (a fact that itself made them a disgruntled and potentially dangerous group within the Central Committee) that they should resign in April rather than wait to be removed at the next regular elections (at the 28th Party Congress due to be held in early 1991), Gorbachev was able at a stroke to reduce substantially the conservative deadweight within that important Party institution. Those who departed included former members of the top leadership team such as Gromyko, Nikolay Tikhonov, Dolgikh, and Boris Ponomarov, as well as Petr Fedoseev—the man who, in his capacity as Vice-President of the Academy of Sciences with special responsibility for the social sciences, bore a good deal of personal responsibility for the sorry state of those disciplines in Brezhnev's time.[71]

As General Secretary, Gorbachev has played a major role in the radicalization of the political reform agenda, but at every stage he has had to carry his Politburo colleagues with him. He began as the most radical member of the Politburo he inherited and, quite apart from the extent to which some of his own views have developed, could not have proposed to that body in 1985 some of the things he advocated in 1987, 1988, and 1989. With the emergence of glasnost, competitive elections, and a legislature in which radicals have been given a forum for public protest, Gorbachev and the progress of perestroika now have liberal as well as conservative critics. While in some ways this makes life even tougher for the Soviet leader, on balance it is to his political advantage. He can play the role of a centrist, albeit one clearly leaning to the liberal side of the centre, while taking on board more of the policies of the liberal critics than of their conservative counterparts. The conservatives, in any event, suffer from their lack of a viable alternative policy or programme. There are those who would wish to turn the clock back only fifteen years and others who would be happier turning it back forty years, but none of them has a vision remotely relevant to the twenty-first century. Gorbachev, by contrast, has in mind a Soviet Union that in the year 2000 will be far more democratic and markedly more efficient economically than ever before. His problem is getting from here to there, for the problems of the transition period are horrendously difficult.

---

[71] Fedoseev's valedictory speech damned 'socialist pluralism' with faint praise and called for the ideological unity of the Party. See *Pravda*, 27 April 1989, p. 4.

THE CHALLENGES AHEAD

The transition to a political system that is qualitatively different from the one that has prevailed in the Soviet Union for so long is well under way. It has made remarkable progress within the space of four years. However, the transition from a centrally administered command economy to one in which market forces play a major role has brought the Soviet Union still closer to economic crisis than did the unreformed economic system Gorbachev inherited. Although some mistakes in economic strategy have been made, the present alarming situation is in no small measure due to the intrinsic difficulties of moving from one type of economic system to another without serious dislocation. The problems of the Soviet leadership have been exacerbated by the drop in the country's foreign earnings as a result of the fall in oil prices, as well as by expensive man-made and natural disasters, including the Chernobyl nuclear accident in 1986 and the Armenian earthquake in 1988.

Money income has risen much faster than the supply of goods, so that shortages of foodstuffs and consumer goods are worse in 1989 than they were in 1985. A major contribution to a dangerously high budget deficit has been made by the cutbacks introduced early in the Gorbachev era in the manufacture of vodka, sales of which have in the past enabled the Soviet state to come much closer to balancing its budget.

Whereas a halfway house of political reform has had mainly beneficial results—raising levels of political consciousness, introducing political accountability, opening up new opportunities for meaningful popular participation in the political process, and pushing back the limits on freedom of expression and debate—a halfway house of economic reform has made things worse. The old economic institutions have lost some of their powers and much of their authority, but the intermediate institutions of a market-oriented system, such as commercial banks and wholesale trading operations, do not yet exist.

The observer of the Soviet scene can quickly move from optimism to pessimism simply by focusing on the economy rather than the polity. Yet there is ultimately, of course, a strong interlinkage between political and economic reform. Some organizations, such as certain departments of the Party Central Committee and many of the ministries, are simultaneously important political and economic institutions. They have, moreover, become an arena of recent change. In the reorganization of the Central Committee apparatus that took place in October 1988, the largest single category of department to be abolished was that of the branch economic departments. In the process of bringing the total number of departments down from twenty to nine, departments responsible for heavy industry and energy, machine-building, the chemical industry, the military industry, and light industry and consumer goods were abolished completely.[72] The sole branch economic department existing today at the Central Committee level is the Agriculture Department. The only other economic department of any description, the Social and Economic Department, has more general oversight responsibilities.[73] So long as there were numerous Central Committee branch economic departments whose structure corresponded broadly to that of Gosplan, the leadership's protestations that it wished to withdraw the Party from detailed economic tutelage rang hollow. The abolition of departments whose raison d'être was to supervise economic ministries and to intervene in economic decision-making is evidence of a new degree of seriousness of that intent.

In June 1989, Nikolay Ryzhkov, after being nominated by Gorbachev to continue in office as Chairman of the Council of Ministers and being confirmed in that post by the Congress of People's Deputies, introduced the most drastic restructuring of the ministerial system ever to have been undertaken in the era of perestroika. He announced a reduction in the number of branch industrial ministries from fifty to thirty-two and, in answer to a deputy of the Supreme Soviet's question about what this would mean in terms of reduction in the size of the administrative apparatus, Ryzhkov said that ministerial staff should be cut by at least 30 per cent.[74] Moreover, the personnel changes among the ministers themselves were dramatic. As Ryzhkov put it to the Supreme Soviet: 'I want to inform you that, of the government which was formed in 1984 and numbered 100 people without counting the chairmen of the union republican Council of Ministers... only 10 people remain in the composition which is being proposed today.'[75] More than half of the members of the Council of Ministers holding office at the beginning of June 1989 were relieved of their offices, and there was a considerable infusion of new blood.

A potentially important appointment was that of one of the Soviet Union's leading academic economists, Leonid Abalkin, hitherto the Director of the Institute of Economics of the Academy of Sciences, to head a new state commission for economic reform with the rank of Deputy Chairman of the Council of Ministers. One of the difficulties with the introduction of Soviet

---

[72] *Izvestiya TsK KPSS*, No. 1 (January 1989), p. 86.   [73] Ibid.
[74] Soviet television, speech of 10 June 1989, as reported in BBC SWB, SU/0483 C/2–6/7, 15 June 1989.
[75] Ibid.

economic reform has been the lack of an overseer of the reforms with a conceptual grasp of what is required and responsibility for avoiding contradictions and ambiguities. The task is greater than Gorbachev or Ryzhkov—with their multifarious other duties—are able to perform, and the appointment of Abalkin and the creation of the new state commission constitute grounds for hope that the strategy for economic reform will acquire greater coherence.

How long the Soviet population will give credence to a leadership that does not produce concrete economic results remains a moot point. The relevance of political reform in this context is that it provides institutional forums for pressure, criticism, and debate, and enough freedom of information and expression to make it hard for conservative Communists to sustain the argument that the problems could be solved by returning to the *status quo ante*. Gorbachev's consolidation of his power at the top of Party and state hierarchy, together with the process of institutional change, has probably secured for the reformers in the Soviet leadership several more years in which to make some improvements in living standards to accompany and reinforce political progress. There are many people, both in the Soviet Union and the West, who would regard that view as overly optimistic and hold that instant improvement is required if a counter-reformation is to be avoided.[76] Since instant enhancement of living standards is impossible, that is a counsel of despair. It underestimates the primacy of politics in the Soviet system (even though developments in the 1980s have been described as 'the revenge of the base on the superstructure') and the new institutions and political climate that would make a Kremlin coup of the kind that overthrew Nikita Khrushchev in October 1964 much more difficult to implement.

Clearly, of course, there exist powerful people who feel that their institutional and individual interests have been undermined. As the April plenum of the Central Committee made clear, such people are to be found in the Party apparatus. It is quite evident that they must also exist in the ministerial apparatus, as well as in the military and the KGB, though opinion in these

---

[76] The Soviet researcher Viktor Belkin, speaking in mid-June 1989, said that 'the economic situation is worse than we can ever have imagined', adding: 'Sometimes I wonder if we can survive until the autumn.' Even the newly appointed Deputy Chairman of the Council of Ministers in charge of economic reform, Leonid Abalkin, gives the Soviet economy only another one-and-a-half to two years to show some signs of improvement if society is not to be 'destabilized' and if 'a rightward swing' of unpredictable form is to be avoided. The leading specialist on agriculture in the Soviet Union, Vladimir Tikhonov, has said that he expects famine 'in the very near future' if peasant farmers are not soon given full control over the land, and Boris Yeltsin has warned that 'a revolutionary situation' will develop in the Soviet Union unless living standards are raised rapidly. These dire warnings from prominent figures in Soviet life appear in a Reuters report published in *The Guardian*, 17 June 1989, p. 24.

bodies is divided. That there is considerable diversity of view even within the army emerged from the line taken by different military candidates in the 1989 elections for the Congress of People's Deputies.

The ethnic unrest in the contemporary Soviet Union cannot go unmentioned. An unintended consequence of perestroika but, at a more profound level, a product of decades of pre-perestroika insensitivity to national feelings and aspirations, ethnic unrest constitutes, along with the critical economic situation, the main danger to the further progress of reform and one of the potential justifications that might be offered for intervention by a potential 'national saviour' offering to restore 'order'. In reality, strong-arm tactics would, of course, be a disaster. The present path, characterized by the Soviet leadership's increasing responsiveness to national grievances and its apparent determination to move towards a full-fledged federalism, offers the best hope of dealing with an almost intractable 'national question'. Even a genuine federalism, however, would by no means solve all the problems, for some of the most bitter conflicts are not between the centre and periphery but between one neighbouring republic and another (above all, the dispute between Armenians and Azeris over Nagorno-Karabakh) or between the titular nationality of a republic and a minority ethnic group within its boundaries (as the case of the Uzbek assault on the Meskhetians in the summer of 1989 starkly illustrated). It is clear that there is a legitimate role for the army or police in protecting one national group from another—especially the minority from the majority in a number of areas—but that any attempts to 'solve' the national question by means of coercion would be doomed to failure.

A combination of severe economic and nationality problems, together with a reduction in the budget of the military and—as must follow if political reform continues—of the KGB, could provoke individuals in those organizations to take action against the reformist leadership. It may be worth noting the high public profile that has been sought by General Boris Gromov, the 45-year-old former commander of the Soviet armed forces in Afghanistan. Gromov vigorously defended the Soviet military and its role in Afghanistan in his speech at the Nineteenth Party Conference in 1988,[77] later ostentatiously announced that he would be the last Soviet soldier to leave Afghanistan, and was subsequently duly filmed crossing the border. Having been elected to the Congress of People's Deputies, he withdrew his candidacy for the Supreme Soviet, since election to that body would have forced him to relinquish his military command, and he deemed it 'inexpedient' to leave his post as commander of the Kiev Military District.[78]

[77] *XIX Vsesoyuznaya konferentsiya kommunisticheskoy partii Sovetskogo Soyuza, 28 iyunya-1 iyulya 1988 goda: Stenografcheskiy otchet*, Vol. 2 (Politizdat, Moscow, 1988), pp. 23–7.
[78] BBC SWB, SU/0470 C/7, 31 May 1989.

However, the traditionally rather effective Soviet political control over the military has acquired new bases of support. A combination of economic hardship and the release of far more information than hitherto about the size of the military burden on the Soviet economy has led a majority of Soviet citizens to support reductions in military expenditure equal to, or even greater than, the 14 per cent announced by Gorbachev at the First Congress of People's Deputies. In an opinion poll published on the front page of *Izvestiya* on 4 June, less than 10 per cent of respondents in each of the six Soviet cities of Moscow, Leningrad, Kiev, Tallin, Tbilisi, and Alma-Ata opposed reductions in military spending.[79] Those against such cuts ranged from 9 per cent in Moscow to 1 per cent in Tbilisi.[80] Despite a significant number of 'don't knows', the total number of respondents who either agreed with a 14 per cent reduction or favoured even larger cuts in military spending ranged from a low of 62 per cent in Leningrad (a city with a substantial military industry) to a high of 82 per cent in the Estonian capital of Tallin (among whom 66 per cent thought that the cuts should have been greater). In Moscow, 75 per cent of respondents were for cuts equal to, or greater than, the ones announced by Gorbachev, with a third of the population of the capital regarding the 14 per cent reduction as insufficient.[81] While the publication of such figures may be unwelcome to the military, they both reveal and reinforce popular support for the Gorbachev leadership's 'new thinking'. Public opinion constraints may not totally rule out an intervention at some point against democratization and the new thinking by an alliance of conservative Communists and the military (as has happened in China), but it is not the most probable outcome. With the balance of power and influence in the higher echelons of the Party moving in favour of the reformers, and with the development of electoral and legislative checks on the holders of executive power, it has become much more difficult to put this process into reverse.

The entire Communist world is in a period of unprecedented volatility. The Chinese gerontocracy has taken fright at the very prospect of political dialogue with its own citizenry, a dialogue that is already an encouraging reality in the Soviet Union. Hungary and Poland have carried political change significantly beyond the stage reached by the Dubček leadership in Czechoslovakia in 1968, which was at that time sufficient to provoke Soviet military

[79] A telephone poll (by a random sample of telephone numbers) of 250–300 people in each of those cities was conducted during the Congress of People's Deputies. See *Izvestiya*, 4 June 1989, p. 1.

[80] The popularity of the military in Georgia has been at a particularly low ebb since a Soviet army unit killed a number of young demonstrators in Tbilisi on 9 April 1989, an event that is now the subject of a commission of inquiry.

[81] *Izvestiya*, 4 June 1989, p. 1.

intervention. (The point is rapidly approaching when it will no longer be meaningful to regard Hungary and Poland as Communist systems.) But the most important change—for better or worse—in terms of its impact on global politics is that occurring in the Soviet Union. The politics and economics of the transition period are imposing almost intolerable burdens on, and challenges to, Gorbachev and committed Soviet reformers. In the political sphere, these reformers have already changed more than even the optimists predicted four years ago, and the sceptics, who doubted the seriousness of their intentions, have been totally confounded. If the Soviet reformers succeed, it will be as great a victory in peace as the Soviet Union just forty-four years ago attained in war.[82] And unlike the latter victory—with its post-war imposition of a Stalinist order on Eastern Europe—it will be possible to welcome it in retrospect as much as the Soviet contribution to the defeat of Nazism was welcomed at the time.

---

[82] *As this was written in 1989, 'forty-four years ago' refers, of course, to the end of the Second World War.*

5

Reconstructing the Soviet Political System[1]

It is important to put into context the remarkably bold attempts of the Gorbachev era to reform the Soviet political system. That means considering both the extent to which the Soviet system had already changed over time and the nature of the system Gorbachev inherited. In this way it should become clearer how the concept of political reform and actual political change under Gorbachev differ from past chapters of Soviet history.

THE HERITAGE OF POWER

The Soviet political system has undergone several changes, inasmuch as the powers of particular institutions have varied from one period to another. Thus, from approximately 1934 until his death in 1953, Stalin was probably more powerful than the rest of the Politburo put together. That was not the case in the 1920s, nor has any one of Stalin's successors wielded such absolute power. Khrushchev did on occasion make policy without adequate consultation with his colleagues, and sometimes acted as if the First Secretary of the Central Committee (as the General Secretary's post was known then) was not bound by any norms of collective responsibility. However, this style of rule—as well as the combination of the post of first secretary with the chairmanship of the Council of Ministers of the USSR—was part of his undoing. He became the first, and thus far the only, leader of the Soviet Communist Party whose political demise preceded his earthly one.

Just as the relative powers of the General Secretary and of the Politburo have varied over time, so have the powers of Party organs and of the ministries. During Stalin's ascendancy, and perhaps especially in the post-war Stalin years, a great deal of power was vested in the ministries. Their authority was also reflected in the fact that a majority of Politburo

[1] *This chapter was written in 1989 and published in Abraham Brumberg (ed.),* Chronicle of a Revolution: A Western-Soviet Inquiry into Perestroika *(Pantheon Books, New York, 1990), pp. 30–49.*

members in the late Stalin years belonged to the ministerial network. Under Khrushchev the abolition of most of the industrial ministries in 1957—and the creation of the regional economic councils (*sovnarkhozy*)—constituted a substantial change in political structures and one which was part of a reassertion of the authority of Party organs vis-à-vis the organs of the state. That reform, however, was hardly a great success, with the 'departmentalism' which had been the besetting sin of the centralized ministries replaced by the 'localism' of economic regions that hoarded materials and took no broader a view of the needs of the country as a whole than the ministries had done. It was no surprise, therefore, when resuscitated ministries and state committees replaced the regional economic councils within a year of Khrushchev's removal from office.

A constant feature in Party-ministerial relations until the recent past has been the existence of Party economic departments supervising the work of state bodies. As noted in Chapter 4, at the Central Committee level, there have generally been at least twenty departments of the apparatus, of which approximately half were made up of economic departments, responsible for the major branches of the economy and supervising one or several ministries. These have included, for example, the Agriculture Department, the Heavy Industry Department, and the Chemical Industry Department. This is an area where structural change has now been quite drastic.

There had, of course, been some changes in the institutional distribution of power in the post-Stalin period. Thus, for example, the development of 'socialist legality' under Khrushchev greatly reduced the element of arbitrariness on the Soviet legal system, although neither then nor in the Brezhnev years did it safeguard such basic liberties as freedom of assembly and of association or the rights of authors and journalists to publish the truth as they saw it concerning past and present social and political injustices.

One of the more important institutional aspects of the new 'socialist legality' under Khrushchev was the removal of the relative autonomy of the security forces which had previously been responsible to Stalin personally and to virtually no one else. In Khrushchev's time, as at least some of Stalin's crimes were exposed, the KGB—already symbolically downgraded from the status of the Ministry of State Security (MGB)—was somewhat on the defensive and was firmly subordinated to the collective Party leadership. Under Brezhnev the subordination of the KGB to the Politburo and Secretariat of the Central Committee (rather than one top leader) continued; but, with the prohibition of public attacks on Stalin and the Stalin period, the security forces were able to shed some of the odium bequeathed to them by their People's Commissariat for Internal Affairs (NKVD) predecessors, and were encouraged to play a substantial role in combating organized dissent in Soviet society.

Other reforms, such as the enhancing of the powers of soviets or the introduction of competitive elections, were sometimes discussed in print during the Khrushchev and Brezhnev period.[2] This showed that even within the parameters of the system there were alternative ways of thinking, but it led to few practical results. Behind the monolithic façade of the post-Stalin but pre-perestroika political system, there were in fact groupings within the Party and society advocating a variety of different views, but these differences could not at that time be given institutional form. The formation of any organized group other than those endorsed and supervised by the Party was regarded as potentially subversive, and considerable resources were devoted to the surveillance and harassment of numerically small groups. People who tried to work for change from within the system could only continue to do so by making substantial compromises. Those who began as within-system reformers, but were of a more uncompromising disposition, such as Andrey Sakharov, were often turned into dissidents by the rigid policies of the Brezhnev leadership.

Thus, the political system Gorbachev inherited—and the one in which he had, of course, worked his way upwards—was palpably anti-pluralistic. It was also one in which the highest authority was vested in Party organs but a great deal of day-to-day decision-making power was lodged in the ministries and, within their own special spheres of activity, in the KGB and the military. On the eve of Gorbachev's accession to power in 1985, discussion was already freer on a number of issues than it had been in Brezhnev's—or indeed Khrushchev's—time. Most political debate, however, remained at a rather esoteric level, lacking both theoretical legitimacy and political institutionalization.

A majority of Western political scientists realized that it was much more misleading than helpful to continue to call this post-Stalin system 'totalitarian'. Yet there was no denying that it remained highly authoritarian. Attempts to characterize it as an example of 'institutional pluralism' or as 'corporatist' involved excessive conceptual stretching, though the granting of considerable discretionary powers to a variety of bureaucratic agencies under Brezhnev did contain some quasi-corporatist elements.[3]

What this system did not contain was much sign of democracy or democratization. In that respect, although not in all, the Brezhnev era represented

---

[2] See, for example, Ronald J. Hill, *Political Science, Soviet Politics and Reform* (Martin Robinson, London, 1980), esp. ch. 2.

[3] See Giovanni Sartori, 'Concept Misformation in Comparative Politics', *American Political Science Review*, 1970, no. 4; and Valerie Bunce, 'The Political Economy of the Brezhnev Era: The Rise and Fall of Corporatism', *British Journal of Political Science*, Vol. 13, pt. 2, April 1983.

a step back from Khrushchev's, where some of the reforms, in a naively populist way, were at least intended to serve the cause of democratization.[4] While the manner in which Soviet political institutions operated had changed greatly by the middle of the 1980s as compared with the Stalin years, the basic structures displayed considerable continuity with those established in the 1920s and 1930s. Moreover, at a conceptual level they were deemed to be the very embodiment of socialism. By socialism, Soviet leaders meant 'actually existing socialism', a term coined under Brezhnev—what was on display in the Soviet Union and in the systems of its orthodox allies in Eastern Europe.

THE MEANINGS OF PERESTROIKA

The changes being discussed and, to some extent, introduced in the Soviet Union today under the rubric of perestroika mark a qualitative advance over previous reform efforts. They are not, of course, devoid of ambiguity. The very term, perestroika, is translated into Western languages in various ways and accorded somewhat different meanings. Increasingly, it is not translated at all, which allows Western readers to impart to it whatever meaning they wish. In that respect, they are not unlike their Soviet counterparts. Practically everyone who makes a public utterance on perestroika in the Soviet Union is, on the surface, in favour of it, but for some the term means only economic modernization, for others a bureaucratic restructuring, for yet others no more than the correct catchword of the epoch, while for its most serious proponents it signifies a fundamental reconstruction of the Soviet political and economic system.

Even among those who belong to the last category, there are important differences of principle. The reformist Communists wish to establish a 'socialist pluralism' in which the Communist Party itself becomes substantially democratized, and its 'leading role' redefined. The reform wing of the Party leadership is undoubtedly serious about political and economic reforms that are dramatic by the standards of anything seen over the past seven decades.

---

[4] Following the Brezhnev years in which Khrushchev was rarely mentioned, and never positively, a number of sympathetic reappraisals of the part played by Khrushchev in Soviet history have appeared in Soviet publications. For a notable example see Fedor Burlatsky, 'Khrushchev', in Yuriy Afanasev (ed.), *Inogo ne dano* (Progress, Moscow, 1988). The first meeting in the Soviet Union entirely devoted to a consideration of Khrushchev's virtues and achievements as well as his faults was held in the auditorium of the Cinematographers' Union on 16 April 1989. It was attended by almost a thousand people and addressed by writers, historians, and survivors of Stalin's prison camps.

The New Economic Policy, which was introduced by Lenin in 1921 and which is held up by many reformers as the model for perestroika, may have been just as radical an economic shift as that now being envisaged. But the political reform currently being pursued is more far-reaching than anything seen in the 1920s or subsequently. Yet the reform from above that has been launched in the Gorbachev era has helped to stimulate pressures from below that threaten to go beyond anything the Communist Party leadership has hitherto been prepared to accept, including demands for a multiparty system.[5]

When the Russian word *perestroika* is translated into English, the word used most often is 'restructuring'. This, however, is adequate only for one part of perestroika—that element in the political and economic reform process which is concerned with rationalizing the economy and reorganizing political institutions. The more radical connotation of the concept is better captured by 'reconstruction'. That term, too, is not an unambiguous one. It may mean rebuilding something which once existed and has been destroyed—NEP, for instance—or it may mean constructing a quite different edifice from the foundations up.

The prominent Soviet historian Yuriy Afanasev noted (in a conversation with this author in 1987): 'We talk about reconstruction, but first of all we need to know what it is that we wish to reconstruct.' This, in turn, presupposes serious research on the whole of Soviet history, the search for foundations worth building on, and a differentiation between structures that may be suitable for renovation and others that are strong candidates for demolition. To a Western observer, it may well appear that no one period of Soviet history offers anything approaching ideal foundations on which to build a new edifice. But history is not architecture, nor is it a blank sheet on which well-meaning (and some ill-meaning) Westerners can prescribe the future of Soviet people who are rooted in their historical experience and their own traditions. Fortunately, that experience is more contradictory, and the traditions much more diverse, than is often assumed—fortunately, because if those who wish to reconstruct the Soviet system find no indigenous foundation on which to build, they will probably fail.

IDEAS—NEW AND OLD

In politics four elements are of pre-eminent importance: ideas, institutions, interests, and culture. I shall consider each of them briefly in the contemporary Soviet context.

---

[5] For an account of the cross-currents, see Abraham Brumberg, 'Moscow: The Struggle for Reform', *New York Review of Books*, 30 March 1989, pp. 37–42.

The idea of socialism has by now a long Russian tradition as well as powerful institutional supports, and most (though by no means all) Soviet reformers wish to reconcile whatever new ideas they espouse with socialist principles as they understand them. But the former Soviet orthodoxy that there were no such things as different models of socialism (though there could be different paths to it) has been explicitly rejected by senior Party intellectuals and by some leading officials. Among the former are prominent reformers such as the director of the Institute of Economics of the World Socialist System, Oleg Bogomolov, and Fedor Burlatsky.[6] The latter include, significantly, the Central Committee secretary responsible for ideology, Vadim Medvedev, and recently—and more explicitly and importantly—Mikhail Gorbachev.[7] They and many other Soviet Communist reformers now publicly acknowledge that a variety of models of socialism do, in fact, exist and that this is not something to be deplored.

The scope and flexibility of socialism as a body of doctrine has been enormously expanded, to the extent that the formerly sharp dividing line between Soviet Communist and social democratic traditions of socialism is becoming blurred. Soviet reformers have argued that a fundamental mistake was made when state ownership was deemed to be the highest form of socialist ownership, and many of them now emphasize the need for a multiplicity of forms of ownership, such as individual ownership, cooperatives, joint ventures (with foreign companies), and even joint stock capital investment (whereby 'working people use their savings to participate in stimulating the kinds of products they are crying out for'),[8] as fully compatible with socialism.

Yevgeniy Ambartsumov, one of the most erudite and reform-minded political analysts in the Soviet Union, has explicitly argued that socialization of the means of production should not be regarded as the main criterion of socialism, but rather that the criteria adopted should be those which follow from the celebrated remark of Marx and Engels in the *Communist Manifesto* on the replacement of 'bourgeois society' by one 'in which the free development of each is the condition for the free development of all'. For Ambartsumov, this means 'the all-round free development of the individual and social justice'.[9]

---

[6] Bogomolov at a press conference reported in BBC Summary of World Broadcasts, 10 February 1989; Burlatsky in 'Problemy razrabotki kontseptsii sovremennogo sotsializma', *Voprosy filosofii*, 1988, no. 11, pp. 31–71.

[7] Medvedev in *Pravda*, 5 October 1988, p. 4; and Gorbachev in *Pravda*, 26 November 1989, pp. 1–3.

[8] Gennadiy Lisichkin, in a Soviet television broadcast on 3 July 1987, as reported in BBC SWB, 11 July 1987.

[9] Ye. A. Ambartsumov, in 'Problemy razrabotki kontseptsii sovremennogo sotsializma', *Voprosy filosofii*, 1988, no. 11, pp. 31–71.

The aspect of Soviet 'new thinking' that has received most publicity in the West is that which has a direct relationship with foreign policy, such as the new priority given to universal values as against class values. But other ideas that are new in the Soviet context, though far from novel in a broader one, have a more direct impact on the reform of the Soviet political system.

For years any idea of convergence between the Soviet and Western systems (which at one time had a certain popularity in Western circles) had been vehemently condemned by Soviet theorists. But Ambartsumov has suggested that it was a mistake to reject this concept completely, pointing out at the same time that Marx's prognosis that socialism would be a post-capitalist system has turned out to be wrong, since 'today we exist simultaneously with capitalist society and will exist simultaneously also in the foreseeable future'.[10]

The need to learn from other political systems has been phrased more cautiously, though interestingly, by Gorbachev's aide, Georgiy Shakhnazarov. Writing in *Pravda*, Shakhnazarov criticizes as 'anti-historical' the former Soviet view that after the rise of socialism, any further progress in the evolution of democratic institutions in the West was impossible. It is fully understandable, he goes on, that 'now, when a profound reform of the political system of our country is unfolding, the experience in this sphere not only of socialist but of all other countries merits attention and study, with the possibility of putting it to creative use'.[11]

Three ideas which have been taken up by Soviet Party reformers in recent years, and which have received the personal endorsement of Gorbachev, deserve special emphasis. They are the concepts of pluralism (usually qualified, in Gorbachev's use of the term, by the adjective 'socialist'), the law-governed state, and 'checks and balances'.[12]

Gorbachev has made a distinction between 'political pluralism' (with its connotations of a competitive party system that he has not thus far accepted) and 'socialist pluralism' or a 'pluralism of opinion', which he has endorsed and advocated. Other Soviet writers, however, have taken up the notion of pluralism, and many of the pressure groups outside the Party (the 'informal groups', in Soviet parlance) champion a more fully fledged version of pluralism. Although Gorbachev's 'socialist pluralism' stops short of legitimizing the activities of independent organizations which are deemed to be 'anti-socialist', and has not yet made room for competing parties, his acceptance of that

---

[10] Ambartsumov, 'Problemy razrabotki kontseptsii'.

[11] G. Shaknazarov, 'Nauka o politike', *Pravda*, 26 September 1988, p. 6.

[12] *As noted in Chapter 4, in which the second of these ideas, in particular, is discussed more fully.* See also my chapter, 'Ideology and Political Culture', in Seweryn Bialer (ed.), *Politics, Society and Nationality Inside Gorbachev's Russia* (Westview, Boulder, CO, 1989).

term in 1987 was an important breakthrough, inasmuch as it provided authoritative support for diversity of opinion and for political debate. The boundaries of the permissible have been pushed ever wider in the subsequent discussions in the pages of officially published Soviet newspapers, journals, and books, not to speak of unofficial publications.

The second idea that is being actively promoted is that of the state based on the rule of law. Many Soviet jurists and others have been pressing for some years for more precisely defined laws and for truly independent advocates and judges. Even in the Gorbachev era, they are some way off from attaining that goal, but the acceptance in principle of the supremacy of law is a considerable advance, as is the acknowledgement by its most active advocates within the Party and outside it that a state ruled by law is still in the process of construction.

A third, and in part at least associated, idea of great importance (as well as novelty) in the Soviet context is the concept of 'checks and balances'. It was broached at a meeting of the Soviet Association of Political Sciences in early 1987 and first endorsed by Gorbachev in late 1988. It is a recognition of the need not only for goodwill or of a return to so-called Leninist norms, but of the necessity of actual institutions that will introduce accountability into the Soviet political system and prevent excessive concentration of power.[13]

INSTITUTIONAL REFORM

The institutional reform now being implemented in the Soviet Union is likely to be—unless perestroika suffers a serious reversal—only the first stage in the reconstruction of the Soviet political system. The most significant changes thus far have been the creation of competitive elections and the formation of an elected assembly that has become a forum for genuine debate and, to some degree, a check on executive power.

It is hardly surprising that the Soviet Union did not move in one fell swoop from completely manipulated, single-candidate elections to fully democratic ones. One-third of the deputies to the Congress of People's Deputies chosen by public organizations—of such varying size and significance as the Communist Party, the Academy of Sciences, the Union of Writers, and the Cultural Foundation—were selected by varying means. In some cases, the choice was made through preliminary soundings, and the elected representatives of the

---

[13] S. Ye. Deytsev and I.G. Shablinsky, 'Rol' politicheskikh institutov v uskorenii sotsial'no-ekonomicheskogo razvitiya', *Sovetskoe gosudarstvo i pravo*, 1987, no. 7, p. 120.

public organization were left to vote for a slate of candidates no longer than the number of seats allocated to their association.

This was notably the case with the one hundred candidates allocated to the Communist Party. However, it was only after the March 1989 elections that Gorbachev was able to persuade a large number of elderly members of the Central Committee to sign a collective letter of resignation. Until then the composition of the Central Committee clearly lagged behind the pace of events and of personnel changes throughout the country. Left to itself, it might have elected a more conservative slate of deputies to the Congress of People's Deputies. (In fact, only when the Party rules are altered at the next Party Congress—to enable Central Committee membership to be renewed, from a pool broader than the ranks of candidate members, between the five-yearly Congresses—will that body become a more appropriate electoral college during a time of rapid political change.) The Central Committee was elected when Gorbachev had been Soviet leader for less than a year and had much less power than he had acquired by 1989.

In the new Soviet climate, however, too little responsiveness to members of the various 'public organizations' could have its dangers, as the Presidium of the Academy of Sciences discovered during the 1989 elections when its initial slate excluded the names of some of the Soviet Union's most outstanding and most outspoken natural and social scientists, including Andrey Sakharov (later, as noted in Chapter 4, to compete and win in a re-run election). The imperfections of the electoral system, but its possibilities as well, were revealed in the contests for territorial constituencies. In about a quarter of the seats the electorate was presented with only a single candidate. But since the new law provided for voting in absolute secrecy (as confirmed by various local and international observers), and for the defeat of any candidate who had not obtained more than 50 per cent of the votes, many Party apparatchiks lost simply by virtue of having their names crossed out by the voters.

The defeat of leading members of the Party establishment was a major consequence of perestroika, if in part an unintended one. So was the over-whelming victory of Boris Yeltsin in Moscow in the face of overt hostility from the highest Party organs. Together they signified the fact that the Soviet people—as distinct from the General Secretary, the Politburo, or the Secretariat of the Central Committee—had changed the balance of forces within the Soviet political system. This step along the road of democratization would make it hard, even for a leadership so minded, to persuade the Soviet electorate to act like automatons again. In addition, the fact that the Congress of People's Deputies and the new-style Supreme Soviet constitute something more like a parliament than the Soviet Union has ever seen has introduced an important new check on the Soviet political executive, though it is still a long way from balancing it.

There is certainly no denying that the new Soviet legislature is already a significant political institution. Both its larger outer body, the 2,250-strong Congress of People's Deputies, and its inner body, the 542-member bicameral Supreme Soviet, have become forums for sometimes searing criticism and for passionate debate. It would be difficult to think of an acute problem of contemporary Soviet society that did not receive an airing either at the First Congress of People's Deputies (which convened in late May 1989 and lasted for thirteen days) or at the Supreme Soviet sessions that followed. By lifting the lid off these burning issues, the new assemblies allowed some of the built-up pressure to escape. Moreover, they proved themselves capable of calling senior officials to account. Important leaders, including Gorbachev himself, were criticized, although Gorbachev in his guidance of the Congress went out of his way to ensure that prominent critics (especially on the liberal wing of the assembly) were given rather more time at the podium than their numerical weight within the legislature strictly warranted.

When the Supreme Soviet was elected by the deputies to the Congress and finally met, it formed a series of committees (with members drawn from both chambers) and commissions (of each chamber, the Soviet of the Union and the Soviet of Nationalities, separately). These provided a new experience for everyone—not least for the Chairman of the Council of Ministers. Nikolay Ryzhkov, who had been confirmed in that role, himself announced fairly sweeping changes in the Soviet ministerial team, including the actual abolition of a number of economic ministries and the important appointment of Leonid Abalkin, the former director of the Institute of Economics, to head a new State Commission on Economic Reform with the rank of a Deputy Chairman of the Council of Ministers.

But the changes were even greater than Ryzhkov and the leadership as a whole had bargained for. The various nominees were cross-questioned by deputies, in some cases quite rigorously. The committees of the Supreme Soviet actually rejected six of Ryzhkov's proposed members of the government, and other nominations were either rejected by the Supreme Soviet as a whole or withdrawn in the face of strong opposition. In the end as many as eleven out of Ryzhkov's seventy-two nominees for the Council of Ministers failed to get through the confirmation process. Those who failed to secure endorsement included Vasiliy Zakharov, who had been Minister of Culture since 1986, as well as the new nominees for such important economic posts as the chairmanship of the State Committee on Prices, the chairmanship of the State Bank (Gosbank) and the Minister of the Oil and Gas Industry.

It is perhaps of special interest—and in accordance with the demands of a number of deputies who spoke at the Congress of People's Deputies and the Supreme Soviet—that among the new committees was one on defence and state security. At least a minority of members of that committee, and of the Supreme Soviet as a whole, have shown a desire to ensure that the defence establishment and the security forces are in future held accountable to some degree for their activities and expenditures. Previously they had been virtually immune from accountability other than to the Administrative Organs Department of the Central Committee and the Politburo—in other words, to Party organs at the highest level rather than to representatives of the people as a whole.[14]

The combination of the General Secretary's post with the new-style presidency—the office of Chairman of the Supreme Soviet—has been a controversial change even within the ranks of Soviet reformers. The Chairman is vested with greater powers (including that of commander-in-chief of the armed forces and the right to appoint the Chairman of the Council of Ministers) than were attached to the former chairmanship of the Presidium of the Supreme Soviet. On the one hand, there are those who welcome the strengthening of the position of a reformist leader, Gorbachev, in the face of all the remaining institutional obstacles to perestroika. On the other hand, there are those who think that the highest political echelons of Party and state hierarchies should reflect the new awareness of the value of 'separation of powers' and 'checks and balances'.[15]

One of the most biting critiques of the institutional framework of the Soviet system, including the reforms adopted thus far, is the article by Sergey Andreev in the Leningrad journal *Neva*.[16] Andreev argues that there is still no guarantee against the emergence of another Brezhnev, and that the key political office in the country remains that of Party General Secretary rather

[14] Communist Party members number about 20 million, out of a total Soviet population of around 286 million.

[15] *While the Russian word* predsedatel' *means equally chairman or president, and this move from Chairmanship of the Presidium of the Supreme Soviet to Chairmanship of the Supreme Soviet was a step in the evolution of the Soviet presidency, it was only in March 1990 that an executive presidency—with the title* Prezident—*was created. As Chairman of the Supreme Soviet Gorbachev initially found himself playing the role, in effect, of Speaker of the new legislature, an impossible burden in addition to all of his other duties. With the creation of the post of* Prezident *the following year the locus of executive power was, to a significant extent, moved from the party leadership to a state institution. For the development of this institution, which had important path-dependent consequences for the institutional structures of the Soviet Union's successor states, see E.L. Kuznetsov,* 'Iz istorii sozdaniy instituta Prezidenta SSSR', Gosudarstvo i pravo, *No. 5, 1996, pp. 95–104.*

[16] Sergey Andreev, 'Struktura vlasti i zadachi obshchestva', *Neva*, 1989, no. 1, pp. 144–73. Andreev's views were echoed by a number of speakers at the First Congress of People's Deputies.

than the presidency. 'But the General Secretary of the Central Committee', he goes on, 'is elected by a narrow circle of people, by a few hundred votes'.[17] A change of General Secretary is obviously of great consequence for the population as a whole, but neither the rank-and-file Party members nor, still more, the approximately 90 per cent of Soviet adult citizens who do not belong to the Party have any say in the matter.

A strong presidency need not necessarily, however, be inconsistent with the further reconstruction of the Soviet political system. Indeed, to the extent that its incumbent wields power by virtue of his or her state, rather than Party, office, the strong presidency can actually be a significant part of the reconstruction. There has already been progress in cutting down the size of the Party apparatus: in 1988 the number of Central Committee departments was reduced from twenty to nine.[18] Lip-service has long been paid to the need for a clearer differentiation of functions between Party and state bodies. The latest restructuring and reduction in the size of the Party apparatus is an indication that this time Gorbachev and his like-minded colleagues in the leadership are serious about it.

Whether a powerful presidency will be compatible with the democratization or even liberalization of the Soviet political system depends essentially on three factors: the further strengthening of the competitive principle in Soviet elections, the extent to which the Supreme Soviet further develops its independence as a representative assembly, and the spirit and letter of the laws being framed to institutionalize freedom of speech and of association. Progress in these areas is still opposed by many within the official structures. Given the reformist disposition of the particular incumbent of the highest Party and state offices at the present time, it is far from evident that stronger curbs imposed on him *within* the executive would further the reformist cause. What matters more is that there should be *checks on*, and *political accountability of*, the executive as a whole.

In this respect, nothing is more important than the institutionalization of freedom of speech and of the press. These forms of freedom must go beyond glasnost, which can still be interpreted, in the words of writer Vladimir Lakshin, as 'only a temporary certificate issued to the public and the press'.[19] Lakshin advocates legal guarantees for a 'real freedom of the press' which will ensure that 'neither a man, nor a good cause, nor a bright idea can be silently trampled upon to the great loss of society'. In the same article

---

[17] Sergey Andreyev, 'Struktura vlasti i zadachi obshchestva', *Neva*, 1989, no. 1, p. 159.

[18] See *Izvestiya TsK KPSS*, 1989, no. 1, pp. 81–8, esp. p. 87. The appearance of this journal (News of the Central Committee of the CPSU) is in itself a remarkable event.

[19] Vladimir Lakshin, 'From Glasnost to Freedom of Speech', *Moscow News*, 1989, no. 15, p. 4.

Lakshin uses the adjective 'socialist' not as a way of restricting a particular right—as has so often been the case in the Soviet Union—but as an argument for broadening it:

Not long ago we shamed and ridiculed the words 'freedom of speech' a thousand times, usually by adding the words 'bourgeois'. Now we agree to recognize that 'bourgeois freedom of the press', contrary to the banal cliché, means the rather wide freedom to criticize your own society and discuss the most varied problems, if they are of interest to the reader. But why shouldn't we wish for a fuller, socialist freedom of the press, where the press does not depend on newspaper monopolists or owners of publishing houses, like [Axel] Springer, and is only under the control of public opinion? The concept of 'socialist' should be combined with a greater level of freedom rather than with a hypocritical reduction of it.[20]

Finally, in any discussion of contemporary Soviet political institutions, mention must be made of one of the most important elements of pluralism, which has in reality, and not only in theory, emerged within a system only partly free of the bonds of authoritarianism: the emergence of genuinely independent political organizations—the 'informal groups', as they are known in the Soviet Union—referred to briefly above. These vary enormously in size and political weight, as well as in political orientation. Thus a huge political gulf separates, for instance, the adherents of Memory (*Pamyat*) from those of Memorial, the similarity of their names in English notwithstanding. The former is a Russian nationalist movement with strongly anti-Semitic overtones; the latter is a reformist, anti-Stalinist association whose aim is to throw more light on the past persecution of citizens for political reasons, and to prevent any repetition of this dark side of Soviet history.

In the Baltic republics, National Fronts have mobilized huge popular support to promote the interests of the titular nationalities of Estonia, Latvia, and Lithuania. In turn this has led to the formation of organizations stressing 'internationalism' within the republics and the interests of Russians and others who have made their home there. Indeed, one of the responses to the ethnic assertiveness of the Baltic peoples has been the rise of Russian nationalism in the Baltic republics and elsewhere.

It must be stressed that up to the present, these manifestations of political pluralism are more de facto than *de jure*. Some of the groups go beyond the limits of 'socialist' in 'socialist pluralism', as that term is understood by either wing of the Party leadership. But the groups are sufficiently widespread and influential to make the present scale of political group activity qualitatively different from the days of the tiny and persecuted dissident groups of the Brezhnev era.

[20] Ibid.

INTERESTS AND NEW CONSTITUENCIES

Interests are by no means only economic interests, although they are often treated as if that were so. Given the extent, however, to which economic interests bulk large in political and social life, those who wish to reconstruct the Soviet system are hampered by the fact that, in the short run, change does not appear to be in the material interest of a majority of citizens. Only a few social groups are better off materially as a result of perestroika, chiefly members of the new cooperatives. They have consequently become the object of envy and sometimes of vandalism.

Moreover, there are groups such as unskilled workers for whom the economic reform does not offer much comfort even in the medium term, since it envisages a widening of pay differentials to reward the acquisition of skills and qualifications. In addition, if even the economic reform already endorsed in principle is fully implemented, it will open up the possibility of job insecurity. Hitherto, Soviet workers in most parts of the country have had a guarantee not only of employment but of employment in the same enterprise. (One result of glasnost has, however, been the revelation of quite high unemployment rates in Soviet Central Asia.) The prospect of forced occupational mobility, which has not been a feature of Soviet life in the post-Stalin period, and the possibility of at least short-term unemployment, seem to be stripping workers of rights they already possessed.

In contrast, the political reforms involve an extension of the rights of workers as well as of other Soviet citizens. Competitive elections (and even, as we have seen, non-competitive ones) have granted them a right to deny local Party bosses a seat in the legislature. This so undermined a number of these officials' authority that it has come close to providing citizens with a veto on the incumbency of local Party officials as well. This is very clearly in the interests of the great majority of Soviet people, just as it is a curtailment of the privileges of Party officials and other local dignitaries. The latter have always been called to account by those above them, but it is a new experience to be accountable to those below. Thus the political reform, especially the move to competitive elections, is in the interests of far more people than those on whose interests it impinges, though the latter still constitute a powerful and increasingly disgruntled group.

Officials who have wielded an irresponsible power have grown used to not being held accountable to the great majority of people whom they nominally serve. Even when they cannot directly oppose policies now emanating from the centre, they can water them down or simply fail to implement them. This, in turn, can promote popular loss of confidence in the success of reform and lead at least a significant minority of Soviet citizens to conclude that Gorbachev is all talk and perestroika just another slogan. As the eminent sociologist Tatyana Zaslavskaya has put it: 'The tendency towards emasculation of the principal ideas of perestroika by the organs of executive power negatively influences social consciousness, undermining people's faith in its success.'[21]

There are several problems for reformers wishing to retain and broaden the appeal of perestroika. One is the interlinkage between economic and political reform. So far as economic reform is concerned, it has produced little if any rise in the standard of living, and the money supply has increased faster than the supply of goods, so that shortages are worse and queues longer. But there are more fundamental difficulties: some essential ingredients of the economic reform, such as a shift to market pricing, are being postponed for fear that the price rises will provoke popular discontent and strengthen the conservative rather than reformist forces.

This is a catch-22 for the reformers. They cannot afford to move to market prices until there is a much better supply of goods, but they cannot greatly increase supplies until they can offer adequate incentives to producers. Even a successful reform will not benefit broad social classes equally. As suggested above, unskilled workers have less to gain even in the medium-term future than skilled workers, and greater intraclass differentiation is likely, as are differing perceptions by diverse social groups of their own interests. Moreover, political reform and also the political climate vary greatly in different parts of the Soviet Union. Many provincial Russian towns have remained relatively immune to perestroika, as has almost the whole of Soviet Central Asia.

One aspect of political change that is clearly in the interests of the majority of workers, as well as intellectuals, is glasnost (not to speak of that freedom of the press advocated by Lakshin). It is in the most direct interest—in terms of work satisfaction—of the creative intelligentsia, though not necessarily of all of them. For the writer of little or no talent, the old ideological guidelines were as much a help as a hindrance, especially since they eliminated some of the potential competition for a place in the literary journals. Thus, there has been a backlash not only from cultural bureaucrats but also from writers who have found it harder to be published in large editions in the face of the newly publishable backlog of works previously taboo. The authors of the latter embrace both dead and living Soviet authors, including some now abroad, as well as foreign authors of books previously as welcome as time bombs and

---

[21] Tatyana Zaslavskaya, 'O strategii sotsial'nogo upravleniya perestroikoy', in Afanasev, *Inogo ne dano*, pp. 9–50, at p. 10.

regarded as their ideological equivalent. In the former category the most remarkable name is that of Aleksandr Solzhenitsyn, whose Soviet publications now include even *Gulag Archipelago*. In the latter category, among the most striking works to be published are Orwell's *Nineteen Eighty-Four* and *Animal Farm* and Koestler's *Darkness at Noon*. All this is welcomed by a majority within the intelligentsia, as the substantially larger rise in the circulations of liberal than of conservative Soviet literary journals indicates.

In one sense, however, glasnost is even more in the interests of workers than intellectuals. In the past, workers were more dependent on the domestic mass media for information on their own country and the outside world than were intellectuals, who had more contacts with foreigners and in many cases could listen to foreign-language radio broadcasts (which, unlike broadcasts to the Soviet Union in Russian and other Soviet languages, were not jammed). The end of jamming of Russian language foreign broadcasts by 1988 is a significant extension of the right to information, though the much greater frankness of the Soviet mass media themselves is still more important.

One of the most difficult tasks facing Soviet reformers is to make perestroika in the near-term economic as well as the political interest of a majority of Soviet citizens and of a wider range of social groups. It is not easy to commend *economic* reform merely on the basis of promises of future prosperity, for such promises must be seen in the context of too long a history of people being asked to sacrifice the present for a future that did not turn out as they had been led to believe. Yet at the same time, Soviet workers, contrary to the view of many Soviet intellectuals and Western observers, have already made it clear—not least through their voting behaviour—that they have a strong interest, in both senses of the term, in *political* reform.

OLD CULTURE AND NEW VISTAS

The cultural context in which perestroika is taking place is often regarded as one of the main obstacles to the success of reform. Just as distrust of economic entrepreneurship and attachment to egalitarianism are part of an economic culture not notably supportive of the principal tenets of the economic reform, so the authoritarian political tradition of the Soviet Union and of pre-revolutionary Russia has produced a political culture in which democratic and libertarian values and aspirations have been relatively weak.

In a fascinating discussion published in *Literaturnaya gazeta* between Soviet Deputy Foreign Minister Anatoliy Adamishin and Fedor Burlatsky, the newspaper's political commentator and the Chairman of the Public

Commission for Humanitarian Cooperation and Human Rights (an official Soviet body), one of the issues touched upon was that of Russian political culture. Burlatsky observed that 'it was the great misfortune of our country's history that Russia did not have a liberal tradition—in other words, individual human rights'. Commenting on the Soviet period, Burlatsky said:

We longed to find forms of democracy that did not continue the old forms but refuted them by demonstrating their bankruptcy. In the process we not infrequently threw out the baby—the common contents of democracy—along with the bourgeois bathwater. The worst of the traditions of old Russia filtered through into the new society via hundreds of different channels—psychological, political, and moral—and made themselves at home here.[22]

While not directly contradicting Burlatsky, Adamishin chose a quite different emphasis in his interpretation of Russian history. He stressed the common roots of Russia and the West, observing that 'Christianity alone ... had a powerful and in many ways similar influence on the political culture of Russia and Western countries. ... Ideas of personal freedoms', he argued, 'and of the limitation of state power in favour of the individual and society were not alien to the Russian people'. It was not such a long time 'in historical terms (half a millennium)' that separated the Soviet Union from the medieval traditions of Pskov and the Novgorod republic and the traditions of the popular assembly (*veche*).[23]

Addressing the 'fashionable' view that 'we are not ready for democracy and that we have no appropriate tradition', Adamishin suggested that this was 'both true and not true'. What Lenin called 'Asian barbarism' had put severe pressure on 'the principles of freedom', but no one had ever succeeded in 'eradicating the Russian democratic impulse', so prominent, he added, in 'such pillars of Russian culture' as Tolstoy and Dostoevsky. Burlatsky, in turn, did not disagree with such an assessment, but drew attention to the 'enormous gulf' between the leading lights of Russian culture, on the one hand, and the mass political culture on the other.[24]

Both contributors to the discussion made valid points. There *is* a sense in which reconstruction of the Soviet political system comes up against greater cultural obstacles than similar attempts in some East European Communist states. Five hundred years may not be such a long time 'in historical terms', but it is a long time in politics. We should, however, guard against the misleading

[22] *Literaturnaya gazeta*, 25 January 1989, p. 2.
[23] Ibid. The *veche* was a town assembly in medieval Russia which in some places shared power with a local prince, but which in Novgorod and Pskov enjoyed full sovereignty.
[24] Ibid.

view, to be found so often in the West and also in certain East-Central European countries (for instance, Poland and Hungary), that interprets the Russian and Soviet mixture of autocracy and oligarchy as the product of an irredeemably authoritarian Russian national character.

People's values, fundamental political beliefs, and expectations—key components of a political culture—do change, and at some times more quickly than at others, for they are the product of concrete historical experience. There are good reasons why such change should have been under way in the post-Stalin USSR, and at an accelerated rate in recent years.

Political cultures are a product of direct experience of political institutions as well as of the ideas disseminated within a society. Glasnost cannot fail to make an impact on Soviet political culture, above all on the values, beliefs, and expectations of the younger generation. Among the institutional changes, the reformed electoral system is particularly significant. The act of voting according to one's individual judgement rather than along the lines laid down from above is the kind of autonomous behaviour likely to lead to political cultural change. There is a large body of evidence from social psychology which suggests that attitudes are reinforced by direct personal experience. Heterodox political views can be strengthened by heterodox political action.

This point applies all the more strongly to those who participated in the dissident movement of the Brezhnev era, but while that movement comprised only a few thousand people, today's nonconformist voters number millions. In the political climate of the Gorbachev era, to vote against the district or even city Party secretary is not an act requiring the boldness of a pre-perestroika overt dissident. Indeed, the very fact that it does not require any special courage to do this may be regarded as one of the greatest achievements of perestroika.

If the re-politicization of millions of formerly apolitical Russians can, on the whole, be seen as a positive contribution to the reconstruction of the Soviet political system, the revitalization of national aspirations in other republics is likely to have a much more ambiguous impact. Only a move towards a much more meaningful federal system that allows for the flourishing of a wide variety of national cultures, including those of peoples not enjoying republican status, can provide the necessary prerequisite for the further democratization—indeed, for the very survival—of the USSR. The process will require continuous and skilful political adaptation. Given the extent to which expectations have been aroused, probably the only alternatives to the symbiosis between perestroika and national cultural diversity are either a return to a higher level of centralization, authoritarianism, and naked force than prevailed during the Brezhnev era, or the disintegration of the Soviet state.

The destabilization of a nuclear superpower would be to the advantage neither of the Soviet population nor of the rest of the world. The road to political pluralism is a much more obstacle-strewn one in the multinational Soviet state than in the East European countries where dramatic, yet peaceful, transitions are now underway. 'The worse the better' has always been an absurdly short-sighted Western sentiment in relation to the Soviet Union. The interest of both West and East lies in the continuing progress of fundamental reform, or reconstruction, of the political system—not in its descent into chaos or extreme coercion.

Part III

6

Institutional Amphibiousness or Civil Society? The Origins and Development of Perestroika

There is a school of thought which interprets transition from Communism as being a result of the development of civil society. In an important article, X.L. Ding questioned the validity of that interpretation in the context of political change in China.[1] Indeed, with the principal exception of Poland, it is doubtful if the growth of civil society should be seen as a source of fundamental political change in the Communist world rather than as a consequence of it.[2] The essence of civil society is the existence of autonomous associations and organizations neither created nor dominated by the state. It is thus at least as misleading to speak of civil society in the Soviet Union prior to perestroika as it has been to see such a development in China. As I noted some years ago:

In the first generation following the death of Stalin—from the mid-1950s to the mid-1980s—a freedom of speech in private gradually developed, but this fell far short of anything which could be called civil society. All organizations were subjected to KGB surveillance and party controls and apart from small and persecuted dissident groups, none could claim to be autonomous social actors. Even religious bodies were penetrated by the political police and the larger and more prominent they were, the higher the price they generally had to pay in political conformism.[3]

That is not to say that social developments over previous decades were irrelevant to the dramatic changes in the Soviet Union of the second half of

---

[1] X.L. Ding, 'Institutional Amphibiousness and the Transition from Communism: The Case of China', *British Journal of Political Science*, Vol. 24, No. 3, July 1994, pp. 293–318.

[2] As David Stark and László Bruszt rightly observe, in Eastern Europe as a whole 'with the exception of Poland, these were extraordinarily weak civil societies'. See Stark and Bruszt, *Postsocialist Pathways: Transforming Politics and Property in East-Central Europe* (Cambridge University Press, Cambridge, 1998), p. 16.

[3] Archie Brown, 'The Emergence of Civil Society', in Archie Brown, Michael Kaser, and Gerald S. Smith (eds.), *The Cambridge Encyclopedia of Russia and the Former Soviet Union* (Cambridge University Press, Cambridge, 1993), pp. 459–61, at p. 459.

the 1980s. If a middle class is defined in terms of lifestyle rather than property ownership, there was a fast-growing middle class in the post-Stalin USSR. A much more highly educated society existed on the eve of perestroika as compared even with Khrushchev's time.[4] Even if the term 'social class' is eschewed, the least that can be said is that a very substantial stratum of well-educated professionals had come into being—a potential social base for liberalizing or democratizing reform. There were, indeed, many informal opinion groupings, as distinct from organized groups, to be found within the Russian intelligentsia.[5] Diversity of view behind the monolithic façade which the Soviet system maintained did not, however, add up to the existence of civil society. Neither did deviant behaviour, whether of a criminal or dissident character. As Ding remarks:

Civility comes first. Civil society is a sphere of civilized human activities. Thus, antisocial behaviour and criminal undertakings, such as the Mafia, are not a constituent of civil society, though they are in the private domain and a part of society.[6]

Ding rightly stresses autonomy as 'the most important element of civil society', noting that in a weak state a civil society of sorts—only in 'a weak sense'—may exist in spite of the declared aims of the state authorities. However:

If the situation in a political community necessitates voluntary associations of citizens having to work underground, a civil society cannot be said to have emerged in that community. For the secrecy of these associational activities is a clear indication of the absence of citizens' political freedom, *de jure* and *de facto*.[7]

On the eve of Konstantin Chernenko's death in March 1985 and, indeed, throughout the first year of the perestroika officially launched at the April plenum of the Central Committee of the Soviet Communist Party, the autonomous organizations characteristic of civil society did not exist. They were subsequently to develop quite rapidly in response to changes initiated at the top of the political hierarchy, but if we are to explain the advent of serious reform of the Soviet system, which was subsequently to develop into systemic transformation, we should look elsewhere than for the development of a non-existent civil society in the pre-1985 Soviet Union.[8] Frederick Starr is among

---

[4] Whereas in 1959 the number of Soviet citizens with higher education stood at 8.3 million, by 1984 the figure had risen to 18.4 million.

[5] Defining 'intelligentsia' sociologically—on the basis of educational and professional attainment—rather than normatively as embracing, by definition, a critical attitude to the state authorities.

[6] Ding, 'Institutional Amphibiousness', p. 295.   [7] Ibid., p. 296.

[8] I am not, of course, talking about pre-revolutionary Russia. In the last decades before 1917 there were some such developments, ably discussed more than forty years ago by Jacob Walkin

those who holds that 'the horizontal communication essential for a civil society' had developed in those pre-1985 years, but the 'unsanctioned, informal groups and networks' to which he alludes neither significantly influenced public policy nor were granted legitimacy prior to the coming to power of Gorbachev, whose role he greatly downplays when he writes: 'All this ferment began prior to Gorbachev's rise to power in 1985. He neither created it nor did much to encourage it, at least initially. Instead, he put his hopes in a campaign for worker discipline and sobriety.'[9]

There was, of course, innovative thinking within the Soviet system in the years between Stalin's death and that of Chernenko.[10] The thinking that had *some* influence then, and that was to develop into a more fundamentally important political phenomenon after Gorbachev succeeded Chernenko, took place, however, within party-state institutions. Among the latter I include research institutes, for even those which came under the jurisdiction of the Academy of Sciences were permeated by the Communist Party and had their *kurator*, or overseer, within the apparatus of the Central Committee.

In what was in many respects an insightful book, Moshe Lewin stretches the concept of civil society unhelpfully (as Ding has also noted)[11] when he writes:

The concept of a civil society operating in the very fortress of statism—among broad layers of officials, political opinion makers, and the party apparatus—challenges conventional thinking about the Soviet state. It is a novel idea about a novel situation.

---

in his *The Rise of Democracy in Pre-Revolutionary Russia: Political and Social Institutions under the Last Three Czars* (Thames & Hudson, London, 1963).

[9] S. Frederick Starr, 'A Usable Past', in Alexander Dallin and Gail W. Lapidus (eds.), *The Soviet Union in Crisis* (Westview, Boulder, CO, 1991), pp. 11–15, at pp. 14–15. Elsewhere Starr writes of 'the civil society that was fitfully coming into being' in the pre-1985 period. See Starr, 'The Road to Reform' in Abraham Brumberg (ed.), *Chronicle of a Revolution: A Western–Soviet Inquiry into Perestroika* (Pantheon, New York, 1990), pp. 17–29, at p. 27. See also Moshe Lewin, *Political Undercurrents in Soviet Economic Debates* (Pluto Press, London, 1975), ch. 10, ' "Civil Society" Recovering', pp. 249–77.

[10] Discussions of it at the time included Archie Brown, 'Pluralism, Power and the Soviet Political System' in Susan Gross Solomon (ed.), *Pluralism in the Soviet Union: Essays in Honour of H. Gordon Skilling* (Macmillan, London, 1983), pp. 146–82; Archie Brown, 'Political Science in the Soviet Union: A New Stage of Development?', in *Soviet Studies*, Vol. XXXVI, No. 3, July 1984, pp. 317–44; Ronald J. Hill, *Soviet Politics, Political Science and Reform* (Martin Robertson, Oxford, 1980); Moshe Lewin, *Political Undercurrents in Soviet Economic Debates*, op. cit.; Jerry F. Hough, *The Struggle for the Third World: Soviet Debates and American Options* (Brookings Institution, Washington, DC, 1986); and Elizabeth Valkenier, *The Soviet Union and the Third World: An Economic Bind* (Praeger, New York, 1983). For fuller, retrospective accounts, see Robert D. English, *Russia and the Idea of the West: Gorbachev, Intellectuals, and the End of the Cold War* (Columbia University Press, New York, 2000); and Archie Brown (ed.), *The Demise of Marxism-Leninism in Russia* (Palgrave Macmillan, London, 2004).

[11] Ding, 'Institutional Amphibiousness...', pp. 299–300.

But insofar as administrators may belong to urban social groups, they may move in and out of the official and social worlds.[12]

In fact, the substance of Lewin's point is valid and significant. He was well aware of diversity of view within the Soviet establishment and of the inter-action of some even within the apparatus of the party and state with those from a different social milieu. As he put it: 'For although the apparaty insiders are often conservative and opposed to reforms and enlightened social change, they are not an island.'[13] One can, indeed, go further. While party and state officials were generally of a conservative Communist disposition, there was a minority who aspired to be serious reformers and who, given unheard-of opportunities (in the Soviet context) to advocate heterodox views following the selection of Gorbachev as General Secretary, were able to exercise dispro-portionately great influence.

The fact that such reform-minded officials were able to hold down positions within party-state institutions and thereby retain the potential to influence policy from the inside was of critical importance.[14] This, however, is a different political phenomenon from civil society. It is one which, in its essence, was recognized by some analysts of Soviet politics, albeit rather a small minority. Jerry Hough was among those who drew attention to the esoteric debate which was conducted within policy-oriented institutes in the Soviet Union, sometimes involving party officials them-selves.[15] It was unfortunate, however, that the name he proposed for this phenomenon was 'institutional pluralism'[16] or, in a worse variant, 'institu-tionalized pluralism'.[17] Writing in the late 1970s—and in the course of providing much insight of substance into Soviet politics—Hough was premature by a decade in arguing that 'the Soviet Union now is character-ized by a type of pluralism'.[18] Pluralism, like civil society, requires auton-omy from the state.

[12] Moshe Lewin, *The Gorbachev Phenomenon: A Historical Interpretation* (Radius, London, 1988), p. 80.

[13] Ibid., p. 81.

[14] See John Gooding, 'Perestroika as Revolution from Within: An Interpretation', *The Russian Review*, Vol. 51, No. 1, January 1992, pp. 36–57.

[15] See, for example, Jerry F. Hough, *The Struggle for the Third World: Soviet Debates and American Options*, op. cit.

[16] Jerry F. Hough, *The Soviet Union and Social Science Theory* (Harvard University Press, Cambridge, MA, 1977), pp. 10–11, 22–4, 33, 43–6, and 69–70.

[17] Jerry F. Hough and Merle Fainsod, *How the Soviet Union is Governed* (Harvard University Press, Cambridge, MA, 1979), p. 547.

[18] Ibid., p. 548.

WORKING FOR CHANGE FROM WITHIN THE SYSTEM

The remainder of this chapter is devoted to arguing that the concept of *institutional amphibiousness*, developed by Ding, is a more useful way of interpreting and conceptualizing the origins and early development of perestroika than civil society. It has, indeed, quite wide applicability to understanding the process of transition from Communist rule in a comparative context. The advent of the 'Prague Spring', for example, was brought about by within-system reformers, among them leading members of the Higher Party School, members of commissions set up by the Central Committee of the Communist Party, and a minority of members of the Central Committee itself.[19] As Ding observes: 'An institution can be used for purposes contrary to those it is supposed to fulfil, and the same institution can simultaneously serve conflicting purposes.'[20] Institutions, which were intended to be pillars of Communist orthodoxy, and in considerable measure were, in a number of cases led a double life. Ding sees a process of 'institutional manipulation' having taken place, whereby institutions that 'were set up by the communist regime for its own use' were 'gradually co-opted by critical forces for counter purposes, all the while keeping up the protective façade that these were still party-state institutions'.[21] This describes very well what happened to a number of Soviet (and, twenty years earlier, Czech) institutions. One should add, however, that even more important than a kind of 'entryism' by 'critical forces' was the gradual evolution of the views of people within these institutions from relative orthodoxy to radical critiques.

Although organized political groups, other than small—and persecuted—dissident groups could not survive in the Soviet Union prior to the era of perestroika, informal friendship groupings were important not only as a way for the average citizen to deal with the vicissitudes of a shortage economy,[22] but as a means of mutual help and political survival for party intellectuals who aspired to make at least a marginal difference to policy outcomes. One group which is itself an example of institutional amphibiousness consists of

---

[19] That precursor of perestroika, it should be recalled, was ended not by indigenous political forces within Czechoslovakia but by Soviet tanks. For my own discussion of the process of change in Czechoslovakia in the late 1960s, see Brown, 'Political Change in Czechoslovakia', in Leonard Schapiro (ed.), *Political Opposition in One-Party States* (Macmillan, London, 1972). For the fullest discussion of the origins and development of the 'Prague Spring', see H. Gordon Skilling, *Czechoslovakia's Interrupted Revolution* (Princeton University Press, Princeton, NJ, 1976).

[20] Ding, 'Institutional Amphibiousness', p. 298.   [21] Ibid., p. 299.

[22] See Alena V. Ledeneva, *Russia's Economy of Favours: Blat, Networking and Informal Exchange* (Cambridge University Press, Cambridge, 1998).

those who spent some years in Prague on the journal of international Communism, *World Marxist Review* (*Problemy mira i sotsializma*—'Problems of Peace and Socialism' in its Russian version). This journal was intended to bind together the international Communist movement but along lines essentially determined from Moscow. From the point of view of its ultimate overseer within the Central Committee, the head of its International Department, Boris Ponomarev (who held that office from 1955 to 1985), the task of the Soviet party intellectuals who worked on the *World Marxist Review* was to propagate Soviet orthodoxy throughout the worldwide Communist movement. To some extent they did that, for the Soviet contingent were the dominant partners in the journal, but they interacted with intellectuals from other Communist Parties, including the Central and West European ones and with representatives of underground parties from, for example, Latin America. The atmosphere was one of free discussion and a good many of the Soviet participants returned from their Prague sojourn more reform-minded and open-minded than before.[23]

In the ranks of those who worked in Prague on the *World Marxist Review* were people who turned into some of the most important political actors of the perestroika period. A number of them were also influential earlier than that, while one or two achieved greater renown in post-Soviet Russia. They included future deputy heads of Central Committee departments and aides or consultants to Gorbachev such as Anatoliy Chernyaev, Georgiy Shakhnazarov, Vadim Zagladin, and Karen Brutents; a future aide to Gorbachev who in the perestroika period edited both the theoretical journal *Kommunist* and (subsequently) *Pravda*, Ivan Frolov; editor of *World Marxist Review* from 1958 to 1964, Aleksey Rumyantsev, who became in the latter year editor of *Pravda*, only to be dismissed for his reformist views in 1965; future Institute directors Georgiy Arbatov, Oleg Bogomolov, Nikolay Inozemtsev, and Timur Timofeev; and other party intellectuals known for their reformist dispositions such as Yevgeniy Ambartsumov, Aleksandr Bovin, Lev Delyusin, Merab Mamardashvili, Gennadiy Gerasimov, Yuriy Karyakin, Vladimir Lukin, Nikolay Shishlin, and Aleksandr Veber.[24]

---

[23] The best account of the experience of working on the *World Marxist Review* in Prague is to be found in A.S. Chernyaev, *Moya zhizn' i moe vremya* (Mezhdunarodnye otnosheniya, Moscow, 1995), pp. 225–36. Also illuminating is Georgi Arbatov, *The System: An Insider's Life in Soviet Politics* (Times Books, New York, 1992), pp. 79–81. I have written about the Prague alumni in *The Gorbachev Factor*, pp. 98–101 and 112, as has Robert D. English, *Russia and the Idea of the West: Gorbachev, Intellectuals, and the End of the Cold War* (Columbia University Press, New York, 2000), pp. 71–3.

[24] There is an interesting overlap between some of the leading members of the Prague group and Yuriy Andropov's team of consultants in the Central Committee of the CPSU in the first half of the 1960s. At that time Andropov was a Secretary of the Central Committee overseeing

Chernyaev notes that within the large staff of the Prague journal there was a division into informal groups on the basis of mutual sympathy,[25] yet he did not know any Soviet party intellectual who had worked on the journal who was *not* against the Soviet invasion of Czechoslovakia in August 1968. A few of them opposed it openly, notably Vladimir Lukin who was in Prague at the time but was speedily put on a plane to Moscow. Thanks to the support of Arbatov (and Arbatov's good relations with Andropov), Lukin was able to move to the Institute of the United States and Canada which, along with the Institute of World Economy and International Relations (IMEMO), was one of the two most influential international institutes in the Soviet Union. Others made private protests to the party leadership—Bovin, for example, wrote to Brezhnev. Most of them condemned it only in conversation amongst themselves. Chernyaev observes: 'We stigmatized ourselves as involuntary accomplices in this historic crime.'[26]

Although their behaviour was less heroic, it is likely that they more effectively served the cause of changing the Soviet Union by remaining within the system than by joining the handful of demonstrators on Red Square. The understandable feelings of guilt of those who did not accept the consequences of publicly condemning the Soviet invasion of Czechoslovakia were not, of course, expiated simply by their progression upwards within the system, for that could be regarded as nothing more than careerism. They redeemed themselves because the positions they moved into gave them the possibility, which most of them seized, to play a significant part in the pluralization of Soviet politics during the perestroika years and to play a constructive role in the ending of the Cold War. This, after all, was the era in which Soviet troops were confined to their barracks while the country on the conscience of the Soviet Prague alumni, Czechoslovakia, went beyond the 'socialism with a human face' of 1968 and became non-Communist and fully independent of Moscow.

relations with Eastern Europe and China. He was then somewhat more open to fresh ideas than his colleagues in the Secretariat, but his subsequent fifteen years as head of the KGB left an indelible mark on him. When he became General Secretary after Brezhnev, Andropov was more innovative than his predecessor but to the extent that he was a reformer, it was within strict limits and, as his KGB years illustrated, he was no liberal. Those who worked both on the *World Marxist Review* in Prague at one time or another and also for Andropov in the Socialist Countries Department of the Central Committee included Arbatov, Bogomolov, Bovin, Delyusin, Gerasimov, and Shakhnazarov. The first head of Andropov's group of consultants in the Central Committee was, however, Fedor Burlatsky who was not a Prague alumnus.

[25] Chernyaev, *Moya zhizn' i moe vremya*, p. 227.

[26] Ibid., p. 236. See also the well-informed account in English, *Russia and the Idea of the West*, pp. 112–13.

Some of the literature on esoteric debates within Soviet politics[27]—as well as the overlapping literature which emphasizes the importance of ideas in the process of political change within the Soviet Union[28]—illustrates the phenomenon of institutional amphibiousness without using that terminology. It does not, however, always place sufficient emphasis on the need for ideas to have an organizational base if they are to be influential under conditions of highly authoritarian rule. Ideas are important in politics, sometimes crucially so, but they generally need institutional bearers. That has been particularly true of Communist systems.

The phenomenon to which the concept of institutional amphibiousness draws attention has been touched upon by people using other concepts, each with different nuances. The most usual term, used by a number of Sovietologists in the Brezhnev era, was 'within-system reformers'. Alexander Shtromas, in a little-known book published in 1981, preferred the term 'intrastructural dissent', which he distinguished from the 'extrastructural dissent' of the dissidents in the normal sense of that term.[29] Shtromas notes the difference between what he calls 'egoistic "intrastructural" dissent'—by which he means individuals pursuing their individual or group economic interests (often by defrauding the state)—from 'altruistic "intrastructural" dissent', which 'consists of pursuit of constructive (but in official terms controversial) political, social, economic or cultural goals'. This, he observes, is 'much less visible than negative, egoistic "intrastructural" dissent but is a much more functional vehicle of political change'.[30]

---

[27] See n. 10.

[28] See, in particular, Brown (ed.), *The Demise of Marxism-Leninism in Russia*, op. cit.; Jeffrey T. Checkel, *Ideas and International Political Change: Soviet/Russian Behavior and the End of the Cold War* (Yale University Press, New Haven, CT, 1997); English, *Russia and the Idea of the West*, op. cit.; Matthew Evangelista, *Unarmed Forces: The Transnational Movement to End the Cold War* (Cornell University Press, Ithaca, NY, 1999); and Julie M. Newton, *Russia, France, and the Idea of Europe* (Palgrave Macmillan, London, 2003).

[29] Alexander Shtromas, *Political Change and Social Development: The Case of the Soviet Union* (Peter Lang, Frankfurt am Main, 1981), pp. 67–87. The fact that Shtromas's book was published in English in Germany helps to account for the fact that it was little cited. It also unfashionably mixed qualitative analysis with impassioned political advocacy. Yet his book is a reminder that even the overt Soviet dissidents, with whom Shtromas strongly identified, were not engaged in a struggle to build capitalism. As Shtromas puts it (p. 142): 'The aim of Soviet dissidents, for whom I seek support, is not to fight "Communism" and even less to establish "Capitalism". The real confrontation in this world is not between economic systems (as represented by Capitalism and Communism), but between those who support the ideals of individual, national, and social freedom, and those who represent the totalitarian forces of oppression.' That is, however, a rather narrow understanding of Communism. As I endeavour to make clear in chapter seven, my own understanding of it embraces much more than the state-owned, non-market economy.

[30] Ibid., p. 75. When Alex Shtromas discussed his manuscript at length with me while writing it, I held to my view that 'within-system reformers' or, in Shtromas's terms, 'intrastructural dissenters' would be more likely to bring about far-reaching change in the Soviet Union than

Interestingly, an archetypal Soviet insider, Yevgeniy Primakov, entitles the first part of his political memoirs 'Dissidents within the System'.[31] Primakov became increasingly influential in each stage of his career—pre-perestroika, during perestroika, and in post-Soviet Russia. During the presidency of Boris Yeltsin, he was successively head of Foreign Intelligence, Foreign Minister, and Prime Minister. In an interview with the author of a history of the major international relations institute, IMEMO, which he headed from 1985 to 1989 (while also playing an influential part in high politics), Primakov elaborated 'the principled difference' between what he called ' "intrasystemic" and "extrasystemic" dissidents'.[32] The former, unlike the latter, he said, 'were not anti-Communists and did not set as their goal the destruction of the existing order'.[33]

This is in essence correct, but in a number of respects an oversimplification. On the one hand, many of the dissidents had much more modest goals than the 'destruction' of the existing system. A frequent appeal was that the Soviet authorities should obey their own laws and observe, for example, the Soviet Constitution of 1977 or the Helsinki Agreement which the USSR had signed in 1975.[34] On the other hand, while Primakov is probably correct in asserting that most Soviet 'intrastructural dissidents' favoured a move towards combining 'necessary elements of a market economy with the Soviet planning system' and that they also wished to take 'the best from the two socio-economic systems—socialism and capitalism',[35] there were other

overt dissidence. Shtromas expressed qualified agreement, although he continued to stress the importance also of 'extrastructural dissent'. He summed up his views in the following way: 'It is probably true . . . that Soviet overt dissent—civic, national, or religious—is not the most important force insofar as inception of political change is concerned. Such change will most probably come not from without but from within the official system; "intrastructural" rather than overt "extrastructural" change will bring it about. Yet it would be wrong to deny that overt dissent is an enormous asset to the whole of the Soviet people's dissident maturation' (ibid., p. 86). In fact, overt dissidents played no part in the inception of perestroika, but once the process was under-way, leading dissidents, especially Andrey Sakharov, were able to play a role in the radicalization of the process. However, by 1989—following the development of freedom of speech and the advent of contested elections—the distinction between 'intrastructural' and 'extrastructural' dissent had become obsolete. In the later perestroika years, of the three forms of overt dissidence mentioned by Shtromas in the passage cited above, national dissent became the most significant.

[31] Yevgeniy Primakov, *Gody v bol'shoy politike* (Sovershenno sekretno, Moscow, 1999), 'Dissidenty v sisteme', pp. 11–98.

[32] Petr Cherkasov, *IMEMO. Institut Mirovoy Ekonomiki i Mezhdunarodnykh Otnosheniy: Portret na fone epokhi* (Ves' mir, Moscow, 2004), pp. 355–6. The exact words Primakov uses are *vnutrisistemnye* and *vnesistemnye*.

[33] Ibid., p. 355.

[34] On the relatively limited goals of mainstream overt dissent in the Brezhnev era, see Peter Reddaway, 'The Development of Dissent and Opposition', in Archie Brown and Michael Kaser (eds.), *The Soviet Union since the Fall of Khrushchev* (Macmillan, London, 2nd edn., 1978), pp. 121–56, esp. p. 122.

[35] Ibid., p. 356.

intrastructural dissidents for whom greater cultural and political freedom was a higher aspiration. Moreover, Shtromas was correct in seeing that even more limited goals, such as those posited by Primakov, were potentially destructive of the political system. Quite apart from the fact that no country has succeeded in establishing a viable mix of plan and market, it became evident in the perestroika period that the political system had to change if such advocacy was to be legitimized and not put at risk of being once again repressed.

None of the foregoing argument means that those who worked for change within the system, testing the limits of its tolerance at any given time (and sometimes going beyond them, resulting in career setbacks), were other than extremely important in relation to the political change of the perestroika years.[36] The author of the institutional history of IMEMO, Petr Cherkasov, uses a less flattering term than 'intrastructural dissenters', 'intra-systemic dissidents', or 'within-system reformers' to describe these party intellectuals. He calls them 'liberal conformists'.[37] By those he thus describes, Cherkasov means *institutchiki* who 'independently of their internal convictions, never spoke out against the existing structure, limiting themselves to more or less sharp criticism of "particular shortcomings"'.[38] They saw their mission to be one of enlightening those who held power at the top of the system through the memoranda, prognoses, and analytical materials sent from their institute to the Central Committee of the CPSU. In this way, he suggests, they cautiously tried to advance movement towards political democratization and towards greater social and economic efficiency of the system.[39] Cherkasov, in spite of preferring the noun 'conformist' to 'dissident', observes that the people he has in mind are essentially in the same category as those described by Primakov as *sistemnye dissidenty* or as *vnutrisistemnye dissidenty* (intrasystemic dissidents) and he shares Primakov's view of their importance.[40]

The contradictory tendencies within the heart of the Soviet Establishment highlighted, in their different ways and somewhat different terminology, by Shtromas, Primakov, and Cherkasov, can also be subsumed under the more subtle notion of institutional amphibiousness. I do not wish to claim too much for the explanatory value of institutional amphibiousness. In a totalitarian regime of the Stalinist type such amphibiousness was all but impossible. For this political phenomenon to emerge, and acquire importance,

---

[36] In the words of Arbatov, 'it was no accident that Gorbachev and his comrades-in-arms who started de-Stalinization and perestroika came from inside, and not from outside, the system'. He adds: 'These also were people burdened with past sins and limitations, imposed by that very system.' See Arbatov, op. cit., p. 242.

[37] Cherkasov, *IMEMO*, p. 356.   [38] Ibid.   [39] Ibid.   [40] Ibid.

some relaxation within the Communist regime is required. Given, however, that minimal level of relaxation, such as took place in the Soviet Union during the Khrushchev era, the presence of reform-minded (or at least open-minded) people within Communist Party institutions, or in research institutes that came under party tutelage, had the potential to generate within-system reform which, in turn, could pave the way for more fundamental change. It is well known that among the most important reformers of the Gorbachev era were party intellectuals who regarded themselves as 'children of the Twentieth Congress', people whose eyes had been (at least partially) opened by Khrushchev's exposure of some of the crimes of Stalin in 1956 and who were unhappy with the imposed moratorium on serious criticism of Stalin and of Stalinism during the Brezhnev years.

That last point serves as a reminder that in the essentially unreformed Communist system the leadership had the power to impose limits on the scope of public discourse and they did not hesitate to exercise it. Anti-Stalinists, in the period between 1964 and 1985[41] had to exercise self-censorship in their public utterances and writings. It was important, nevertheless, that they interacted with one another informally and that they kept their positions within the political establishment, whether within policy-oriented research institutes or (still more significantly) as senior officials in the apparatus of the Central Committee of the CPSU.

DEPARTMENTS OF THE CENTRAL COMMITTEE

The international departments of the Central Committee—the International Department itself and the Socialist Countries Department (which were amalgamated in 1988)—were exceptionally important examples of institutional amphibiousness. The International Department was meant to ensure that Soviet foreign policy remained faithful to Marxist-Leninist ideology and to influence non-ruling Communist parties and other parties of the left throughout the world. The Socialist Countries Department was set up to keep a close watch on all the other Communist countries, especially those of East Europe, and to help ensure that they moved along straight and narrow Marxist-Leninist lines. While to a large extent both departments fulfilled those allotted roles, they included more people of high educational standards and knowledge of the outside world (including foreign languages) than

---

[41] There was only minor change for the better in this respect during Andropov's General Secretaryship and a step back under Chernenko when Stalin's long-term ally, Vyacheslav Molotov, was symbolically readmitted to party membership.

any other Central Committee departments. People from the International Department, in particular, contributed disproportionately to the 'New Thinking' of the Gorbachev era, especially on foreign policy.

Indeed, the long-term significance of the International Department is more as an example of institutional amphibiousness than as the key player in the making of Soviet external policy. Leonard Schapiro, who made a major contribution to the study of the Soviet Communist Party,[42] overstated the functions of the Department when he argued (in an article in the mid-1970s) that it played the 'dominant role in foreign policy'.[43] Anatoliy Chernyaev, who was a deputy head of the International Department from 1970 until he became principal foreign policy aide to Gorbachev in February 1986, sees the relationship with non-ruling Communist Parties as being the main function of the Department, even though the Department aspired to provide ideological guidelines for external policy more generally. Writing on the basis of his diary entries of the 1970s, Chernyaev observes that the superfluousness of the International Department from the point of view of Brezhnev's *Realpolitik* made ever more meaningless the Department's claim to exert influence on Soviet foreign policy.[44] The redundancy of the International Department would have become even more obvious, Chernyaev says, but for the claim of its head, Boris Ponomarev, to play the role of a theoretician.

Chernyaev notes that the International Department did play a foreign policy role in the Middle East, but otherwise was not particularly relevant to the state-to-state relations that were the concern of Brezhnev and the Ministry of Foreign Affairs under its long-serving minister, Andrey Gromyko. The only Western Communist Parties taken seriously by the Politburo were the French and Italian, since they appeared to have a solid support base in their own countries. Moreover, personal relations also contributed to the fact that the International Department was *not* the dominant influence on Soviet foreign policy. Brezhnev strongly disliked Ponomarev,[45] but had good relations with Gromyko, whose authority was enhanced when he became a full member of the Politburo in 1973.[46] Gromyko had hitherto not been

---

[42] Above all in his historical account, *The Communist Party of the Soviet Union* (Eyre & Spottiswoode, London, 1960; 2nd rev. edn., 1970).

[43] Leonard Schapiro, 'The International Department of the CPSU: key to Soviet policy', *International Journal*, Vol. XXXII, No. 1, Winter 1976–7, pp. 41–55, at p. 45. It must be added that we have vastly more information at our disposal on the inner workings of the Soviet system today than was available to scholars in the 1970s.

[44] Anatoliy Chernyaev, *Moya zhizn' i moe vremya* (Mezhdunarondnye otnosheniya, Moscow, 1995), p. 276.

[45] Ibid., pp. 260–1.

[46] From that time on Gromyko's political influence increased, contrary to the arguments of Schapiro in his *International Journal* article (see n. 42), p. 44.

even a candidate member of the Politburo, only a member of the Central Committee, and thus in party terms he had ranked below Boris Ponomarev. Now, however, he leapfrogged over him, for Ponomarev remained a candidate member, a position he held in combination with his Secretaryship of the Central Committee. The Soviet system was extremely hierarchical and formal party rank translated into political authority.[47]

Chernyaev entitles a lengthy chapter of his memoirs 'In the Regime of Doublethink (the International Department of the Central Committee)'. The head of the Department, Ponomarev, was sincere in his condemnation of 'revisionists' within the international Communist movement. He was a conservative Communist whose world view rested on his orthodox interpretation of the writings of Lenin. There were, however, other members of the Department who while, to a greater or lesser extent, publicly opposing 'revisionism', were themselves internal revisionists. That is to say, they sympathized more with the reformist tendencies within European Communist Parties—the embrace of pluralism by the Italian and Spanish Communist Parties, in particular, which became known as 'Eurocommunism'—and, indeed, with the European socialist parties of a social democratic character, than with Marxism-Leninism.

Sometimes the heterodoxy of the views of party intellectuals within the International Department led to their removal from it, but even then they usually had enough support from within the party hierarchy to have a soft landing. Thus, Yuriy Krasin, who in the words of Chernyaev was 'an expert on Lenin and for precisely that reason became a "revisionist" long before perestroika',[48] was moved out of the Department in the mid-1970s—his punishment for being a source of information for Roy Medvedev (whose work on Soviet history and politics could not be published in the Soviet Union, but was much read abroad). However, Krasin became, first, the Pro-Rector of the Academy of Social Sciences and then a professor in an institution under the aegis of the International Department, the Institute of Social Sciences, whose students came from Communist and revolutionary movements in the Third World.

---

[47] An illustration of Gromyko's higher authority as compared with Ponomarev can be seen in the top secret document on the invasion of Afghanistan prepared for the Politburo by Yuriy Andropov, Gromyko, Ponomarev, and Ustinov. Although in the Cyrillic as well as the Latin alphabet, the names should appear in that order, this 31 December 1979 document has the signatures of Andropov, Gromyko, and Ustinov in alphabetical order across one line and two lines lower the signature of Ponomarev. See HIA, Fond 89, Archives of the Communist Party and Soviet State, Reel 1.993, opis 14, file 35, p. 5.

[48] Chernyaev, *Moya zhizn' i moe vremya*, p. 247.

A former First Deputy Head of the International Department, Karen Brutents, notes, in his memoirs, that the International Department was closely connected with many academic institutions—more closely than other agencies concerned with foreign policy (in which category he includes, presumably, the Ministry of Foreign Affairs and the KGB). The academic establishments he particularly mentions are 'the Institute of World Economy and International Relations [IMEMO], the Institute of the USA and Canada, the Institute of Oriental Studies, the Institute of Latin America, and the Institute of Africa'. Brutents goes on:

On the instructions of the Central Committee, and sometimes on their own initiative, they prepared analytical materials and included recommendations. Unfortunately, on the whole, the influence on our 'output' of these contacts was not very great.[49]

That changed with perestroika. The influence of these institutes, not least IMEMO, whose Director from 1983 to 1985 was Aleksandr Yakovlev (who was succeeded by Yevgeniy Primakov), and Georgiy Arbatov's Institute of the United States and Canada increased dramatically after Gorbachev became General Secretary. Yakovlev was already an informal adviser of Gorbachev from the time he was appointed IMEMO Director. His return to Moscow from ten years of dignified exile as Soviet Ambassador to Canada had been ended on Gorbachev's recommendation to Andropov, following Gorbachev's 1983 visit to Canada, during which he established a close personal and political rapport with Yakovlev. (Their relations were later to become more complicated, and they were for a time estranged in the 1990s. However, although their relationship never regained its former warmth, they had re-established contact well before Yakovlev's death in late 2005. Yakovlev was a guest at Gorbachev's seventieth birthday celebration in 2001 and participated in several conferences, marking the twentieth anniversary of the launch of perestroika, in 2005.)[50]

It was especially between 1985 and 1988 that the role of Yakovlev was important in the radicalization of the concept and content of perestroika. It is, however, entirely wrong to see Yakovlev as the prime mover even in the early years of perestroika. His role as a staunch advocate of reform within the leadership—and as a counterweight to the conservative Communists who were numerically predominant—was one *deliberately facilitated* by

---

[49] K.N. Brutents, *Tridstat' let na Staroy ploshchadi* (Mezhdunarodnye otnosheniya, Moscow, 1998), p. 168.

[50] One such conference at which Gorbachev presided, held in Turin in March 2005, resulted in a useful book to which Yakovlev contributed: Andrei Grachev, Chiara Blengino, and Rossella Stievano (eds.), *1985–2005: Twenty Years that Changed the World* (Editori Laterza for World Political Forum, Rome, 2005).

Gorbachev. His extraordinarily fast promotion from non-membership of the Central Committee at the beginning of 1986 to full membership of the Politburo and a Secretaryship of the Central Committee by the summer of 1987 would have been unthinkable had Gorbachev not put his full weight behind Yakovlev's advance into the inner leadership of the Communist Party.

It was crucially important that there were within the International Department and, to a lesser extent, in the Socialist Countries Department of the Central Committee people on whom Gorbachev could draw who would be committed supporters of a radical break with the past. No less important was the fact that there were many talented people working in research institutes who, as a result of attacking particular 'shortcomings' rather than any of the fundamentals of the system, had held on to their party membership and their jobs through the 'era of stagnation'. Now they were more than ready to be enlisted in the process of perestroika. The system was such that the change had to be initiated from the top, but the fact that there were major Central Committee Departments and large research establishments characterized by what Ding calls 'institutional confusion, systemic ambiguity and double identity'[51] was a precondition for progress in the early years of perestroika when conservative Communists were still thoroughly entrenched in the headships of Central Committee departments, in the leadership of the republican and most regional party organizations, and at the top of most ministries, not to mention the deep conservatism of the military–industrial complex and the leadership of the KGB.[52]

Gorbachev took a lead in changing the priorities of the International Department, although even during the perestroika years—one might, indeed, say increasingly in that period—the Ministry of Foreign Affairs remained more important in the making of foreign policy than the Department. That was partly again for personal reasons. Gorbachev had a very close working relationship with Eduard Shevardnadze. It also reflected the trajectory of the reform process itself. In the later stages of perestroika, Gorbachev was presiding over a conscious shift from party to state power. In a new instruction of 6 May 1986, Gorbachev insisted that the first priority of the International Department had to be fresh thinking about international relations. As Brutents puts it:

In the first place the main problems of the party's foreign policy and problems of international relations as a whole, and second (second! K.B.) the links of the CPSU

---

[51] Ding, 'Institutional Amphibiousness and the Transition from Communism', p. 313.

[52] In the case of the KGB, there were, however, officers who had worked as intelligence agents in Western countries whose experience there had made them only too well aware of the limitations of the Soviet command economy.

with Communist and worker, social-democratic and labour, and other parties and organisations, with national-liberation movements and anti-war forces.[53]

Whereas the advice from the *mezhdunarodniki*—specialists on foreign countries and international relations in the research institutes—had, as I have already noted Brutents contending, only a limited influence prior to perestroika, the head of IMEMO during the Brezhnev years, Nikolay Inozemtsev, and the head of the Institute of the United States and Canada, Georgiy Arbatov, made the Soviet leadership better informed than it otherwise would have been and they were voices of reason and prudence in the foreign policymaking process.[54] On some of the most momentous issues, such as the invasion of Czechoslovakia in 1968 and of Afghanistan in 1979, not only were the leading specialists ignored. In the case of the latter intervention, even the Politburo as a whole was presented with a fait accompli. The policy was initiated by Defence Minister Dmitriy Ustinov, Foreign Minister Andrey Gromyko, and KGB chief Yuriy Andropov and presented to Brezhnev at a meeting on 12 December 1979. Later the same day a Kremlin meeting involved Ponomarev and others (though not the full Politburo), but the essential choice, which had such far-reaching consequences, had been made by just four people.[55]

HETERODOX THINKING WITHIN OFFICIAL INSTITUTIONS

So far as social democracy is concerned, Karen Brutents, from his vantage point of First Deputy Head of the International Department, notes that 'M.S. Gorbachev and his associates strove in an unbiased way to examine the experience of western countries in general and of social democracy in particular'.[56] Within the research institutes, and even within the two international departments of the Central Committee, there were people who were already sympathetic to a social democratic version of socialism. Georgiy Shakhnazarov, whose role has already been noted in earlier chapters of this book, was a striking case in point. Shakhnazarov was a deputy head of the Socialist

---

[53] Brutents, *Tridtsat' let na Staroy ploshchadi*, p. 169.

[54] See Primakov, *Gody v bol'shoy politike*; Cherkasov, *IMEMO*; and English, *Russia and the Idea of the West*.

[55] See HIA, Fond 89, 1.993, 14, 32; Anatoly Dobrynin, *In Confidence: Moscow's Ambassador to America's Six Cold War Presidents (1962–1986)* (Times Books, New York, 1995), pp. 437–8; and Anatoly Chernyaev, *My Six Years with Gorbachev* (translated and edited by Robert English and Elizabeth Tucker, State University of Pennsylvania Press, 2000), p. 26.

[56] Brutents, *Tridsat' let na Staroy ploshchadi*, pp. 157–8.

Countries Department from 1970 to 1986 and First Deputy Head from then until 1988.[57]

Other significant 'new thinkers' from within the heart of the Central Committee establishment included Vadim Zagladin and, especially, Anatoliy Chernyaev. Zagladin was a deputy head of the International Department from 1967, and its First Deputy Head from 1975 until 1988 when he became an adviser to Gorbachev. Chernyaev was a deputy head of the Department from 1970 to 1986. In February of that year he joined the staff of the General Secretary as Gorbachev's principal aide (*pomoshchnik*) on foreign policy. Shakhnazarov, who had earlier been consulted on an ad hoc basis by the General Secretary, became a full-time *pomoshchnik* of Gorbachev in February 1988. Although the office of the General Secretary included other capable people such as Ivan Frolov, and treacherous ones—notably Valeriy Boldin— Chernyaev and Shakhnazarov became Gorbachev's two most important (and most enlightened) aides. Shakhnazarov's responsibilities were to advise the General Secretary not only on Eastern Europe (given his long experience in the Socialist Countries Department) but also on reform of the Soviet political system.

Neither Chernyaev nor Shakhnazarov came remotely close to fitting the popular image of an apparatchik. They maintained links with intellectual circles, including both the cultural intelligentsia and social scientists. They were both among those who frequented the politically and artistically daring productions of the Taganka Theatre, which, under its director, Yuriy Lyubimov, was a constant thorn in the flesh of the Soviet cultural and ideological establishment in the earlier Brezhnev years. Chernyaev and Shakhnazarov were among the party officials who worked behind the scenes (e.g. by going over the head of the Department of Culture of the Central Committee to Brezhnev's closest aides) to protect the theatre from censorship and possible dismemberment. Lyubimov had his supporters also in the scientific and artistic world—among them the renowned physicist Petr Kapitsa and the composer Dmitriy Shostakovich—but relying only on them, Chernyaev notes, Lyubimov would not have been able to stand his ground.[58] (Those who had worked for Andropov—among them Arbatov, Burlatsky, Delyusin and Shakhnazarov—also used their connection with him to intervene on

---

[57] Writing a decade ago, I recorded that Shakhnazarov told me, in an interview I had with him in the Kremlin in December 1991, that his point of view had been that of a social democrat *since the early 1960s*. I added: 'It has to be said that this viewpoint was often very well disguised; equally, it *had* to be unless Shakhnazarov had been prepared to exchange work in the Central Committee apparatus for persecution as a dissident.' See Brown, *The Gorbachev Factor* (Oxford University Press, Oxford, 1996), pp. 339–40.

[58] Chernyaev, *Moya zhizn' i moe vremya*, p. 242.

the Taganka Theatre's behalf. Burlatsky suggests that Andropov may have seen Lyubimov's theatre as a safety valve.[59]) In addition to his links with the artistic and cultural world, Shakhnazarov, a man described by his friend, Fedor Burlatsky, as having 'deep roots in the intelligentsia',[60] had especially close links with the academic community. He was President of the Soviet Association of Political Sciences, a body within which some members, with the encouragement and protection of Shakhnazarov, attempted even in the Brezhnev era to move closer to an objective analysis of politics.[61]

It was important, too, that Shakhnazarov was the *kurator* within the Central Committee of the Institute of Economics of the World Socialist System, perhaps the most radically reformist of all the policy-oriented official institutes in the years immediately preceding perestroika and during it. The Director of the Institute from the time of its foundation until it ceased to exist under that name in the perestroika period (there no longer being even the semblance of a 'world socialist system') was Oleg Bogomolov, a long-standing friend of Shakhnazarov.[62] They had worked together in Yuriy Andropov's team of consultants in the Socialist Countries Department of the Central Committee in the 1960s. The Institute was a classic example of an institution which subverted the role it was designed to play. Its most influential members spent less time impressing on the East-Central Europeans the unique advantages of the Soviet way of doing things and more time learning from the experience of reform—both its successes and failures—in the other European Communist states. Bogomolov himself was a keen observer of economic reform in Eastern Europe. He was also bolder than most Institute Directors, as exemplified by the memorandum his Institute sent to the Central Committee of the CPSU on 20 January 1980 in which they spoke about the

[59] Burlatsky, *Khrushchev and the First Russian Spring* (translated by Daphne Skillen, Weidenfeld & Nicolson, London, 1991), p. 190. No less important, in all probability, was the fact that Andropov's daughter was married to an actor of the Taganka company. See Zhores Medvedev, *Andropov: His Life and Death* (Blackwell, Oxford, rev. edn., 1984), p. 65; and Aleksandr Baygushev, *Russkaya partiya vnutri KPSS* (Algoritm, Moscow, 2005), p. 220. Lyubimov emigrated in 1983 and as late as 1988 it took a special memorandum from Eduard Shevardnadze and Aleksandr Yakovlev for permission to be granted to him to return to the Soviet Union to see his relatives. Even in that letter advocating that permission be granted, Shevardnadze and Yakovlev write disapprovingly of Lyubimov's having made anti-Soviet statements in media appearances, although he had made favourable assessments of the changes underway in others. See HIA, Fond 89, Reel 1.995, opis 19, file 39, memorandum of E. Shevardnadze and A. Yakovlev, 4 May 1988.

[60] Burlatsky, *Khrushchev and the First Russian Spring*, p. 187.

[61] See Hill, op. cit.; and Archie Brown, 'Political Science in the USSR', *International Political Science Review*, Vol. 7, No. 4, October 1986, pp. 443–81.

[62] The institute, which continued to take an interest in developments in Eastern Europe, and with which Bogomolov retained a connection as its honorary president, was renamed the Institute of International Economic and Political Research.

'hopelessness and harmfulness' of the Soviet military intervention in Afghanistan.[63] Yet Bogomolov was self-critical enough to say by 1990 that he should have done more to oppose the system during the 'eighteen years that the party was headed by a dull-witted individual' (meaning, of course, Leonid Brezhnev).[64]

While such a remark reflects well on Bogomolov, it does not necessarily accord with the reality of the dynamics of political change in the Soviet Union. It was to the ultimate advantage of transformative change in the second half of the 1980s that Bogomolov, and others holding positions of authority within the system who harboured critical views, *kept* those posts, and that they did *not*, therefore, publicly call Brezhnev 'dull-witted' during his lifetime. The transformation of an indigenous Communist system[65]—and, indeed, of any consolidated authoritarian regime—is not a simple process. Premature radicalism on the part of its within-system critics would have meant that the balance of forces, when reform got seriously underway a year or more after Gorbachev succeeded Chernenko, would have been tilted significantly further in favour of conservative Communists. Within party-state agencies as a whole, serious reformers were in a minority, but having the General Secretary on their side was a crucial advantage. Gorbachev, however, needed the ideas, support, and, indeed, pressure from the reformist wing of society, almost as much as they needed him, as a counterweight to the forces of inertia and conservatism which were far from easy to overcome.[66]

It is notable how many people from Bogomolov's Institute, who had often stretched official tolerance to its limits (and sometimes beyond) in pre-perestroika times, emerged as important contributors to the public political debate which became especially lively from 1987 onwards. That, as already noted in an earlier chapter, was the year in which Gorbachev became the first person to break the taboo on speaking positively in print of *pluralism*—and only the General Secretary could do this—when he advocated both a 'socialist pluralism' and a 'pluralism of opinion'.[67] From the summer of 1986 and

[63] Bogomolov first drew public attention to the existence of that memorandum in *Literaturna gazeta*, 16 March 1988.

[64] O. Bogomolov, 'Ne mogu snyat' s sebya vinu', *Ogonek*, No. 35, 1990, pp. 2–3.

[65] The transformation of the East European Communist systems could occur much more quickly and easily once fundamental change had taken place in the Soviet polity and in Soviet foreign policy, for the regimes were largely perceived as alien impositions. They were kept in place only by the ultimate threat of Soviet intervention and the risk for the populations of East-Central Europe of making a bad situation worse.

[66] For Bogomolov's own interesting reflections on perestroika, see Oleg Bogomolov, 'Istoricheskiy perelom: razdum'ya ochevidtsa', in V.V. Kuvaldin (ed.), *Proryv k svobode: o perestroyke dvadtsat' let spustya (kriticheskiy analiz)* (Al'pina Biznes Buks, Moscow, 2005), pp. 188–98.

[67] See *Pravda*, 15 July 1987, pp. 1–2, at p. 2; and *Pravda*, 30 September 1987, p. 1. In one of the conversations I have had with Anatoliy Chernyaev, Chernyaev said that he did not think

especially from 1987 onwards a real diversity of political opinion was already in reality gaining expression in parts of the mass media and in the 'thick journals'. One example, which made a huge impact at the time, was the hard-hitting and well-argued attack on the existing Soviet economic system published by Nikolay Shmelev in *Novy mir* in June 1987.[68] Shmelev, the current Director of the Institute of Europe of the Russian Academy of Sciences, worked for some twenty years at Bogomolov's Institute before moving to the Institute of the United States and Canada in 1982. The scholars from Bogomolov's Insitute who made a great impact on the political discourse of the perestroika years did so from various standpoints, though a majority of them were at the time to be found towards the radical end of the political spectrum. They included Yevgeniy Ambartsumov, Anatoliy Butenko, Igor Klyamkin, Otto Latsis, Gennadiy Lisichkin, Andrannik Migranyan, Oleg Rumyantsev, Lilia Shevtsova, Aleksandr Tsipko, and Ruben Yevstigneev.

Latsis, Lisichkin, and Yevstigneev became prominent advocates of market reform in the perestroika years. Klyamkin, Shevtsova, and Rumyantsev were committed democrats, the first two as scholars and commentators, the latter as an active political organizer. Rumyantsev was one of the leaders of the Moscow Democratic Perestroika Club, founded in 1987, and he openly espoused social democratic views as early as that year. He became one of the founders of the Russian Social Democratic Party which was formally created at a congress in Moscow in May 1990.[69] Migranyan was at the centre of controversy with his argument in 1988 and 1989 that in order for Russia to progress to a market economy and democracy a period of enlightened authoritarian rule would be required.[70] Aleksandr Tspiko caused a sensation when he attacked Marx and Lenin (not just Stalin) while holding down a position in the Central Committee apparatus. He was working in Bogomolov's Institute until 1986 when, as he relates, Gorbachev—'at Shakhnazarov's request'—agreed to his joining the apparatus of the Socialist Countries Department of the Central Committee.[71] Tsipko had earlier come to

Gorbachev introduced the term 'pluralism' on the prompting of any of his aides or advisers but very much on his own initiative, as part of his offensive against conservative Communist opponents.

[68] N.P. Shmelev, 'Avansy i dolgi', *Novy mir*, No. 6, 1987, pp. 142–58.

[69] See Alexander Lukin, *The Political Culture of the Russian 'Democrats'* (Oxford University Press, Oxford, 2000), pp. 90–1.

[70] See Igor Timofeyev, 'The Development of Russian Liberal Thought since 1985', in Archie Brown (ed.), *The Demise of Marxism-Leninism in Russia* (Palgrave Macmillan, London, 2004), pp. 70–1 and 110.

[71] Alexander Tsipko, 'The Collapse of Marxism-Leninism' in Michael Ellman and Vladimir Kantorovich (eds.), *The Destruction of the Soviet Economic System: An Insiders' History* (M.E. Sharpe, Armonk, 1998), pp. 169–86, at p. 183.

Gorbachev's attention because he had been attacked by an enemy they had in common, Richard Kosolapov, the highly orthodox editor of the theoretical journal, *Kommunist*.[72] (Gorbachev made sure that Kosolapov was replaced as editor as early as 1986, his successor in the editorial chair being Ivan Frolov who was later to become an aide to Gorbachev and later still editor of *Pravda*.)

Tsipko captures the mood of even the most disillusioned of intellectuals in the Soviet Union in the mid-1980s when he writes:

Perhaps the most important thing to remember about that time is that I never believed that the USSR could quickly and peacefully free itself from Communism, even when perestroika had begun. The ban on the CPSU and the dismantling of the KGB were beyond our expectations. I know of no intellectual in the USSR or abroad who anticipated such a dramatic capitulation of Communism in the Soviet Union. Our inner fear deterred us from even dreaming about such things. Our only hope was the emergence of a new leader, who would come and liberalize the system from above.[73]

The case of Tsipko—who, although explicitly anti-Marxist, is more of a liberal Russian nationalist than liberal or social democrat—is an especially interesting example of institutional amphibiousness. Tsipko says that from his arrival in the Central Committee apparatus he believed 'there was no limit to Gorbachev's ideological flexibility'. In 1988, the Socialist Countries Department he had initially entered was merged into a larger International Department, supervised by Aleksandr Yakovlev, and at this point Tsipko decided 'to spill out all the dormant ideas' he had 'nurtured over the course of many years'.[74]

The first in his series of articles critically discussing both Marx and Lenin and the Communist record in the Soviet Union appeared in the popular science journal *Nauka i zhizn'* in November 1988. Tsipko notes that it was only because he was working in what was at the time still the most authoritative institution within the Soviet Union—the apparatus of the Central Committee of the CPSU—that his articles were accepted for publication. The deputy chief editor of the journal, Rada Adzhubei, who happened to be the daughter of Nikita Khrushchev, took responsibility for publishing them only after both she and the conservative leadership of the censorship office (which was still working, though by now in some confusion) had satisfied themselves that Tsipko was not only employed in the Central Committee apparatus but was also in good standing there. They were relieved to hear that he had close ties with Vadim Medvedev and not only with Aleksandr Yakovlev, since the former was 'perceived to be neither a democrat nor a liberal'.[75]

---

[72] Ibid., pp. 176–8.   [73] Ibid., p. 183.   [74] Ibid.   [75] Ibid., p. 184.

For Glavlit—the censorship office—such a perception was reassuring and a commendation. It was also, from a different perspective, unfair to Medvedev. He was a more cautious reformer than Yakovlev, but he was evolving from the position of reformist Communist into a supporter of democratic socialism (meaning Scandinavian-style social democracy), and both then and subsequently he remained very loyal to Gorbachev.

The most essential point, however, is that it was only because Tsipko was working within the Communist institutional stronghold of the Central Committee that he was able to extend significantly further what it was possible to publish with impunity. As he put it, he conducted his 'argument with Marxism and Communism' legally and, in a paradox dramatically illustrative of institutional amphibiousness, Tsipko says: 'My struggle with the Soviet regime was conducted according to the Soviet rules of the game.' The fact that no one in the Central Committee reprimanded him for his writings set a precedent—'in effect', observes Tsipko, 'legitimizing anti-Communism'.[76]

If a remarkably large proportion of the leading researchers in Bogomolov's Institute were people of independent mind and of a variety of heterodox viewpoints, there were many other institutes which exemplified institutional amphibiousness both before perestroika and in the early stages of its radicalization. IMEMO, which has already been mentioned, was a source of informed advice to the top party leadership (with successive Directors of the institute having access to the General Secretary) and to the International Department of the Central Committee. It had its enemies, however, in the more conservative parts of the Central Committee apparatus and even within the Academy of Sciences of the USSR. Yevgeniy Primakov observes that the Academy could (at least up to a point) be regarded as an 'island of free thought' during 'the years of stagnation', even though a substantial number of the natural scientists—who set the tone in the Academy—were directly or indirectly connected with the military–industrial complex.[77]

---

[76] Ibid., pp. 184–5. There is an irony in the fact that Tsipko's views became quite acceptable to many in the Central Committee apparatus who were *not* reformers. Most of them had very little interest in Marxism. Their outlook was more nationalist and statist. Thus, it was the committed social democrats such as Shakhnazarov who were most unhappy with the direction taken by Tsipko's published reflections, though Yakovlev (who had evolved into a liberal more than a social democrat) was eager to keep Tsipko within the Central Committee apparatus. He remained in the International Department for more than a year after the publication of his controversial articles, 'but as soon as Gorbachev set his mind on revamping the CPSU along social democratic lines, my letter of resignation was accepted' (ibid., p. 186). Tsipko left the Central Committee in March 1990. As of 2006, he is a political columnist on the Writers' Union weekly newspaper *Literaturnaya gazeta*.

[77] Primakov, *Gody v bol'shoy politike*, p. 22.

Primakov argues that IMEMO was an especially non-dogmatic institute, to which 'progressively minded scholars', working in other scholarly establishments, gravitated.[78] From the outset, it is important to note, its connection with politicians in high places was a necessary condition for IMEMO's flourishing as a place of relatively free inquiry. These links provided some protection, though the institute's researchers had to observe the rules of the game in their publications.

The first Director of IMEMO, Anushavan Arzumanyan, who held that office from 1956 to 1965, owed both his appointment and his ability to protect the Institute to the fact that his wife was the sister of the wife of Anastas Mikoyan, one of the most senior members of the Politburo and an ally of Khrushchev. According to Primakov, Arzumanyan hated Stalin, but his connection with Mikoyan made it 'difficult for the party reactionaries to interfere and to turn around the institute'.[79] He might, indeed, have survived the political demise of Khrushchev and Mikoyan, for Arzumanyan had a close connection with Brezhnev going back to the war years, and as IMEMO's historian remarks: 'Brezhnev... not only did not forget old friends, he also promoted them to the highest posts.'[80] Arzumanyan died, however, in 1965. Inozemtsev, appointed his successor in 1966, served throughout almost the whole of the Brezhnev era until his own death in 1982. The arch-reactionary head of the Department of Science in the Central Committee, Sergey Trapeznikov, who was close to Brezhnev, tried more than once to settle scores with Inozemtsev and IMEMO and there were times when he came close to succeeding.

In the early 1980s even the pre-perestroika muted liberalism, or moderate reformism, found in institutes such as IMEMO, the Institute of the United States and Canada, and the Institute of Economics of the World Socialist System, came under severe attack in a conservative backlash, bolstered by the collapse of détente. The struggle for the future orientation of the Soviet Communist Party was closely connected with the clandestine succession struggle, in the light of Brezhnev's very evident physical and mental decline. An attempt to put paid to the relatively free thinking that went on in the best of the policy-oriented institutes was launched by a serious onslaught on IMEMO in 1982. On this occasion not only Trapeznikov but also Moscow Party First Secretary and Politburo member Viktor Grishin were overtly involved in the attack. One consequence was the arrest of two young IMEMO researchers who had been involved in circulating samizdat critical of the imposition of martial law in Poland. They were falsely accused of having links with Western intelligence.[81] On this occasion, as the attack on

[78] Ibid., p. 33. This view of IMEMO is substantiated at length by Cherkasov, *IMEMO*, op. cit.
[79] Primakov, ibid., p. 20.   [80] Cherkasov, *IMEMO*, p. 198.
[81] Primakov, *Gody v bol'shoy politike*, p. 21.

IMEMO broadened, Inozemtsev was unwilling to use his access to Brezhnev, by whom he was often consulted when major speeches or documents on international affairs were being prepared, to contact the General Secretary directly. However, Arbatov and Bovin did so on his behalf. Perhaps for good tactical reasons, they identified Grishin rather than Trapeznikov as the politician who was pressurizing Inozemtsev and his institute. A telephone call from Brezhnev to Grishin ended that particular assault on IMEMO, but the institute's enemies remained.[82]

During the perestroika period many of IMEMO's leading scholars played a significant part in the policy process, able now to express themselves publicly as well as freely. In Inozemtsev's time, Cherkasov observes, there was a kind of 'gentlemen's agreement' whereby the Director would 'guarantee' the institute researchers' freedom of inquiry in return for their observing the 'rules of the game' and doing nothing to undermine the Institute.[83] With each successive year of perestroika, there was less need for self-censorship on the part of *institutchiki* in general, even in their utterances aimed at a broad public. Encouraged to be bold in their analyses, many of the IMEMO researchers responded. Nodari Simonia, who in the past had run into difficulties for deviations from orthodoxy in his published works,[84] was both a new

---

[82] Primakov, *Gody v bol'shoy politike*, p. 22. On that episode, see Arbatov, *The System*, pp. 236–41; and English, *Russia and the Idea of the West*, pp. 170–1. For a fuller account of IMEMO's enemies and friends within the Soviet political establishment, see also Cherkasov, *IMEMO*, esp. pp. 466–530. Some of the IMEMO employees who had to leave the institute because they were senior colleagues within the same departments as the two arrested researchers saw the episode as part of the struggle between Chernenko and Andropov. In that view, not just Grishin and Trapeznikov, but also the more senior Chernenko, were behind the attempt to crack down on the international institutes, since they were perceived to be more supportive of Andropov, a hate figure for Russian nationalists within the party apparatus. Andropov, in turn, had to demonstrate that he was not soft on, or beholden to, liberal *mezhdunarodniki*. The arrest by the KGB of IMEMO employees demonstrated the limits of the protection that could be offered even by such a respected establishment figure as Inozemtsev. This raises a broader issue. In discussing institutional amphibiousness, I have focused on the party officials and party intellectuals who were part of a reformist, social democratic and internationalist tendency. An equally long chapter could be written on the Russian nationalist tendency within the party apparatus and a section of the intelligentsia, much of it directed against the presence, and perceived influence, of Jews within the major Moscow research institutes and in parts of the Central Committee apparatus. A representative of that nationalist group and thus of a very different strand of institutional amphibiousness within an ostensibly Marxist-Leninist party is Aleksandr Baygushev, whose book on the 'Russian party inside the CPSU' sees Soviet political history as largely a struggle between Jews and cosmopolitans, on the one side, and Russian patriots, on the other. Characteristically, Yuriy Andropov figures in this book as 'Andropov-Faynshteyn', his mother's name being Evgeniya Faynshteyn. See Baygushev, *Russkaya partiya vnutri KPSS*, op. cit., pp. 200, 220, 222, 225, 274, 295, 367, 387, and 445.

[83] Cherkasov, *IMEMO*, p. 356.

[84] He was supported, however, by his long-standing friend, Primakov. Simonia worked in the Institute of Oriental Studies from 1958 to 1988, and for some years combined that research post

thinker on foreign policy and a social democrat with his own individual reading of Marx and Lenin. Much later (2000–6) he was to become Director of IMEMO. Other notable new thinkers on international relations were Vladimir Baranovsky and Nikolay Kosolapov, with the latter co-opted by Yakovlev to work with him in the Central Committee. Among the leading economic reformers in IMEMO during perestroika, Primakov picks out Aleksandr Dynkin and Rair Simonyan who, *inter alia*, produced analyses of industrial transformation in advanced Western countries, including Sweden and the Federal Republic of Germany, for Nikolay Ryzhkov and the Council of Ministers.[85]

Among the many other IMEMO researchers deserving of mention, including German Diligensky and Georgiy Mirsky,[86] it would be wrong to overlook a political economist who became an active politician. A notable 'intrastructural dissident' and critic of the Soviet system from long before he joined the staff of IMEMO in 1977, Viktor Sheynis went on to play a significant part in the new pluralist politics. He was elected to the Congress of People's Deputies of the Russian republic, and to its Supreme Soviet, in 1990, and was later to become one of the leading figures in the post-Soviet liberal party, Yabloko. As early as 1956 Sheynis had shown his independence of mind and character when he criticized the Soviet invasion of Hungary. As a punishment he was not allowed to engage in teaching or research for the next eight years, six of which he spent as a factory worker. In 2005 Sheynis published two substantial volumes which are in part political memoirs and in part political analysis entitled 'The Rise and Fall of Parliament: Critical Years in Russian Politics (1985–1993)'.[87]

There were a good many other institutes apart from those already mentioned which exemplified institutional amphibiousness both before

with a professorship at the Institute of Social Sciences. Primakov was Director of the Institute of Oriental Studies from 1977 until 1985 when he returned to IMEMO as Director. (He had been IMEMO's Deputy Director from 1970 to 1977.)

[85] Primakov, *Gody v bol'shoy politike*, p. 27. As of early 2006, Dynkin, Baranovsky and Kosolapov are still at IMEMO—Dynkin as First Deputy Director, Baranovsky as Deputy Director and Kosolapov as a head of department. Simonyan is Chairman of the Board of Morgan Stanley, Russia.

[86] Diligensky and Mirsky were the two most senior members of IMEMO to lose their jobs in 1982 as the heads of department of the two arrested young researchers. However, they both returned to play prominent roles in the institute and in public debate during the perestroika era. From 1988 until his death in June 2002 Diligensky was editor of the institute's journal, *MEMO*. An obituary of him appears in *MEMO*, Vol. 8, August 2002.

[87] They have appeared only in Russian. See Viktor Sheynis, *Vzlet i padenie parlamenta: perelomnye gody v rossiyskoy politike (1985–1993)* (Moscow Carnegie Centre and INDEM Foundation, Moscow, 2005), 2 vols. Sheynis, who was born in 1931, remains an active scholar and professor on the staff of IMEMO as of 2006. He was part of the team which produced the current Russian Constitution, adopted in 1993.

perestroika and in the early stages of its radicalization. One such was the Central-Mathematical Economic Institute (TsEMI), the institutional base of an important politico-economic actor of the Gorbachev era, Nikolay Petrakov. In the Brezhnev years Petrakov ran into trouble on occasion for being too well disposed towards marketizing reforms, but he, nevertheless, held on to the position of Deputy Director of TsEMI from 1965 to the end of 1989 when he was appointed economic adviser to Gorbachev.[88] It was only from the beginning of 1990 that Gorbachev had a professional economist as one of his aides. Petrakov worked with Gorbachev for a year and played a significant part in persuading him, in principle, of the need to move to a market economy. He was part of the team which in the summer of that year produced what was almost certainly an over-optimistic '500-Day Plan' of transition of the Soviet Union from a command to market economy. Gorbachev was excited by the policy and at first supportive, but he subsequently tried to find a compromise between these radical measures and the strong opposition to them of the Chairman of the Council of Ministers, Nikolay Ryzhkov, whose scepticism was shared by most of the governmental and party apparatus.[89] (Petrakov resigned from his position as economic aide in January 1991 and was succeeded by a more cautious Leningrad economist, Oleg Ozherelev.)

An economic institution whose leading members played, in fact, a greater role than TsEMI in the genesis and early development of perestroika is the Institute of Economics and Organization of Industrial Production of the Siberian Academy of Sciences in Novosibirsk. The Institute's Director from 1967 to 1985 when he moved to Moscow to become one of Gorbachev's advisers was Abel Aganbegyan. During the Brezhnev years Aganbegyan received more than one reprimand for his unorthodox views, and he was not allowed to travel to Western countries.[90] One of his most influential colleagues in the early stages of perestroika was Tatyana Zaslavskaya.[91] She was consulted by Gorbachev on occasion when he was the Central Committee Secretary responsible for agriculture—for the first time in April 1982 when

[88] Yegor Gaydar, who attended Petrakov's seminars at TsEMI, noted the atmosphere of 'deideologized, open discussion and sharp formulation of the problems'. See Gaydar, *Dni porazheniy i pobed* (Vagrius, Moscow, 1997), p. 31.

[89] See Brown, *The Gorbachev Factor*, ch. 5; and Gordon M. Hahn, *Russia's Revolution from Above, 1985–2000: Reform, Transition, and Revolution in the Fall of the Soviet Communist Regime* (Transaction Publishers, New Brunswick, NJ, 2002), ch. 5.

[90] Aganbegyan observes: 'Until 1985 I managed to visit only Bulgaria and Hungary—and then only for short periods. And although I went through the due processes several times I was refused exit visas.' See Abel Aganbegyan, *Moving the Mountain: Inside the Perestroika Revolution* (Bantam Press, London, 1989), p. 155.

[91] It was through Zaslavskaya that Aganbegyan was first connected with Gorbachev (as Aganbegyan told me in a conversation I had with him in November 1987).

Brezhnev was still General Secretary. Zaslavskaya achieved fame abroad and unpleasantness at home when a paper she presented to a closed seminar several years before Gorbachev became General Secretary was leaked and published in the West. Its highly critical analysis of Soviet economic and social institutions was along lines which became almost commonplace several years later but they were regarded in orthodox party quarters as heretical before 1985. Zaslavskaya received a party reprimand from her regional party committee, but, like Aganbegyan, moved to Moscow to become part of the reformist establishment after Gorbachev came to power.[92] In 1988 she became the first Director of a new institution of great political importance, the All-Union Centre for the Study of Public Opinion (VTsIOM).[93] It carried out professional survey research on even the most sensitive political issues, including Soviet citizens' perceptions of their country's history and their opinion of the country's political leaders at that time. By publishing the results, it made a huge contribution to glasnost and facilitated better-informed political discussion.

Yet another striking example of institutional amphibiousness was the Institute of Social Sciences, which, as noted earlier in this chapter, came under the direct jurisdiction of the International Department of the Central Committee. Its official role was to teach foreign students, especially from the Third World, with the aim of producing influential Communist propagandists or even (it was hoped) leaders within their home countries. Their teachers, however, included people who had worked in the Central Committee apparatus but had been insufficiently orthodox (or careful) to keep their posts there during the conservative Brezhnev era. Yuriy Krasin, who, as has already been noted, had worked in the International Department, moved to the Institute of Social Sciences in 1975. He was promoted to be Rector of the Institute in 1987, benefiting from the change in the balance of political forces already evident early in the Gorbachev era. He became an informal Gorbachev adviser and in the post-Soviet period worked at the Gorbachev Foundation.

From 1975 until 1989 the head of the Department of Philosophy at the Institute of Social Sciences was Fedor Burlatsky, a prolific writer, astute political analyst, and—in the perestroika period—politician. As early as 1965 he became the first advocate of a separate discipline of political science

---

[92] See the interview with Zaslavskaya in Stephen F. Cohen and Katrina vanden Heuvel in *Voices of Glasnost: Interviews with Gorbachev's Reformers* (Norton, New York, 1989), pp. 115–39.

[93] The establishment of this Institute was warmly welcomed by the most reformist members of the party leadership. At a Politburo meeting held on 8 September 1988, Shevardnadze said that for 15–20 years there had been talk about how it was necessary to study public opinion. 'Thank God', he said, 'that issue has now been resolved precisely and clearly' (HIA, Fond 89, 1.003, opis 42, file 22, p. 182).

in the Soviet Union with an article in *Pravda* which raised hopes that for many years were not fulfilled.[94] A number of his writings in the pre-perestroika years broke new ideological ground and he was adept at saying more between the lines than could be proclaimed overtly. Although no Sinologist, he wrote articles and a book on China which were Aesopian ways of criticizing Soviet reality during the Brezhnev years.[95] This, indeed, was quite a widespread device to which a number of anti-Stalinist Soviet scholars resorted during the Brezhnev years. Open criticism of Stalin and the political regime which developed during his years in power was at that time forbidden, and so 'Mao' in some of these writings was a surrogate for Stalin.[96] The Institute of Social Sciences itself was an example of an overtly ideological, party-sponsored educational establishment which fitted well with Ding's contention that there can be parts of 'the state system' which 'simultaneously work for functions and purposes contradictory to those of the state',[97] given the dominant tendencies within the Soviet state during the Brezhnev era.

Most institutes in the social sciences and humanities, and, indeed, in the natural sciences in the post-Stalin years of the Soviet Union, contained people of a variety of views. Some of these institutes had a preponderance of researchers who were well disposed towards change, while other institutes were predominantly conservative. Even institutes which had a mainly conservative reputation did, however, have their intrastructural dissidents and reflected—albeit to a lesser degree than institutes such as Bogomolov's, Aganbegyan's, Arbatov's, or IMEMO—institutional amphibiousness.

A case in point is the Institute of State and Law of the Academy of Sciences in Moscow. During the directorship of Vladimir Kudryavtsev—from 1976 to 1989—the Institute contained a minority of bold reformers as well as those who more cautiously tried to promote a rule of law. Kudryavtsev himself was much more reform-minded than his predecessor as director, the highly conservative, only partially reconstructed Stalinist, Viktor Chkhikvadze. The institute's journal *Sovetskoe gosudarstvo i pravo* (Soviet State and Law, which continues to be published, though now minus the first word of its old title) contained some innovative work, especially after Mikhail Piskotin became its editor-in-chief in 1978, a post he held until 1987. Although in the later

---

[94] F. Burlatskiy, 'Politika i nauka', *Pravda*, 10 January 1965, p. 4.

[95] See Fedor Burlatskiy, *Mao Tsedun i ego nasledniki* (Mezhdunarodnye otnosheniya, Moscow, 1979).

[96] On this, see Gilbert Rozman, *A Mirror for Socialism: Soviet Criticisms of China* (Princeton University Press, Princeton, NJ, 1985), and Alexander Lukin, *The Bear Watches the Dragon: Russia's Perceptions of China and the Evolution of Russian–Chinese Relations Since the Eighteenth Century* (M.E. Sharpe, Armonk, NJ, 2003). Its title notwithstanding, most of the latter volume is devoted to Russian perceptions of, and relations with, China during the Soviet period.

[97] Ding, 'Institutional Amphibiousness', op. cit., p. 313.

perestroika period and in post-Soviet Russia, Piskotin moved closer to Russian nationalist positions, he was as broad-minded an editor of a journal devoted to sensitive legal and political issues as was feasible prior to perestroika.[98] Some of the boldest articles advocating a socialist market economy to be published in the years immediately preceding perestroika were written by a former KGB colonel on the staff of the Institute of State and Law, Boris Kurashvili. Later he was to become a strong critic of developments in the last years of perestroika, for he truly believed in a *socialist* market economy and was appalled by movement in the direction of capitalism as well as by the breakup of the Soviet Union.

A more root-and-branch critic of the Soviet system, Valeriy Kalensky, published a series of books prior to perestroika which were covertly critical of the Soviet order, but when he turned to overt criticism and wrote letters to the Communist Party leadership criticizing the invasion of Afghanistan and the political exile from Moscow of Academician Andrey Sakharov, he was marginalized within the institute and told by its Director, Kudryavtsev, that he had no future there. He was permitted to emigrate from the Soviet Union to the United States in 1985—on the eve of a period in which he could have given vent to his critical views with impunity.[99]

The Institute of State and Law was the organizational base for the Soviet Association of Political Sciences which made some modest progress towards more objective study of politics before perestroika. The fact that the President of the association, Georgiy Shakhnazarov, was a senior official within the Central Committee apparatus gave the organization a measure of protection. The achievements of the association were, however, more at a conceptual than an empirical level up until the mid-1980s, although Aleksandr Obolonsky— one of the few senior researchers in the Institute of State and Law who never joined the Communist Party—was able to begin serious study of bureaucracy in the unreformed Soviet Union by focusing his detailed research on the administration of Soviet sport.[100] Another Institute researcher, who was later

[98] Following the establishment of the new legislature in 1989, Piskotin was appointed editor-in-chief of its official journal, *Narodnyy deputat*. A letter in the Central Committee archives proposing him for that post was written by Anatoliy Lukyanov on 5 October 1989. (See HIA, Fond 89, 1.999, opis 30, file 15.) Lukyanov was at that time First Deputy Chairman of the Supreme Soviet. He had long-standing links with the Institute of State and Law and good relations with Piskotin personally.

[99] On Kalensky's writings, see Archie Brown, 'Political Science in the USSR', *International Political Science Review*, Vol. 7, No. 4, 1986, pp. 443–81; and Brown (ed.), *The Demise of Marxism-Leninism in Russia*, op. cit., pp. 5–6 and 22.

[100] Even with sport as his case study, Obolonsky was refused permission to publish most of the empirical data he had gathered. See, however, A.V. Obolonskiy and V.D. Rudashevskiy, *Metodologiya sistemnogo issledovaniya problem gosudarstvennogo upravleniya* (Nauka, Moscow, 1978); and see also the innovative article by Obolonsky, 'Formal'nye i neformal'nye

to become head of its political science section, William Smirnov, played a significant role in the institutionalization of the controversial discipline of *politologiya* (political science) as General Secretary of the Soviet Association of Political Sciences, working closely with Shakhnazarov.[101] Smirnov was the main organizer of the triennial congress of the International Political Science Association when it was held (for the first time in a Communist country) in Moscow in 1979. The event brought many hundreds of 'bourgeois' political analysts to Moscow and led the KGB to cordon off the Moscow University rooms in which the meetings were held for fear of ideological contamination. Some contamination, however, undoubtedly occurred.[102] Shakhnazarov had, indeed, struggled hard to get the event approved by the Soviet leadership who were concerned that the event would attract Sovietologists.[103]

In view of the lack of opportunity for, and legitimacy of, independent political activity prior to Gorbachev's coming to power, many people of ability with an interest in politics and life in foreign countries worked in policy-oriented research institutes where Communist Party membership generally went with the job. Even more important, as has already been emphasized in this chapter, was the minority of talented people of reformist disposition who worked within the Central Committee apparatus. Aleksandr Yakovlev and Vadim Medvedev, who held the highest political ranks during the perestroika period, were two strikingly important examples of Soviet-style 'in-and-outers'. In between their spells in the Central Committee apparatus both men spent time in policy-related academic institutes.[104] It was especially important for Gorbachev that Yakovlev was not only someone whose ideas chimed with his own, but that he knew the Central Committee apparatus from the inside. Having given Yakovlev the opportunity to refresh his

gruppy v apparate gosudarstvennogo upraveleniya', *Sovetskoe gosudarstvo i pravo*, No. 5, May 1983, pp. 28–35.

[101] For Smirnov's observations on the key role played by Shakhnazarov, see 'Politicheskaya nauka v Rossii: vchera, segodnya, zavtra. Materialy nauchnogo seminara', *Polis*, No. 1, 2006, pp. 141–2.

[102] As a participant in that congress, I can both testify to the heavy presence of the KGB and vouch for the useful interaction between Soviet and Western scholars which, nevertheless, took place.

[103] Early in the post-Soviet period Shakhnazarov told me that the response he encountered in the party leadership in the 1970s, when the issue of holding the International Political Science Congress in Moscow was broached, was: 'Politolog znachit sovetolog znachit antisovetchik' ('Political scientist means sovietologist which means an anti-Soviet').

[104] As already noted, Yakovlev was Director of IMEMO from 1983 to 1985. Medvedev was Rector of the Academy of Social Sciences of the Central Committee—a different establishment from the Institute of Social Sciences which was merely 'pri TsK'—from 1978 to 1983. The main task of the Academy of Social Sciences was to provide further education for Soviet domestic Communist Party cadres. Medvedev re-entered the Central Committee apparatus as head of the Department of Science and Education (1983–6) before rising significantly higher.

intellectual batteries as Director of IMEMO, along with an advisory role to him during his two years there,[105] Gorbachev lost no time in bringing Yakovlev back into the Central Committee building once he had succeeded Chernenko.

Yakovlev and Medvedev knew each other of old. Medvedev had taught economics in Leningrad before becoming in 1968 the secretary of the Leningrad city party organization responsible for ideology. He moved to the Central Committee in Moscow in 1970 as a deputy head of the Propaganda Department where until 1973 his immediate superior was Aleksandr Yakovlev. In the Gorbachev era not only Yakovlev but Medvedev, too (although less dramatically), received unusually rapid promotion to Secretaryships of the Central Committee and full membership of the Politburo.[106]

CONCLUSIONS

In the early years of the development of perestroika, especially between 1986 and 1988, the most striking examples of institutional amphibiousness were to be found in very high places, indeed—not just in the major institutes, as has been elaborated in the preceding pages and not only in one or two particular departments of the Central Committee. They were to be found also within the Secretariat of the Central Committee and, even more pertinently, in the office of the General Secretary. Already in the opening chapter of this book, I have drawn attention to the struggle between conflicting tendencies at the top of the Communist Party which was present throughout the perestroika period, even though it was less immediately obvious than the stand-off between the party and the openly oppositional forces which emerged in the last years of the Soviet Union. Far from speaking with one voice, the Secretariat of the Central Committee sent out different signals to the party and society, with Yegor Ligachev representing more traditional views and Yakovlev helping to extend the boundaries of the permissible, not least through appointments in the mass media and his backing for editors who took maximum advantage of Gorbachev's policy of glasnost. While some authors have argued that elite consensus is a requirement of transition from authoritarian rule, there was no greater stimulus to political pluralism in the Soviet Union than the overt elite dissension embodied by the leadership of the Communist Party during

[105] Yakovlev was a member of the group Gorbachev brought to Britain in December 1984, during which the future General Secretary had his momentous first meeting with Prime Minister Margaret Thatcher.

[106] As noted in chapter 1 (n. 39), Gorbachev elevated Medvedev above Yakovlev within the Secretariat in late 1989.

perestroika. According to their own disposition, editors and commentators could take their cue from different Secretaries of the Central Committee.

The views of the General Secretary had, of course, the greatest resonance. One of the paradoxes of perestroika was that a combination of the extremely *hierarchical* nature of the Soviet system, the *authority* traditionally accorded the top party leader, and the *power* of appointment enjoyed by the General Secretary facilitated Gorbachev's dismantling of the pillars of the system he had been bequeathed and the secularization of the party through whose ranks he had risen. In some ways Ding's 'systemic ambiguity and double identity' were to be found in Gorbachev's own person. As was noted during the perestroika years, he was both Pope and Luther. As General Secretary of the CPSU, he was expected to defend Marxist-Leninist holy writ. Yet, as a reformer by disposition who by 1988 had turned into a systemic transformer, he rejected more and more of Lenin*ism*, a point that is elaborated in chapter ten. At the same time, Gorbachev retained more respect for Lenin (viewing the late Lenin as a reformer who had seen the error of his earlier ways) than the latter deserved.[107] Or as John Gooding aptly observed: 'At once insider and outsider, apparatchik and revolutionary, true believer and iconoclast, [Gorbachev] would use his ambivalence as a vitally effective political weapon.'[108] The General Secretaryship (whose staff included, on the one hand, the future putschist Valeriy Boldin and, on the other hand, Chernyaev and Shakhnazarov) turned out to be the most important example of institutional amphibiousness of all.

In the later years of perestroika there *was* a burgeoning civil society, but the real breakthrough in the dismantling of the Communist system occurred at the Nineteenth Party Conference in 1988.[109] The decisions to pluralize the

---

[107] Surprisingly perhaps, even in his recent book, Gorbachev writes: 'I trusted Lenin, and trust him now.' He goes on to make clear that it is Lenin in his last years he most approves of, the Lenin of NEP who recognized that serious mistakes had been made. Gorbachev adds that there is no need to make an idol of Lenin. See Mikhail Gorbachev, *Ponyat' perestroiku... pochemu eto vazhno seychas* (Al'pina Biznes Buks, Moscow, 2006), pp. 17–18. Yet Gorbachev's reluctance to give up his life-long respect for Lenin sits oddly with the development of his own social democratic views and, indeed, with his opinion (expressed in a television interview with Clive Anderson during his visit to Britain in October 1996) that the Bolshevik Revolution was a mistake, that the February Revolution of 1917 was enough, and that the various socialist and democratic forces should thereafter have found a way of working together. I have more to say about Gorbachev's relationship to Lenin and Leninism in Chapter 10.

[108] Gooding, 'Perestroika as Revolution from Within: An Interpretation', *The Russian Review*, Vol. 51, No. 1, 1992, pp. 36–57, at p. 38.

[109] As late as December 1987 even the leading reformers within the Soviet leadership, among them Yakovlev and Shevardnadze, remained suspicious of former dissidents taking civil society initiatives. Yakovlev and Shevardnadze were co-signatories with KGB Chairman Viktor Chebrikov and Central Committee Secretary Lev Zaykov of a secret memorandum proposing ways to scupper the initiative of a group of citizens, who had clashed with the authorities in

political system were taken by Gorbachev and a group of informal advisers, including *some* members of the Politburo and not others.[110] The fact that the Yakovlevs, Chernyaevs, and Shakhnazarovs were available, when perestroika was launched, to be co-opted from senior positions to posts of still greater authority and influence was of crucial importance. Neither a party versus society nor a state versus civil society dichotomy does justice to the complex reality. An examination of the origins and early development of perestroika adds weight to Ding's contention that 'as an analytical concept institutional amphibiousness has the broadest applicability in late communist societies and can help us understand the dynamic processes of the transition'.[111]

pre-perestroika times, who were preparing to hold an international seminar on human rights in Moscow. The authors of the document, however, proposed more subtle ways than in the past to minimize the impact of the seminar, arguing that this 'provocation' would damage the Soviet authorities not only if it succeeded and set a new precedent for the breadth of glasnost, but also if it were to be stopped, for that would be turned into an 'anti-Soviet sensation'. See 'O namerenii antiobshchestvennykh elementov provesti v Moskve tak nazyvaemyy "seminar" po pravam cheloveka', HIA, Fond 89, 1.995, opis 19, file 37.

[110] Yakovlev and Medvedev were frequent participants in the narrower and informal group discussions, which Gorbachev convened outside Moscow at weekends, in which many of the innovative ideas, such as those which went into the documents presented to the Nineteenth Party Conference, were discussed. Chernyaev, Frolov, Primakov, and Shakhnazarov were also often present, as was Gorbachev's chief of staff, Valeriy Boldin, whose later disloyalty came as a particular shock to Gorbachev.

[111] Ding, 'Institutional Amphibiousness', p. 318. I have been concerned in this chapter primarily with the period up to and including 1988. While arguing for the greater relevance of institutional amphibiousness as compared with civil society in interpreting political processes of that time, I would not wish for a moment to deny the significance of a developing civil society in the later perestroika years and the great importance of institutions independent of the state such as the 'Democratic Russia' movement during 1990–1.

7

The Dismantling of the System and the Disintegration of the State[1]

It is frequently asserted that the Soviet Union was unreformable, but as earlier chapters of this book have shown, a vast amount of reform took place during the perestroika years. Some of those who argued prior to perestroika that serious reform could not occur in the Soviet Union subsequently modified that position to say that what they really meant was that it could not ultimately be successful. Whether even that modified claim holds water depends on the criteria one adopts for measuring success. Does the advent of political pluralism and the introduction of a wide range of freedoms, including freedom of speech and association, and cultural and religious freedom, count for less than the fact that fifteen states now stand on the territory where one stood before? Opinions vary also on how the disintegration of the Soviet state should be evaluated, as they do on the question whether it was an ineluctable consequence of radical reform of the system or whether the greater part of the Union could have been reconstructed and preserved had a handful of political actors behaved differently.

The late Alexander Dallin and Stephen Cohen are among those who have noted the oversimplifications and 'retrospective determinism' characteristic of much writing on the end of the Soviet system and of the Soviet Union.[2] Cohen rightly points out that reform occurred at various times in Soviet history and that many of those who say the USSR was 'unreformable' are simply not using 'reform' in the normal sense of the term. Cohen, however,

[1] This chapter is a revised and expanded version of an article entitled 'The Soviet Union: Reform of the System or Systemic Transformation?', published in *Slavic Review*, Vol. 63, No. 3, 2004, pp. 489–504.

[2] As Dallin put it: 'To claim that the Soviet system was bound to collapse amounts to committing what Reinhard Bendix . . . called "the fallacy of retrospective determinism"— denying the choices (however constrained) that the actors had available before acting.' See Alexander Dallin, 'Causes of the Collapse of the USSR', *Post-Soviet Affairs*, Vol. 8, No. 4, pp. 279–302, esp. pp. 296–300; and Stephen F. Cohen, 'Was the Soviet System Reformable?', *Slavic Review*, Vol. 63, No. 3, Fall 2004, pp. 459–88. See also Archie Brown, *The Gorbachev Factor* (Oxford University Press, Oxford, 1996), esp. pp. 315–18.

is also among those who at times conflates *system* and *state*—the issue of whether the system was reformable and that of whether a Union could have been maintained.[3]

On a normal understanding of the meaning of reform, there is no doubt that this occurred at various times in Soviet history. Nikita Khruschchev's reforms significantly modified the way the system worked and minor reform took place under Leonid Brezhnev and Aleksey Kosygin. Aside from Kosygin's modest economic reform of 1965, it was no trivial change when the mass terror of 'high Stalinism' was replaced from the late 1950s onwards by a regime in which people could retreat into their private lives and be reasonably sure they would not be arrested because of anonymous denunciation or the political police's need to fill a quota. This undoubted advance, which was accompanied by an improvement in living standards, did not come even remotely close to creating a civil society, still less a democratic polity, but for the Soviet citizen the difference between life in 1938 and 1978 was not trivial. The changes that occurred after the death of Stalin made life more predictable and more bearable, even though, paradoxically, there were almost certainly more true believers in a radiant future during the worst years of mass terror than forty years later.

It is also far from inconsequential that a freedom of speech in private developed two to three decades before the freedom of speech in public of the second half of the 1980s. A Russian literary scholar of dissident views, Leonid Pinsky, made an important point when he gave much of the credit for this to Khrushchev's house-building programme that enabled large numbers of people to acquire for the first time a front door they could close to the outside world.[4] When communal apartments gave way to self-contained flats, conversation was liberated. There was a new freedom among trusted friends to say exactly what they thought about their society or to make jokes about their leaders. While that could reasonably be regarded as an unintended political consequence of social policy, it was accompanied also by a change of attitude on the part of the authorities. Critical views in private did not always go unnoticed, and they could deprive an individual of the chance of promotion, but they were no longer likely to lead to imprisonment or worse.

Moreover, to all but the ideologically blinkered, it was obvious that explicitly political reform, and *major* reform at that, occurred under Gorbachev

---

[3] On this point, see also Mark Kramer, 'The Reform of the Soviet System and the Demise of the Soviet State', *Slavic Review*, Vol. 63, No. 3, Fall 2004, pp. 505–12.

[4] In a conversation I had with him in Moscow in 1976. On the high-speed (if low-quality) apartment-block building boom under Khrushchev which was particularly notable in Moscow, see Timothy J. Colton, *Moscow: Governing the Socialist Metropolis* (Harvard University Press, Cambridge, MA, 1995), pp. 367–76.

even before it evolved into transformative change. Conservative politicians on both sides of the Atlantic, such as Ronald Reagan and Margaret Thatcher, together with Secretary of State George Shultz and Foreign Secretary Sir Geoffrey Howe, were among those who recognized this, even if others, such as Robert M. Gates of the CIA and Dick Cheney, the first Defense Secretary of President Bush, were slow to appreciate the fundamental character of the changes Gorbachev was, by the summer of 1988, introducing into the Soviet system.[5] Politicians were not helped towards understanding by writers who defined all Communist regimes as totalitarian and simultaneously argued that whereas authoritarian regimes could be changed from within, totalitarian regimes could not.[6] The revolutionary change that occurred from below in Hungary in 1956, the radical reform that took place from within the Communist Party of Czechoslovakia in 1968, and the rise of Solidarity in Poland a further twelve years later were all indigenous movements and they were stopped not by the internal strength of the regimes but by Soviet intervention in the first two cases and the veiled threat of intervention in the third. Had the Soviet leadership taken the non-interventionist position that Gorbachev adopted in 1989, systemic change in East-Central Europe would have occurred much earlier.

For many years there was a useful subdiscipline in political science that bore the name, 'Comparative Communism'. This recognized not only that Communist systems had a number of defining features in common but also that there were very important differences among them—not least, the extent to which they had been reformed. In the later Kádár years, Hungary was still an authoritarian state but it was a relatively mild authoritarianism in

---

[5] See Jack F. Matlock, Jr., *Reagan and Gorbachev: Ending the Cold War* (Random House, New York, 2004); Ronald Reagan, *An American Life* (Simon & Schuster, New York, 1990); George P. Shultz, *Triumph and Turmoil: My Years as Secretary of State* (Scribners, New York, 1993); Robert M. Gates, *From the Shadows* (Simon & Schuster, New York, 1996); Margaret Thatcher, *The Downing Street Years* (HarperCollins, London, 1993); and Geoffrey Howe, *Conflict of Loyalty* (Macmillan, London, 1994).

[6] An influential exponent of such a view was Jeane Kirkpatrick. In her article, 'Dictatorship and Double Standards', *Commentary*, November 1979, she wrote: 'Although there is no instance of a revolutionary "socialist" or Communist society being democratized, right-wing autocracies do sometimes evolve into democracies—given time, propitious economic, social, and political circumstances, talented leaders, and a strong indigenous demand for representative government' (p. 37). The historical generalization became a prediction when she observed (p. 44): '[T]he history of this century provides no grounds for expecting that radical totalitarian regimes will transform themselves.' Kirkpatrick notes, in a later publication: 'It was spring 1989 before I concluded that Gorbachev did in fact desire sweeping internal reforms of the Soviet system and also that he "needed" international peace to pursue them' (Jeane J. Kirkpatrick, *The Withering Away of the Totalitarian State... and Other Surprises*, American Enterprise Institute, Washington, DC, 1990), p. 24.

comparison even with Husák's Czechoslovakia, not to speak of Ceauşescu's Romania (whether one calls that regime 'totalitarian' or 'Sultanistic'[7]) or Hoxha's Albania.[8] In particular, the reforms in Hungarian agriculture, introducing market elements and increasing the independence of the peasantry, raised living standards in the countryside and greatly improved the supply of foodstuffs to the towns.[9]

Change within the countries that belonged to the Warsaw Pact was constrained, however, by the limits of tolerance of the Soviet leadership in Moscow. Thus, until the dramatic changes of the perestroika era, the question whether there could be a viable reformed Communism was not fully tested. What was called the 'Brezhnev doctrine' encapsulated the Soviet leadership's self-appointed right to intervene to 'defend socialism' in any part of 'the socialist commonwealth' where 'socialism' was under threat.[10] If, however, the system which Soviet leaders called 'socialist' was to be threatened within the Soviet Union itself, no one else was going to send troops to sustain it. Thus, the Soviet Union was the ultimate testing-ground of the limits of reform. A reformed Communism could not, I believe, have been a lasting settlement, and the whole issue of *reform of the system* versus *systemic transformation* becomes clearer if we use the term 'Communist' for the polity and economy that existed in the Soviet Union until the late 1980s rather than 'socialist'.

Whether a Soviet Union could have been held together is a separate issue. After, first, addressing the terminological and conceptual problem (Communism or socialism), I shall look at the issue of reform versus transformation (or dismantling) of the *system* before going on to consider whether the complete breakup of the Soviet *state* was unavoidable once a process of democratization was underway. In doing so, I shall refer to the major decisions that could have gone the other way and ask how much of a difference that might have made.

---

[7] Or 'totalitarianism-cum-sultanism', in the terminology of Juan Linz and Alfred Stepan. See Linz and Stepan, *Problems of Democratic Transition and Consolidation: Southern Europe, South America, and Post-Communist Europe* (Johns Hopkins University Press, Baltimore, MD, 1966), pp. 344–65.

[8] See Juan Linz, *Totalitarian and Authoritarian Regimes* (Lynne Rienner, Boulder CO, 2000) and Archie Brown, 'The Study of Totalitarianism and Authoritarianism' in Jack Hayward, Brian Barry and Archie Brown (eds.), *The British Study of Politics in the Twentieth Century* (Oxford University Press for the British Academy, Oxford, 1999), pp. 345–94.

[9] On the Hungarian economic reforms—which got underway in the late 1960s—see, for a useful contemporary account, William F. Robinson, *The Pattern of Reform in Hungary: A Political, Economic and Cultural Analysis* (Praeger, New York, 1973). For an insightful work completed just at the point at which a Communist system in Hungary ceased to exist, see Elemér Hankiss, *East European Alternatives* (Oxford University Press, Oxford, 1990); and for a major study conducted in the post-Communist period, see Rudolf L. Tőkés, *Hungary's Negotiated Revolution: Economic Reform, Social Change, and Political Succession, 1957–1990* (Cambridge University Press, Cambridge, 1996).

[10] See Jaromír Navrátil (ed.), *The Prague Spring 1968: A National Security Archive Documents Reader* (Central European University Press, Budapest, 1998), pp. 502–3.

COMMUNIST SYSTEMS

The five defining characteristics of Communist systems can be summarized as (1) the monopoly of power of the Communist Party; (2) democratic centralism; (3) state ownership of the means of production; (4) the declared aim of building communism—a society in which the state would have withered away—as the ultimate, legitimizing goal; and (5) the existence of, and sense of belonging to, an international Communist movement.[11] The fact that Communist leaders and ideologists in the unreformed Soviet Union, and in other Communist states, described their systems as 'socialist' is hardly a good reason for following suit. The same Communist leaders and guardians of ideology described their systems as 'democratic'. 'Socialist democracy' and 'Soviet democracy' were used almost interchangeably in the pre-perestroika USSR. Few Western analysts would wish to accept the description by Soviet leaders and ideologists of their system as 'democratic'. While to call the system 'socialist' is less evidently absurd, the fact that this is what the system was named by Soviet politicians and theoreticians up until the later years of perestroika[12] is not a sufficient ground for adopting it as an analytically useful term.

The adjective 'socialist' is applicable to a far wider range of social movements, political parties, and governments than those which have professed allegiance to Marxism-Leninism.[13] It is a less discriminating term than

[11] The points are elaborated in Archie Brown, 'Communism', in N.J. Smelser and Paul B. Baltes (eds.), *International Encyclopedia of the Social and Behavioral Sciences* (Pergamon, Oxford, 2001), pp. 2323–5; and also Brown, *The Gorbachev Factor*, pp. 309–15.

[12] Gorbachev, at the beginning of his General Secretaryship, regarded the system as 'socialist', albeit a flawed socialism in need of reform. He subsequently came to embrace a social democratic conception of socialism and, as a corollary, held that the Soviet Union had never been socialist. The change in Gorbachev's position was a gradual one. As he put it in conversation with one of his oldest friends: 'But to deny the idea that the Soviet system was identical with socialism, to deny that it embodied the advantages of socialism, I reached that point only after 1983, and not all at once even then': Mikhail Gorbachev and Zdeněk Mlynář, *Conversations with Gorbachev: On Perestroika, the Prague Spring, and the Crossroads of Socialism* (Columbia University Press, New York, 2002), p. 65. Gorbachev also observed: '[I]n 1985, and for some time after that, our desire was to improve, to make more socialist a system that was not truly socialist.... It is a big step forward that we are no longer trying to create ideal models and force the life of our society to fit into a preconceived mold. We have eliminated totalitarian governmental power, provided freedom of choice and democratic pluralism, and that is the main thing for the cause of socialism, which is inseparable from democracy' (ibid., p. 200).

[13] It is worth noting that the meaning of 'socialism' for the socialist parties of Western Europe has also changed. Few in the leadership of any of the mainstream parties that belong to the Socialist International believe any more in the possibility of building a distinctive socio-economic system that would bear the name of socialism. 'Socialism', in so far as they continue to use the term (and it is used less today by the leadership of the British Labour Party than by their Socialist International counterparts in continental Europe) has come to mean different values and priorities rather than an entirely distinctive system. Gorbachev reached a similar

'Communist' to apply to the Soviet Union and those countries recognized by it as forming part of the international Communist movement. It is not difficult to distinguish between a Communist (with a capital 'C') system and (lower-case) 'communism', the stateless utopia that provided the ultimate justification for the 'leading role' of Communist Parties, since it was the Party, as Lenin had argued, that provided the theoretical insight and organizational basis to guide less advanced citizens to this harmonious, classless society. (It is doubtful, of course, whether there was a single true believer in this mythical future society in Brezhnev's Politburo in the 1970s, but that is not to deny its remaining ideological significance—until it was abandoned even as a theoretical construct in the late 1980s, as part of a wider rejection of Marxism-Leninism.[14]) There should be little danger of confusing the Communism of actually existing Communist systems (*real'nyy sotsializm* in the terminology of Brezhnev's Soviet Union) with the utopia of 'full communism'. There is, however, vast conceptual stretching, and blurring of crucial distinctions, involved in applying the same term, 'socialist', to, for example, socialist governments in Fifth Republic France and to the Soviet government pre-Gorbachev. It is more precise, as well as far less misleading, to apply the term 'Communist' to the latter. Many Western analysts have refused to accept the official Soviet terminology of 'socialist' as an apt term for Communist Party dictatorship, and they feel no need for concern that this causes discomfort to surviving, unreconstructed Communists (and perhaps also to those from a very different point in the political spectrum who are happy, for opportunistic reasons, to blur the distinction between the 'socialism' espoused by social democrats and the 'socialism' once defended by the KGB).

The use of the term 'socialism' to describe the Soviet system can be a major source of misunderstanding when, for instance, one reads that Mikhail Gorbachev's views remained essentially unchanged, because he continued to proclaim support for 'socialism'.[15] This is a view expressed much more in

position. As he put it in conversation with his close friend, Zdeněk Mlynář: 'I see that it was wrong from the start to regard socialism as a special formation that represents something historically inevitable in the development of humankind. My whole experience has convinced me that a value-based conception of socialism is more correct. It is a process in which people seek to realize certain values, and in this process all progressive and democratic ideas and practical experiences are integrated' (Gorbachev and Mlynář, *Conversations with Gorbachev*, New York, 2002, pp. 154–5).

[14] See Archie Brown (ed.), *The Demise of Marxism-Leninism in Russia* (Palgrave Macmillan, Basingstoke, 2004); and Robert D. English, *Russia and the Idea of the West: Gorbachev, Intellectuals, and the End of the Cold War* (Columbia University Press, New York, 2000).

[15] For a recent example of this elementary error, see Leon Aron, 'The "Mystery" of the Soviet Collapse', *Journal of Democracy*, Vol. 17, No. 2, April 2006, pp. 21–35, where he writes (p. 29): 'Gorbachev hardly changed. Until his resignation in December 1991, he firmly believed in the "socialist choice" of the Russian people and was given to quoting Lenin.'

the United States and in Russia than in Western Europe, and there is a good reason for that. Neither the United States nor Russia, in sharp contrast with Western Europe, has experience of successful democratic socialist political parties. Accordingly, fewer scholars in these countries see the importance of maintaining a clear distinction between Communism and the variety of democratic beliefs and practices which the concept of socialism has embraced in the European experience. The fact that Gorbachev had moved from being an adherent of Soviet-style 'socialism' to believing in the superiority of the kind of 'socialism' exemplified by mainstream West European social democratic parties amounted to a spectacular political evolution. Even as normally perceptive an analyst as Valerie Bunce is led astray when she writes of Gorbachev's 'overriding concern' with 'saving Soviet socialism and protecting his reforms....'[16] This is to miss the qualitative change represented by Gorbachev's embrace of a social democratic variant of socialism, the significance of which is obscured when seen simply as a continuing attachment to 'socialism'.[17]

COMMUNIST ECONOMY TO ECONOMIC LIMBO

It is abundantly clear that those who held that the Soviet Union could not be changed from within—and changed radically—were wrong. While, however,

[16] Valerie Bunce, *Subversive Institutions: The Design and Destruction of Socialism and the State* (Cambridge University Press, New York, 1999), p. 134.

[17] Endorsing the view that the Soviet regime and those modelled on it should be called Communist rather than socialist, Andrew Roberts observes: 'Reasoned debate, not to mention efficient scholarly communication, requires that we distinguish the unique regimes of eastern Europe from other regime types. More self-conscious labelling of regime types may help us to accomplish this. Words do matter both in politics and scholarship.' See Roberts, 'The State of Socialism: A Note on Terminology', *Slavic Review*, Vol. 63, No. 2, Summer 2004, pp. 349–66, at p. 366. Gorbachev, as he made clear on innumerable occasions, was acutely conscious of different meanings of socialism, including the extent to which the appeal to 'socialism' could be a rationalization of vested interests or a veiled defence of Stalin's despotism. In one of a series of meetings he held with obkom first secretaries in April 1988, Gorbachev referred to a letter he had been sent by a pensioner in the Crimea, accusing him of having 'the aim to destroy everything that was created by Iosif Vissarionovich [Stalin]'. Gorbachev responded: 'But he "created" also the year 1937' (it was in 1937–8 that the purges reached their height). In essence, Gorbachev said, this call for a return to class war was the message also of the Nina Andreeva letter: 'In a word, give us again "the year 1937"'. The Andreeva letter was an attack on Gorbachev's reforms published in the newspaper, *Sovetskaya Rossiya*, on 13 March 1988 with the support of influential elements within the Central Committee apparatus. It was the backing for this reactionary point of view from within the Communist Party bureaucracy that concerned Gorbachev. Addressing the party secretaries, he said: 'Andreeva—God be with her! But if any of you share her philosophy, you had better get out!' ('Vstrecha Gorbacheva s tret'ey gruppoy sekretarey obkomov, 18 Aprelya 1988 goda', Chernyaev notes, Gorbachev Foundation Archives).

some reform of the economy took place in the USSR and other Communist states at different times, radical reform posed fundamental problems connected with the operational principles of the systems and exacerbated, in the Soviet case, by some special circumstances peculiar to Russia. Robert Dahl has persuasively argued not only that a command economy is incompatible with democracy but that this applies also to a pure market economy.[18] He observes: 'Historically, all democratic countries have developed mixed economies in which markets, though highly important, are significantly modified by government intervention'.[19] This is partly in response to the activities of groups defending interests that would be too severely damaged if the market were the *only* criterion for authoritative economic decision-making.

An economy may be essentially a command economy, operating on the basis of administrative allocation of resources, but some concessions will be made to the law of supply and demand—for example, the existence of private tuition even in the unreformed Soviet Union. In a market economy it is axiomatic that prices are not determined administratively, but business is always (and rightly) subject to a degree of state regulation. A mixed economy exists, to a greater or lesser degree, in all essentially market economies. It may well involve elements of public ownership, such as nationalized railways or municipally owned airports, and will generally include extensive state intervention to modify the workings of the market, such as high taxes on tobacco to discourage use of substances damaging to health—and more recently, in many countries with essentially market economies, legislation to prevent smoking in restaurants and bars.

However, although pure models do, indeed, exist only in textbooks, an economic system must be *primarily* one thing or another. Despite the modifications to the ideal types of a command economy and a market economy which exist in the real world, the latter has a different logic from the former. To move from a command economy to a market economy is a fundamental shift, fully deserving use of the term 'transition'. In the Soviet Union there was a basic tension between trying to *make the existing economic system work better* and *replacing that system by an essentially market economy* which would operate on *different principles*. As a result, much of the well-intentioned economic legislation of the Gorbachev era—for example, the Law on the State Enterprise of 1987 and the Law on Co-operatives of 1988—had unintended consequences. In a command economy as long-established as the

---

[18] Robert A. Dahl, 'Why All Democratic Countries Have Mixed Economies', in John W. Chapman and Ian Shapiro (eds.), *Democratic Community* (New York University Press, New York, 1993), pp. 259–82.

[19] Ibid., p. 259.

Soviet one there was no easy way of making the transition from one system to another, as the experience of post-Soviet Russia has only served to underline. At some point most prices had to become essentially market prices and the attempt to improve the pre-existing 'administrative-command system' had to give way to its replacement by a regulated market economy (although Gorbachev was subjected to much ignorant criticism for attaching the word 'regulated' to 'market economy').

Notwithstanding the fact, however, that the goal of an essentially market economy had been embraced by Gorbachev by 1989, the economic system between then and the end of the Soviet Union was neither one thing nor another. The country's economy was in limbo—no longer a functioning command economy but not yet a market economy. The reforms had introduced what were, from the standpoint of central planners, perverse incentives, while market institutions remained weak and the crucial marketizing measure of freeing the majority of prices was postponed. In *this* sense the Soviet economic system was unreformable. Partial reforms could and did take place, but the operating principles of an economic system have to be, *in the main*, one thing or another. To point to the dilemma is not to suggest that there was an easy solution. To add to the systemic problem, there were Russian specifics which made economic transition far more difficult in the Soviet Union than in the countries of East-Central Europe. Not only had the administrative-command system been operating for far longer, but the size and climatic conditions of Russia, coupled with the inheritance left by Soviet planning, imposed (and still impose) far greater difficulties even for politicians eager to embrace the market than is the case, for instance, in Hungary or the Czech Republic. The work of Fiona Hill and Clifford Gaddy, analysing the heavy economic burden of extensive urban development in Siberia, eloquently illustrates the point.[20] Dahl's observations about the prohibitive social and political costs of observing *only* market economic criteria are fully applicable to this case.[21] Entire cities, even if they have no prospect of becoming economically viable, cannot be closed down overnight.

COMMAND POLITY TO POLITICAL PLURALISM

Although some Western political commentators began to echo Russian radicals—very often Soviet citizens who had been perfectly conformist before

---

[20] Fiona Hill and Clifford Gaddy, *The Siberian Curse: How Communist Planners Left Russia Out in the Cold* (Brookings Institution, Washington, DC, 2003).

[21] Dahl, 'Why All Democratic Countries Have Mixed Economies', op. cit.

Gorbachev made the Soviet Union safe for dissent—and thus condemn the slowness of political reform in the USSR under Gorbachev, the speed of change was dramatic between 1987 and 1990. East European regimes, needless to say, changed even more quickly—in 1989—but that is hardly surprising. The Communist institutions that were there so quickly cast aside were seen by a majority of people in East-Central Europe as an alien imposition. They were sustainable only so long as the Soviet leadership was prepared, in the last resort, to use armed force to defend unpopular systems and leaders. For Russia—with its authoritarian pre-revolutionary tradition and seven decades of oppressive Communist rule, whether autocratic or oligarchical—to move within three years from a highly authoritarian political system to political pluralism and contested elections was a breakthrough of breathtaking speed.[22]

Only a minority of Western observers paid much attention prior to perestroika to the fact that behind the monolithic façade the CPSU presented to its own citizens and the outside world there was a wide diversity of view.[23] The most influential political actors not only in the perestroika period but also in post-Soviet Russia have been former members of the CPSU; indeed, in many cases they have come from the ranks of the _nomenklatura_. Even with the pluralization of the political system, it was the career party official, Boris Yeltsin, who became the standard-bearer of the radical democrats.[24]

There was a huge element of contingency in the transformation of the Soviet system coming when it did. The views of the other members of the Politburo at the time when Gorbachev became General Secretary of the

---

[22] From 1988 Gorbachev saw the essence of perestroika as a gradual democratization of the political system, although by 1990–1 gradualism had to give way to improvisation under the pressure of events. He frequently emphasized to his Politburo colleagues how far they still had to go and urged the necessity of patience in the face of public criticism. For example, at a Politburo meeting on 21 July 1988, Gorbachev said: 'We are only beginning perestroika, taking only the first steps; this is felt from below and there is dissatisfaction with it. Public opinion is not yet fully formed . . . we need to react patiently to criticism directed at us, so as not to put a stop to the general process' ('Politbyuro, 21 Iyulya 1988 goda, zapis' [V.A.] Medvedeva', Gorbachev Foundation Archives).

[23] Stephen Cohen was one of those who did draw attention to that important political phenomenon whose significance became clearer to many more observers with the onset of perestroika. See, for example, Stephen F. Cohen, Alexander Rabinowitch, and Robert Sharlet (eds.), _The Soviet Union since Stalin_ (Indiana University Press, Bloomington, IN, 1980), in particular, Cohen's chapter, 'The Friends and Foes of Change: Reformism and Conservatism in the Soviet Union', pp. 11–31.

[24] His chosen successor, Vladimir Putin, was not only a former KGB colonel, but also a former member of the CPSU, a requirement for KGB officers.

Central Committee in March 1985 are by now well known to those who have
bothered to search, both from contemporary documents and the rich memoir
literature.[25] None of them would have pursued a policy remotely similar to
that of Gorbachev. One of them, Heidar Aliev, has said that at the time of
Chernenko's death he had no idea that Gorbachev would be a reformer, and
clearly it was not because of any reformism that the Politburo endorsed
Gorbachev as the new General Secretary. As Aliev put it in an interview:
'Gorbachev was the youngest of all, he was the second person in the party,
power, so to speak, was already in his hands' (italics added, AB).[26] Gorbachev's
own views also underwent rapid evolution which reflected both a reformist
disposition and an openness to new ideas unusual (to put it mildly) at the level
of the Politburo. That open-mindedness was crucially important. The only
realistic alternative leaders of the Soviet Union, far from breaking the taboo

[25] No one voted against the nomination of Gorbachev at either the pre-selection meeting by
the Politburo or the endorsement of his name by the Central Committee on 11 March 1985.
Indeed, at the Politburo meeting everyone present spoke in fulsome terms about Gorbachev's
suitability for the post. (See Fond 89, 1.1001, opis 36, file 16, 'Zasedanie Politburo TsK KPSS 11
Marta 1985 goda'.) That, however, was because Gorbachev, as second secretary, had been in a
very strong position to structure the succession process and because those Politburo members
who were opposed to him (*a*) did not wish to jeopardize their careers by opposing a certain
victor, and (*b*) had no idea of the scope of Gorbachev's potential radicalism. If they had
understood just how different his mindset was from theirs, they would have mobilized the
conservative majority within the Politburo and Central Committee. An earlier, but unsuccessful,
attempt to halt Gorbachev's ascent to power had been made by Chernenko on the urging of
those around him. On the eve of Gorbachev's important speech to a conference on ideology in
Moscow in December 1984 (at which, in a sense, Gorbachev first 'outed' himself as a reformer),
Chernenko—who had been sent an advance copy of the speech—telephoned Gorbachev and
complained about a series of ideological errors in the text. (The detailed critique of the speech
had been helpfully prepared for him by one of Gorbachev's enemies, Richard Kosolapov, the
editor of *Kommunist*). More remarkably, given that the event was about to take place, Chernenko told Gorbachev that the conference should be postponed. Gorbachev, as Aleksandr
Yakovlev (who was with Gorbachev when he took Chernenko's call) notes, flatly refused to go
along with the General Secretary's wishes in what, Yakovlev says, was a 'a surprisingly for me
tough tone'. See Aleksandr Yakovlev, *Sumerki* (Materik, Moscow, 2003), p. 369. Gorbachev's
firm resistance to Chernenko's wishes on this matter is also recorded by Vadim Medvedev who
notes, additionally, that—in an action unprecedented for an organ of the Central Committee—
Kosolapov subsequently refused to publish Gorbachev's speech in *Kommunist*. See Vadim
Medvedev, *V kommande Gorbacheva* (Bylina, Moscow, 1994), p. 22. For the text of the speech,
see M.S. Gorbachev, 'Zhivoe tvorchestvo naroda', in Gorbachev, *Izbrannye rechi i stat'i* (Politizdat, Moscow, 1987), Vol. 2, pp. 75–108. This speech was discussed in my 1985 *Problems of
Communism* article which is reproduced as chapter two of this volume. See also Brown, *The
Gorbachev Factor*, pp. 78–81 and 121–2. On other efforts in 1984—by Konstantin Chernenko
and Nikolai Tikhonov—to frustrate Gorbachev's political ambitions, see Vadim Medvedev,
Prozrenie, mif ili predatel'stvo? K voprosu ob ideologii perestroiki (Evraziya, Moscow, 1998),
p. 84. See also Mikhail Gorbachev, *Zhizn' i reformy* (Novosti, Moscow, 1995), vol. 1, p. 266.
[26] Interview with Aliev on 9 February 1990 in Andrey Karaulov, *Vokrug Kremlya: kniga
politicheskikh dialog* (Novosti, Moscow, 1990), pp. 262–73, at p. 267.

on speaking positively about 'pluralism', as Gorbachev did,[27] would have used all the numerous levers at their command—among them, censorship, party discipline and the KGB—to make sure that change did not get out of hand.[28]

Some of the important decisions Gorbachev pushed through the 19th Party Conference in the summer of 1988 became political reality only in 1989. The most fundamental of such changes were the contested elections for a legislature with real power (power enough to reject 13 per cent of Nikolay Ryzhkov's nominations of ministers in 1989).[29] By this time 'reform' is an inadequate word to describe the transformation that occurred within the Soviet system. Gorbachev, with justification, sees the Nineteenth Conference as a turning point. His major speech to the conference, he has said, concerned nothing other than an attempt to make a 'peaceful, smooth *transition from one political system to another*' [italics added, AB].[30] Change moved beyond liberalization to democratization, but democratization is a process and not the same as an established democracy. If the system did not become a full-fledged democracy either under Gorbachev or under his successors in post-Soviet Russia, it did become politically pluralistic and different in kind from the Communist system. The Soviet Union came to an end in 1991 but Communism in the Soviet Union ended in 1989.

Consider the five defining characteristics of a Communist system already enumerated. First, the monopoly of power of the Communist Party was

---

[27] See *Pravda*, 15 July 1987, pp. 1–2, at p. 2; and *Pravda*, 30 September 1987, p. 1.

[28] The conservative Communist views of Grishin emerge clearly enough from his book, *Ot Khrushcheva do Gorbacheva: politicheskie portrety pyati gensekov i A.N. Kosygina: memuary* (Moscow, 1996). Yakovlev observes not only that Grishin aspired to the post of General Secretary but also that Chernenko's closest circle had 'already prepared the speeches and political programme' for a Grishin general secretaryship. See Yakovlev, *Sumerki*, p. 459. Grishin knew the game was up when Chernenko died at 7.20 p.m. on 10 March and a first meeting of the Politburo was convened by Gorbachev for that very evening. Gorbachev and his allies had also been preparing the ground for a smooth succession. This included doing a deal with Andrey Gromyko. See Yakovlev, *Sumerki*, pp. 459–63, and Anatoliy Gromyko, *Andrey Gromyko. V labirintakh kremlya: vospominaniya i razmyshleniya syna* (Avtor, Moscow, 1997), pp. 94–5. Gorbachev does not use the language of deal-making, but in his latest book he reveals that he met with Andrey Gromyko for half an hour prior to the Politburo meeting on the evening of Chernenko's death. Gorbachev told him that many problems both internally and externally were overdue for resolution and that tackling them could not be postponed any longer. 'I invited Gromyko to combine our forces at this crucial moment.' Gromyko's answer, says Gorbachev, was definite: 'he said that he fully shared my assessment and [we]agreed to work together' (Mikhail Gorbachev, *Ponyat' perestroyku: pochemu eto vazhno seychas* (Al'pina Biznes Buks, Moscow, 2006), p. 11. Anatoliy Gromyko suggests that Grigoriy Romanov, even more strongly than Grishin, aspired to be General Secretary and that this explains his rapid removal from the Politburo by Gorbachev once the latter had succeeded Chernenko (*Andrey Gromyko*, pp. 96–8).

[29] Nikolay Ryzhkov, *Perestroyka: istoriya predatel'stv* (Novosti, Moscow, 1992), p. 291.

[30] Gorbachev, *Zhizn' i reformy*, vol. 1, p. 395.

abandoned when the Constitution was changed in March 1990 to remove the guaranteed 'leading and guiding role' of the CPSU, but independent political organizations and embryonic political parties already existed in 1989.[31] Second, democratic centralism had been disappearing fast from 1986 onwards and by 1989 it was totally abandoned when Communists, with radically different policies and standpoints, opposed one another in the contested elections. Third, state ownership of the means of production survived to a greater extent than any of the other main features of Communism, but in 1988 the Law on Co-operatives made serious inroads into it, going much further than the Law on Individual Labour Activity of 1986. Co-operatives quickly developed into thinly disguised private enterprises. Fourth, the ideological commitment to 'communism' disappeared even as a distant aspiration for Gorbachev and his allies and from the programmatic documents of the CPSU. And, fifth, after 1989 there was no international Communist movement for the Soviet Union to lead or belong to.

This amounted to systemic transformation, even if the transition from Communism was less than a transition to democracy. In some ways, it ill behoves a British author to pass critical judgement on the fact that the democratic transition was not more complete, especially by 1990 or (in some respects still less) by 2006. Britain's movement to democracy was so gradual that, unlike the case of Russia, it is virtually impossible to point to a year or even a decade as *the* time of *systemic* change. Already in the eighteenth century there was 'mixed government', an argumentative and significant parliament, and political pluralism, but not until the twentieth century, when the franchise was extended to women, did the parliamentary government which had developed further in the nineteenth century become parliamentary democracy. In Russia the transition *from* Communism is clear enough, but it has been to a system constituting a mixture of democracy and arbitrariness in the post-Soviet period.[32]

---

[31] See, for example, Geoffrey A. Hosking, Jonathan Aves, and Peter J.S. Duncan, *The Road to Post-Communism: Independent Political Movements in the Soviet Union, 1985–1991* (Pinter, London, 1992); M. Steven Fish, *Democracy from Scratch: Opposition and Regime in the New Russian Revolution* (Princeton University Press, Princeton, NJ, 1995); and Michael Urban with Vyacheslav Igrunov and Sergei Mitrokhin, *The Rebirth of Politics in Russia* (Cambridge University Press, Cambridge, 1997).

[32] Stephen Cohen, in his article, 'Was the Soviet System Reformable?', cites the work of John Hazard on the unreformed Soviet system. With modifications, Hazard's formulation could be applied to post-Communist Russia. Writing in the Khrushchev era, Hazard interpreted Soviet politics as 'incorporating democratic forms, counterweighted with totalitarian controls', (John N. Hazard, *The Soviet System of Government* (University of Chicago Press, Chicago, 2nd edn., 1960), p. 9). Rather than becoming a democracy, post-Soviet Russia has seen the evolution of a system in which democratic forms are counterweighted with varying degrees and types of authoritarian control.

Counterfactuals have their limitations, but it is at least seriously arguable that if Gorbachev had come down on the opposite side of the argument in two particular instances, a more vibrant and more effectively institutionalized democracy might have emerged.[33] The first such fateful decision was to have the President of the USSR elected indirectly by the legislature in March 1990 rather than directly by the whole people. If the decision had gone in favour of direct election in the spring of 1990 (and not just for *future* presidential elections, as was intended),[34] that would have been even more important in relation to the attempt to keep most of the republics within a new and voluntary Union (of which more below).

The second fateful decision was Gorbachev's postponement of an overt split in the Communist Party. If this could have been carried through, it would have been important in establishing legitimate political institutions that cut across republican boundaries, thus bolstering a Union, and would have been still more important from the point of view of the future consolidation of democracy. That in private he was ready to contemplate party competition is well known. When as early as 1985 Aleksandr Yakovlev wrote a private memorandum to Gorbachev suggesting that the Communist Party be divided into two in order to introduce contestation into the political system, Gorbachev did not react as if this were a sin against the holy ghost

[33] See Brown, *The Gorbachev Factor*, pp. 202–7; and Cohen, 'Was the Soviet Union Reformable?', op. cit., pp. 476–9.

[34] The law, in fact, stipulated direct election by the people as a whole. The same Congress of People's Deputies which took the decision that the first President would be elected by that body approved the following new article (127-1) of the Soviet Constitution: 'A citizen of the USSR not younger than 35 and not older than 65 years may be elected the President of the USSR. One and the same person may not be President of the USSR for more than two terms. The President of the USSR shall be elected by citizens of the USSR on the basis of universal, equal, and direct suffrage by a secret ballot for a term of five years. The number of candidates for the post of President of the USSR shall not be limited. Elections of the President of the USSR shall be considered to be valid if not less than fifty per cent of the electors have taken part. A candidate who has received more than half of the votes of the electors who took part in the voting, for the USSR as a whole and in a majority of union republics, shall be considered to be elected' (translation by William E. Butler in Butler (ed.), *Basic Documents of the Soviet Legal System*, Oceana, New York, 1991, p. 33). The original document, 'Ob uchrezhdenii posta Prezidenta SSSR i vnesenii izmenii i dopolnenii v Konstitutsiyu (Osnovoy Zakon) SSSR' is to be found in *Vedomosti s" ezda narodnykh deputatov SSSR i Verkhovnogo soveta SSSR*, No. 12, Item 189 (21 March 1990), p. 230. Gorbachev received conflicting advice within his own entourage on whether he should strive for popular election from the outset or whether, in view of the pressing need to set up presidential institutions that would fill the gap left in executive authority by the downgrading of the CPSU, he should go for quick election by the Congress. If Gorbachev had not accepted the advice which erred on the side of caution, he could doubtless have persuaded the Congress of People's Deputies to implement the new constitutional provision for direct election by universal suffrage in that very year.

of party unity. Instead, he said that the idea was 'premature'.[35] Clearly, in practical political terms it *was* premature; it would have been impossible for a recently selected General Secretary, surrounded in the Politburo by Communists of orthodox views, to split the Party, especially given the animus reserved in Leninist parties for splitters.

The best time for Gorbachev to have taken the risk of splitting the CPSU would have been either in 1989 or at the 28th Party Congress in June 1990, with the Congress possibly representing the optimal moment. At that point several million members would almost certainly have followed Gorbachev into a Social Democratic Party and those who remained 'true Communists' would also have been able to form a large party.[36] A liberal party could, moreover, have emerged from the CPSU, for the membership of that ideologically variegated organization included Yegor Gaidar and most of those who were to come to prominence as proselytizing marketeers. This would have been an optimal way of giving birth to a competitive party system with mass membership and mass support and, if the Party's property had been divided among the successor parties, with strong financial bases. To make the last point is, however, to raise doubts as to whether such an open embrace of Western-style party competition to the detriment of the CPSU could have been agreed in a kind of pact-making process.

It is likely that the Party *apparatchiki*, a majority of whom were already highly suspicious of Gorbachev's social democratic leanings, would have been the backbone of the Communist rump party. But might they not have made common cause with the military and the KGB to put a stop to the split? That cannot be ruled out, and a coup over a year earlier than the August 1991 putsch would have had a greater chance of success.[37] In 1990 the same people

---

[35] Yakovlev, *Sumerki*, p. 383.

[36] Shakhnazarov advised Gorbachev in 1990 to change the name of the Communist Party of the Soviet Union to the Social Democratic Party of the USSR 'and to tell those who disagreed to stay away' from the forthcoming Party Congress. See the interview with Shakhnazarov by E.L. Kuznetsov in *Demokratizatsiya*, Vol. 2, No. 2, Spring 1994, pp. 228–33, at p. 230 Gorbachev, however, was not yet ready to take the risk of attempting to bring the party's name into line with the evolution of his own views and those of the party's reformist wing.

[37] Gorbachev's own reasons for not splitting the CPSU at that point were not so much that he feared a coup as that he believed it important to maintain his control over the Party apparatus. That apparatus, he has argued on numerous occasions, was still potentially a powerful organization, one capable—if headed by a General Secretary of conservative views—of reversing many of the changes of the perestroika years. It was for the same reason that he held on to the General Secretaryship, even after he had become President, for the levers of power of the former office were too great a gift to offer to the 'opponents of perestroika'. Shakhnazarov was among several of Gorbachev's advisers who proposed to him in 1990 that he give up the General Secretaryship now that he was President of the USSR. Later he decided that Gorbachev had been correct to resist that advice. As he put it: 'Everybody believed that some day he would

who led the actual coup attempt would not have been faced with their August 1991 problem of claiming to speak for the people as a whole when the Russian people, at least, had just elected a person of quite different views, Boris Yeltsin, as President two months earlier. Yeltsin would have had no such formidable democratic legitimacy in the summer of 1990—unless he had been the victor in an election by universal suffrage for a *Soviet* presidency in the spring of that year. That is where the counterfactual of direct election of the President of the USSR assumes great significance (and is discussed in the next section of this chapter).

While it has to be acknowledged that it would have been a real risk for Gorbachev to take the initiative in splitting the Communist Party, the risks of keeping the Party superficially united were even greater. When Aleksandr Yakovlev returned to the theme of splitting the Party in 1990, Gorbachev told him not to be in such a hurry, saying that the division (*raskol*) would take place at a Party Congress in November 1991.[38] Of course, no such Congress was ever held—the August putsch put paid to it—but in the meantime Gorbachev's position had weakened so much that the optimal moment for him to initiate an overt schism had, even without the coup, long passed.

THE BREAKUP OF THE SOVIET STATE

Soon after the breakup of the Soviet state, Robert Conquest wrote that for anyone with 'even a moderate knowledge of Soviet nationality problems', it had long been clear that a 'democratic Soviet Union' would be 'a contradiction in terms'.[39] I would agree with that view to the extent that a 'democratized Soviet Union' is taken to refer to all fifteen republics. The Baltic states were, and should have been treated as, a special case. Forcibly incorporated in the Soviet Union against their will as relatively recently as 1940, Estonians,

---

have to resign the post of general secretary. The question was whether the time had come or not. I think Mikhail Sergeevich was right at the time. Having resigned the post of general secretary, he would have left the Party in the hands of people who would have pushed it back, resulting in the emergence of a dual power' (interview, *Demokratizatsiya*, Vol. 2, No. 2, Spring 1994, p. 230). Gorbachev could, indeed, interpret his success in getting a social democratic platform approved by the 28th Congress of the CPSU as meaning that he had won the Party over. It was to become evident, however, that the majority of party officials who voted for principles and policies of which they disapproved did so with no intention of implementing them.

[38] Andrei Grachev, *Gorbachev* (Vagrius, Moscow, 2001), pp. 227–9.

[39] Robert Conquest, Foreword to Ian Bremmer and Ray Taras (eds.), *Nations and Politics in the Soviet Successor States* (Cambridge University Press, Cambridge, 1993), p. xvii.

Lithuanians, and Latvians predictably opted for independent statehood when the risks of making such demands were sufficiently reduced. Given that their reference group of countries was their Scandinavian neighbours, who had enjoyed far greater prosperity as well as flourishing democracy, it is not surprising that the Balts' political aspirations should have been very different from those of the peoples of Soviet Central Asia.

There are, however, ways in which a smaller, voluntary Union could have survived. The election of a Soviet President by universal adult suffrage across the whole of the USSR (or even excluding the three Baltic states) in the spring of 1990 would surely have played a significant part in that. There is, furthermore, no reason to suppose that the breakup of the Soviet Union whereby fifteen independent states stand on the territory that had been occupied by just one state was necessarily a more democratic outcome than a Union containing nine or even twelve republics. (Some of those states—especially in central Asia, but including also Belarus—are more authoritarian in 2006 than they were in the last years of the Soviet Union.) If a larger political entity, embracing different nationalities, can be held together by consent, that need not be inferior as a democratic polity to a state based on a particular nation's claim to statehood. Indeed, the belief that every nation has an absolute right to its own state raises as many problems as it resolves. Within virtually every projected 'nation-state' there are smaller national groups, sometimes occupying territorial enclaves which, following the breakup of the larger political entity (as we have seen both in the former Soviet Union and former Yugoslavia), may form the basis of *their* claim to 'nation-statehood'. This raises the possibility of an almost infinite regress to ever smaller states, to civil war and to the spectre of ethnic cleansing.

Most members of the Central Committee of the CPSU would have been extremely unhappy had Gorbachev endorsed the idea of direct election of a Soviet president in early 1990, for anti-Communist sentiment had grown within the Soviet Union, stimulated by economic problems, by the sharpening of the 'nationalities question', and, not least, by the demonstration effect of events in Eastern Europe when in the course of the previous year Soviet citizens were able to watch on their own television screens Communist rulers being held responsible for the peoples' manifold discontents and summarily dispatched from office.[40] Moreover, the two most popular politicians in the country at the time, according to the best survey research then, that of VTsIOM, were Gorbachev and Yeltsin. In March 1990 Gorbachev was still

---

[40] For the Baltic nations—a point which is discussed further in the next chapter—the sight of East-Central European countries becoming fully independent and non-Communist was particularly important.

ahead of Yeltsin; in May–June of that year, with Gorbachev on a downward trajectory and Yeltsin's popularity increasing, the positions were reversed.[41]

If Gorbachev had won the election, that would have been bad news for the Party traditionalists. Having a mandate from the whole people, he would have been even freer from pressures by the Politburo and Central Committee than he was as an indirectly elected President. If Yeltsin had won the election—and he would surely have contested it, given his growing popularity—that would have doubtless have struck the *apparat* as a still worse outcome. Yet, if Gorbachev had sprung a decision for election of a President by universal suffrage on a surprised Party, just as he sprung the move to contested legislative elections on them at the Nineteenth Party Conference, he would probably have got away with it.

Juan Linz and Alfred Stepan have argued that the chances of holding the Soviet Union (or, at least, the greater part of it) together as a new, voluntary federation were weakened because competitive elections in the republics preceded elections at all-Union level.[42] Their general point about sequencing is a substantial one, but it could have been more powerfully applied to the presidential elections than to the parliamentary elections which are the focus of their argument. There was not such a qualitative difference between the elections for the Congress of People's Deputies of the USSR in 1989 and for the Congress of People's Deputies of the RSFSR in 1990 as Linz and Stepan suggest. Moreover, the first *multiparty* elections in Russia did not occur until 1993 and make a poor candidate for a 'founding election', since they attracted

---

[41] For the VTsIOM survey data, I am grateful to Professor Yuriy Levada who supplied the relevant materials to me in the early 1990s. All too often one encounters ludicrously wrong-headed assessments of Gorbachev's popularity between 1985 and 1991 based on something as irrelevant as his derisory vote in the Russian presidential election of 1996. Not only had that much later event nothing to do with Gorbachev's popularity at a time when most Russians still appreciated their new freedoms and the ending of the Cold War, but the 1996 election hardly even tested Gorbachev's (admittedly much diminished) popularity in Russia by then. The contest was framed by the mass media in terms of *either* Yeltsin *or* a return to the worst years of Communism. The survey data show clearly that Gorbachev's popularity was, indeed, in steep decline during his last eighteen months in office, but the contemporary hard evidence, as distinct from retrospective and selective memory, also shows that he was the most popular politician in Russia and the Soviet Union as a whole for the greater part of his time as Soviet leader. Or, as the leading VTsIOM researcher, Boris Dubin has noted, between 1988 and the early 1990s the two people who emerged from survey research as 'heroes of the year' were, at first, Gorbachev, and, later, Yeltsin. See Dubin, 'Stalin i drugie. Figury vysshey vlasti v obshchestvennom mnenii sovremennoy Rossii', *Monitoring obshchestvennogo mneniya*, No. 1, January–February 2003, pp. 13–25, at p. 16. In addition to the VTsIOM surveys, serious sociological research commissioned by the Academy of Social Sciences showed that Gorbachev's standing was still high in 1989, although less spectacularly so than earlier. In late 1989, 62.6 per cent of respondents evaluated him, on the whole, positively. In 1988 the percentage who gave him a positive evaluation was 70 per cent and in 1986 it was more than 80 per cent. See Vadim Medvedev, *Prozrenie, mif ili predatel'stvo?*, p. 213.

[42] Linz and Stepan, *Problems of Democratic Transition and Consolidation*, esp. pp. 381–5.

the lowest turnout of all national elections between 1989 and 2004. The contrast could not have been greater with the genuine excitement surrounding the first contested elections, those of 1989, notwithstanding their compromise character. If, however, a free election had taken place for the executive presidency of the USSR in 1990—i.e. a full year before the actual elections for presidents of the republics—this would have been an event of extraordinary political import. It would have given not only the winner but also a renewed Union greater legitimacy. In his book on perestroika published in Moscow fifteen years after perestroika came to an end, Gorbachev makes the point that if he had been elected President in 1990 in a vote by universal suffrage, then 'in the decisive moments of 1991 the more convincing legitimacy of authority of the President would have allowed the taking of firmer steps against the liquidators of the USSR'.[43] In fact, with the President of the Soviet Union elected by universal suffrage, the August 1991 coup plotters might have thought more than twice about attempting to seize power. It would have been still more difficult to imagine a President of Russia joining forces with the heads of state of Ukraine and Belarus to wind up the federal union if the great majority of citizens of Russia, Ukraine and Belarus had taken part in electing the Union President.

Indeed, from the point of view of preservation of a Union of nine or more republics, a Yeltsin victory in an election for the Presidency of the Soviet Union would have been of particular significance.[44] Although a number of scholars have aptly pointed to the importance of the institutional resources that could be mobilized in each of the Union republics once local elites, in a reformed and more tolerant Soviet Union, had decided to seek sovereignty,[45] there was something paradoxical about Yeltsin's assertion of Russian 'independence' from the Union. Since—as the Balts, presumably, would be the first to agree—the Union had been, in a sense, a greater Russia, and since, apart

---

[43] Gorbachev, *Ponyat' perestroyku*, p. 374. Gorbachev also observes: 'The presence of a strong conservative tendency in the Politburo and in general in the higher echelons of the party, led to the fact that not infrequently we were late in taking urgent decisions' (ibid.).

[44] Yeltsin's victory would have been far from guaranteed. To institute a popular election for the presidency would have given a new boost to Gorbachev's flagging popularity and he would surely have gained from being the first supreme leader in Russian history who, having inherited vast power, voluntarily chose to put his power at the disposal of the people. Cumulatively, Gorbachev's reforms did just that, but the point would have emerged much more clearly if direct elections for a Soviet presidency had occurred when Gorbachev (in the short term) still had a lot to lose.

[45] See, for example, Rogers Brubaker, *Nationalism Reframed: Nationhood and Nationalism in the New Europe* (Cambridge University Press, Cambridge, 1966); and Valerie Bunce, *Subversive Institutions: The Design and Destruction of Socialism and the State* (Cambridge University Press, Cambridge, 1999). See also Linz and Stepan, *Problems of Democratic Transition and Consolidation*, esp. ch. 19.

from a very brief period in late 1991, a majority of Russians favoured preservation of the Soviet Union (both before and after its breakup),[46] it was hardly in Russia's long-term interest for Yeltsin to argue that Russian law had supremacy over Union law and that Russia should seek its 'independence'.[47] In terms of his ambition to replace Gorbachev in the Kremlin, this made sense, but that was evidently higher on his scale of priorities than preservation of a larger Union. Clearly, if Yeltsin had been elected *Soviet* president in 1990, he would have had no incentive whatsoever to assert *Russian* independence—quite the reverse.

The breakup of the Soviet Union into fifteen successor states was facilitated by the new freedom and political pluralism that Gorbachev played the major role in introducing in the second half of the 1980s. Those who blame Gorbachev for the breakup of the Soviet Union—and it is the main thing for which he is criticized in contemporary Russia—should be clear that they are indicting him for introducing political freedom.[48] Yet that disintegration of the state was the ultimate unintended consequence of his actions. The more proximate causes of the breakup (the Baltic states apart) were Yeltsin's playing of the Russian card against the Union and the intervention of the putschists who took their action when they did to prevent the signing of the agreed Union Treaty (which would have devolved massive powers to the republics) and, in their folly, hastened what they had sought to prevent.

CONCLUSION

Liberalization and the substantial measure of democratization represented by competitive elections were bound to put great strain on the Union, but they did not rule out the possibility of movement from pseudo-federalism to

[46] See Matthew Wyman, 'Russians and Non-Russians on the Collapse of the USSR' in his book (which, title notwithstanding, deals with the late Soviet as well as post-Soviet period), *Public Opinion in Postcommunist Russia* (Macmillan, Basingstoke, 1997), pp. 149–73.

[47] In May 1990 Yeltsin insisted that Union laws must not contravene those of Russia, rather than the other way round. See Leon Aron, *Boris Yeltsin: A Revolutionary Life* (HarperCollins, London, 2000), p. 377. The fate of the Union not only for Yeltsin but also for his ambitious entourage was secondary to the struggle for power.

[48] One Russian scholar, who had been part of the 'Democratic Russia' movement in the last years of the Soviet Union, to whom I made this point in Moscow in March 2006, responded: 'You need to be careful which people you are giving freedom to.' A good many of those who criticized Gorbachev for being an insufficiently thoroughgoing liberalizer and democratizer during the later perestroika years now blame him for what they view as his excessive political liberalism.

a genuine (albeit loose) federation embracing a majority of Soviet republics on the basis of a new and voluntary Union Treaty. That this did not happen owed a great deal to the actions and ambitions of Boris Yeltsin. A smaller, loosely federal Union could have emerged from the negotiations that took place among the representatives of a majority of the Soviet union republics, a process disrupted by the August 1991 coup mounted by hard-line opponents of this diminution of central authority—people who also had good reason to believe that they would not be holding their high positions for much longer.[49] If, on that issue, I am in agreement with Stephen Cohen[50] and Mark Kramer,[51] I part company with Cohen's contention that there was a 'Soviet system' that could survive by being reformed.

The only way in which a peaceful transition to a pluralistic political system could take place in as firmly established a Communist system as that of the Soviet Union was by reform from above. At some stage, though, the issue of transition—or systemic transformation—was bound to arise if the reforms were radical enough to allow open discussion of all possible options by an awakened society. Moreover, reform of the Soviet command economy could not but bring out the limitations of reform of such a system, thus pointing to the need to move to an economic system operating on different principles, even though transition from one system to the other could scarcely avoid making things worse before they got better. Reform of the command polity could proceed more smoothly to change of the fundamentals of the system. Yet, that required a high degree of political skill and dexterity on the part of Gorbachev, not least in 'tranquillizing the hardliners', and thus avoiding a reversal of the changes at a time when their opponents could have brought

[49] A meeting on 30 July 1991 at which Yeltsin, Kazakhstan Communist Party First Secretary Nursultan Nazarbaev and Gorbachev discussed the appointments to the posts of Prime Minister, Defence Minister, and Chairmanship of the KGB that would follow the signing of the Union Treaty was bugged by the KGB. Thus, Vladimir Kryuchkov was well aware that he was going to be replaced as KGB chief, and that Valentin Pavlov and Dmitriy Yazov were also going to be removed from the prime ministership and office of Minister of Defence respectively. On this, see Gorbachev, *Ponyat' perestroyku*, pp. 326–8.

[50] Cohen, 'Was the Soviet System Reformable?', op. cit.

[51] Mark Kramer, 'The Reform of the Soviet System and the Demise of the Soviet State', op. cit, pp. 505–12. Kramer is, I think, wrong when he says (p. 505) that the Soviet system and the Soviet state 'ended coterminously', but right when (p. 506) he holds: 'There is ample reason to believe that the Soviet *state* could in fact continue to exist even if the Soviet *system* had disappeared.' The switch of opinion in Ukraine from majority acceptance (in the March 1991 referendum) of a renewed Union to majority support for separate statehood was, along with Yeltsin's assertion of Russian independence from the Union, of decisive significance in bringing about the disintegration of the Soviet state. The August putsch was of great importance in this instance. Ukraine's time-serving leader Leonid Kravchuk initially supported the hard-line coup and to cover up his opportunism rapidly had to reinvent himself as a spokesman for Ukrainian independence and democracy.

this about by as simple a device as votes in the Politburo and Central Committee to replace him as General Secretary.[52]

Gorbachev was faced by intense pressures coming from different directions—from conservative Communists occupying strong positions in the party apparatus, the security forces, and the military-industrial complex; from national elites demanding, in some cases, separate statehood, for which, in the Baltic states in particular they enjoyed mass support; and from a highly politicized Russian society now able to voice its discontent at the persistence of economic shortages and social problems. Nevertheless, by the end of the 1980s Russia and the Soviet Union as a whole had moved beyond reform of the system to systemic transformation. That this is not merely playing with words is suggested by Gorbachev's recognition already by 1988 of the need for 'a transition (*perekhod*) from one political system to another'.[53] Tactical retreats and hesitations (some of which were counterproductive) notwithstanding, Gorbachev and his closest supporters pursued the strategic goals of dismantling the system they inherited. The political system was transformed dramatically—and for the better. Change in the economic system was, however, inconsistent and far from successful. The growing dissatisfaction with economic conditions, in turn, bolstered the support of those national élites in the European republics of the Soviet Union who embraced the goal of separate statehood. As I shall argue in chapter eight, that movement was also given a massive fillip by developments elsewhere in Eastern Europe.

---

[52] On the need to 'tranquillize the hardliners', as a general problem of political transition, see Guillermo O'Donnell and Philippe C. Schmitter, *Transitions from Authoritarian Rule: Tentative Conclusions about Uncertain Democracies* (Johns Hopkins University Press, Baltimore, MD, 1986), p. 44. Or, as Andrei Grachev (Gorbachev's last presidential press spokesman) has put it: 'People seldom ask how many coups d'états Gorbachev managed to avoid in six and a half years of reform. Any of these potential coups could have occurred under much less favorable circumstances, when Gorbachev's position in the Politburo and Central Committee was such that he was virtually isolated from the Party of which he was the leader.' See Andrei S. Grachev, *Final Days: The Inside Story of the Collapse of the Soviet Union* (Westview, Boulder, CO, 1995), p. 101.

[53] Gorbachev, *Zhizn' i reformy*, Vol. 1, p. 395. Or, as Gorbachev puts it in his most recent book, 'the logic of development' meant that what was needed was 'not to improve the system but to encroach on its very foundations, to change those foundations'. What was occurring was 'a gradual transition to a social market economy and to a political structure built on the supremacy of law and the full guaranteeing of human rights' (Gorbachev, *Ponyat' perestroyku*, p. 22).

8

Transnational Influences in the Transition
from Communism[1]

The transition from Communism, it hardly needs saying, has to be distinguished from transition to democracy. Of the thirty-one formerly Communist states, not more than half of them can today be firmly categorized as democratic.[2] Many possess significant democratic elements, including contested elections—a necessary but not sufficient condition for democracy. A number of them are *hybrid* or *mixed polities*—a broad category into which post-Soviet Russia belongs. It was premature to classify Yeltsin's Russia as a democracy and still more conceptual stretching would be required to include Putin's Russia in that category.[3] Other states have made the transition from a distinctively Communist type of post-totalitarian authoritarianism to a different kind of authoritarian regime. The criteria for determining how much democracy makes a state democratic are, of course, debatable. Following Robert Dahl, most scholars are conscious that the states we normally call 'democracies' are 'polyarchies', although, like Dahl himself, we do not subsequently eschew the word, 'democracy', in writing about the political systems conventionally embraced by that concept.[4]

[1] This chapter is a revised and expanded version of an article with the same title published in *Post-Soviet Affairs*, Vol. 16, No. 2, April–June 2000, pp. 177–200.

[2] There are twenty-nine post-Communist states if one includes the German Democratic Republic (GDR), but since it became not a successor state but part of the larger Federal Republic of Germany, it is a case apart. The number of states is likely to increase, partly as a result of continuing fissiparous tendencies in the former Yugoslavia.

[3] For a fuller discussion of these issues, see Archie Brown (ed.), *Contemporary Russian Politics: A Reader* (Oxford University Press, Oxford, 2001); Alex Pravda (ed.), *Leading Russia: Putin in Perspective* (Oxford University Press, Oxford, 2005); Graeme Gill and Roger D. Markwick, *Russia's Stillborn Democracy? From Gorbachev to Yeltsin* (Oxford University Press, Oxford, 2000); Peter Reddaway and Dmitri Glinsky, *The Tragedy of Russia's Reforms: Market Bolshevism Against Democracy* (United States Institute of Peace Press, Washington, DC, 2001); and Lilia Shevtsova, *Putin's Russia* (revised and expanded edition, Carnegie Endowment for International Peace, Washington, DC, 2005).

[4] See four works of Robert A. Dahl, in particular: *Polyarchy: Participation and Opposition* (Yale University Press, New Haven, CT, 1971); *Dilemmas of Pluralist Democracy: Autonomy vs Control*

It should be easier to get agreement on what constitutes transition *from* Communism than to agree on what these various states are in transition *to* or to achieve common ground concerning what point in a transition process (to democracy or a market economy) they have reached. Yet, there is a need to distinguish even the most authoritarian of post-Communist regimes from the Communist systems out of which they emerged, especially since the continued presence of former Communist leaders in positions of power has led some commentators to suggest that that perhaps the 'post' may be misplaced in 'post-Communism'.[5] It is important, then, to be clear about what we mean by *Communism*. I have outlined in Chapter 7 what I take to be its major defining features. Taken together, they differentiated Communist systems from other authoritarian or totalitarian regimes and, still more fundamentally, from pluralist systems in which socialist parties of a social democratic type have held office. I have argued in Chapter 7 that the Soviet Union ceased to have a Communist *system* as early as 1989—long before the generally favoured end-dates for Soviet Communism, i.e. when the CPSU was banned on Russian territory by Yeltsin's decree of August 1991 or when the Soviet flag was lowered from the Kremlin in December of that year. It might be objected that it was not until March 1990 that the monopolistic position of the Communist Party was removed from the Soviet Constitution, but, in practice, that constitutional change *followed* the loss of the party's unchallenged and unchallengeable hegemony rather than *preceding* it.

This chapter is concerned with the process of dismantling, or breaking with, a Communist system rather than with the transition in a longer post-Communist perspective, and, most specifically, with the international dimension of that earlier process. Transitions—certainly in the case of transition from Communism—can be divided into three stages: erosion, breakthrough,

---

(Yale University Press, New Haven, CT, 1982); *Democracy and its Critics* (Yale University Press, New Haven, CT, 1989); and *Democracy* (Yale University Press, New Haven, CT, 1998). See also the concise, but remarkably broad-ranging and insightful, work by John Dunn, *Setting the People Free: The Story of Democracy* (Atlantic Books, London, 2005).

⁵ In the words of Valerie Bunce: 'One analyst's democratization is another's postcommunism—and a third might question whether postcommunism is so "post".' See Valerie J. Bunce, 'Should Transitologists be Grounded?', *Slavic Review*, Vol. 54, No. 1, 1995, pp. 111–27, at p. 119. The presence of former Communists in positions of authority has been more readily accepted in some countries than others. In Poland, Andrzej Walicki has suggested, 'hostility towards the old political elite was caused *not by its opposition* to market economy and democracy *but by its successful adaptation* to these new conditions'. The 'more successful the former communists appear to have been in using the democratic rules of the game and in promoting economic reforms', observes Walicki, 'the louder have been the demands for decommunization...' (Walicki, 'Transitional Justice and the Political Struggles of Post-Communist Poland', in A. James McAdams (ed.), *Transitional Justice and the Rule of Law in New Democracies*, University of Notre Dame Press, Notre Dame, IN, and London, 1997, pp. 185–237, at p. 204).

and reconstruction. The stages are clearer in some countries than others. In Poland and Hungary it really was a long goodbye to Communism. The stage of erosion of the system was a lengthy one. Yet, for *all* of these European Communist states the year of definitive breakthrough was 1989. This was followed by the stage of transition not just *from* Communism but *to* something different, the era of reconstruction in the sense of constructing a new system. Transnational influences in that third stage have, of course, become increasingly obvious. *After* the crucial breaks with a Communist polity and a relatively isolated command economy were made, the political elites became ever more receptive to Western advice and the incentives offered by Western governments and Western-dominated international economic institutions.[6] The post-Communist economies became increasingly intertwined with, and dependent on, the global economy, and the summer of 1998 produced spectacular examples of transnational economic contagion, although the effects of the East Asian economic turmoil on the former Communist countries were by no means entirely capricious. The East-Central European countries—where progress in political and legal institution-building and in economic management has been, on the whole, far greater than in the successor states to the Soviet Union—weathered the storm with fewer traumas than, to take the most important example, Russia. There, in the words of the 1998 Report of the European Bank for Reconstruction and Development, 'the turbulence following the East Asian crisis exposed in a dramatic fashion the frailties of [Russia's] economic governance and reforms'.[7]

Yet, even before the break with Marxism-Leninism the economies of Communist countries were, naturally, not immune from international economic trends. The Soviet Union, as an energy-exporting economy, benefited hugely in the short term from the rise in oil prices in the 1970s, although this helped to disguise from the Brezhnev leadership deep-seated problems of lack of economic innovation as well as the secular decline in the rate of growth. Equally, the decline in the price of oil in the second half of the 1980s did nothing to cushion Gorbachev's reforms, although it did make clearer the

---

[6] That the cosy relationships which ensued were often counterproductive for the broader societies and of benefit (particularly in the case of Russia) chiefly to a relatively narrow circle of donors, consultants, and recipients is a major theme of Janine R. Wedel's work. See especially Wedel, *Collision and Collusion: The Strange Case of Western Aid to Eastern Europe, 1989–1998* (Macmillan, London, 1998); and Wedel, 'Rigging the U.S.–Russian Relationship: Harvard, Chubais, and the Transidentity Game', *Demokratizatsiya: The Journal of Post-Soviet Democratization*, Vol. 7, No. 4, 1999, pp. 469–500.

[7] *European Bank for Reconstruction and Development: Transition Report 1998* (EBRD, London, 1998), p. 3. See also Yoshiko M. Herrera, 'Russian Economic Reform, 1991–1999', in Zoltan Barany and Robert G. Moser (eds.), *Russian Politics: Challenges of Democratization* (Cambridge University Press, Cambridge, 2001), pp. 135–73.

need for far-reaching economic transformation. To a significant degree, however, Communist states had a choice in *pre*-transition times about the extent of their involvement in the world economy. Thus, Poland, with its heavy borrowing from Western banks in the first half of the 1970s, exacerbated its economic problems and found itself more dependent both on the West, to which it was indebted, and on the USSR which was prepared to bail it out at a political price—the price of greater regime responsiveness to Soviet political pressures. Czechoslovakia, in contrast, although it, too, suffered from the backwardness of its industry, had very little debt burden at the time of the collapse of the Soviet bloc, as a result of the caution of its conservative Communist rulers and their fear, ever since 1968, of greater involvement with the West.

Although these states have continued to adapt to a post-Communist world in a variety of different ways, by the end of the 1980s they had already (*a*) made a breakthrough to political pluralism, and (*b*) largely abandoned a command economy and the world of five-year plans. In some cases, notably those of Hungary and Yugoslavia, substantial concessions to the market had come much earlier. Five questions, in particular, are addressed (though not seriatim) in the remainder of this chapter: (1) Are the transitions from Communism part of what is known in the political science literature as the *Third Wave* of democratization? (2) How significant were *Western* influences directly *on Eastern Europe* in the transition from Communism? (3) How important was the influence of *East European countries on one another or on the Soviet Union* in the transition process? (4) How consequential were *Western influences on the Soviet Union* in producing the transformation of the Soviet system? And (5) How significant was *change in the Soviet Union vis-à-vis the East European transitions*?

THE FOURTH WAVE

Samuel Huntington is among the many comparativists who includes developments in the East European countries in the second half of the 1980s in the 'Third Wave' of democratization which he sees as having begun with Portugal in 1974.[8] It is clear that to include transitions from Communism, in general, in the 'Third Wave' of *democratization* must be an oversimplification, for a majority of the transitions are to a non-Communist form of hybrid or

[8] Samuel P. Huntington, *The Third Wave: Democratization in the Late Twentieth Century* (University of Oklahoma Press, Norman, OK, and London, 1991).

authoritarian rule. That does not in itself exclude the possibility of including a majority of the *European* transitions from Communism in the 'Third Wave'. There are, however, other good reasons why one should refrain from doing so. Even in the cases of transition from Communism which *have* involved a democratization process, the influence in Eastern Europe of the transition to democracy in southern Europe (Spain, Portugal, Greece) in the 1970s was marginal and the influence of the transition process in a number of Latin American countries non-existent. Moreover, both the domestic context, on the one hand, and the international stimuli and facilitating conditions, on the other, were very different in the second half of the 1980s from the first half of the 1970s. The Iberian changes of the 1970s did have an impact on Latin America, where there were not only ties of language and culture but also a regional great power, the United States, supportive (especially during the Carter administration) of democratization. In contrast, in Eastern Europe there was a profound lack of political change during the 1970s in the dominant power, the Soviet Union, and intense distrust on the part of the Brezhnev leadership of even liberalization, never mind democratization.[9]

It is, of course, the case that those who speak about a Third Wave of democratization which embraces also the cases of former Communist countries do not necessarily suggest that they are all interconnected. What needs emphasis, however, is that there *are* strong interconnections among the transitions from Communism which constitute a *Fourth Wave* of democratization. ('Democratization' is understood here as a *process* which may be incomplete and does not exclude the possibility of backsliding.) These transitions share a common stimulus and common facilitating condition. One cannot make a clear distinction in terms of *time* between the Third Wave of democratization and the Fourth, for the Marcos dictatorship in the Philippines ended in 1986, and there was progress towards democratization in South Korea and Taiwan between 1986 and 1988.[10] That overlapped in time with the transformation which had got underway in the Soviet Union, but those Soviet changes would not appear to have been of particular importance in relation to the liberalization and partial democratization of conservative authoritarian regimes in Asia. What happened in Moscow was, in contrast, of

---

[9] The one area in which a very limited 'liberalization' was squeezed out of a reluctant Soviet leadership was the selective permission for German and Jewish emigration and the temporary lifting during part of the 1970s of jamming of many, though not all, Western broadcasts. The Helsinki process, culminating in the Final Act of 1975, provided the major transnational pressure that induced this partial compliance with 'Basket Three' of the Accords. Direct American pressure and a feeling that troublesome refuseniks were more of a nuisance inside the Soviet Union than out also played their part in ameliorating Soviet policy on emigration.

[10] Huntington, *The Third Wave*, p. 23.

such decisive importance for the transition from Communism in Europe—
and so interconnected are all those transitions—that it makes sense to see
them as representing a discrete political phenomenon. If the notion of waves
means anything more than a temporal bunching, and it is of limited use if
that is *all* it means, then the changes in East and East-Central Europe
constitute a Fourth Wave of democratization.[11]

At a relatively late stage of the transition some of the incentives for East
European countries became similar to those which applied to Spain and
Portugal—in particular membership of the European Union and, to a much
lesser extent, NATO. It would be stretching credulity, however, to argue that
either aspiration was seen as a practical possibility in East-Central Europe as
comparatively recently as 1985. Yet it is important that Western Europe
offered a more attractive alternative to Communism over a generation later
than it had done in the immediate post-war years, though even then Communist systems had to be imposed in Eastern Europe by Soviet force of arms
(with the exceptions of Albania and Yugoslavia and the partial exception of
Czechoslovakia). Once transition was seriously underway, then for democratic reformers both within southern and East-Central Europe, the European
Union was a pole of attraction. For some, but not other, regimes emerging

[11] South Africa should also be seen as belonging to the Fourth, rather than Third, Wave of
democratization. The changes in Moscow and the collapse of Communism in Eastern Europe
had a decisive impact both on the African National Congress (ANC) and, still more, on the
ruling National Party, led by F.W. de Klerk. Soviet foreign policy under Gorbachev was clearly
orientated toward political settlements rather than armed struggle and Moscow had no interest
in fomenting revolutionary violence and unrest in Africa or Asia. The fundamental shifts in
both the domestic and foreign policy of the Soviet Union in the second half of the 1980s
strengthened the forces of moderation within the ANC, while the collapse of Communism in
Eastern Europe in 1989 made the Marxist-Leninist rhetoric of many of its leading figures appear
outmoded. On the other side, de Klerk's genuine fears of Communist encroachment into South
Africa, with the ANC as its vehicle, were stilled by the end of the Cold War and Soviet non-
intervention when one East European country after another ceased to be a Communist state.
Moreover, the ending of the Cold War removed the one well-worn shred of legitimation
(holding Communism at bay) which a pragmatic conservative politician such as de Klerk
could offer in justification of the banning of the ANC and the South African Communist
Party. As Adrian Guelke has noted, 'the National Party government' had become 'increasingly
reliant on anti-communism to justify its policies internationally, particularly as any residual
sympathy for racial oligarchy in the Western world faded' (Guelke, 'The Impact of the End of
the Cold War on the South African Transition', *Journal of Contemporary African Studies*, Vol. 14,
No. 1, 1996, p. 97). But anti-Communism required some semblance of a plausible Communist
threat if it was to carry any weight. After 1989 that conviction could not be sustained and it was
no accident of timing that on 2 February 1990, de Klerk announced the lifting of the ban on the
ANC and on the South African Communist Party, followed by the dramatic news of the
imminent release of Nelson Mandela after twenty-seven years of imprisonment. On the crucial
relevance of the Soviet and East European changes for South Africa, see—in addition to Guelke's
useful article—the valuable analysis by David Welsh and Jack Spence, 'F.W. de Klerk: Enlightened Conservative', in Martin Westlake (ed.), *Leaders of Transition* (Macmillan, London, 2000).

from authoritarian or specifically Communist rule, NATO membership was also seen as a goal worth pursuing. These international organizations attempt to uphold the principle of democracy as a condition of membership and the European Union also insists on the member states being part of a regulated market economy. Accordingly, once the transition was in progress, the prospect of membership of the European Union, in particular, provided incentives for the establishment of democratic institutions and practices, first, in southern and, later, in Eastern Europe. In the case of the East Europeans it also strengthened the hand of those who pushed for a speedy marketization of the economy. That was not an issue in Spain or Portugal where an essentially market economy already existed.

A specific feature of the transitions of the Fourth Wave has been the by now well-accepted point that the dismantling of Communist regimes involved the special difficulty of simultaneously transforming the political system and the economic system. That is not, however, to say that students of transitions from Communism cannot gain insights from the comparative transitological literature, based disproportionately though it is on cases drawn from Latin America and southern Europe. In addition to the work of, for example, Guillermo O'Donnell,[12] Laurence Whitehead,[13] and Giuseppe Di Palma,[14] the significant books embracing both Eastern Europe and Latin America by Adam Przeworski,[15] by Juan Linz and Alfred Stepan,[16] and by Larry Diamond[17] are striking testimony to the contrary. It is worth noting, however, that in much of the literature on democratic transitions transnational influences were accorded very little attention until the changes in Eastern Europe brought them more sharply into focus. In the studies which

[12] See especially O'Donnell, 'Illusions about Consolidation', in Larry Diamond, Marc F. Plattner, Yun-han Chu, and Hung-mao-Tien (eds.), *Consolidating the Third Wave Democracies: Themes and Perspectives* (Johns Hopkins University Press, Baltimore, MD, 1997); and O'Donnell, 'On the State, Democratization, and Some Conceptual Problems: A Latin American View with Glances at Some Postcommunist Countries', *World Development*, Vol. 1, No. 8, 1993, pp. 1355–69.

[13] Laurence Whitehead (ed.), *The International Dimensions of Democratization: Europe and the Americas* (Oxford University Press, Oxford, 1996); and Whitehead, *Democratization: Theory and Experience* (Oxford University Press, Oxford, 2002).

[14] Giuseppe Di Palma, *To Craft Democracies: An Essay on Democratic Transition* (University of California Press, Berkeley, CA, 1990).

[15] Adam Przeworski, *Democracy and the Market: Political and Economic Reforms in Eastern Europe and Latin America* (Cambridge University Press, Cambridge, 1991); and Przeworski, *Sustainable Democracy* (Cambridge University Press, Cambridge, 1995).

[16] Juan Linz and Alfred Stepan, *Problems of Democratic Transition and Consolidation: Southern Europe, South America, and Post-Communist Europe* (Johns Hopkins University Press, Baltimore, MD, 1996).

[17] Larry Diamond, *Developing Democracy: Toward Consolidation* (Johns Hopkins University Press, Baltimore, MD, 1999).

concentrate specifically on southern Europe and Latin America, Laurence Whitehead was an early and rare exception to that general rule.[18] Ten years after his first substantial essay on the subject, he returned to the theme of *The International Dimensions of Democratization* in his edited book of that title.[19] In contrast with Huntington, Whitehead sees the process of democratization in Eastern Europe as a 'fourth wave', but he does not elaborate the point.[20]

It surely makes sense to classify the transitions from Communism in Europe (though hardly those in Asia) as constituting a *fourth wave* of democratization. *First*, as already noted, the democratization of conservative authoritarian regimes did not act as a trigger to democratization in Communist Europe. These regimes did not in the 1970s or 1980s constitute a major reference group for either elites or citizenry in East European countries. *Second*, there is the simultaneity problem. The fact that both the command economy and the command polity had to be dismantled together and rebuilt on quite different foundations (producing a fundamental contradiction, not least in the Soviet Union, between getting the economic system to work better and dismantling that system) made the transitions from authoritarian rule more complex and difficult in Russia and Eastern Europe than in Spain and Portugal. *Third*, the countries of Eastern Europe constituted an interconnected whole. Even though Albania and Yugoslavia were no longer part of a *Soviet* bloc, in the sense that they were not members of the Warsaw Pact,

---

[18] Whitehead, 'International Aspects of Democratization' in Guillermo O'Donnell, Philippe Schmitter and Laurence Whitehead (eds.), *Transitions from Authoritarian Rule: Comparative Perspectives* (Johns Hopkins University Press, Baltimore, MD, 1986).

[19] This includes a useful chapter by Whitehead entitled 'Democracy and Decolonization: East-Central Europe', pp. 356–91. See also Geoffrey Pridham, Eric Herring and George Sanford (eds.), *Building Democracy: The International Dimension of Democratization in Eastern Europe* (University of Leicester Press, Leicester, rev. edn., 1997).

[20] 'Three International Dimensions of Democratization', p. 4. The first wave, in Whitehead's formulation, was that of countries—beginning with the USA—whose democratic institutions developed in the process of decolonization from the British Empire; the second was that of states whose political freedoms stemmed from the Allied Victory in the Second World War; and the third was that of the countries which underwent transition from conservative authoritarian rule in the period between 1973 and the (fourth wave) fall of Communism in Europe. (The 'three international dimensions' of Whitehead's title are 'contagion', 'control', and 'consent'.) Another early use of the notion of the 'Fourth Wave' to embrace the changes in Eastern Europe is to be found in Klaus von Beyme, *Transition to Democracy in Eastern Europe* (Macmillan, London, 1996). For a more recent, and more detailed, analysis, see Michael McFaul, 'The Fourth Wave of Democracy *and* Dictatorship: Noncooperative Transitions in the Postcommunist World', *World Politics*, Vol. 54, No. 2, January 2002, pp. 212–44. Philippe Schmitter has also written: 'We are currently in the fourth wave of democratization', but it is one which he says began in Portugal in April 1974. In short, it is other writers' 'Third Wave' and does not acknowledge how separate and specific were the transitions from Communist rule triggered by change in the Soviet Union. See Schmitter, 'The Influences of the International Context upon the Choice of National Institutions and Policies in Neo-Democracies', in Whitehead (ed.), *The International Dimensions of Democratization*, pp. 26–54, at p. 37.

they possessed (in their very different ways) most of the attributes of Communist systems, Albania, of course, more than Yugoslavia. All East European Communist states—given their common ideological and socio-political foundations—could not avoid being affected by what was happening in neighbouring Communist countries. *Fourth*, and of fundamental importance, the changes in the Soviet Union were decisive for this new wave of democratization. As the regional hegemon, the Soviet Union had determined the parameters within which political change could occur throughout Eastern Europe. The pluralization of the Soviet political system and the new, conciliatory foreign policy its leaders pursued after 1985 changed the entire context in which political developments occurred in the region.[21]

Whitehead, accordingly, is almost right when he identifies the trigger for this latest group of transitions from authoritarian rule as 'the collapse of Soviet power'.[22] The *changes* in the Soviet Union did, indeed, constitute the essential facilitating condition and the most decisive impulse to democratization in Eastern Europe. But that is not to agree that it was Soviet *collapse* which played such a role. There were two crucial changes in Russia which directly stimulated and made possible the dramatic events of 1989. First, there was the demonstration effect of liberalizing and pluralizing change within the Soviet political system itself. Second, but no less crucial, there was the change of Soviet foreign policy whereby it was in the mid-1980s decided, and by 1988 publicly communicated, that there would be no more military interventions by Soviet troops to uphold regimes in East-Central Europe which could not command the support of their own people.[23] The 'collapse of Soviet power' was, in *part*, a *consequence* of the rapidity with which Communist regimes were removed in Eastern Europe, *not* an *antecedent* of them. There are a number of interrelated and profoundly important political events which need to be kept analytically distinct. They are: the transformation of the Soviet system, the transition from Communism in Eastern Europe, the end of the Cold War, and the breakup not only of the Soviet Union but also of the two other Communist states with federal institutions, Czechoslovakia and Yugoslavia.[24]

---

[21] On this, see also Valerie J. Bunce, *Subversive Institutions: The Design and Destruction of Socialism and the State* (Cambridge University Press, New York, 1999), pp. 66–76.

[22] Whitehead, *The International Dimensions of Democratization*, p. 4.

[23] A.S. Chernyaev, *Shest' let s Gorbachevym* (Kul'tura, Moscow, 1993); Mikhail Gorbachev, *Zhizn' i reformy*, Vol. 2 (Novosti, Moscow, 1995); Vadim Medvedev, *Raspad* (Mezhdunarodnye otnosheniya, Moscow, 1994); and Georgiy Shakhnazarov, *Tsena svobody* (Rossika Zevs, Moscow, 1993). See also Jacques Lévesque, *The Enigma of 1989: The USSR and the Liberation of Eastern Europe* (University of California Press, Berkeley and Los Angeles, CA, 1997).

[24] Clearly, institutional path-determinacy had an important part to play in these outcomes. For discussion of this, see Bunce, *Subversive Institutions*, op. cit.; and Alfred Stepan, 'Russian

Some waves of democratization can largely be explained by a single event. That is surely true of the restoration (or, in the case of Japan, establishment) of democratic institutions which followed the allied victory in the Second World War. In the case of the transformation of Communist systems between 1988 and 1990, the changes in the Soviet Union are overwhelmingly the most important part of the explanation, although certainly not the whole story. These changes in Russia, in particular, require more analysis and explanation than the demise of Communism in East-Central Europe, since East Germany, Czechoslovakia, and even Hungary and Poland were penetrated political systems with very limited national autonomy, albeit varying considerably in the degree to which national elites or citizens pressed to those limits and sometimes succeeded in widening them. In all of these countries Communist systems represented an essentially foreign imposition, although this was less clear-cut in the case in the Czech lands of Bohemia and Moravia than in that of the other countries of the region until the Soviet armed intervention of August 1968.[25] It was predictable, therefore, that *liberalization* in the Soviet Union would have a profound and disproportionate impact on Eastern Europe and that *democratization* in Russia would lead to a still speedier democratization in the countries of East-Central Europe, in particular. Even when the international environment had been extremely unfavourable, democratic upsurges had occurred in Hungary, Czechoslovakia, and Poland. These, of course, met with Soviet invasion in the first two cases and intense pressure from Moscow (with the risk in the last resort of Soviet armed intervention) in the third—during the rise of Solidarity, 1980–1.[26]

Federalism in Comparative Perspective', *Post-Soviet Affairs*, Vol. 16, No. 2, April–June 2000, pp. 133–76.

[25] See H. Gordon Skilling, *Czechoslovakia's Interrupted Revolution* (Princeton University Press, Princeton, NJ, 1976); and Jaromír Navrátil (ed.), *The Prague Spring: A National Security Archive Documents Reader* (Central European Press, Budapest, 1998).

[26] The leadership of the Polish United Workers' Party (PUWP) was strongly pressured by the Soviet Politburo to crack down on 'Solidarity' and on anyone within the PUWP who showed signs of being soft on the Polish opposition. The CPSU Politburo on 21 November 1981 approved the text of a firm letter to Vojciech Jaruzelski from Leonid Brezhnev. In his lengthy missive, Brezhnev wrote, inter alia: 'Some among you assert that there now exist three tendencies within the party: left, right and centre, and they advise you to chop off the left and the right, inflicting similar blows on them. That is dangerous advice. Who, strictly speaking, are being called the "left" or "diehards"? Communists, who stand firmly on the positions of Marxism-Leninism, by no means denying the necessity of correcting admitted mistakes and distortions. And who are the right? These are people advocating revisionist views and, in the final analysis, closing ranks with "Solidarity".' It was time, Brezhnev went on, to get rid of the revisionists, including those in the party leadership. See 'Vypiska iz protokola No. 37 zasedaniya Politbyuro TsK KPSS ot 21 Noyabrya 1981 goda', HIA, Fond 89, reel 1.1010, opis 66, file 5. Marshal Viktor Kulikov, the Commander-in-Chief of the Warsaw Pact forces, was believed to have hinted at the possibility of Soviet military action, but at a Politburo meeting on 10 December 1981 an invasion was ruled out. The chairman of the Politburo's special commission on Poland, Mikhail

Jeane Kirkpatrick, in an influential article published in November 1979 (discussed briefly in Chapter 7) argued against any expectation that 'radical totalitarian regimes will transform themselves'.[27] But the Hungarian revolution had come close to transforming Hungary in 1956; the 'Prague Spring', the culmination of a reform movement which emerged from within the Communist Party, was rapidly pluralizing the Czech polity; and Kirkpatrick was writing on the very eve of the emergence of Solidarity as a massive social movement. In other words, it should have been clear even then (and to some of us it was) that if you were (*a*) to identify all Communist systems as totalitarian and (*b*) to say that totalitarian states could not be radically altered from within, then at least one of those propositions had to be wrong.[28] Either these countries were not totalitarian or the generalization about totalitarian regimes was misleading. Fundamental change *had*, in fact, taken place within those societies—both from above and below—and it was Soviet intervention, or the potential for intervention in the case of Poland, which put a stop to it. It could have been argued, of course, and frequently was, that there would be no possibility of change in the Soviet Union, but that, too, turned out to be wrong.[29]

REFERENCE GROUPS

In emphasizing the decisive importance of change in Moscow, one should not ignore other highly significant transnational influences. The exact weight of each cannot be measured, especially in retrospect, but varied from one

Suslov, KGB Chairman Yuriy Andropov and Minister of Defence Dmitriy Ustinov all spoke against it. Nevertheless, Ustinov noted that the existing Soviet army garrisons in Poland were being strengthened ('Zasedanie Politbyuro TsK KPSS 10 Dekabrya 1981 goda', HIA, Fond 89, 1.1010, opis 66, file 6). See also Carl Bernstein and Marco Politi, *His Holiness: John Paul II and the Hidden History of Our Time* (Doubleday, New York, 1996), esp. pp. 237–86; and A.S. Chernyaev, *Moya zhizn' i moe vremya* (Mezhdunarodnye otnosheniya, Moscow, 1995), pp. 410–13.

[27] Jeane Kirkpatrick, 'Dictatorship and Double Standards', *Commentary*, November 1979, pp. 34–45, at p. 44.

[28] I made these points at the time—in my Henry L. Stimson Lectures, 'Political Change in Communist Systems', at Yale University in the fall of 1980.

[29] The Soviet Union's imperviousness to change was almost an article of faith within the North Atlantic political establishment. At a conference of foreign policymakers, influentials and analysts from both sides of the Atlantic in which I participated in *February 1985*, there were only two participants (Jerry Hough and myself) who challenged the consensus and said that under Gorbachev, who, we confidently predicted, would soon be Soviet leader, important change would follow (though, admittedly, it went further and faster than even Hough and I, whose views later diverged, could claim to have expected). Nevertheless, the Chair of the final session of the conference, a former British Ambassador, summing up the proceedings, said (to nods of general approval): 'There's one thing we all know. The Soviet Union isn't going to change.'

country to another. For most of the nations there was the alternative source of information that emanated from contact with their diasporas, less restricted in the case of Poland and Hungary, more restricted (especially after 1968) in Czechoslovakia. There was widespread listening to foreign radio, particularly Radio Free Europe, and the influence, even idealization, of the United States which resulted from this. There was also the increasing prosperity of East-Central Europe's 'near abroad'—the European Community (now European Union)—which was made manifest in the growing numbers of well-heeled tourists who arrived from the countries of the European Union, especially the Federal Republic of Germany. The contrast between the two halves of Europe was far more familiar to the citizens of Poland than to those of Albania, but, in general, was becoming better known throughout the eastern part of the continent.

It is difficult to compare perceptions of the outside world of East and Central Europeans over time—across the post-war decades—because in some countries there was no survey research until just before or just after the fall of Communism. In others, where such studies were conducted earlier, there was, nevertheless, little serious research on public opinion until the 1970s and 1980s and, even then, variations in the extent to which the most sensitive political questions could be asked and, if posed, answered honestly. But the image of Western Europe could not *but* be better in the 1980s than it had been in the 1950s or even the 1960s. That was especially true of its leading economic power, West Germany, as memories of the war faded and it became increasingly clear that this was a different Germany from that which had been the cause of so much suffering across the continent. The Chancellorship of Willy Brandt—in combination with Brandt's anti-Nazi wartime record—played an important part in changing perceptions.

All that notwithstanding, however, it is highly probable that the countries of Eastern Europe would have rapidly ceased to be Communist in *any* decade from the 1950s onwards had their peoples not accurately perceived that behind their own national rulers stood the might of the Soviet army and a Soviet leadership ready to use whatever level of coercion would be necessary to uphold a pro-Soviet Communist regime in countries which it viewed as the main fruits of victory in the Second World War. The transition *to* Communism had owed more to the Soviet army than to domestic revolutionaries except, as noted earlier, in Yugoslavia and Albania. In Albania's case Yugoslav help was more important than that of the Soviet Union. Czechoslovakia was an ambiguous and intermediate case. There were no Soviet troops on Czech soil when the Communist Party seized full power there in 1948, but since the end of the war Stalin had regarded Czechoslovakia as being within the Soviet sphere of influence, and Czech politicians on both sides of the political divide felt the pressures from Moscow.

In the transition *from* Communism much depended on what a particular nation's or group of nations' reference group was. Thus, for example, the Czechs liked to compare themselves with Austria. The most orthodox Communists apart, they never failed to remind Western visitors to Communist Czechoslovakia that between the wars they had been every bit as prosperous as Austria, whereas once they were locked into the Soviet bloc and a Communist system, the Austrians had left them far behind.[30] In the Soviet Union the reference group for the three Baltic states was their Scandinavian neighbours. It is hardly surprising that this accentuated dissatisfaction with their Soviet lot. That those Scandinavian countries had far greater freedom, greater wealth *and* much superior welfare states to the Soviet one was all too evident.

Once democratization processes got seriously underway in Eastern Europe in the late 1980s transnational influences became still more directly effective. The Communist regimes were never entirely able to stop ideas crossing national boundaries, and by the late 1980s they were totally *in*capable of preventing detailed information being made available by radio and even television of events in neighbouring countries they would rather their populations did not know about. News from a more distant country could, in principle, affect people's beliefs about what was *politically desirable*, but it was news of what was happening in neighbouring countries that convinced them of what was *politically possible*. To some extent, one could say that this was what Whitehead calls 'contagion through proximity',[31] although, arguably, that may better explain Spain following fast on the heels of Portugal than the changes of East-Central Europe, to which the failure of democratization in Yugoslavia (as Whitehead himself notes) stands out in the Fourth Wave. Philippe Schmitter observes that 'Eastern Europe may provide the best possible case for contagion', but he also makes the crucial qualification that this was 'even though the initial impetus for regime change was given by an exogenous event, i.e. the shift in Soviet foreign and defence policy vis-à-vis the region'.[32]

---

[30] I made five study visits to Czechoslovakia when it was still a Communist state—in 1965, 1968, 1969, 1976, and 1983—and heard the comparison with Austria from a wide variety of different people every time.

[31] Whitehead, *The International Dimensions of Democratization*, p. 5.

[32] Schmitter, 'The Influence of the International Context upon the Choice of National Institutions and Policies in Neo-Democracies', in Whitehead (ed.), *The International Dimensions of Democratization*, p. 40.

LIBERALIZATION AND DEMOCRATIZATION

All serious writers on transitions from authoritarian rule make a distinction between liberalization and democratization. This is undoubtedly relevant in analysis of the transition from Communism, even if in some cases the two processes were so compressed as to be almost simultaneous. But well before the late 1980s liberalization in one European Communist state could have an influence elsewhere. The special and overwhelmingly most important case is, once again, the Soviet Union. It is enough to recall the impact in East-Central Europe—above all in Poland and Hungary—of the 20th Party Congress in Moscow in 1956 and Khrushchev's 'Secret Speech'. But there were intellectual and reformist influences from one East-Central European country to another. I clearly recall seeing prominently displayed in Prague shop windows in 1965 the works of the Polish economic reformer, Włodzimierz Brus (some years later to become an Oxford colleague), whose writings had been translated from Polish into Czech. He was among the important influences on Ota Šik and the Czech economic reformers. Later the current of influence went into reverse. The crushing of the 'Prague Spring', following the Soviet invasion of August 1968, reinforced conservative Communists throughout Eastern Europe, even in Poland. (Brus was among the leading Polish intellectuals who emigrated at the end of the 1960s or beginning of the 1970s, in Brus's case in 1972 to Britain.)

What, however, occurred in Eastern Europe up until the changes in the Soviet Union which began in 1985–6—and became much more profound in 1987–8—was, at best, pockets of liberalization, not democratization. Thus, it is impossible to agree with those who see Pope John Paul II as the great democratizer of Eastern Europe, although the Catholic Church was the strongest independent institution in several Communist countries, most obviously in Poland. Huntington quotes with approval Timothy Garton Ash writing that the Pope's 'first great pilgrimage' to Poland was the 'beginning of the end' of Communism in Eastern Europe.[33] But *post hoc* does not mean *ergo propter hoc*. One could, with greater plausibility, say that Khrushchev's 1956 'Secret Speech' was the beginning of the end of Communism in Eastern Europe, but that end was a long time in coming.

Certainly the election of a Polish Pope in 1978 was far from good news for the Polish Communist leadership. When Stanislaw Kania telephoned Gierek to break the bad tidings, the response of the first secretary of the Polish United Workers' Party was to exclaim: 'Holy Mother of God'![34] Even at

---

[33] Huntington, *The Third Wave*, p. 83.   [34] Bernstein and Politi, *His Holiness*, p. 175.

the time it was clear that having a fellow-countryman in the Vatican—a man who as a Bishop and Cardinal had stood up to the Communist authorities and who became the first non-Italian Pope for four and a half centuries—had galvanized the Polish opposition and given them a sense that God was on their side. It surely played a significant part in the rise of Solidarity. But Solidarity, while it was an admired example in much of Eastern Europe, was not one which was followed anywhere. Moreover, its success, before the imposition of martial law in December 1981, was relatively short-lived— until, that is, the changes in the Soviet Union much later in the decade created a political climate in which, between 1988 and 1990, it could re-emerge victorious. Solidarity worried the Soviet Politburo intensely even in its first phase,[35] but that did not lead them to liberalize, still less democratize. Quite the reverse. At best it sent a very ambiguous message to the Soviet Union. For some of the more enlightened party intellectuals in research institutes in Moscow and the more thoughtful members of the Central Committee apparatus it was a useful lesson that the working class could be in the vanguard not of society's triumphal progress on the path to Communism but in the rejection of Communism. It could be interpreted as reinforcing the need to avoid too excessive and visible inequalities in society but also as emphasizing the necessity of stamping hard on dissident groups before they got out of hand. As a matter of historical fact, the crackdown on the Soviet dissident movement was especially harsh post-1979 and up to, and including, Chernenko's thirteen months as General Secretary. The leading Western specialist on Soviet dissent, Peter Reddaway, referred at the end of 1983 to the 'post-1979 purge of dissent' and, at the same time, acknowledged that 'the dissenting groups and movements...have made little or no headway among the mass of ordinary people in the Russian heartland'.[36]

The Pope unquestionably made a huge impact on Polish society and politics and helped to put the party-state authorities on the defensive. To the extent that he helped to inspire the Polish opposition in 1979, 1980, and 1981, he had an impact, too, on the Soviet Politburo as they pressed the leadership of the PUWP to take a firmer stand against the growing pluralization of Polish politics. If Huntington is right, the Pope also played a part in the

---

[35] A special commission of the Politburo to deal with the Polish question was set up on 25 August 1980. Chaired by Suslov, its other eight members included Andrey Gromyko, Yuriy Andropov, Dmitriy Ustinov and Konstantin Chernenko (HIA, Fond 89, 1.1010, opis 66, file 1). Other deliberations of the Soviet leadership on Poland are to be found in HIA, Fond 89, 1.1003, opis 42, file 34; Fond 89, 1.1010, opis 66, file 5; and Fond 89, 1.1010, opis 66, file 6. See also Bernstein and Politi, *His Holiness*, pp. 247–57; and Chernyaev, *Moya zhizn' i moe vremya*, pp. 410–13.

[36] Peter Reddaway, 'Dissent in the Soviet Union', *Problems of Communism*, Vol. 32, No. 6, 1983, p. 14.

democratization of Brazil, the Philippines, Argentina, Guatemala, Nicaragua, El Salvador, Haiti, Korea, Chile, and Paraguay with his visits to those countries.[37] That is quite an impressive list and, in terms of impact, one could easily add Lithuania. But there again democratization did not follow an election in Rome or events in Poland, but radical change in Moscow.

Once the sequence of democratization in Eastern Europe was underway, the transnational influences in the form of demonstration effects were obvious. If the Poles and Hungarians could get away with it (with Communist rulers and Opposition leaders agreeing on new democratic rules of the game in the course of Roundtable discussions in the spring and summer of 1989), why, thought the Czechs and East Germans, the Romanians and Bulgarians, should not they? In November and December of the same year, in a variety of ways (but violently only in Romania) they did. And once Moscow had conceded the independence of 'the outer empire', it gave added confidence to the citizens of the most restive parts of the 'inner empire' in the Baltic states, ever more boldly from 1989, to press the case for *their* independence. One of the most important examples of demonstration effects—and, in this case, *literally*, the effect of *demonstrations*—was the impact that the massive and public rejection of Communist rule in Eastern Europe had on the attitudes to the Communist Party of *Russians*. While a lot of information on the misdeeds of their Soviet rulers was being published in the USSR, especially from 1986–7 onwards, Russians came much later than most East Europeans to associate their misfortunes specifically with the rule of the Communist Party.

However, between March and August 1989 there was a sharp fall in the proportion of the Soviet population who expressed 'full trust' in the CPSU—from just under 40 per cent to a little over 20 per cent.[38] There were certainly major domestic factors involved in this, among them the televised broadcasts of the sessions of the new Soviet legislature—the Congress of People's Deputies—which broke new ground with their airing of public criticism of Communist Party leaders and policies. But the culmination of the changes in Eastern Europe in November–December 1989 coincided with a sharp rise in the number of Soviet respondents who said they had 'no trust' in the Communist Party. The percentage of citizens in that category almost doubled (to just under 40 per cent) between December 1989 and March 1990.[39] For a majority of the population the 'leading role' of the Communist Party had

[37] Huntington, *The Third Wave*, pp. 82–5.
[38] Matthew Wyman, *Public Opinion in Postcommunist Russia* (Macmillan, London, 1997), p. 63.
[39] Ibid.

simply been taken for granted until almost the end of the 1980s. There was hardly anyone alive who could remember anything else. While people were far from satisfied with their lot, there had been no mass movement from below to change the fundamentals of the system. What Soviet citizens saw, however, on their own television screens—as a result of glasnost—of the massive demonstrations against Communist rulers and the Communist system in Prague, Bucharest and several cities of East Germany helped to give a much more radically anti-Communist character to their dissatisfaction.

WESTERN INFLUENCES

Once a wave of democratization had begun in Communist Europe, the importance of contagion, proximity, and demonstration effects is fairly clear. But, as Whitehead says of the contagion hypothesis, it 'cannot tell us how a sequence begins, why it ends, what it excludes, or even the order in which it is likely to advance'.[40] And, of course, correlation, as always, must be separated from causation, for it may be 'the policy of a third country that explains the spread of democracy from one country to the next'.[41] Many people in the United States, in East-Central Europe and some even in Russia would argue that the third country which should be credited with causing the democratization of Eastern Europe was *not* the Soviet Union at a certain, late phase of its history but the United States, thus addressing in one of its variants the question raised earlier in this chapter of the impact of the West on the Soviet Union. The influence of the United States is certainly not to be discounted, but writers such as Richard Pipes have exaggerated its causative, as distinct from facilitating, role in bringing about democratization in Eastern Europe.

During Ronald Reagan's first term as President international tension was acute and East European independence remote. Neither the archival evidence nor the recollections of significant foreign policy actors in the Soviet Union during the 1980s support the view that the hard-line aspects of Reagan's foreign policy had the positive impact that has been claimed for them on debates within the Soviet leadership.[42] It was the changes introduced on the initiative of the Soviet side, in which 'new thinking' was followed by 'new behaviour', which persuaded not only British Prime Minister Margaret

[40] Whitehead (ed.), *The International Dimensions of Democratization*, p. 6.
[41] Ibid., p. 9.
[42] I return to that theme in chapter nine. For an earlier discussion, see Brown, *The Gorbachev Factor*, pp. 225–42 and 315–18.

Thatcher but also President Reagan that this was a leader they could 'do business with'. Gorbachev was the fourth Soviet General Secretary to overlap with the Reagan presidency, and nothing changed for the better either in East–West relations or in the autonomy accorded Eastern Europe until he succeeded Chernenko. He then proceeded to create, very early on, a new foreign policy team, in which Aleksandr Yakovlev, Eduard Shevardnadze, Vadim Medvedev, Anatoliy Chernyaev, Georgiy Shakhnazarov, and Yevgeniy Primakov were among those who played the most significant parts. All owed their promotion to Gorbachev and several were surprise choices for the posts they were asked to fill.

This raises another extremely important source of transnational influence—the impact on these leading political actors of their experience of the West, a different aspect of Western impact on Soviet policy. There cannot, of course, be a simple equation between foreign travel and a more positive view of Western political and economic systems or of Western intentions. Gromyko, after all, had spent much time in Western countries and Shevardnadze scarcely any before he entered the Ministry of Foreign Affairs. Shevardnadze, however, had by far the more open mind of the two and was undoubtedly influenced by his Western interlocutors after he moved from Tbilisi to Moscow and embarked on his travels as Foreign Minister. The most important example by far, though, of reassessment of former stereotypes as a result of foreign travel was that of Gorbachev. This occurred well before he became General Secretary, although he did not broadcast these views outside a trusted circle. Vadim Medvedev, Chernyaev, and Shakhnazarov have all reported Gorbachev saying to them at different times that it was his trips to Western Europe which first made him realize how little in common much of Soviet propaganda concerning the West had with reality.[43]

Gorbachev had visited several East European countries in the 1960s, but his earliest visit to Western Europe was to Italy in 1971.[44] It was followed in that decade with visits to Belgium, Holland, France (in 1976 and 1977), and the Federal Republic of Germany. In the first half of the 1980s three of Gorbachev's visits to North America and Western Europe had an especially important impact on him. The first of these was to Canada in 1983 (where he also had long and important conversations with the Soviet Ambassador, Aleksandr Yakovlev, in which they talked frankly and achieved a political and

---

[43] Chernyaev, Shakhnazarov, and Medvedev all independently mentioned this in interviews between 1991 and 1993 when I asked them what impact, if any, Gorbachev's visits to Western Europe in the 1970s had made on him.

[44] Gorbachev, *Zhizn' i reformy*, vol. 1, p. 159. Chernyaev, who first met Gorbachev on a trip to Belgium and Holland in 1972, was mistaken in thinking that this was Gorbachev's first visit to the West (Chernyaev, *Shest' let s Gorbachevym*, p. 8).

personal understanding).[45] Gorbachev has written of the powerful impetus to thought his Canadian visit provided, especially his exposure to the efficiency of Canadian agriculture.[46] The second was to Italy in June 1984 when Gorbachev led the Soviet delegation to the funeral of the popular leader of the PCI, the 'Eurocommunist' Enrico Berlinguer. The head of the International Department, Boris Ponomarev, had assumed that *he* would head the Soviet group, but both Chernenko's foreign policy adviser, Andrey Aleksandrov-Agentov, and the First Deputy Head of the International Department, Vadim Zagladin, warned the Politburo that this would be an insensitive choice, given the extent to which Ponomarev had castigated the 'Eurocommunists' as dangerous revisionists. Following consultations with the PCI, Mikhail Gorbachev was chosen to lead the group.[47] He was astounded by the scale and emotion of the support for a Communist leader and by the sight of hundreds of thousands of Italians joining in the mourning. 'What we saw in Rome', Gorbachev wrote, 'left in our souls a deep, unforgettable impression'.[48] Gorbachev found especially remarkable the fact that the President of Italy, on behalf of the nation, bowed before the coffin of the departed Communist leader. This, Gorbachev remarked, was a manifestation of 'a different political culture'—one which clearly appealed to him.[49]

The third visit to make an especially significant impact on Gorbachev, and one in which he made no less of an impression on his hosts, was the week he spent in Britain in December 1984. During it he addressed Members of Parliament, met the Leader of the Opposition, Neil Kinnock, and the Labour Shadow Foreign Secretary, Denis Healey, and, most importantly, had lengthy meetings with the Prime Minister, Margaret Thatcher, and Foreign Secretary, Sir Geoffrey Howe. He established a rapport with Margaret Thatcher which was to stand them both in good stead in the years ahead. She was especially important initially in persuading Ronald Reagan that Gorbachev was a different Soviet leader from those they had been used to dealing with: 'he was much less constrained, more charming, open to discussion and debate, and did not stick to prepared notes'.[50] They disagreed on many matters, but

---

[45] See Aleksandr Yakovlev, *Sumerki* (Materik, Moscow, 2003), pp. 353–4.

[46] Gorbachev, *Zhizn' i reformy*, vol. 1, pp. 238–9.

[47] Ibid., p. 255.   [48] Ibid.   [49] Ibid.

[50] From the official—now declassified—memorandum of a conversation between Prime Minister Margaret Thatcher and President Ronald Reagan, 28 December 1984, at Camp David. The document is available both in the Reagan Library and at http://www.margaret-thatcher.org/archive. The American Secretary of State at the time, George Shultz, noted the importance of Margaret Thatcher's visit to the United States immediately after Gorbachev had been to Britain. He wrote: 'Our knowledge of the Kremlin was thin, and the CIA, I found, was usually wrong about it.... Our appetite was whetted by Gorbachev's performance on a visit to London'. Shultz cites in his memoirs Margaret Thatcher's public statement in London: 'I like

on the basis of mutual respect.[51] Summing up the relationship with Margaret Thatcher in his most recent book, Gorbachev writes:

For us Thatcher was not an easy partner, especially having in mind her anti-Communism, which sometimes prevented her from seeing things more realistically. Although in many cases she was able to illustrate her accusations with facts, which later we ourselves began to subject to reappraisal.[52]

In his memoirs Gorbachev draws attention to the great importance to him in a variety of ways of these foreign visits; they filled gaps in his knowledge left by the paucity of reliable information about Western countries dispensed in the Soviet Union; they enabled him to discover, and be impressed by, the lack of hostility to Soviet citizens; he learned that in Western Europe people had a higher standard of living than in the Soviet Union and that, in turn, prompted him to ask the question 'why?' Gorbachev's favourite interlocutor among foreign statesmen was the Spanish Prime Minister—and socialist of a social democratic complexion—Felipe González.[53] Writing in 2006 of the important conversation lasting many hours which they had had twenty years earlier in Moscow, Gorbachev described González as 'one of the representatives of a new generation of leaders of the Socialist International, a genuine democrat' and confirms that their dialogue had been important for him.[54] Most significantly of all, Gorbachev observes that after he had seen a functioning civil society and the political systems of Western Europe, his '*a priori* faith in the advantages of socialist over bourgeois democracy was shaken'.[55]

Learning from seeing was important also for key members of Gorbachev's entourage. Yakovlev's ten-year stint (1973–83) as Soviet Ambassador to Canada gave him unusual exposure to a Western country for a Soviet official who had been acting head of the Department of Propaganda of the Central Committee and who was to continue to be much concerned with ideological issues.[56] Those who worked with him at IMEMO during his time

Mr Gorbachev. We can do business together', and notes that in private also 'she was enthusiastic about Gorbachev' (George P. Shultz, *Turmoil and Triumph: My Years as Secretary of State* (Scribner's, New York, 1993), pp. 507 and 509).

[51] Gorbachev, *Zhizn' i reformy*, vol. 1, pp. 257–9.

[52] Mikhail Gorbachev, *Ponyat' perestroyku . . . pochemu eto vazhno seychas* (Moscow: Al'pina biznes buks, 2006), p. 190.

[53] On this, see Brown, *The Gorbachev Factor*, pp. 116–17.

[54] Gorbachev, *Ponyat' perestroyku*, pp. 102–3.

[55] Gorbachev, *Zhizn' i reformyi*, vol. 1, p. 169.

[56] On qualitative change in Soviet political learning more generally, see George Breslauer and Philip E. Tetlock (eds.), *Learning in U.S. and Soviet Foreign Policy* (Westview Press, Boulder, CO, 1991), especially the chapters by Robert Legvold (pp. 684–732) and Breslauer (pp. 825–56).

as its Director, 1983–5, mention how frequently, and positively, he referred to Canada (as distinct from the United States, of which he had remained critical after spending a year at Columbia University in 1959). Gorbachev's two most important aides, in policy advisory terms, Chernyaev and Shakhnazarov, were also frequent travellers to the West as well as, in the case of Shakhnazarov (as a senior official in the Socialist Countries Department of the Central Committee) to Eastern Europe. Both were closet social democrats within the Central Committee apparatus.[57]

Of course, there were many other changes in Communist societies apart from those induced by transnational influences. A focus on the transnational is a recognition of its importance, not advocacy of unicausal explanation. In the Soviet case, there were important domestic factors at work and, indeed, the *timing* of Soviet reforms stemmed from domestic policy choices made by the new Kremlin leadership. Some of the significant Western influence was on Establishment social scientists, for they, in contrast with non-Party members, had far better opportunities to travel to the West and to make personal contact with their Western counterparts. But until early 1989 the most crucial influence of the West, even for the East-Central European transition, was through its impact on key decision-makers in Moscow. The more favourable perceptions of Western policies and institutions by Gorbachev and his allies in the Soviet leadership and their determination to make radical changes in both domestic and foreign policy constituted the most important facilitating condition for what followed in Eastern Europe in 1989. Indeed, the programme of reform which Gorbachev persuaded the Nineteenth Party Conference to accept in the summer of 1988 went beyond that of the 'Prague Spring' reformers of twenty years earlier. It thus provided not just a green light for but also a direct stimulus to reform in East-Central Europe. In Hungary, David Stark and László Bruszt observe, János Kádár liked to boast that 'what Gorbachev is trying to do now, we already accomplished decades before', but he was replaced as Hungarian party leader in May 1988 by a coalition of opponents who were aware that 'Hungary was actually lagging behind the Soviet Union in the field of political reform'.[58]

---

[57] Shakhnazarov emphasized, in an interview I had with him on 16 December 1991, how important seeing other countries for himself had been for the evolution of *his* views. There is scope for further research on that section of the Soviet political elite which backed Gorbachev's reforms and played an important part in the break with previous Soviet foreign policy.

[58] David Stark and László Bruszt, *Postsocialist Pathways: Transforming Politics and Prosperity in East-Central Europe* (Cambridge University Press, Cambridge and New York, 1998), p. 21.

EAST-CENTRAL EUROPE: SELF-ASSERTION
AND CONTAGION

The Hungarian Revolution of 1956 was even harder for Soviet leaders to come to terms with than the Prague Spring, for it had been a violent uprising and had involved the hanging of Communist secret policemen from lamp-posts. Thus, the most reformist member of the Hungarian Politburo, Imre Poszgay, caused a sensation when he announced in January 1989 that a commission he headed which had examined 'the events of 1956' had come to the conclusion that this had been a 'popular insurrection'.[59] The head of the International Department of the Soviet Communist Party's Central Committee, Valentin Falin, immediately drafted a memorandum restating the Soviet position that this had been a counter-revolution. But, to the astonishment of those Hungarians who waited with baited breath for Moscow's reaction, there *was* no reaction, for Falin's memorandum was never sent. Gorbachev refused to endorse it, invoking his policy of non-interference.[60] The Hungarian reassessment was in itself important beyond the borders of Hungary, but so was the Soviet response or, more precisely, non-response.

A Hungarian decision which had even more far-reaching consequences was the opening of the border to Austria in late May 1989. This led to tens of thousands of East Germans using Hungary as a route to West Germany and put colossal pressure on the East German authorities. It was a decision which led by November of the same year to the opening of the Berlin Wall. While the Hungarian government had grounds for stating that they took this momentous decision independently, Jacques Lévesque, who interviewed many of the principal political actors, adds two 'nuances' to that statement. Some days before the Hungarian decision was made public in May, Foreign Minister Gyula Horn went on a secret visit to Bonn where he met Chancellor Helmut Kohl and extracted a promise of a loan of one billion DM in return for opening the border. He asked the Germans to allow a 'decent' delay after the doors were opened before announcing the credits.[61] The second, and even more important, 'nuance' is that the Hungarian Foreign Ministry also sent a note to Soviet Foreign Minister Shevardnadze some days in advance of the

---

[59] See Rudolf L. Tőkés, *Hungary's Negotiated Revolution: Economic Reform, Social Change, and Political Succession* (Cambridge University Press, Cambridge, 1996), pp. 298–9; and Lévesque, *The Enigma of 1989*, p. 129.

[60] Ibid., pp. 129–30. For Valentin Falin's own critical assessment of the conduct of Soviet foreign policy under Gorbachev, see Falin, *Bez skidok na obstoyatel'stva: politicheskie vosponimaniya* (Respublika, Moscow, 1999), pp. 380–458.

[61] Lévesque, *The Enigma of 1989*, p. 153.

announcement of opening the borders. The purpose was, according to Hungarian Deputy Foreign Minister László Kovács, 'to inform the USSR about the probable direction we were intending to take'. The Soviet reaction was again to do nothing. Shevardnadze's terse reply said simply: 'This is an affair that concerns Hungary, the GDR and the FRG.'[62] At this stage a Soviet hands-off policy was still a decisive element of transnational influence. By the end of the year, the precedents which had built up were such that Soviet non-intervention was being taken for granted, so that from then on Soviet (and Russian) influence over Eastern Europe was dramatically diminished. For over forty years both East European rulers and peoples had been obliged to think about the likely reaction in Moscow to what they did. In the course of 1989 that changed irrevocably.

The closer East European states and Russia got to dismantling the Communist system, the more salient and direct became Western influences. No longer were they mediated by Gorbachev and like-minded colleagues who wished to preserve as much of a regional alliance—and, especially, as much of the Soviet Union—as could be kept together without recourse to sustained coercion. Moreover, while that radically reformist wing of the Soviet leadership was in favour of movement to an essentially market economy, they hesitated to remove all controls before new political and economic institutions were functioning. By 1990–1 the Soviet Union was in crisis, and 'the moments of greatest freedom', Peter Gourevitch has suggested on the basis of comparative study of international economic crises, 'are crisis points' with choices 'more constrained in stable times'.[63] For the radical opposition in Russia during 1990–1—not only to the old regime but to Gorbachev, by this time castigated for what were held to be 'half-measures'—transnational influences were enormously important. Many activists in, and supporters of, the 'Democratic Russia' movement made an uncritical association between the West, democracy, a market economy and greater prosperity.[64] One manifestation of this was the growing popularity of Margaret Thatcher in the Soviet Union in the late 1980s. She had impressed viewers when she was interviewed on Soviet TV in 1987. When a VTsIOM poll conducted in December 1989 asked respondents to name the 'woman of the year', the then British Prime Minister emerged as the clear winner.[65]

---

[62] Ibid., p. 153.

[63] Peter Gourevitch, *Politics in Hard Times: Comparative Responses to International Economic Crises* (Cornell University Press, Ithaca, NY, and London, 1986), p. 240. For a critique of Gourevitch's and related work, see Gabriel A. Almond, 'Review Article: The International–National Connection', *British Journal of Political Science*, Vol. 19, No. 2, 1989, pp. 237–59.

[64] A substantial body of evidence on this is to be found in Alexander Lukin, *The Political Culture of the Russian 'Democrats'* (Oxford University Press, Oxford, 2000).

[65] *Obshchestvennoe mnenie v tsifrakh*, 6/13, February 1990 (VTsIOM, Moscow), p. 14.

Boris Yeltsin, enjoying the enthusiastic support of 'Democratic Russia', increasingly portrayed Gorbachev as only a very partially reconstructed Communist. Presenting himself as a truer democrat and better friend of the West, he resolutely moved into political space created by Gorbachev's pluralizing reforms. Yeltsin's self-portrait was misleading in important respects, but his lack of concern about legal and democratic institution-building became clear only later. The decisive steps in the transition from Communism had been taken by Gorbachev and he was the sole Westernizer to hold the office of General Secretary of the CPSU.

CONCLUSIONS

Transnational influences came directly from the West to Eastern Europe, partly through diasporas, partly through radio broadcasts aimed directly at the East European populations, partly through foreign travel in both directions. Of the many ways in which such influence came to the Soviet Union from the West, perhaps the most important—and least attended to—was the direct impact of Western interlocutors and Western travel on a new generation of Soviet policymakers and, in particular, on Gorbachev. There was very definite influence from one Eastern European country to another, most spectacularly in the year of transformation, 1989, more subtly before that. East-Central Europe had an ambiguous impact on the Soviet Union. When, from the point of view of Soviet within-system reformers, East European reforms went too far and too fast, this could strengthen the hand of hardliners within the Soviet Establishment and so hold up by years Soviet reforms. Thus, while the Prague Spring was welcomed (in private) by the more radical Russian reformers, closet reformers within the higher echelons of the Communist Party feared that it was going to result in a severe setback for them. When the Soviet military intervention in August 1968 took place to put an end to the Czech reforms, that was, indeed, a victory for conservative forces in Russia which saw them through the remainder of the Brezhnev era—another fourteen years—without disturbance.

Similarly, the rise of Solidarity did nothing to strengthen Soviet reformers but led to a more severe crackdown on Russian dissidents. In contrast, because Hungarian reform under Kádár was cautious and evolutionary, Russian economic reformers were able to draw upon the work of their Hungarian colleagues in their own writings, though it took two leadership changes before they gained a hearing at the top of the party hierarchy. The process of listening began with Andropov, stopped under Chernenko, and began again—and accelerated—under Gorbachev. In 1989 what happened in Eastern Europe had a huge impact on the Soviet Union itself. East-Central European independence stimulated and emboldened demands for outright independence in a number of Soviet republics, especially the Baltic states, and also gave a more anti-Communist character to the growing opposition movement in Russia. It was, however, the changes in the Soviet Union in the second half of the 1980s which altered the entire political context in which East-Central and Eastern European peoples lived and politicians acted. *That* transnational influence was the decisive trigger and indispensable facilitator of transition from Communist rule and of the Fourth Wave of democratization—from Budapest and Berlin to the Baltic states.

9

Ending the Cold War

The debate on *why* the Cold War ended when it did has been intense. There remains disagreement, indeed, over *when* precisely it could be said to be over. There are a good many Russian political commentators and at least one prominent Western analyst who have argued that the Cold War is not over yet.[1] In a number of respects, some fifteen years after the Soviet Union ceased to exist, relations between the United States and Western Europe, on the one hand, and Russia, on the other, have again become clouded by mutual suspicion. Moreover, this is against a backdrop of NATO enlargement and of continued expenditure both in the United States and in Russia on weapons of mass destruction. Increasingly in the West, Russia is seen as moving backwards towards more authoritarian rule, a perception matched by a widespread Russian view that the United States is behaving in the twenty-first century like an imperial power and, together with its 'coalition of the willing', acting in contravention of international law in Iraq.

---

[1] For example, Valentin Aleksandrov, a senior official in the Socialist Countries Department and (from 1988) the International Department of the Central Committee, referred in an interview to his 'deep conviction that, unfortunately, the "cold war" has not ended'—p. 43 of transcript of the interview on 12 November 1998 by Viktor Kuvaldin and Gordon M. Hahn (The Hoover Institution and the Gorbachev Foundation, Moscow, Oral History Project, Accession No. 98067–16.305, Box 1, Hoover Institution Archives). Vitaliy Tretyakov, the founding editor of Russia's first large-circulation independent newspaper in the perestroika period, *Nezavisimaya gazeta*, and—as of 2006—editor of *Moskovskie novosti*, declared at a conference held in Moscow in October 2004, whose proceedings were published in 2005: 'But I say that the "cold war" is continuing today. And war between the United States and Russia continues.' See Tretyakov, 'Da, Rossiya vsegda ne takaya moshchnaya, kak ona sama o sebe dumaet, no i vsegda ne takaya slabaya, kak o ney dumayut drugie', in V.I. Tolstykh (ed.), *Perestroika dvadsat' let spustya* (Russkiy put', Moscow, 2005), pp. 202–8, at p. 204. Picking up on the statement of an American participant in the conference that a 'normal country' is one in which 'you are threatening no one and no one is threatening you', Tretyakov put the question: 'and is the United States today a normal country? Is it really threatening no one today? And is no-one really threatening it?' (ibid., p. 203). At another conference (in which I participated), devoted to the Cold War and held at the Gorbachev Foundation on 1 March 2006, an American scholar, Stephen F. Cohen, took a very different view from that castigated by Tretyakov, arguing, like him, that the Cold War has not ended yet. (See also Cohen's article, 'The New American Cold War', *The Nation*, 10 July 2006.)

However, the changing evaluations on both sides have led to only a mild deterioration in the relations between the world's most formidable military power and the country richest in energy resources. The relationship between the United States and Russia remains qualitatively different from the highly ideologized struggle that characterized the Cold War in the most meaningful sense of that term. In that long-lasting conflict each side was prepared to risk nuclear holocaust rather than be forced to adopt the political system of the adversary. It was a clash of systems, not just of interests and values, important though both of the latter were. The 'First World'—an anti-Communist alliance headed by the United States—and the 'Second World', the Communist bloc controlled by the Soviet Union (though with important outriders, especially China) competed directly for bases and influence in the 'Third World'.[2] Both sides emphasized the superiority of their social, economic, and political systems, and devoted vast sums to propagating their systemic advantages.

COLD WAR AS CLASH OF SYSTEMS

The tensions between Russia and the United States today are not of the same order, and it is reasonable to reserve the term 'Cold War' for the clash of *systems*. Although both Communist leaders and their Western antagonists often made pragmatic, rather than ideological, decisions and came to temporary agreements and compromises, the struggle was seen on both sides as a zero-sum game, one that could end only with the triumph of Communism or with the triumph of democracy or—in an alternative emphasis in the systemic struggle—of capitalism. As the Communist system came to an end, one of the most important dividing lines not only among Russians but also—and at least as important—in the West was between those for whom democracy was the more important alternative and those who, while paying lip-service to 'freedom' and 'democracy', were primarily interested in building capitalism. That, indeed, is a theme which merits more detailed attention from students of post-Soviet Russia.

There can be no definitive—still less 'scientific'—answer to the question, 'when did the Cold War end?', since the expression, 'Cold War', is, after all, a metaphor. The reality it encompassed was both an extraordinarily important and extremely dangerous stage of affairs, but the fact remains it was *not* a war.

---

[2] For an exceptionally thorough overview of the struggle for the 'Third World', see Odd Arne Westad, *The Global Cold War* (Cambridge University Press, Cambridge, 2005).

Granted, however, that it was the designation for the stand-off between the United States and its allies, especially in Western Europe, on the one side, and the Soviet Union and the Communist bloc, on the other, there is a very strong argument for holding that the Cold War, in the most meaningful sense of the term, ended in 1989 when the Soviet bloc itself ceased to exist. The Cold War began with the Soviet takeover of Eastern Europe in the form of acquisition of power by Moscow-dominated Communist Parties. It ended when the countries of Central and Eastern Europe became non-Communist and independent.

As already noted, the Cold War was an *ideologized* struggle—and not only on the Soviet side. A lot of the rhetoric in the United States—about the 'free world', for example—only partly corresponded to objective reality. The 'free world' embraced some highly unpleasant and authoritarian states (as well, of course, as many democratic ones) which were accorded a place in this pantheon of 'freedom' because of the anti-Communist credentials of their dictatorial leaders. The de-ideologization of foreign policy actually occurred more quickly in Moscow than in Washington in the second half of the 1980s as part of the process of conceptual revolution that was taking place in Russia, and the Soviet Union as a whole, during the perestroika period.[3] In that context, it should be noted that from an ideological standpoint, the Cold War was concluded in 1988—a year before it ended on the ground. It was in 1988—first of all, in his major Nineteenth Party Conference speech in the summer of that year and again in December when he spoke at the United Nations—that Mikhail Gorbachev stressed the right of the people of every state to choose their own political and economic system.[4] In the context of post-Second World War history, that was a momentous proclamation. Its significance was fully understood, even in Eastern Europe, only in 1989 when Soviet deeds, to the surprise of some Western cold warriors, fully corresponded with Gorbachev's words. Soviet troops remained in their barracks and did not interfere with the process that brought Communist rule to an end in the countries which, along with the Soviet Union, had formed the Warsaw Pact.

Why this happened is debated much more than the *when*. Not many people would date the end of the Cold War any more recently than the

---

[3] The fundamental character of that conceptual revolution in different areas of thought and policy is discussed in Archie Brown (ed.), *The Demise of Marxism-Leninism in Russia* (Palgrave Macmillan, Basingstoke, 2004).

[4] See M.S. Gorbachev, *Izbrannye rechi i stat'i* (Politizdat, Moscow, 1989), vol. 6, pp. 323–97, at p. 347; and Gorbachev, *Izbrannye rechi i stat'i*, vol. 7 (1990), pp. 184–202, at p. 188. The language Gorbachev used about the universality of this principle at a time when 'the survival of civilization' was at stake was very similar in both the conference speech of 28 June and the UN speech of 7 December 1988.

unification of Germany in 1990, the last date for which a serious argument can be made.[5] Even that, however, followed logically from Gorbachev's decision not to use force to preserve the status quo in Eastern Europe and from his acceptance of the spontaneous demolition of the Berlin Wall the previous November. Moreover, although the 'free to choose' announcement was made public and explicit only in 1988, Gorbachev came to office in 1985 with the intention of doing all in his power to end the Cold War. From the outset, he aimed to end as early as possible Soviet military involvement in Afghanistan, though the process took longer than he wished. At a Politburo meeting on 17 October 1985 Gorbachev told the assembled company that he had made it clear to Babrak Karmal, the Afghan leader (who had been 'dumbfounded'), that by the summer of 1986 they would have to learn how to defend their revolution themselves. They would also have 'to lean on the traditional authorities' and broaden the base of their regime.[6] Chernyaev, who was at the Politburo meeting, reported that Gorbachev read aloud to those present 'several heart-rending letters, all of them not anonymous' from Soviet mothers. Gorbachev was raising the emotional temperature in an attempt to persuade the Politburo that the Soviet presence in Afghanistan was a very bad mistake. He concluded the discussion by saying: 'With or without Karmal we will follow this line firmly, which must in a minimally short amount of time lead to our withdrawal from Afghanistan.'[7]

In a corresponding break with the past, as early as March 1985, at Konstantin Chernenko's funeral, Gorbachev told the East European Communist leaders to expect no more Soviet military interventions to keep

---

[5] In other words, the Cold War was over before Boris Yeltsin became Russian President and, earlier than that, Yeltsin played no part in its ending. As Pavel Palazchenko, Gorbachev's interpreter, put it in his significant contribution to the history of perestroika-era international relations: 'Yeltsin took little interest in foreign policy, and even less interest in theoretical concepts such as "new thinking".... He had a gut feeling for what the people wanted, and the people supported Gorbachev's foreign policy. There was therefore little that Yeltsin could do or say on foreign policy issues with a clear benefit to himself.' See Pavel Palazchenko, *My Years with Gorbachev and Shevardnadze: The Memoir of a Soviet Interpreter* (Pennsylvania State University Press, University Park, PA, 1997), p. 372. Frank Carlucci, who was successively National Security Adviser and Secretary of Defense in the second Reagan administration, when asked about 'the role of Yeltsin in transforming the international system', replied: 'He was not a player': The Hoover Institution and the Gorbachev Foundation (Moscow) Oral History Project, HIA, Frank Carlucci interview of 5 June 2000, p. 36.

[6] Anatoly S. Chernayev Diary 1985, NSA website, http://www.gwu.edu/~nsarchiv, entry for 'October 17th 1985'.

[7] Ibid. The process of extricating Soviet forces from Afghanistan took longer than Gorbachev had hoped—the last soldiers left in February 1989—but the intention to pull the troops out was in Gorbachev's mind (though not in that of all his Politburo colleagues) from the earliest months of his General Secretaryship.

them in power.[8] It was up to them to maintain or win the trust of their own people. It was only later that Gorbachev was forced to recognize that no Communist leaders were likely to succeed in gaining majority support in Eastern Europe. When that became clear, he could have reacted as previous Soviet leaders would have done and backed the use of coercion, preferably by the leadership of that particular country, but in the last resort by Soviet force of arms. Instead, he accepted the logic of the principle he had elaborated that the peoples of any country were entitled to choose the form of government they desired for their own state. Consistent with that, he stressed the impermissibility of intervention by foreign powers. In a six-page paper Gorbachev prepared for the Politburo meeting of 26 June 1986, he was critical of past Soviet practice of claiming for itself the function of sole preserver and defender of Marxist-Leninist teaching. The Soviet Union should not be the unique authority, and still more should not issue directives, but should, rather, exert ideational-political influence, deepen cooperation through constructive initiatives, and provide the force of example rather than the example of force. The relationship with the socialist countries, he concluded, should be on the basis of equality and it must be fully voluntary. The opinions of their friends in these countries should be studied not as a matter of form but of substance. The one part of Gorbachev's statement which did not correspond with his behaviour was his claim that 'for all the significance of our relations with the United States, and with the major states of Western Europe, the connections with the socialist countries must be in the first place'.[9] Throughout the post-war period that order of priority held good for Soviet leaders. Gorbachev, however, was to devote much more attention to relations with the United States and with Western Europe than to ties with Eastern Europe. Indeed, it was Western Europe—and especially its experience of social democracy—that attracted him more than the countries of East-Central Europe as a source of ideas, with welfare-state socialism, combined with a pluralist polity, providing a qualitatively different political model from that of Soviet-style Communism.[10]

[8] From the outset, Gorbachev has written, he was determined that that there would be no repeat of 'what happened with the "Prague Spring" in Czechoslovakia, when the people wished independently to build socialism "with a human face", and we answered them with tanks'. See Gorbachev, *Ponyat' perestroyku...pochemu eto vazhno seychas* (Al'pina Biznes Buks, Moscow, 2006), p. 33.

[9] M. Gorbachev, 'O nekotorykh aktual'nykh voprosakh sotrudnichestva s sotstranami, 26 Iyunya 1986 g.', Volkogonov Collection, NSA, R10049.

[10] Gorbachev was also influenced by, and felt close to, the analyses of international security issues produced by West European social democrats, among them Willy Brandt and the Palme commission. On this, see Thomas Risse-Kappen, 'Ideas do not float freely: transnational coalitions, domestic structures, and the end of the cold war', *International Organization*, Vol. 48, No. 2, Spring 1994, pp. 185–214, esp. pp. 201 and 210; Matthew Evangelista, *Unarmed Forces: The Transnational Movement to End the Cold War* (Cornell University Press, Ithaca, NY, 1999); and Robert D. English, *Russia and the Idea of the West: Gorbachev, Intellectuals, and the End of the Cold War* (Columbia University Press, New York, 2000).

'REALIST' EXPLANATIONS

In the debate among international relations scholars on the end of the Cold War, there have been various attempts to provide a single parsimonious explanation of this momentous outcome. Since none of them has been successful, it makes sense to accord due weight to a variety of contributory factors. The explanation which is politically dominant today, and whose proponents seek to make intellectually dominant, is that associated with the 'realist' school in international relations with its emphasis on material resources, military strength, and changes in the international balance of power, or expectations of impending shifts in that balance.[11] This school—or more, precisely, grouping of schools[12]—attracts rational choice analysts for whom the change in Soviet behaviour was a recognition that the Soviet Union could no longer compete in the superpower game. Accordingly, their interest lay in coming to an accommodation with the West and, in particular, with its pre-eminent power, the United States.

Realists hold that the primary cause of international change is the uneven growth of material capabilities among states. For James W. Davis and William C. Wohlforth, this, above all, was what underlay Soviet behaviour during the

[11] The 'realist' view is far from dominant among professional scholars. Odd Arne Westad summarizes the popular view that 'two giant countries faced each other and battled it out for world supremacy by most means short of an all-out war, until one of them was too exhausted to fight any longer'. He goes on: 'It is interesting to note that this commonly held view—often called "Realist", for lack of a better term—differs from the views held by an increasing number of historians and international relations experts in the West, who believe that their materials tell them that the Cold War was more about ideas and beliefs than about anything else.' See Westad (ed.), *Reviewing the Cold War: Approaches, Interpretations, Theory* (Frank Cass, London, 2000), p. 1. There are, of course, different strands of realist doctrine and one must distinguish attempts to detect broad regularities of behaviour in international relations from the effort to explain change in the foreign policy of any particular country. Some realists would say, indeed, that their concern is with the former and thus they need not concern themselves with the specifics of the transformation of Soviet foreign policy under Gorbachev, even though that is a momentous case by any standards. For a scholarly account of the development of realist thinking over the last 500 years, see Jonathan Haslam, *No Virtue Like Necessity: Realist Thought in International Relations since Machiavelli* (Yale University Press, New Haven, CT, and London, 2002) and for a thoughtful discussion of contemporary realist and neorealist thinking, see Gideon Rose, 'Neoclassical Realism and Theories of Foreign Policy', *World Politics*, Vol. 51, No.1, 1998, pp. 144–72. From the perspective of those who see interests as social constructions and, in contradistinction from the realists, emphasize culture and ideas, a particularly influential exposition of this 'constructivist' approach is Alexander Wendt's *Social Theory of International Politics* (Cambridge University Press, Cambridge, 1999).

[12] Haslam, *No Virtue Like Necessity*; and Rose, 'Neoclassical Realism and Theories of Foreign Policy'.

end of the Cold War and in the lead-up to German unification.[13] They argue
that even 'old thinkers' did not advocate the use of force to preserve Soviet
hegemony in Eastern Europe and, given relative Soviet economic decline, they
pose the question: were there alternative policies that would have reversed
Soviet decline?[14] In another article, William Wohlforth, this time with Stephen G. Brooks as co-author, holds that there was a high degree of consensus
in the Soviet elite on the foreign policy of the perestroika years and on
the need for such a break with the past. Arguing against an emphasis on the
importance of ideas, these authors write:

If the meaning and consequences of the material pressures facing the Soviet Union
depended on ideational shifts, then people with different ideas should have had
dramatically different strategic reactions to observable indications of material change.
But this was not the case: A critical mass of old thinkers in the military, defense
industry, foreign ministry, Communist Party apparatus, and KGB saw essentially the
same material constraints Gorbachev did, and so not only acquiesced to but were
complicit in Gorbachev's strategic response.[15]

While a stress on ideas to the exclusion of such an important factor as the
secular decline in the rate of Soviet economic growth would also be a mistake,
it would be less wide of the mark than the interpretation offered by Wohlforth
et al. With all due recognition of the long-term decline in the rate of Soviet
economic growth from the 1950s to the 1980s, the weight of evidence that a
command economy was less efficient than a market economy (with the
exception of a limited range of specially privileged sectors, such as military
industry, aviation and space research), and the likelihood that some kind of
radical economic reform was in the long-term interest of the people as a whole,
it was far from clear in *whose particular interests* among Soviet elites such
reform was. The same applies to a radical reduction in military expenditure,
including unilateral arms reductions. At the Politburo meeting which followed
the failure of Gorbachev and Reagan to reach agreement at the Reykjavik
summit of 1986, the KGB Chairman Chebrikov said: 'The Americans understand only strength', adding that the Soviet Union must oppose them 'with the
unity of the people around the party' while strengthening further 'the patriotic
education of the workers'.[16]

[13] James W. Davis and William C. Wohlforth, 'German Unification', in Richard K. Herrmann
and Richard Ned Lebow (eds.), *Ending the Cold War: Interpretations, Causation, and the Study of
International Relations* (Palgrave Macmillan, New York, 2004), pp. 131–57.
[14] Ibid., pp. 138–9.
[15] Stephen G. Brooks and William C. Wohlforth, 'Power, Globalization, and the End of the
Cold War: Reevaluating a Landmark Case for Ideas', *International Security*, Vol. 25, No. 3,
Winter 2000–1, pp. 5–53, at p. 44.
[16] 'Zasedanie Politbyuro TsK KPSS, 14 oktyabrya 1986 goda', Volkogonov Collection, NSA,
R9744, p. 9.

The KGB and the Soviet military did well within the unreformed Soviet economy. The Soviet ministries, especially the many connected with the military-industrial complex, had a secure place within the system that would be endangered by marketizing reform. And the party apparatus had a supervisory role within the economic system that would become superfluous in a market economy. So far as the top leadership of the country was concerned, the Soviet Union was a superpower partly because it was the largest country on earth, and one rich in natural resources, but mainly because of its military strength. It was far from obvious what the most privileged sections of the Soviet elite had to gain from radical economic reform or from asymmetrical arms reductions.

The balance of material resources was much more strongly in favour of the United States and against the Soviet Union when Stalin subjugated the countries of East-Central Europe to Soviet-style rule and proceeded to consolidate Soviet hegemony over the eastern half of the European continent. The Soviet Union achieved a rough military parity with the United States only in the 1970s. Even though the slowdown in Soviet economic growth posed a long-term problem for the USSR, and even if Reagan's America was outspending the Soviet Union in military build-up, the Soviet side possessed more than enough nuclear weapons to destroy the United States—and, indeed, life on earth. President Reagan's Strategic Defense Initiative (SDI) was only on the drawing-board. Even on Reagan's own optimistic scenario, developing 'defensive weapons that would render nuclear missiles obsolete . . . might take 20 years or more but we had to do it'.[17] Although it caused concern to the Soviet Union because of its likely technological spin-offs, the head of Soviet space research, Roald Sagdeev, was among Gorbachev's advisers who scoffed at the idea that it could ever provide a foolproof umbrella against an incoming missile attack and at the notion that the Soviet Union should attempt to copy the SDI programme.[18] The Soviet Union's existing force of intercontinental ballistic missiles with multiple warheads was more than ample to make any potential American reliance on SDI catastrophically risky.

[17] Ronald Reagan, *An American Life: The Autobiography* (Simon & Schuster, New York, 1990), p. 571.

[18] Sagdeev recalled that in a small group meeting in Gorbachev's office in the Kremlin, he almost died from suppressing his laughter when he heard an official from the Soviet space industry telling Gorbachev: 'We are losing time while doing nothing to build our counterpart to the American SDI program.' Nevertheless, Sagdeev accepts that 'if Americans oversold SDI, we Russians overbought it'; however, the attention devoted to the issue, by leading to the conclusion that even a fully developed SDI could be counteracted much more cheaply, 'saved the country a few billion rubles'. See Roald Sagdeev, *The Making of a Soviet Scientist: My Adventures in Nuclear Fusion and Space from Stalin to Star Wars* (Wiley, New York, 1994), p. 273.

A combination of the United States military build-up and Reagan's anti-Communist rhetoric—in separate speeches in March 1983 he described the Soviet bloc as an 'evil empire' and made public his support for SDI—caused concern in the Kremlin. However, the idea that the Soviet Union had no option but to pursue the policy which Gorbachev implemented—as 'realists' of different hues suggest—is far-fetched in the extreme. Yuriy Andropov presided over a Politburo meeting on 31 May 1983, at which all the leading figures in the CPSU leadership discussed the new threat, as they perceived it, from the United States and its allies, including the decision 'to deploy Pershing II and cruise missiles in Europe in the fall of 1983 to counter the threat of the [Soviet] SS-20s'.[19] The Politburo response had four main elements: to maintain to the full the Soviet Union's own armaments programme; to take diplomatic initiatives to improve relations with both Japan and China; to convene a meeting of the Soviet Union's East European allies in Moscow in order to establish a common line and maintain a united front; and to intensify both international and domestic propaganda against the 'anti-Soviet fabrications' emanating from Reagan.[20]

At that Politburo meeting the Minister of Defence, Dmitriy Ustinov, said: 'Everything that we are doing in relation to defence we should continue doing. All of the missiles that we've planned should be delivered...'[21] He also proposed a 50 per cent symmetrical cut in East–West nuclear weapons, the 50 per cent on the Western side to include the French and British weaponry, and advocated another diplomatic attempt to prevent the placing of Western medium-range missiles in Europe. Gorbachev, at this meeting, followed (as was customary) the lead of the General Secretary and of such senior Politburo members as Ustinov and Gromyko, and said that he fully supported the measures proposed, including the military line and the convening of a conference of fraternal countries. Andropov concluded the meeting by, as it were, telling the assembled party oligarchy to pull their socks up. Gorbachev was instructed to talk less about the weather and to get on with organizing 'the struggle for the harvest'. And in the kind of stock response of the Soviet leadership to any perceived intensification of external danger, Petr Demichev, the cultural overseer, was instructed to be stricter in his attention to theatre repertoires since there were many deficiencies in that area![22]

Under Brezhnev, Andropov, and Chernenko, the Soviet leadership reacted very much as in the past to what they saw as an enhanced threat emanating

---

[19] Reagan, *An American Life*, p. 551.
[20] 'Zasedanie Politbyuro TsK KPSS, 31 maya 1983 goda', HIA, Fond 89, Reel 1.1003, Opis 42, File 53.
[21] Ibid., p. 7.   [22] Ibid., p. 13.

from the United States. Given the fact that, even on Reagan's assumptions about the long-term viability of the SDI programme, mutually assured destruction (MAD) would prevail for another two decades, it is quite wrong to imagine that the Soviet leadership was *forced* to change its foreign policy comprehensively. Deborah Welch Larson and Alexei Shevchenko, arguing against the assumption of the 'realists' that the Soviet leadership had no option but to adopt the dramatic changes espoused by Gorbachev once he controlled the levers of power, suggest two other alternatives.[23] One, which they describe as 'détente plus', would have involved some reduction in defence expenditure and overseas commitments until the Soviet Union had recovered its power, after which they could resume expansion.[24] Although it is not part of these authors' argument, it is worth noting that the price of oil plummeted during the second half of the 1980s but has risen dramatically in the last decade and a half, especially—happily for Vladimir Putin—since the turn of the millennium. The Soviet exchequer would have benefited from that in much the same way as Russian state finances have during the Putin presidency. The long-term trend in oil and gas prices was always likely to be upwards, given that energy is a finite resource and given the growing, almost insatiable, demand for it from recently industrialized countries, most notably China.[25]

Another policy alternative suggested by Larson and Shevchenko was one of 'abandoning Marxist-Leninist ideology as a guide to Soviet foreign policy in favor of a traditional realpolitik interpretation of Soviet/Russian interests'.[26] This would have included 'swift rapprochement with the People's Republic of China', withdrawal from Afghanistan, and a radical shift of policy towards Japan, negotiating 'technological and economic assistance and investments in exchange for conceding the Kurile islands'. The issue, though, of how much

---

[23] Deborah Welch Larson and Alexei Shevchenko, 'Shortcut to Greatness: The New Thinking and the Revolution in Soviet Foreign Policy', *International Organization*, Vol. 57, Winter 2003, pp. 77–109.

[24] Ibid., p. 83.

[25] In any event, the economic reform, deemed to be inescapable by the 'realists', was the least successful area of Gorbachev's innovations. Even in the post-Soviet period, Russian natural resources have contributed overwhelmingly to foreign earnings. The export of Russian manufactured goods pales into insignificance in comparison with the success in this sphere of Communist China. Indeed, there are many Russian politicians who believe that the China model was the one that Gorbachev should have adopted. For a variety of reasons that would have been difficult in the Soviet context, quite apart from the fact that it would have required a different mindset from that of Gorbachev and his 'new thinking' allies. By definition, it would have meant *not* introducing a wide range of political, civil and religious freedoms and refraining from promoting democratization.

[26] Larson and Shevchenko, 'Shortcut to Greatness', p. 83.

Marxist-Leninist doctrine actually guided Soviet foreign policy is not a straightforward one, for the ideology had been redefined in such a way that it was a buttress for what the leadership perceived to be Soviet 'national' interests. In many ways, the foreign policy pursued by Gromyko was already one of Realpolitik, although Gromyko—as his contributions to Politburo discussions make clear—regarded himself as a Leninist and an undeviating Communist. As Nigel Gould-Davies has observed, the new archival sources 'show that Soviet officials and leaders, in forums never intended for public scrutiny, took ideology very seriously'.[27] As he puts it:

It is sometimes argued that the Soviet leadership did not really believe Marxism-Leninism, and that the ideology was rather a means of legitimating, in the eyes of the population, power wielded and policies pursued for self-interested reasons. This view was always inherently implausible. It assumed that elites, intensely socialized into the official ideology during a long career in the party-state apparatus, were less likely to have internalized it than the 90 per cent of the population who were not even party members. It also begged the question of why the regime should choose to base its claims to authority on beliefs so incongruent with Russian culture and tradition rather than draw on others, such as nationalism or religion, with deeper roots.[28]

It is true that Lenin was much invoked even in Politburo meetings and in other occasions not intended for public view, though it is also the case that this was a language of politics that was open to differing emphases and interpretations. Some politicians and ideologists manipulated it cynically, and, in general, there is little doubt that ideology was less of a motivating force by the 1970s and 1980s than it was in Lenin's, Stalin's, or Khrushchev's time. As Gould-Davies contends, there were still many party and state officials who believed that the Soviet Union was the great exemplar of socialism and that they were following in the footsteps of Lenin. One such person, admittedly of an older generation, was the long-serving head of the International Department, Boris Ponomarev, as he emerges in the private conversations reported by Anatoliy Chernyaev.[29] However, given the malleability of the body of doctrine, it would have been possible to redefine what was in the interests of the Soviet state without entirely abandoning what was its legitimating ideology, and to that extent the argument of Larson and Shevchenko needs

---

[27] Nigel Gould-Davies, 'Rethinking the Role of Ideology in International Politics During the Cold War', in *Journal of Cold War Studies*, Vol. 1, No. 1, Winter 1999, pp. 90–109, at p. 92.

[28] Ibid.

[29] See, for example, 'The Diary of Anatoly Chernyaev' for the year 1985, NSA website, http://gwu.edu/~nsarchiv.

to be modified. Even Gorbachev believed he was returning to purer Leninist norms at the very time he was turning Marxism-Leninism on its head.[30]

It is likely that any leadership, shorn of at least three of the four people who had been instrumental in putting Soviet troops into Afghanistan—Brezhnev, Andropov, Ustinov, and Gromyko—would have began to look for a way out of that particular impasse. This was not the most controversial part of Gorbachev's foreign policy, although both he and the military chiefs had the problem (which other political leaders in other countries have had both before and since) of avoiding the impression that so many lives had been lost in vain. In the case of the Soviet withdrawal, worries about abandoning allies to an uncertain fate and about leaving a vacuum which might be filled by Islamist fundamentalism gave members of the Politburo more pause for thought than any lingering hope of implanting Marxist-Leninist ideology in Afghanistan.

In the Politburo meeting already cited, over which Yuriy Andropov presided on 31 May 1983, some elements of the second alternative policy suggested by Larson and Shevchenko were indeed mooted. Andropov was strongly in favour of rapprochement with China and, in his desire to woo Japan away from support for Reagan's foreign policy, he went so far as to suggest raising with the Japanese joint economic development of the disputed islands. Gromyko seemed to be prepared to go still further and to be ready to consider negotiating some of the smaller islands away. Andropov also called for an effort to involve Japan in 'more active co-operation with the Soviet Union in the economic sphere'.[31] Yet no real progress was made in any of these areas and when Chernenko succeeded Andropov, Soviet foreign and defence policy continued along entirely traditional lines under the firm control of Gromyko and Ustinov. Although Gorbachev had by then become the Central Committee Secretary overseeing foreign policy and Romanov the Secretary overseeing the military and military industry, so long as Gromyko and Ustinov were, respectively, Minister of Foreign Affairs and Minister of Defence (Ustinov died in December 1984, causing Gorbachev to cut short by a day his visit to Britain), their vast experience made them the supreme authorities within their separate, but linked, domains. One may legitimately ask: if the policy pursued by Gorbachev was (as Western 'realists' have claimed, albeit only retrospectively) the sole serious option for the Soviet leadership, why did such hard-bitten 'realists' as Gromyko and Ustinov (or, for

---

[30] For more on that, see Archie Brown (ed.), *The Demise of Marxism-Leninism in Russia* (Palgrave Macmillan, Basingstoke, 2004); and especially the discussion in Chapter 10 of the present volume.

[31] 'Zasedanie Politbyuro TsK KPSS, 31 maya 1983 goda', op. cit., pp. 3–4 and 6.

that matter, Brezhnev, Andropov, or even Chernenko) not turn to it at some point during the first five years of Reagan's presidency?

In a more recent attempt to justify a realist interpretation of the end of the Cold War, involving explanation of the radical change in Soviet foreign policy in the second half of the 1980s, Brooks and Wohlforth maintain that 'three factors stand out' in the light of recent research: '(1) Soviet decline was more marked, occurred earlier, and generally placed a much greater strain on maintaining the foreign policy status quo than scholars had previously assumed; (2) the costs of Soviet isolation from the globalization of production were growing rapidly; and (3) the Soviet Union "arguably confronted modern history's worst case of imperial overstretch"'.[32]

The first two points are not as central to the end of the Cold War as Brooks and Wohlforth appear to imagine and the third is wholly fanciful. The relative decline in Soviet economic performance, as compared with advanced Western countries and with the newly industrialized countries of Asia, was one of the factors spurring the early stage of Soviet reform after 1985, but the reform of the Soviet economy during the era in which the Cold War ended did not come even close to matching the transformation of the Soviet polity. In fact, as noted in an earlier chapter, it was symbolic of Gorbachev's priorities that when two particularly important plenary sessions of the Central Committee for the furtherance of reform took place in 1987, it was the plenum on political reform that came first—in January—followed by the plenum on economic reform in June.[33] If one looks at Soviet domestic reform, as distinct from

[32] Stephen G. Brooks and William C. Wohlforth, 'From Old Thinking to New Thinking in Qualitative Research', *International Security*, Vol. 26, No. 4, Spring 2002, pp. 93–111, at p. 95. See also William C. Wohlforth, 'Realism and the End of the Cold War', *International Security*, Vol. 19, No. 3, Winter 1994–5, pp. 91–129; and Wolforth, 'A Certain Idea of Science: How International Relations Theory Avoids Reviewing the Cold War', in Westad (ed.), *Reviewing the Cold War*, pp. 126–45.

[33] That is not to say that the widening of the technological gap between the Soviet Union and other Communist countries, on the one hand, and the United States and the advanced Western countries, on the other, was a side-issue. It was for Gorbachev an important reason for seeking both economic reform and international arms control agreements. At a meeting on 4 October 1986 (shortly before the Reykjavik summit) with a group of advisers and senior officials, among them Lev Zaykov, who was by that time supervising the military and military industry within the Central Committee Secretariat, Chief of General Staff Sergey Akhromeev, and KGB Chairman Viktor Chebrikov, Gorbachev made clear that he was seeking the liquidation of nuclear weapons and wanted 'a political approach, not an arithmetical one' at the negotiations. He also, however, emphasized the need to avoid a new phase of competition in armaments not only because of the dangers of a world in which a hundred missiles could already destroy Europe and much of the Soviet Union, but also because of the economic pressures an accelerated arms race would bring. Therefore, it was 'the task of tasks' to prevent 'a new stage of the arms race', for if that occurred 'the pressure on our economy would be unbelievable'. It may well be that Gorbachev thought that the economic argument was his strongest card when talking with

foreign policy, the measures of democratization—especially the movement to contested elections of 1988–9 and the expansion of a wide range of freedoms—were far more important in relation to the end of the Cold War than economic reform. The Soviet Union was no more part of the global economy at the end of the 1980s than it was at the beginning. As already noted, even in the post-Soviet era, the main exports are Russian natural resources. During the period of rapid economic growth under Putin, there remains suspicion of foreign companies acquiring a majority holding in any of Russia's energy companies which, in comparison with the Yeltsin years, have come under increasing state control. Thus, the economic issue, while a stimulus to the first phase of (moderate) Soviet reform during the perestroika era, was far less important than political reform (itself only tangentially related to the decline in economic growth) so far as the end of the Cold War was concerned.

The domestic political reform, in turn, was not as decisive as the change of policy towards the outside world. This applies, above all, to the willingness to see the countries of Eastern Europe go their separate ways. So far as 'modern history's worst case of imperial overstretch' is concerned, a contiguous empire was a good deal easier to control than the distant lands of the British Empire, embracing India and large tracts of Asia and Africa. It was also militarily and psychologically harder for the Soviet Union to give up what appeared to be a buffer zone (to which NATO expansion has subsequently given some credence) and the reward for victory in the Second World War. Vladimir Kryuchkov, who succeeded Chebrikov as Chairman of the KGB in 1988, did not put his head above the parapet to oppose German unification in 1990, but subsequently he was to make his view of it sufficiently clear:

In general, the treachery of M.S. Gorbachev knows no bounds. When the fate of the GDR [East Germany] was being decided, the interests of the Soviet Union were trampled upon by M.S. Gorbachev in the open. He was not made to wait long for praise from the West for that step. In 1990 the former Minister of Foreign Affairs of

---

leading representatives of the military-industrial complex and the security forces, given that he would be proposing cuts at Reykjavik in Soviet as well as American arsenals. 'Realists' are not wrong in emphasizing economic pressures on the Soviet leadership, but misleading when they elevate it above all else. The imperative of preventing war, the influence of ideas about interdependence and of a 'reasonable sufficiency' of defence needs, and concerns about the level of Soviet technology by world standards were not mutually exclusive, but mutually reinforcing. See 'Zapisi pomoshchnika general'nogo sekretarya TsK KPSS, Prezidenta SSSR, sdelannye na zasedaniyakh Politbyuro, drugikh razlinchnykh soveshchaniyakh, uskikh i shirokikh, s uchastiem M.S. Gorbacheva, 1986–1990 gg.', Anatoliy Chernyaev transcripts, entry for 4 October 1986, Gorbachev Foundation archives.

Germany, H.-D. Genscher said the following: 'The German people will always be grateful to Gorbachev for what he did to make possible our unity.'[34]

While Kryuchkov goes on to stress the difficulties many East Germans have faced in a united Germany, and, according to Kryuchkov, 'experience great nostalgia for the socialist regime',[35] only a minority would prefer to be back in the GDR. How subjective the assessment of national interest can be is illustrated by the former KGB head's evident belief that keeping Germany divided against the will of a majority of its inhabitants was in the Soviet and Russian interest—as against Gorbachev's conviction that to facilitate unification, once the demand for it had become sufficiently strong, was more likely to lead to long-term, good-neighbourly relations.

INSTITUTIONAL POWER AND SYSTEMIC NORMS

To explain why Soviet leaders who were far from being 'new thinkers' went along with the foreign policy pursued by Gorbachev (with the help of such important political actors as Shevardnadze and Yakovlev and, in an advisory capacity, Chernyaev and Shakhnazarov), one has to pay careful attention to Soviet institutional power and systemic norms. More generally, it is impossible to understand how the Cold War came to an end—and why it ended when it did—without an understanding of the Soviet domestic political context. Lack of such knowledge limits the usefulness of many of the contributions to the debate on the end of the Cold War by international relations specialists. That applies, still more, to the oversimplifications and distortions on the end of the Cold War by a fair number—though certainly not all— of those who served in the Reagan administration. The analyses of Jack Matlock[36] and the memoirs of George Shultz[37] are in sharp contrast to the

---

[34] Vladimir Kryuchkov, *Lichnost' i vlast'* (Prosveshchenie, Moscow, 2004), p. 174. For a Russian nationalist view that 'Gorbachev did not have the historic right to put a stop to the activity of the Warsaw Pact', see also Aleksandr Dugin, 'Perstroyka po-evraziyski: upushchennyy shans', in V.I. Tolstykh (ed.), *Perestroyka dvadtsat' let sputstya* (Russkiy put', Moscow, 2005), pp. 88–97, at p. 96.

[35] Kryuchkov, *Lichnost' i vlast'*, p. 176.

[36] See Jack F. Matlock, Jr., *Autopsy on an Empire: The American Ambassador's Account of the Collapse of the Soviet Union* (Random House, New York, 1995); and especially Matlock, *Reagan and Gorbachev: How the Cold War Ended* (Random House, New York, 2004).

[37] See George P. Shultz, *Turmoil and Triumph: My Years as Secretary of State* (Macmillan, New York, 1993). See also Shultz interview of 20 June 2000, Hoover Institution Oral History Project, HIA, Acc. No. 98067–16.305.

ignorance of, for example, Caspar Weinberger.[38] Matlock knew more than any of the others about how Soviet politics worked on the ground and Shultz gained much first-hand experience of the evolution in the thinking of Soviet key players in his discussions with Gorbachev and Shevardnadze.

Considering both the policy of the United States and the indigenous pressures in the Soviet Union, Vladislav Zubok—a prominent Russian specialist on Cold War history now based in America—gets the balance right when he observes:

The pressure from the West in the early 1980s revived Cold War tensions, but it is hard to see it as a decisive factor in the end of the Cold War world order. The ending was, in a way, a 'victory' of the West, but the attempts of some US leaders to take credit for this victory cannot be corroborated by the new evidence from the Soviet side. The role of longer-term processes within the Soviet Union (the erosion of ideology, the pent-up desire for relaxation) played a much greater role than the short-term measures of the Reagan or Bush administrations.[39]

Even though Gorbachev was engaged in a process of changing the norms of the system, some elements of institutional inertia worked to his advantage. The old rules of the game, conventions, and habits of mind—together with the General Secretary's considerable power to appoint and to dismiss—meant that other members of the top leadership team found themselves suppressing doubts and going along with policies that differed almost 180 degrees from those they had espoused hitherto. Although there was real discussion in Politburo meetings, and Gorbachev found it prudent to make some concessions (though not usually on fundamentals) 'to the opinions of other members of the leadership',[40] those who wished to disagree with Gorbachev generally did so in a highly respectful way, avoiding head-on collision. The authority of the General Secretary was immense. Even someone with the intellectual limitations of Brezhnev, especially in his last years, or Chernenko,

---

[38] In an interview given on 20 October 1998, Weinberger observed: '[W]e were able to sustain a major peacetime build up for about five years, which was longer than had ever happened before in our history, and which gave us the necessary strength so that Gorbachev, whose I think only real contribution to the cold war was recognizing that they couldn't win a war, recognized that and then began to change his rhetoric. I don't think he ever changed his philosophy. He talked a lot about perestroika, glasnost, all of those things, but he never really changed.' Hoover Institution Oral History Project, Acc. No. 98067–16.305, HIA, Weinberger interview, p. 7.

[39] Vladislav M. Zubok, 'Why Did the Cold War End in 1989? Explanations of "The Turn" ', in Westad (ed.), *Reviewing the Cold War*, pp. 343–67, at p. 361. Zubok also resists the view that 'the "non-use" of force in 1989 was "overdetermined" ' and contends that Gorbachev's choice to avoid force 'proved to be decisive' (ibid., p. 367).

[40] Mikhail Gorbachev and Zdeněk Mlynář, *Conversations with Gorbachev: On Perestroika, the Prague Spring, and the Crossroads of Socialism* (Columbia University Press, New York, 2002), p. 211.

in his thirteen months as General Secretary, was addressed with deference by his colleagues.

In Gorbachev's case, the power and authority of the office, allied to his immense self-confidence and intellectual ability, meant that Politburo members and Central Committee Secretaries were frequently swept along by his advocacy of a change of course. Once things started going badly wrong for the party leadership—with the rise of separatist movements in the Soviet Union and Yeltsin's growing popularity in 1990–1—the tone of the exchanges in the Politburo changed. At the Politburo meeting held on 16 November 1990, which immediately preceded the abolition of the Presidential Council that Gorbachev had formed earlier in the year, heavy criticism about the way things were going, and Gorbachev's responsibility for this, was levelled by one participant in the discussion after another.[41] By this time, however, the switch from party to state power—while reversible—had gone sufficiently far that Gorbachev had been able to bypass the Politburo on key issues. Formally, the body which seemed in some respects to be a successor organ to the Politburo was the Presidential Council, but it had a disparate membership and unclear functions; it was essentially an advisory body rather than a powerful executive committee at the apex of the system which the Politburo had been in the past. Even during the Presidential Council's short-lived existence (from March to November 1990), a lot of key decision-making took place in a more informal group, convened by Gorbachev, which likewise had the effect of bypassing the Politburo. Its most regular members in 1990 were Yakovlev, Medvedev, and Primakov from the Presidential Council and Chernyaev, Shakhnazarov, and Ivan Frolov from Gorbachev's aides.[42] They were valuable to Gorbachev, Shakhnazarov suggests, not only because they were like-minded to him and not afraid to express their views, but also because they were able to write, and they could put the 'new thinking' into programmatic form.[43] The Politburo was also bypassed completely when Gorbachev, in association with Yeltsin, set up the team which produced the '500-Days Plan' to transform the Soviet economic system from a command into a market economy.[44] Gorbachev also had a lot of leeway to take crucial decisions while engaged in talks with

---

[41] 'Zasedanie Politbyuro TsK KPSS ot 16 Noyabrya 1990 goda', HIA, Fond 89, Reel 1.003, Opis 42, File 30.

[42] Shakhnazarov, *Tsena svobody*, p. 144.   [43] Ibid.

[44] As noted in an earlier chapter, after initial support for this project for rapid transition to a market economy, Gorbachev drew back in the face of intense opposition to it from Ryzhkov and the Council of Ministers and from the Supreme Soviet of the USSR as well as from the party bureaucracy. He also had second thoughts himself about the viability of the measures being advocated by the team of economic specialists headed by Stanislav Shatalin and Grigoriy Yavlinsky.

other heads of government—most notably, by 1990, President George Bush and Chancellor Helmut Kohl.

Gorbachev reached the peak of his power in many respects in 1988 and the first half of 1989.[45] By then he had removed a significant part of the old guard from the Politburo and had brought in several supporters, even though he was constrained by the party rules to restrict his choice to people who were already members of the Central Committee. Consequently, there was never a majority of wholehearted reformers or foreign policy 'new thinkers' in the Politburo throughout the entire perestroika period. It was yet another convention of the system, however, that the General Secretary—in addition to having broad oversight of policy—had a special concern with foreign policy. By the time of the dramatic changes of 1989, the composition of the Politburo itself had changed and included some genuine supporters of the 'new thinking', most notably, Yakovlev, Shevardnadze, and Medvedev. The main reasons, however, why Gorbachev's foreign policy was not challenged in the Politburo even then were the General Secretary's acknowledged leading role in the conduct of foreign policy and the extent to which the entire international climate had been changed, and expectations aroused, by the policies already pursued.[46]

Stepping back to the composition of the Politburo at the time of Chernenko's death in March 1985, it is clear that no one within that body would independently have advocated a foreign policy, or domestic liberalization (still less democratization), of the kind pursued by Gorbachev. The political climate at home, and the expectations in East-Central Europe, would in 1989, under a Grishin or Romanov, have been very different from what they were under Gorbachev.[47] Even the second youngest full member of the Politburo in March 1985 (Gorbachev, at 54, was the youngest by five years), Vitaliy Vorotnikov, was scathingly critical of Gorbachev in his memoirs, saying, among many uncomplimentary things, that he 'abandoned at a difficult

[45] He was freer of constraints from within the Communist Party after he had created a state presidency with executive power in March 1990, but by that time there were many other constraints upon his power, emanating from the leadership of the Russian republic in the person of Boris Yeltsin and in the form of nationalist and other pressures from a society now free to voice and act upon its discontents.

[46] Or, as Viktor Kuvaldin expresses the first of these points: 'Although in the Politburo all were equal, one was more equal than others.' See V. Kuvaldin, 'Gorbachev i ego vneshnyaya politika', *Mirovaya Ekonomika i Mezhdunarodnye Otnosheniya*, no. 11, 2005, pp. 14–22, at p. 19.

[47] Although Shakhnazarov was one of those who was acutely conscious of the pressing need for radical change in the Soviet Union, he insists that there was a huge element of chance in Gorbachev being in the right place at the right time, for 'everything would have been as in the past if in March 1985 Viktor Vasil'evich Grishin had been elected General Secretary' (Shakhnazarov, *Tsena svobody*, p. 36).

moment our friends from the countries of the socialist commonwealth'.[48] He also acknowledges some of Gorbachev's strengths in Soviet politics, describing him as a 'magnificent master of apparat affairs'.[49] On more than one occasion in his book, Vorotnikov refers to Gorbachev's powers of persuasion as well as his institutional power as General Secretary. And he blames himself (though to a much lesser extent than Gorbachev) for going along with policies in which he did not believe:

During discussion in the Politburo of the Central Committee of the reforms planned by Gorbachev I not infrequently had doubts about their essence and timeliness, and argued and raised objections.... But in the end I often yielded to the logic of his conviction. In that lies my guilt. The thing is that I long believed in Gorbachev and placed my hopes in him.[50]

The views of Grishin and Romanov—both of whom had aspired to succeed Chernenko, but were outranked and outwitted by Gorbachev—are sufficiently well known.[51] There was no chance of either of *them*, in particular, introducing policy change remotely as radical as that driven by Gorbachev. It was a policy which far exceeded the expectations in the mid-1980s even of the minority within the International Department of the Central Committee (and much smaller minority within the Central Committee apparatus as a whole) who had espoused elements of the new thinking in advance of Gorbachev's becoming General Secretary.

A conventional view of Soviet state interests, which had prevailed up until the point when Gorbachev became General Secretary, was that the more territory the Soviet Union controlled in Eastern Europe and beyond (politically, militarily, and ideologically), the better, and the more weapons it accumulated, the more it would be respected. On this understanding, Soviet

---

[48] V.I. Vorotnikov, *A bylo eto tak... Iz dnevnika chlena Politbyuro TsK KPSS* (Sovet veteranov knigoizdaniya, Moscow, 1995), p. 264.

[49] Ibid., p. 259.

[50] Ibid., p. 461.

[51] The ambitions of both Grishin and Romanov to succeed Chernenko are discussed in Chapter 7. Roald Sagdeev, who headed Soviet space research and so came to know the Soviet military-industrial complex at first hand, observes that he and his friends were disappointed when Andropov brought Romanov from Leningrad to Moscow, making him a senior party secretary in 1983, for 'Romanov symbolized the most anti-intellectual kind of party apparatchik'. Although Romanov had been given responsibility for overseeing the military–industrial complex, Sagdeev observes that he did not immediately involve himself in it: 'My friends in the Defense Department of the Central Committee told stories that their new boss was spending most of his time conferring with regional party secretaries influential in the overall picture of the Central Committee. It was up to them to decide in the most critical period of Soviet history who would be the next general secretary of the Communist party' (Sagdeev, *The Making of a Soviet Scientist*, pp. 258–9).

prestige in the world rested on its military might.[52] When Gorbachev presented his draft report for the Nineteenth Party Conference to a Politburo meeting on 20 June 1988 for the members to give their comments, he pointed out that in the first draft of a passage on the reduction in the threat of nuclear war, this had been characterized as 'thanks to our [military] strength (*blagodarya nashey sile*)'. That, he said, was incorrect. It should be 'thanks to the new thinking'.[53] Gorbachev described this emphasis as one of realism,[54] though his emphasis on removing the reasons for conflict—and the huge doctrinal change away from irreconcilable ideological and class differences to

---

[52] Not surprisingly, that was the view of the Secretary of the Central Committee (from 1988 to 1991), Oleg Baklanov, who supervised military industry and who became First Deputy Chairman of the Defence Council (Gorbachev was the Chairman) in the last year of the Soviet Union's existence. He attempted to defend his position in conversation with Gorbachev, but within the conventions of the system. How he expressed himself both in private and subsequently was very different. At the conference jointly organized by the Mershon Center of Ohio State University (Columbus, Ohio) and the Institute of General History of the Russian Academy of Sciences in Moscow in June 1999, at which the main participants on the Russian side were those who took part in the August coup of 1991, Baklanov—a Soviet-style 'realist'—spoke of the Soviet Union's achievement of military parity with the United States in the following terms: 'Parity was created as a result of the tremendous efforts made by all peoples comprising the Soviet Union, and this parity held the world in a delicate balance, but a balance nonetheless. And in my opinion, the horrible sin, the horrible sin of Gorbachev and his stooges . . . consisted in the fact that this parity was violated, and we ended up with what we have now' (Moscow Cold War Conference, Tape 2, Mershon Center, Ohio State University).

[53] 'Politbyuro 20 Iyunya 1988 goda, Obsuzhdenie proekta doklada Gorbacheva k XIX partkonferentsii', Chernyaev notes, Gorbachev Foundation Archives. Gorbachev did not get his way on everything connected with his report to the Nineteenth Party Conference. At a meeting of the Secretariat of the Central Committee on 23 April 1988 he announced that the title of his presentation to the Conference would be 'On the course of perestroika and the further democratization of the society and the party.' In fact, the eventual title (of what was, nevertheless, a path-breaking speech) was the altogether more traditional 'On the course of fulfilment of the decisions of the XXVII Congress of the CPSU and the tasks of deepening perestroika'. The 27th Party Congress came too early in the Gorbachev era for it to have set a particularly radical agenda, but it was a Soviet convention that between congresses, the entire party should be devoting itself to fulfilling the tasks set out at the last such gathering of the CPSU's highest policymaking body (so far as the party statutes were concerned). The title eventually chosen for the report was very much in line with the view expressed by one of the Politburo members who had shown no enthusiasm for the changes espoused by Gorbachev, Mikhail Solomentsev. He said that the essence of the conference speech should be about fulfilling the decisions of the 27th Party Congress and deepening them, to which Gorbachev responded that the role of the conference would be not less than that of the Congress. They clashed also on the role of the party. Solomentsev warned against any weakening of the party, for it alone could unite different interests. Gorbachev replied that for that to happen, the party had to be freed 'from its executive functions'. Cf. 'Sekretariat TsK 23 Aprelya 1988 goda (zapis' Medvedeva)', Gorbachev Foundation Archives; and 'O khode realizatsii resheniy XXVII s"ezda KPSS i zadachakh po uglubleniyu perestroyki. Doklad na XIX Vsesoyusnoy konferentsii KPSS 27 iyunya 1988 goda', in M.S. Gorbachev, *Izbrannye rechi i stat'i* (Politizdat, Moscow, 1989), Vol. 6, pp. 323–97.

[54] 'Politbyuro 20 Iyunya 1988 goda', ibid.

an embrace of universal interests and 'all-human values'—was not the kind of 'realism' purveyed by the realist or neo-realist schools of international relations theorists.[55] In his most recent, retrospective thoughts on perestroika, Gorbachev describes the new thinking, both on foreign and domestic policy, as 'an attempt to think and act in accordance with normal human *common sense*' [italics Gorbachev's].[56]

Gorbachev's foreign policy, notwithstanding his ascription to it of realism and common sense, was, in many respects, idealistic. While willing to use force as a very last resort, he was always eager to seek negotiated settlements. Thus, while in the end, he supported the US military response to drive the Iraqi forces of Saddam Hussein out of Kuwait in 1991, he had hoped to prevent war by using Yevgeniy Primakov, who combined high political standing with vast experience of the Arab world (including long acquaintanceship with Saddam Hussein), as an emissary who could persuade Saddam to retreat and thus avoid armed conflict.[57] More generally, Gorbachev was serious about creating a new world order and even one entirely free of nuclear weapons, a point to which I shall return. In place of the Soviet Union's previous utopian goal of building communism worldwide (which in reality had become greatly attenuated by more pragmatic practice), Gorbachev saw a world which was interdependent, in which interests and values common to the whole of humanity had acquired priority over all others.[58] This—given the problems of the age, with the nuclear threat well to the forefront of his mind—called for cooperation across the old ideological divide. As he later put it, the new thinking involved 'recognition that there exists a single interconnected and interdependent world... that is complex and full of contradictions, but is nevertheless a single, inseparable whole.... But cooperation, and ultimately partnership could not push conflict out of the way as long as the division of

---

[55] As Richard Ned Lebow observes, if Gorbachev had been only a moderate reformer and had pursued a foreign policy that was 'essentially an extension of Brezhnev's', adherents of the realist school would have regarded this 'as entirely consistent with their theoretical expectations'. In advance of the actual policy Gorbachev pursued, the idea that he would have introduced democratic reforms, agreed to the dissolution of the Warsaw Pact and to the reunification of Germany within NATO, among other things, 'would have been greeted derisively as the height of *unreason*' (Lebow, 'The Long Peace, the End of the Cold War, and the Failure of Realism', *International Organization*, Vol. 48, No. 2, Spring 1994, pp. 249–77, at p. 264).

[56] Gorbachev, *Ponyat' perestroyku*, p. 39.

[57] See Yevgeny Primakov, *Russian Crossroads* (Yale University Press, New Haven, CT, 2004), ch. 3, 'The War That Might Not Have Been', pp. 42–71; and Pavel Palazchenko, *My Years with Gorbachev and Shevardnadze* (Pennsylvania State University Press, University Park, PA, 1997), ch. 9, 'The Gulf War Test 1990–1991', pp. 207–36.

[58] See, for example, Gorbachev's speech to the Nineteenth Party Conference on 28 June 1988: M.S. Gorbachev, *Izbrannye rechi i stat'i* (Politizdat, Moscow, 1989), vol. 6, pp. 323–406, at p. 346.

the world into opposing military-political blocs existed.'[59] The realism that underlay the idealism was expressed by Gorbachev when he said: 'The roots of the new thinking lay in the understanding that there would be no winners in a nuclear war and that in any such event both "camps" would be blown to kingdom come.'[60]

Gorbachev's perception of what lay in the interests of the Soviet Union was different from that of the other members of the Politburo, although the latter began adjusting their positions once Gorbachev had become party leader and was accordingly able to exercise disproportionate influence over the Politburo. Instead of believing that the Soviet Union needed to spend ever more on armaments in order to keep up with the United States, Gorbachev sought to resolve the major international disputes and make such heavy military expenditure unnecessary. Yet his primary foreign policy concern in 1985—and especially after the Chernobyl catastrophe in 1986—was not budgetary, but the prevention of nuclear war. Gorbachev was well aware that in periods of high tension, war could begin by accident as well as design. As recently as 1983, there had been genuine worries in Moscow that the United States might be preparing a pre-emptive strike on the Soviet Union and that Reagan's heightened anti-Communist rhetoric was a kind of psychological preparation of Western publics for this. Britain's double agent within the KGB, Oleg Gordievsky, had reported these concerns to his superiors in London, and a NATO exercise was altered, as a result, to make it abundantly clear that this was not going to be a disguised first strike.[61]

[59] Mikhail Gorbachev and Zdeněk Mlynář, *Conversations with Gorbachev: On Perestroika, the Prague Spring, and the Crossroads of Socialism* (Columbia University Press, New York, 2002), p. 139.

[60] Ibid. Elaborating further on global interdependence, Gorbachev said: 'The logical result of acknowledging the interconnection and interdependency of the world should, after all, be the recognition that general human values and needs must take precedence over class conflicts; also, the viewpoint that violence is the driving force in history must be renounced' (ibid., p. 145).

[61] Geoffrey (now Lord) Howe, who was British Foreign Secretary at the time, notes his surprise that 'the Soviet leadership did really believe the bulk of their own propaganda' and in 1983 feared an American attack. The Korean airliner, KAL 007, which blundered into Soviet airspace and was shot down, was believed by the Soviet authorities to be part of a stratagem planned from Washington. Howe goes on: 'Within the next few weeks Gordievski gave us warning of another alarming example of Soviet fearfulness. From 2 to 11 November 1983 the NATO exercise "Able Archer" was scheduled to take place. This simulated crisis was designed to lead to nuclear conflict and involved "incidents" and active participation by senior Western ministers. Gordievski left us in no doubt of the extraordinary but genuine Russian fear of real-life nuclear strike. NATO deliberately changed some aspects of the exercise so as to leave the Soviets in no doubt that it was only an exercise. Gordievski's own reports to his nominal masters reinforced the message, and the crisis passed.' See Geoffrey Howe, *Conflict of Loyalty* (Macmillan, London, 1994), p. 350. There is a fuller discussion of this in the memoirs of the former CIA Director, Robert M. Gates, *From the Shadows* (Simon & Schuster, New York, 1996), pp. 270–3. He notes that the CIA 'did not really grasp how alarmed the Soviet leaders might have been until some time after the exercise had been concluded'. Gates cites the British view that 'the threat of a preemptive strike was taken very seriously in Moscow in mid-1983 and early 1984' (p. 272).

Western leaders—with the interesting and significant exception of Ronald Reagan—found it hard to believe that Gorbachev was serious in his declared intention of seeking to outlaw all nuclear weapons by the year 2000. Yet Gorbachev was, in fact, deadly serious. After Chernobyl, he spoke both within his circle of advisers and in the Politburo about how the accident at that nuclear power plant had strengthened his conviction of the need to banish nuclear weapons completely. That was certainly not 'realism' in the sense in which that term is used in academic discourse, but, rather, one feature of what was essentially an idealistic foreign policy which Gorbachev pursued. Following the Reykjavik summit, Gorbachev told the Politburo in mid-October 1986 that a 'qualitatively new situation' had arisen. 'The discussion about nuclear disarmament reached a new, higher position, from which it is now necessary to expand further the battle for the liquidation and complete prohibition of nuclear weapons and to actively conduct our peace offensive.'[62] While Soviet 'peace offensives' in the past had often amounted to no more than propaganda, in this case the propaganda was underpinned by a deep conviction that it was necessary to banish nuclear weapons worldwide. The accident at the Chernobyl nuclear power station in April of the same year had made a profound impact on Gorbachev. In an interview in 1999 Gorbachev referred again to Chernobyl in the context of reflecting on his foreign policy while in power. He noted that nuclear conflict threatened the very existence of humankind and that in just one rocket there 'lurked a hundred Chernobyls'.[63] After Ronald Reagan and George Shultz, accompanied by their spouses, had spent an evening at the home of Gorbachev and his wife, Raisa, in the company also of Eduard Shevardnadze and his wife, during Reagan's visit to Moscow in the summer of 1988, Shultz sent Reagan a memorandum giving his impressions of the evening while 'the memory is still fresh'. It is reproduced by Reagan in his memoirs. Shultz wrote:

I was struck by how deeply affected Gorbachev appeared to be by the Chernobyl accident.... Gorbachev noted with seemingly genuine horror the devastation that would occur if nuclear power plants became targets in a conventional war much less a full nuclear exchange. Gorbachev agreed that Chernobyl was a 'Final Warning'.... It was obvious from that evening that Chernobyl has left a strong anti-nuclear streak in Gorbachev's thinking.[64]

---

[62] 'Zasedanie Politbyuro TsK KPSS 14 oktyabrya 1986 goda', Volkogonov Collection, NSA. R9744.

[63] Interview with M.S. Gorbachev, 22 March 1999, Hoover Institution and Gorbachev Interview Project on the Cold War, p. 7. (For the text of this interview I am grateful to the Gorbachev Foundation and, in particular, to Viktor Kuvaldin, one of the interviewers.)

[64] Reagan, *An American Life*, p. 710.

Alexander Bessmertnykh, who was Soviet Minister of Foreign Affairs during the first eight months of 1991, and before that an influential participant in arms reduction talks, has spoken of Gorbachev's discovery in 1985–6 that 'many leaders in both camps' preserved 'pre-nuclear notions of the world' at a time when 'thirty thousand nuclear warheads were sitting in storages on both sides'.[65] This, says Bessmertnykh, is why Gorbachev, as his first priority, 'invited other nations to fight the Cold War as a common enemy'.[66]

Those who wish to salvage a 'realist' interpretation of the end of the Cold War make the point that 'no old thinker advocated the use of force in 1989, and none has since suggested that such a decision would have served Soviet interests'.[67] This they link to the long-term decline in the rate of Soviet economic growth, a point which has already been addressed. The same authors aver 'that hard-liners like Kryuchkov and Yazov were also unwilling to contemplate the large-scale use of force to rescue the GDR in 1989. All of these patterns of evidence make it harder to sustain the counterfactual that German unification would not have happened had Gorbachev not been in power'.[68] The last part of that statement is a non-sequitur. It is true that no member of the top leadership team advocated the use of force in Germany or elsewhere in East-Central Europe either in the Politburo or in public in 1989. The changes in Soviet theory and practice which had altered the entire political climate in East-Central Europe were, however, the work of Gorbachev and his closest 'new thinking' allies, notably (at Politburo level) Yakovlev, Shevardnadze, and Medvedev. In 1985 it had not entered the heads of citizens in Warsaw Pact countries that by the end of that decade they might be living in non-Communist, independent countries.[69]

A unified Germany was the result of the heightened expectations of Germans which the developments across the whole of East-Central Europe in 1989 had brought about. Those expectations, as I have tried to show both

[65] Andrei Grachev, Chiara Blengino, and Rossella Stievano (eds.), *1985–2005: Twenty Years that Changed the World* (The World Political Forum and Laterza, Rome, 2005), p. 149.

[66] Ibid.

[67] James W. Davis and William C. Wohlforth, 'German Unification', in Herrmann and Lebow (eds.), *Ending the Cold War*, p. 138.

[68] Ibid., p. 148.

[69] To take just one example, a good Czech friend of mine, Rita Klimová, who became the first post-Communist Ambassador to the United States, told me that the most she and her friends dared hope for with the change of General Secretary in Moscow in 1985 was that Czechoslovakia might be allowed some modest economic reform up to the limits of that introduced in Hungary under János Kádár. And Klimová was not a conformist. By the mid-1980s she was active in the small opposition movement in Czechoslovakia. It was she who, interpreting for her friend, Václav Havel, in 1989, put the words 'velvet revolution' into the English language.

in this chapter and the previous one, were a direct result of liberalization and democratization in Moscow and of Gorbachev's explicit break with the 'Brezhnev doctrine'—his enunciation in 1988 of 'the right to choose', although from the beginning of his General Secretaryship Gorbachev had been determined to put the Soviet Union's relations with Eastern Europe on a different footing.[70]

There is a sense in which earlier 'realist' assumptions that the Soviet Union's gains from the Second World War—control over Eastern Europe— were non-negotiable were 'less wrong' than the post hoc version that any Soviet leadership in the second half of the 1980s would have had to let them go. Robert English has put the point in the following way:

The majority of Cold-War Sovietologists who discounted the possibility of a radical reform movement coming from within the system, or who doubted that Moscow would voluntarily disarm or peacefully yield its core security zone in Eastern Europe, were properly skeptical. All of these *were* highly unlikely. Realist scholars who foresaw the likelihood of a conflictual resolution to the dilemma of Soviet national decline in fact assessed the odds correctly. Their failing lay instead in a rather more understandable inability to foresee how ideas and leadership could combine to overcome such difficult odds.[71]

It is going too far to say that those who ruled out radical reform coming from within the system were 'properly skeptical'. This had already happened within the Communist Party of Czechoslovakia in the 1960s, and reformist tendencies could be discerned within the more highly educated part of the CPSU by those who looked hard enough. That *should* have alerted more than a handful of scholars to the fact that reform from within and above was, at least, a serious possibility. It was, of course, far from certain that a reformist rather than a nationalist tendency would prevail.

---

[70] At his meetings with leaders of the Warsaw Pact countries at Chernenko's funeral, Gorbachev recalls telling them: 'I wish to state as General Secretary of the Central Committee of the CPSU that we place full faith in you, that we make no claim to control or give instructions. You carry out the policy dictated by national interests and take full responsibility for it. So far as our common interests are concerned, we'll meet, work out a line and act.' That, Gorbachev affirms, was said clearly and openly and in the presence of Tikhonov and Gromyko. Those present, he accepts, may have thought this to be just a 'routine declaration of a general secretary'. However: 'In essence this was the establishment of the end of the "Brezhnev doctrine".' Subsequently, the Soviet leadership did not depart from it even once, although there were appeals to them to do so—for example, from Ceaușescu who, in contrast to his earlier line on the independence of East European states, suddenly decided it was 'necessary to defend socialism in Poland'. See interview with M.S. Gorbachev of 22 March 1999 (Hoover Institution and Gorbachev Foundation Interview Project), op. cit., p. 3.

[71] Robert English, 'The Sociology of New Thinking: Elites, Identity Change, and the End of the Cold War', in *Journal of Cold War Studies*, Vol. 7, No. 2, 2005, pp. 43–80, at pp. 79–80.

The failure of those in high places in Moscow who disapproved of the turn of events in Europe to press their case has to be seen partly in the context of the conceptual revolution which occurred in the Soviet Union between 1985 and 1989.[72] Although the innovative ideas and concepts had been germinating for a long time, as noted in chapter six, the thinking became much less constrained after Gorbachev came to power. The conceptual revolution, like perestroika in general, was also in many respects a revolution from above, stimulated by the new vocabulary of politics Gorbachev used and by his support, and that of Yakovlev, for the bolder editors of weeklies and journals. Another part of the context was the revolution of rising expectations in East-Central Europe. The idea that a Grishin or a Romanov—or any other surviving member of Chernenko's Politburo—would have given an iota of encouragement to the development of such expectations is wholly at odds with what we know of the mindset of those 'old thinkers'.

Before expectations were aroused, the veiled threat of force would have been enough to keep Eastern Europe under Communist rule. Even in Poland, the most obstreperous barracks in the camp, Solidarity was able to lead only a subdued underground existence after the imposition of martial law in December 1981—until 1988, following the changes in Moscow. Gorbachev had introduced new ideas and used his institutional power to the full, contributing hugely to the changed political climate both in the Soviet Union and in East-Central Europe. His agenda-setting was bolstered by the great domestic authority which, as already noted, resided in the office of General Secretary. At a Moscow conference in 1999, Anatoliy Gromyko, the son of the long-serving Soviet Foreign Minister, said: '[I]t seems to me that foreigners have a hard time understanding to what extent the post of general secretary was influential in the Soviet mentality. You see, to object to the general secretary, or even worse, to debate his opinions in public—at that time I don't think anyone would dare to do that.'[73] By 1989 freedom of speech had developed to the point at which some people *were* beginning to venture public criticism of Gorbachev, but they were either those who had never had any power to lose or, in the exceptional case of Boris Yeltsin, someone who had already been removed from high office and who was boldly preparing to use the new institution of contested elections to attempt a comeback.[74]

---

[72] See Brown (ed.), *The Demise of Marxism-Leninism in Russia*, op. cit.

[73] Moscow Cold War Conference of June 1999, Tape 2, Mershon Center, Ohio State University.

[74] As already noted, Yeltsin's criticisms did not, however, touch on the Soviet Union's relations with other countries.

Only Gorbachev within the Chernenko Politburo was dissatisfied with Gromyko's conception of Soviet interests and conduct of foreign policy. Interests can be perceived very differently,[75] and Gromyko's outlook, a product of a different era, is summed up by Dobrynin, the long-serving Soviet Ambassador to Washington who became a Secretary of the Central Committee and head of the International Department under Gorbachev:

His chief priority was the defense of our national interests as he saw them and, first of all, upholding our gains of the hard war that defeated Nazi Germany. A disciple of Stalin's, he did not attach much importance to moral aspects of foreign policy such as human rights, although he was an honest and decent man. He did not believe that such abstract notions could be a serious factor in policy, or in the possibility of early and radical agreements with the West.[76]

By 1989 Gorbachev had secured acquiescence in the Soviet Union for his foreign policy. The fact that it was popular with the general public at that time—President Reagan's friendly visit to Moscow in 1988 seemed to provide confirmation that the threat of nuclear war had vanished—made it harder for discontented elements within the elite to oppose. With the advent of serious survey research and, still more important, competitive elections, public opinion had begun to matter. The fact that debate on foreign policy in the Politburo was muted does not, however, mean that there was a genuine consensus. The Minister of Defence, Dmitriy Yazov, disagreed with many of Gorbachev's policies, but face to face with him, he was very deferential. He told a friendly interviewer, Oleg Skvortsov, that Gorbachev would become upset when told of opposition in the military to his policies. Gorbachev would ask: 'Why are you opposed? What do you want, nose to nose, bayonet to bayonet?' Gorbachev, Yazov reported, told him: 'You have to look ahead.' Skvortsov said: 'And did you ask, in which direction?' That led to the following revealing exchange:

Yazov: 'At that time Gorbachev was general secretary.'
Skvortsov: 'Did he use his authority to apply pressure?'
Yazov: 'It's not that he used his authority to apply pressure, but we had to use a certain tact with him.'[77]

---

[75] Rejecting an ideas–interests dichotomy, Alexander Wendt argues that 'only a small part of what constitutes interests is actually material. The material force constituting interests is human nature. The rest is ideational: schemas and deliberations that are in turn constituted by shared ideas or culture' (*Social Theory of International Politics*, pp. 114–15).

[76] Dobrynin, *In Confidence*, p. 574.

[77] O.I. Skvortsov interview with Yazov, 11 March 1999, cited by Matthew Evangelista, 'Turning Points in Arms Control', in Herrmann and Lebow (eds.), *Ending the Cold War*, pp. 83–105, at p. 93.

LEADERSHIP

In the final section of this chapter, I consider the crucial role of leadership in the ending of the Cold War. Change on the Soviet side was more important in relation to that outcome than shifts in American policy, since more *needed* to be changed in Soviet policy if the deadlock between the two blocs and two systems were to be broken. Although his role has often been exaggerated, a significant part in the process was played by President Ronald Reagan.[78] I have already discussed Gorbachev's use of the power of his office that enabled him to sideline the military-industrial complex which had been such a powerful institutional interest in Brezhnev's Soviet Union. Reagan's presidential power, combined with his convincing second term electoral victory, also put him in a strong position to negotiate. Reagan himself, and many in his administration, believed that increased spending on defence, including SDI, improved the chances of successful negotiations, although that view is disputed by some of the principal foreign policy actors on the Soviet side who argue that this led to pessimism in the Soviet Union about the chances of improving East–West relations and complicated Gorbachev's task of overcoming domestic institutional opposition.[79]

While promoting democratization within Soviet society, Gorbachev often used his power to the full within the leadership to get his way on matters he

[78] Margaret Thatcher, who is identified by most of the leading figures in the Reagan Administration who were interviewed for the Hoover Oral History Project on the end of the Cold War, as the foreign leader who had most influence over Reagan and to whom he was closest, played a far smaller role than Gorbachev or Reagan (or, for that matter, Chancellor Helmut Kohl during the period when German unification was being discussed and negotiated). However, in the first years of perestroika—and, indeed, earlier, when the British Prime Minister flew to Washington to brief Ronald Reagan immediately after Gorbachev's first visit to Britain in December 1984—Thatcher played a significant part in encouraging the American President to believe that he would be able to 'do business' at last with a Soviet leader.

[79] In Dobrynin's view: 'The impact of the American hard line on the internal debates of the Politburo and the attitudes of the Soviet leadership almost always turned out to be just the opposite of the one intended by Washington. Rather than retreating from the awesome military buildup that underwrote Reagan's belligerent rhetoric, the Soviet leaders began to absorb Reagan's own distinctive thesis that Soviet–American relations could remain permanently bad as a deliberate choice of policy. Only gradually did both sides begin to realize they were doomed to annihilation unless they found a way out. But it took a great deal of time and effort to turn from confrontation and mutual escalation, probably much more than if this course had never been taken in the first place' (Dobrynin, *In Confidence*, p. 544). Anatoliy Adamishin, who was more of a 'new thinker' within the Ministry of Foreign Affairs than Dobrynin (not to speak of Gromyko), has stated that the notion that Reagan's hard line led to the appearance of the new political thinking and perestroika was the opposite of the truth. Reagan's pressure, he said, 'gave unnecessary arguments to our "hawks" and created difficulties for Gorbachev...', Interview with A.L. Adamishin of 5 August 1999, The Hoover Institution and the Gorbachev Foundation (Moscow) Collection, Acc. No. 98067–16.305, HIA, p. 5.

regarded as essential. Michael Howard (the historian, not the former Leader of the British Conservative Party), defending Gorbachev from the charge that 'he was not really a democrat', observed:

Yet it was only such an arbitrary exercise of power that made it possible for him to bring the Cold War to an end at all. It took an experienced *apparatchik* like Gorbachev to manipulate the system, eliminate the irreconcilables, and push through the votes to enable such a seismic transformation of Soviet policy to take place. Gorbachev may not have been nice in the way that he did it, but nobody was imprisoned, nobody was exiled, and certainly nobody was shot.[80]

The example of Gorbachev using the flight of the young German, Matthias Rust to Red Square as a way of removing the Minister of Defence and a number of the most senior military officers from their posts has been discussed in greater detail in chapter one. This was, at least in part, a political stratagem to weaken opposition from within the defence establishment to his policies.[81] Another instance of Gorbachev pushing to the limits of his authority came in the Spring of 1989 when, as noted in Chapter 4, Gorbachev induced—at extremely short notice—almost one hundred full and candidate members of the Central Committee to sign a request that they relinquish their powers as members of that body. The group included several former members of the top leadership team, among them Andrey Gromyko, Vladimir Dolgikh, and Nikolay Tikhonov. In general, these were people who had lost the functions that entitled them to membership of the Central Committee in the first place, a fact that made them a potential repository of support for any group within the leadership willing to take the risk of moving against Gorbachev.[82]

[80] Michael Howard, 'Winning the peace: How both Kennan and Gorbachev were right', *Times Literary Supplement*, 8 January 1993, p. 8. Howard remarks that it is a matter for amazement that 'the end of the Cold War was accomplished with so much good will', adding: 'For an all too brief moment it seemed as if the affairs of mankind had been taken in hand by some Higher and very much more sensible Power. Not, alas, for very long' (ibid.).

[81] See Dobrynin, *In Confidence*, pp. 625–6. The former KGB Chairman, Vladimir Kryuchkov, claims that Gorbachev used the case of Rust 'to strike a blow to the Ministry of Defense, which in his opinion was not wholly subordinate to him, and didn't carry out his will or follow his train of thought'. A similar view is expressed by Marshal Dmitriy Yazov, the immediate beneficiary of Gorbachev's action as he succeeded Marshal Sergey Sokolov as Minister of Defence. See Moscow Cold War Conference transcripts, Mershon Center, Ohio State University, Tape 3.

[82] In the laconic official language, the April 1989 plenum of the Central Committee 'complied with the request of 110 members and candidate members of the Central Committee of the CPSU and of the Central Auditing Commission of the CPSU' to relinquish their positions 'in the central elected organs of the party in connection with their transfer to a pension on account of their age and the condition of their health'. See *Ezhegodnik bol'shoy sovetskoy entsiklopedii 1990* (Sovetskaya entsiklopediya, Moscow, 1990), p. 19. In their valedictory speeches, a number of the 'dead souls'—as, with apologies to Gogol, the functionless Central Committee members became known at the time—expressed varying degrees of disillusionment with the way perestroika was going. See Vorotnikov, *A bylo eto tak*, pp. 257–8.

Leadership is not identical with power, albeit intertwined with it in the case of chief executives. The parts played by Gorbachev and Reagan have to be seen in the context of their ideas and values—which were very different but which intersected at certain points. Reagan, unlike some leading figures in his administration, did believe in the possibility of change in the Soviet Union and he not only shared Gorbachev's horror of nuclear weapons but, like him, was prepared to consider attempting to eliminate them entirely from military arsenals. The best-informed, insider account of Reagan's policy towards the Soviet Union is the study of the end of the Cold War by Jack F. Matlock, Jr., who was on the staff of the National Security Council in Washington from 1983 until the end of 1986 as senior director for European and Soviet Affairs and then, from 1987 to 1991, an exceptionally well-qualified US Ambassador to Moscow.[83]

Matlock does not endorse the myth that Ronald Reagan, through his weapons buildup and embrace of SDI, brought the Soviet Union to its knees and left its leadership with no alternative to but to acquiesce in the independence of Eastern Europe, seek arms reductions, and end the Cold War. Like Shultz, he notes that Reagan wished to negotiate from strength, but he *did* wish to negotiate. Matlock emphasizes the significance of the national security directive of January 1983, classified at the time, which set out the principles governing the Reagan administration's relations with the Soviet Union. The document expressed the desire to 'engage with the Soviet Union in negotiations which protect and enhance U.S. interests and which are consistent with the principle of strict reciprocity and mutual interest'.[84] Matlock dismisses as 'rationalization after the fact' statements by some former members of the Reagan administration that the policy had been 'to bring the Soviet Union down'. President Reagan, he insists, 'was in favour of bringing pressure to bear on the Soviet Union, but his objective was to induce the Soviet leaders to negotiate reasonable agreements, not to break up the country'.[85]

---

[83] Jack F. Matlock, Jr., *Reagan and Gorbachev: How the Cold War Ended* (Random House, New York, 2004).

[84] Ibid., pp. 52–4. The document, National Security Decision Directive Number 75 (NSDD-75) is summarized on pp. 53–4.

[85] Ibid., pp. 75–6. In order to try to reduce the inter-agency differences, Shultz inaugurated a series of Saturday morning breakfasts, attended by himself, National Security Adviser McFarlane, Secretary of Defense Weinberger, CIA chief Casey and Vice-President George Bush. The first such meeting was held on 19 November 1983 with Matlock appointed as the organizer and note-taker at these meetings, whose very existence was kept confidential. Matlock's outline notes of the first meeting mention three elements which it was agreed were *not* goals of US policy: 'a. Challenging legitimacy of Soviet system; b. Military superiority; c. Forcing collapse of the Soviet system (as distinct from exerting pressure on Soviets to live up to agreements and abide by civilized standards of behaviour)', *Reagan and Gorbachev*, p. 76.

While the gulf in values and beliefs within the Reagan administration was less wide than that within the leadership of the Soviet Communist Party during the perestroika years, there were, nevertheless, very important differences. Just as it was crucial that Gorbachev endorsed the approach of the 'new thinking' element within the Soviet foreign policy establishment—with Yakovlev and Chernyaev especially influential—so it was important that Reagan, in the final analysis, preferred the judgement of Secretary of State George Shultz to that of Secretary of Defense Caspar Weinberger and CIA Director William Casey.[86] Most departments, Matlock observes, 'would obey a decision by the president' but 'one could never be sure that Weinberger would'. If the Secretary for Defense disliked a decision, he would bring public pressure on Reagan through 'distorted leaks to favored journalists—perhaps not from Weinberger himself, but obviously from someone in his department'.[87] Indeed, Matlock writes, 'Ronald Reagan's favourite phrase during the last years of his presidency, "Trust, but verify", was directed not only at Gorbachev... but also at those in his own administration who, like Weinberger, persisted in opposing realistic negotiations with the Soviet Union.'[88]

On the American side, Shultz's role was almost as important as that of Reagan. Certainly the appointment of Shultz in succession to Alexander Haig made progress easier than it otherwise would have been once the Soviet Union had a leader ready to embrace change. Reagan found that Haig made a difficult subordinate, saying that he discovered 'only a few months into the administration that Al [Haig] didn't want anyone other than himself, me included, to influence foreign policy while he was secretary of state' and he 'was never shy about asserting this claim'.[89] Matlock notes that General Haig 'was less sanguine than Reagan and Shultz that the Soviet Union could change, and therefore posed more limited goals for U.S. policy than they eventually did'.[90] That statement may not be entirely fair to Haig, given that it was the change in the Soviet Union under Gorbachev—which had very clearly *not* taken place when Haig left office in 1982—that enabled Reagan and Shultz 'eventually' to have less limited goals. What is absolutely clear, however, is that

---

[86] Ibid., pp. 102–3. Reagan, Matlock says (p. 102), resented the efforts of hard-liners within his administration to undermine and even remove from office Shultz and National Security Adviser Robert McFarlane because 'he knew they were carrying out his policies more faithfully than Weinberger and Casey'. A 1984 entry in Ronald Reagan's diary, cited in his memoirs, bears this out. Observing that the dispute between Weinberger (backed by William Casey and Edwin Meese) and Shultz 'is so out of hand George sounds like he wants out. I can't let that happen. Actually George is carrying out my policy. I'm going to meet with Cap [Weinberger] and Bill [Casey] and lay it out to them. Won't be fun but has to be done' (*An American Life*, p. 606).

[87] Matlock, *Reagan and Gorbachev*, p. 114. [88] Ibid., pp. 114–15.

[89] Reagan, *An American Life*, p. 360. [90] Matlock, *Reagan and Gorbachev*, p. 24.

nothing changed for the better in relations between Washington and Moscow, between the Soviet Union and Western Europe, or for the peoples of Eastern Europe during the first term of Reagan's presidency when he 'co-existed' with three different General Secretaries of the CPSU—Brezhnev, Andropov, and Chernenko.

That in itself would suggest that the different values, ideas and priorities that Gorbachev embodied made the more crucial difference. Yet the Reagan factor was important in many ways, not least because, although he listened to the hard-liners within his administration and outside it as well as to Shultz, he had a persistent preference for the policy of dialogue of which Shultz was a key proponent. Reagan's importance lay also in the fact that his long-standing anti-Communist credentials stood him in good stead with conservative Republicans and he was, accordingly, far less troubled by the domestic opposition of hard-liners than a Democratic President would have been.[91] It is significant also that Reagan set great store by personalities and on his personal relations. The fact that he liked Gorbachev and thought him sincere played a very positive role in making it possible for them to come to far-reaching agreements. Reflecting on his first meeting with Gorbachev in Geneva on 19 November 1985, Reagan said: 'As we shook hands for the first time, I had to admit—as Margaret Thatcher and Prime Minister Brian Mulroney of Canada predicted I would—that there was something likable about Gorbachev. There was warmth in his face and his style, not the coldness bordering on hatred I'd seen in most senior Soviet officials I'd met until then.'[92] Following three additional summit meetings, Reagan went further: 'Looking back now, it's clear that there was a chemistry between Gorbachev and me that produced something very close to a friendship.'[93]

In contrast with Jack Matlock's even-handed account of the roles of Gorbachev and Reagan in ending the Cold War (with only a mild and understandable bias in favour of the administration in which he served), the latest book on the Cold War by one of its most prominent historians, John Lewis Gaddis, presents a more conventional Washington view of its ending.[94] The fact that the Soviet leadership had a strong preference for a domestic

---

[91] In the past Reagan's anti-Communism had sometimes led him into making monumental misjudgements. He was one of those who for years believed that the Sino-Soviet split was an elaborate ruse to deceive the West.

[92] Ronald Reagan, *An American Life: The Autobiography* (Simon & Schuster, New York, 1990), p. 635.

[93] Ibid., p. 707.

[94] John Lewis Gaddis, *The Cold War: A New History* (Penguin Press, New York, 2005). See also Gaddis, *Strategies of Containment: A Critical Appraisal of American National Security Policy During the Cold War* (Oxford University Press, New York, 2005), revised and expanded edition; and Gaddis, *We Know Now: Rethinking Cold War History* (Clarendon Press, Oxford, 1997).

Polish crackdown over an invasion by their forces in 1981 leads Gaddis to assume, wrongly, that the 'Brezhnev doctrine' had already been abandoned before Gorbachev came to power. That was not the view of anyone within the Soviet elite at the time or the belief of the peoples of Eastern Europe. Otherwise, the Poles, and not only the Poles, would have tested the limits of the possible in the first half of the 1980s. Gaddis is also surely wrong in suggesting that if John Hinckley, Jr.'s bullet had killed Ronald Reagan in 1981, the Cold War would not have ended because 'there would probably not have been an American challenge to the Cold War status quo'.[95] That view exaggerates the qualitative change in the attitude to the Soviet Union of the Reagan administration as compared with American administrations from Truman to Carter. More importantly, it underestimates the extent to which Gorbachev and his 'new thinking' allies were able to reach their own judgements on the changes required within their system and in Soviet foreign policy without guidance from Washington. It also implies a rather pessimistic view of the American political system by suggesting that no other president could have emerged who would have been capable of responding to change in Moscow (if one abandons the implausible premise that this change was mainly Reagan's doing). As has already been noted, Reagan's policies, which were for Gorbachev a *further* reason for seeking to end the Cold War, were for more conventional Soviet thinkers, including the members of the Politburo during the Andropov and Chernenko General Secretaryships, reasons for maintaining existing military expenditure and for cracking down on the slightest sign of dissent or ideological deviation at home.

If Reagan had died in the attempt on his life in 1981 he would have been succeeded by George H.W. Bush. No more than Reagan would Bush have been able to do serious business with Brezhnev, Andropov, and Chernenko. Indeed, between 1980 and 1984, with the partial exception of Andropov's fifteen months at the helm, Gromyko and Ustinov were even more important than the general secretary when it came to determining Soviet foreign and defence policy. If Bush had won the 1984 presidential election, he would before long have found that his counterpart was Mikhail Gorbachev. Departing from the counterfactual and looking at Bush's actual policy when, following the 1988 election, he succeeded Reagan, we see that he was, indeed, slow to realize how much things had changed in Moscow and in Soviet foreign policy. At a Politburo meeting largely devoted to international affairs, held over two days on 27–28 December 1988 (following Gorbachev's UN speech and meetings in the United States with both Reagan and Bush), Gorbachev

---

[95] Gaddis, *The Cold War*, p. 222.

described Bush as 'a very cautious politician'.[96] Shevardnadze and Yakovlev at the same meeting endorsed that view and Yakovlev said that the previous day he had met with the American Ambassador Matlock. Compared with Reagan, Yakovlev reports Matlock as saying: 'Bush is more professional, more informed, but at the same time more cautious. He tried to suggest that [Bush] always took part in the working-out of concrete decisions, was interested in details, and knew a lot—that is, he tried to display the new president in an advantageous light.'[97] Yakovlev went on to say that it was necessary to continue to work towards the disappearance of the 'enemy image'; that would 'pull the rug from under the feet of the military-industrial complex'.[98]

Indeed, the first President Bush, after a lull in active diplomacy, in due course established relations of trust with Gorbachev. If, from the Oval Office, he had already experienced the frustration of trying to make headway with Brezhnev, Andropov, and Chernenko, he would probably have embraced him all the earlier. Any American President with an ounce of common sense should, with Gorbachev as a partner, have been able to preside over the end of the Cold War. It is true that Bush—still more a Democratic president—would have had a tougher domestic fight on his hands to persuade Washington hard-liners that the Soviet Union was seeking more than a breathing-space before resuming its quest for world domination. It is unlikely that the latter would have prevailed, given the growing popularity of Gorbachev with the American public, the withering away of the 'enemy image', and the fact that European governmental and public opinion was still more in favour of entering into dialogue and negotiations with Gorbachev.

A more subtle case for Reagan's indispensability than that made by Gaddis is presented by George W. Breslauer and Richard Ned Lebow when they set themselves the 'counterfactual thought experiment' of judging the outcome after Hinckley's bullet killed Reagan in 1981 and the Central Committee of the CPSU in 1985 'unanimously elected Comrade Viktor Grishin as General Secretary'. They have no difficulty in showing that the Cold War would not have ended under Grishin's stewardship, for the dramatic change in both domestic and foreign policy which Gorbachev initiated, and with whose unintended as well as intended consequences he was prepared to live, would simply not have occurred. Gorbachev changed the balance of power within

---

[96] 'Zasedanie Politbyuro TsK KPSS 27–28 dekabrya 1988 goda', HIA, Fond 89, 1.1003, opis 42, file 24, p. 329.

[97] Ibid., p. 344.

[98] From the context, Yakovlev was clearly speaking about the American military-industrial complex, but from his remarks on other occasions, it is reasonable to deduce that he believed the same would usefully apply to its Soviet counterpart.

the governing structures of the Soviet Union and the balance of influence among advisers. Grishin's allies and advisers had very different mindsets from Gorbachev's. The views of the latter had been evolving over a lengthy period which began long before Reagan entered the White House.[99]

Breslauer and Lebow make the case for Reagan's crucial role on the basis of the following psychological argument:

People with less developed schemas are initially more likely to maintain their schemas intact in the face of discrepant information, but to change them dramatically in the face of a consistent stream of discrepant information. People with more complex and developed schemas are more likely to find ways of interpreting discrepant information in a manner consistent with their schemas, or of making small, incremental changes in their schemas to accommodate this information.[100]

Thus, the very fact that Reagan, in the words of Breslauer and Lebow 'held strong views on many subjects and had little knowledge to back up those views' and that 'he repeatedly demonstrated his ignorance of the Soviet Union, in public and private' made it easier for him to change his position dramatically. Thus, they conclude, it was not surprising that 'Reagan, who entered office with the most fervently anti-Soviet views, retired as the biggest dove in the administration'.[101] In contrast, Reagan's advisers, with their 'more elaborate schemas of the Soviet Union' were able 'to explain away Gorbachev's reforms and interest in arms control and accommodation as clever, duplicitous, and seeking to weaken the West by appealing to the antiwar sentiments of European and American public opinion'.[102] While there is certainly something in that analysis, it needs to be amplified by the fact that when Shultz succeeded Haig as Secretary of State (and, one might add, when Jack Matlock succeeded Arthur Hartman as American Ambassador to Moscow) the sophistication of understanding of the Soviet Union within the administration was on the side of those who wished to enter into serious negotiations with their Cold War antagonist. And, while Reagan might listen to Weinberger or Casey

---

[99] See on this Jeffrey T. Checkel, *Ideas and International Change: Soviet/Russian Behavior and the End of the Cold War* (Yale University Press, New Haven, CT, 1977); Robert D. English, *Russia and the Idea of the West: Gorbachev, Intellectuals, and the End of the Cold War* (Columbia University Press, New York, 2000); Neil Malcolm, *Soviet Policy Perspectives on Western Europe* (Royal Institute of International Affairs and Routledge, London, 1989); and Julie M. Newton, *Russia, France, and the Idea of Europe* (Palgrave Macmillan, Basingstoke, 2003). See also Chapter 6 of the present volume; and Robert English, 'The Sociology of New Thinking', op. cit.

[100] George W. Breslauer and Richard Ned Lebow, 'Leadership and the End of the Cold War: A Counterfactual Thought Experiment', in Herrmann and Lebow (eds.), *Ending the Cold War*, pp. 161–88, at p. 182.

[101] Ibid. This last point is a slight exaggeration. Reagan was no more 'dovish' than was Shultz who was also a rather less ideological and more pragmatic conservative.

[102] Ibid., p. 182.

genially enough, he ultimately preferred the judgement of Shultz on developments in the Soviet Union and on US–Soviet relations.[103]

There are a number of disparate reasons why the presence of Reagan in the White House was conducive to the Cold War ending when it did. A variety of them are offered by Breslauer and Lebow, Matlock, Shultz and Gaddis, and others have been mentioned in this chapter. Ultimately, however, it is hard to believe that the American political system would have been incapable of adapting to the new opportunities offered by Gorbachev's ascent to the General Secretaryship or that either George Bush the elder (with his more developed schemas) or a Democratic alternative would have been impervious to the changes in Soviet domestic and foreign policy which had both domestic roots and far more complex transnational roots than the policies of Ronald Reagan. Ultimately, Gorbachev was substantially more important than Reagan because *none* of the possible alternative leaders of the Soviet Communist Party was remotely as reform-minded or as open-minded as he was. There *were* alternative American leaders with a realistic chance of becoming president (as one of them, George H.W. Bush, did) who were at least as open-minded as Reagan and who did not, *pace* Breslauer and Lebow, seem unduly handicapped by knowing a bit more about the outside world.[104]

CONCLUSIONS

The Cold War began with Stalin's imposition of Soviet-type regimes in Eastern Europe. It ended in 1989 when the countries of Eastern Europe were allowed, peacefully, to gain their independence.[105] Not a shot was fired

---

[103] It is worth noting, additionally, that his wife Nancy was a dovish influence, as was the historical writer, Suzanne Massie, whom he frequently consulted. Massie was convinced of the seriousness of the changes underway in the Soviet Union under Gorbachev and she also helped Reagan to appreciate the Russians as people rather than as cogs in a Communist machine. On Massie, see Matlock, *Reagan and Gorbachev*, pp. 92–3 and 134; and Shultz, *Turmoil and Triumph*, pp. 720, 724, 746, and 872–3.

[104] See Richard Ned Lebow and Janice Gross Stein, 'Understanding the End of the Cold War as a Non-Linear Confluence', in Lebow and Herrmann (eds.), *Ending the Cold War*, pp. 188–217, at p. 192.

[105] Moreover, although the changes in Eastern Europe went further and faster than Gorbachev had bargained for, he actively mediated in 1989 to ensure that—in those countries where he had real influence over the rulers (which excluded Romania)—the transformation would occur without backlash or bloodshed. The Soviet Union was quick to accept the legitimacy of the Mazowiecki government elected in 1989 at a time when there were those in the PUWP who were not disposed to tolerate such an outcome. As Mark Kramer sums up the situation: 'The experience with Poland was typical of Gorbachev's policy toward eastern Europe as a whole. In each case, the Soviet Union helped to bring about sweeping political change while effectively

by a Soviet soldier. This dramatic turn of events was produced, above all, by a change of leader in the Soviet Union who used his power of appointment to replace the top foreign policy team and who introduced a surprising element of idealism into relations with the rest of the world, displacing the previous unpromising mixture of Leninist dogma and Realpolitik.[106] On the Western side, while military capability was far from inconsequential, it was less important than the facts that non-Communist democratic states had combined far greater political freedom with much more substantial economic prosperity and social welfare than was to be found in Communist Europe. As noted in the previous chapters, the first-hand exposure to Western countries of many of those who were to become leading figures in the formulation of Soviet foreign policy during the perestroika years—Gorbachev, among them—had a significant impact on their way of looking at the world. That is one of the transnational influences which has already discussed in Chapter 8.

The sources of change are to be found in an interdependent mixture of ideas, leadership, and institutional power. Harry Truman's frustration at times with the limitations on the powers of the American presidency was famously rephrased by Richard Neustadt as: 'Presidential *power* is the power to persuade.'[107] Mikhail Gorbachev had formidable powers of persuasion—and he used the 'power to persuade' to the full—but to a still greater extent than the American President, with the latter operating in a separation-of-powers system, these were underpinned by the vast power and authority of his office.

The long-term causes of the end of the Cold War include the indubitable fact that democracies, with all their imperfections, turned out to be more just, more efficient, more prosperous and, it goes without saying, freer societies than the Communist regimes of the Soviet Union and Eastern Europe. If the Cold War were to end peacefully, far greater changes were required in the polities and societies under Communist rule than in Western Europe or North America. However, in this chapter I have been concerned with the issue of why the Cold War ended when it did. The constructive response of the

---

depriving hard-line communist leaders of the option of violent repression' (Kramer, 'Gorbachev and the demise of East European communism', in Silvio Pons and Frederico Romero (eds.), *Reinterpreting the End of the Cold War: Issues, Interpretations, Periodizations* (Cass, London, 2005), pp. 179–200, at p. 191).

[106] The new foreign policy team—with Shevardnadze, Yakovlev, Chernyaev, and Shakhnazarov especially key players—has been touched upon only briefly in this chapter, notwithstanding its enormous importance. That is because it is discussed in greater detail in Chapters 3 and 6. See also Brown, *The Gorbachev Factor*, ch. 4, 'The Power of Ideas and the Power of Appointment', pp. 89–129, and ch. 7, 'Gorbachev and Foreign Policy', esp. pp. 212–20.

[107] Richard E. Neustadt, *Presidential Power: The Politics of Leadership from FDR to Carter* (Wiley, New York, 2nd edn., 1980), pp. 9–10.

American side in negotiations between the two principal rivals between 1985 and 1990—with, first, Reagan and Shultz in the leading roles and, subsequently, Bush and James Baker as the key actors—played an important part in ending the stand-off. However, more decisive factors were the coming to power of Gorbachev, his selection of a new foreign policy team who shared his values, and his willingness to liberalize the Soviet system and then to embark on its democratization. Gorbachev's rejection of the ideological underpinnings of the East–West conflict led, in turn, to a new emphasis on freedom of choice and the crucial rejection of the use of force to uphold Communist regimes loyal to Moscow. The end of the division of Europe, which followed from this, marked the end of the Cold War.

10

Gorbachev and His Era in Perspective

This concluding chapter addresses a series of controversial issues concerning Gorbachev and perestroika, but I should first make clear what I am *not* arguing. In pointing to the decisive role played by Mikhail Gorbachev in the initiation of perestroika—and the dramatic change this brought about in the Soviet Union and in the climate of world politics in the second half of the 1980s—I am offering neither a 'Great Man' interpretation of history nor an explanation of the breakthrough primarily in terms of charismatic leadership.[1] That is notwithstanding the fact that Gorbachev had, indeed, some of the attributes associated with Weber's ideal type of 'charismatic authority'. For Weber, of course, such authority is unconnected with office-holding or expert knowledge. A person possessing charismatic authority is a 'natural' leader, although charisma can be 'lost' if the leader's deeds 'do not fare well'.[2]

In the way in which the term, 'charismatic', has come to be used in ordinary political discourse, Gorbachev has good claim to be a charismatic leader.[3] His authority emerged before he held any political office, and during his years as General Secretary his popular standing was immense in many countries where

[1] Or, as Thomas Carlyle, in his classic (and florid) statement of the former case, puts it: 'Universal History, the history of what man has accomplished in this world, is at bottom the History of the Great Men who have worked here. They were the leaders of men, these great ones; the modellers, patterns, and in a wide sense creators, of whatsoever the general mass of men contrived to do or to attain; all things that we see standing accomplished in the world are properly the outer material result, the practical realisation and embodiment, of Thoughts that dwelt in the Great Men sent into the world; the soul of the whole world's history, it may justly be considered, were the history of these' (Carlyle, *On Heroes, Hero-Worship, and The Heroic in History* (Chapman & Hall, London, 3rd edn., 1846), pp. 1–2). And, as the no less classic (but more down-to-earth) Max Weber writes of charismatic authority: 'The natural leaders in distress have been holders of specific gifts of the body and spirit; and these gifts have been believed to be supernatural, not accessible to everybody.... Charisma knows only inner determination and inner restraint. The holder of charisma seizes the task that is adequate for him and demands obedience and a following by virtue of his mission' (*From Max Weber: Essays in Sociology* (translated and edited by H.H. Gerth and C. Wright Mills, Routledge & Kegan Paul, London, 1948), pp. 245–6).

[2] *From Max Weber*, pp. 245 and 249.

[3] That, however, is far from being the most positive thing that can be said about Gorbachev's leadership. Charisma, in Weber's sense, is value-neutral. A charismatic leader can be a Hitler or a Martin Luther King.

the writ of the Central Committee of the CPSU did not run. His Moscow University friend and contemporary, Zdeněk Mlynář, has testified that as a student—and one from a much humbler background than most of his fellows—Gorbachev 'won an informal and spontaneous authority'.[4] Even after the strictly hierarchical character of the Soviet system had been altered by Gorbachev's own reforms, and after the powers of the General Secretary-ship had accordingly been somewhat curtailed, Gorbachev was frequently able to carry the day in a Politburo in which like-minded reformers were in a minority.[5] His natural authority, self-confidence, and powers of persuasion, albeit allied to the authority bestowed by his office, led conservative Communists to support actions—and benign inaction—they later regretted. Vitaliy Vorotnikov, for example, a sufficiently conservative member of the Politburo to have instinctively sided with the neo-Stalinist response to perestroika associated with the Nina Andreeva letter,[6] 'often yielded', as noted in chapter nine, 'to the logic of [Gorbachev's] persuasion'.[7]

Gorbachev's leadership qualities, which were readily apparent to others, were very important.[8] The way one of his closest associates, Georgiy Shakh-nazarov, put it was as follows:

Undoubtedly, no small role was played by his charismatic appearance. An intelligent, smiling face with correct features, extraordinarily expressive eyes (for five years it was my lot to see Mikhail Sergeevich tired, sleepless, ill, but I never saw him lack-lustre), the birth-mark on his forehead as an impressive sign of a chosen one; a fine, a little full, but smart figure; a confident manner of behaviour; openness and benevolence in combination with strictness and a commanding air. In a word, his every fibre exuded charm, and this was sufficient from his first appearances on the screen and on the street to win sympathy.[9]

---

    [4] *L'Unità*, 9 April 1985, p. 9. As I also noted in Chapter 2, Denis Healey, the most experienced and outstanding politician in the British Labour Party in the field of foreign affairs in the second half of the twentieth century, was struck by Gorbachev's 'immense authority' when he met him in 1984—before Gorbachev had reached the top of the Soviet political hierarchy.

    [5] By the time Politburo members had shaken off their traditional deference to the General Secretary, neither the General Secretaryship nor the Politburo were the highest repositories of power. See, for example, the discussion later in this chapter of the Politburo meeting of 16 November 1990.

    [6] See Chapter 7, n. 17; 'O stat'e N. Andreevoy i ne tol'ko o ney' in M.S. Gorbachev, *Gody trudnykh resheniy*, pp. 98–110; and Archie Brown, *The Gorbachev Factor*, pp. 172–5.

    [7] V.I. Vorotnikov, *A bylo eto tak . . . Iz dnevnika chlena Politbyuro TsK KPSS* (Sovet veteranov knigoizdaniya, Moscow, 1995), p. 461.

    [8] Gorbachev himself has observed: 'From my earliest days I liked to be a leader among my peers—that was my nature. And this remained true when I joined the Komsomol . . . and later when I joined the party—it was a way of somehow realizing my potential.' See Mikhail Gorbachev and Zdeněk Mlynář, *Conversations with Gorbachev: On Perestroika, the Prague Spring, and the Crossroads of Socialism* (Columbia University Press, New York, 2002), p. 15.

    [9] Georgiy Shakhnazarov, *Tsena svobody: Reformatsiya Gorbacheva glazami ego pomoshchnika* (Rossika zevs, Moscow, 1993), p. 37. Yakovlev has described Gorbachev as 'an emotionally gifted

Less glowing accounts of Gorbachev's persona are, needless to say, provided by some of those who turned against him and who took part in mounting the August 1991 attempted coup. The KGB chief at the time, Kryuchkov, and the chief of staff of Gorbachev's presidential office, Boldin, portray Gorbachev as chronically suspicious of others in the leadership and as devious.[10] It has to be said that both of them, especially Kryuchkov, put much energy into the attempt to make Gorbachev suspicious of the most liberal members of his team in order to drive a wedge between him and them. Gorbachev could have done with being *much more suspicious* of Kryuchkov and Boldin. At times he gave them more credence than they deserved—when, for example, they brought him disinformation on particular personalities or presented dubious evidence that exaggerated the dangers of violent unrest in the Baltic states or even in Moscow.[11] However, in the final analysis, Gorbachev was far readier to listen to the recommendations of Chernyaev, Shakhnazarov, or Yakovlev, when determining the main lines of policy, especially foreign policy, and he resisted immense pressure from the hard-liners to use force to 'solve' the nationalities problem in the Soviet Union's most restive republics. It was because Gorbachev so seldom *acted* on the advice of Kryuchkov and his like-minded associates that they attempted to take matters into their own hands in August 1991.

Gorbachev did not, of course, rise through the Soviet system to become General Secretary of the Central Committee of the CPSU without being able to watch his back. Aleksandr Yakovlev probably protested too much in post-Soviet Russia about Gorbachev's lack of open support for him in the last years of the Soviet Union.[12] Gorbachev had used his power and authority to the full to accord Yakovlev exceptionally accelerated promotion and to give him a major role in policymaking, particularly during the first four years of perestroika. Although Gorbachev's own position became weaker during his last two years in office, he kept Yakovlev in the leadership team, albeit with reduced influence, at a time when Yakovlev was both the *bête noire* of Russian nationalists and a focus for virulent criticism from conservative Communists. Gorbachev did not, however, publicly come to Yakovlev's defence. To have

person and in many respects artistic'. He has, says Yakovlev, 'a distinctive charm', especially evident during meetings in a small group (Aleksandr Yakovlev, *Sumerki*, Materik, Moscow, 2003, p. 494).

[10] See V.I. Boldin, *Krushenie p'edestala: Shtrikhi k portretu M.S. Gorbacheva* (Respublika, Moscow, 1995), pp. 373–81. Gorbachev, according to the former KGB chairman, Kryuchkov, 'thought one thing, said another, and did a third'. See V.A. Kryuchkov, *Lichnost' i vlast'* (Prosveshchenie, Moscow, 2004), p. 195. Kryuchkov's portrayal of Gorbachev and of the perestroika period—which, quite apart from being pro-Stalin and anti-Gorbachev, contains many factual errors—is to be found on pages 157–99.

[11] See Yakovlev, *Sumerki*, pp. 507–9.   [12] See, for example, Yakovlev, *Sumerki*, pp. 495–9.

done so might have won him back some support from liberal intellectuals at the cost of further alienating him from those who, in the most literal sense, had the big battalions on their side. The latter were perceived by Gorbachev to be the greater danger to the continuation of perestroika and his own political survival.

Gorbachev's tactical retreat in the winter of 1990–1, when he became less close to the most radically reformist elements in the Soviet leadership and more responsive than before (or after) to the conservative forces, was partly a reaction to the fact that much of the liberal part of the intelligentsia had transferred their support from him to Boris Yeltsin. Weakened on one flank, Gorbachev became more dependent on the other. Overall, the tactical shift was probably a strategic error—and Yakovlev, for one, gives many reasons in his memoirs for regarding it as a tragic mistake.[13] One cannot rule out, however, the possibility that if Gorbachev had compromised less in the winter of 1990–1 the date of the coup might have been brought forward. A winter coup in, say, January 1991, would, as I argued in Chapter 7, have had more chance of succeeding. Yeltsin had not yet been accorded the legitimacy bestowed by a Russia-wide general election, and a restored Communist system might well have lasted for a number of years. Nevertheless, by tacking in the direction of those who would gladly have restored the *status quo ante*, and being insufficiently sceptical of Kryuchkov's misinformation, Gorbachev discomfited some and wholly alienated others among his natural supporters.[14] Gorbachev was not the only person to be deceived and betrayed by Kryuchkov. Earlier, when he was plotting to replace Chebrikov as Chairman of the KGB, Kryuchkov gained the strong support of none other than Yakovlev who is very open in his memoirs about his recommendation of Kryuchkov for that post and about how quickly he was to regret it.[15]

---

[13] See, for example, Yakovlev, *Sumerki*, pp. 502–20.

[14] Kryuchkov, for example, attempted to implant in Gorbachev's head the idea that Yakovlev, Minister of the Interior Vadim Bakatin and General Mikhail Moiseev, Chief of the General Staff, were meeting together and conspiring against him. As a result Yakovlev got a telephone call from Gorbachev when he was in the countryside. Gorbachev wanted to know what he was up to, and Yakovlev replied: 'Gathering mushrooms.' 'And so what are you doing together with Bakatin and Moiseev?' Gorbachev inquired. An astonished Yakovlev told Gorbachev that he had not seen them that day. Kryuchkov's methods, Yakovlev notes, were in the worst traditions of the KGB, but this was one of a number of instances where Gorbachev—partly as a result of Kryuchkov's efforts to portray himself as a great supporter of perestroika—was not sceptical enough of the concoctions of the KGB chairman. See *Sumerki*, pp. 535–7.

[15] Yakovlev, *Sumerki*, pp. 533–5. Yakovlev devotes quite a lot of space in his memoirs to Kryuchkov and to the machinations, under his leadership, of the KGB. See *Sumerki*, pp. 372, 426–30, 492, 494, 532–42, and 579–80. In one of his earlier attempts to win over Yakovlev, Kryuchkov portrayed himself as the more radical of the two. For every desirable reform Yakovlev mentioned, Kryuchkov proclaimed his readiness to go further. He also cursed Chebrikov for his conservatism and weak professionalism (ibid., p. 372).

The features of Gorbachev described by Shakhnazarov were part of the reason why he gained early popularity when, as General Secretary, he visited Leningrad, the far north of Russia, the Urals, and the Russian south; they help to account also for the favourable impression he made both on foreign leaders and the public at large on his trips abroad. These aspects of Gorbachev's personality would, however, have achieved nothing remotely comparable to the ending of the Cold War and the pluralization of Soviet politics but for the presence of a number of other factors. More important than the charm was the mindset—and the ideas which had been germinating not only in Gorbachev's mind but in the minds of a significant minority within the Soviet elite (as discussed in Chapter 6). More essential than Gorbachev's early appeal to broad swathes of Soviet society (even though that further bolstered his authority) was the push he gave to reform within the highest echelons of the Soviet system. His intra-elite manoeuvring, tactical skill, and flexibility were much more crucial in getting liberalization and democratization underway than his popular standing. To insist, then, on the decisive importance of Gorbachev is partly to stress his different outlook from that of every other member of the Politburo in the first half of the 1980s and to take account of his leadership qualities. It is, additionally, to reiterate the central point about the institutional structures of the Soviet Union—the vast power and authority concentrated in the office of General Secretary of the Central Committee of the CPSU.

Gorbachev's leadership must also be seen in socio-political context, not least that of a particular political generation. Gorbachev spent the ages from 10 to 14 in a Soviet Union that was fighting a merciless war which killed 27 million of its citizens. His own village was occupied by German troops for almost five months. For Gorbachev this was a searing experience. He has said of it:

We were wartime children who survived. Nothing of the life and deeds of our generation is understandable unless we take this into consideration. Because we shouldered the responsibility for our families' survival and for our own subsistence, we little boys became instant grownups. Peace, and with it our ordinary lives, collapsed before our eyes.[16]

Gorbachev, moreover, saw himself not only as a product of a wartime childhood but as a *shestidesyatnik*—a term first used for progressive social thinkers in the 1860s and then applied to reformers within the Soviet system

---

[16] Mikhail Gorbachev and Daisaku Ikeda, *Moral Lessons of the Twentieth Century: Gorbachev and Ikeda on Buddhism and Communism* (translated by Richard L. Gage, Tauris, London, 2005), p. 14. See also Mikhail Gorbachev, *Zhizn' i reformy*, vol. 1, pp. 42–51, esp. p. 51.

in the 1960s.[17] The latter wished to carry on where Khrushchev had left off, taking further the anti-Stalinism launched at the 20th Party Congress in 1956 and more openly discussed at the 22nd Congress in 1961.[18] Gorbachev, who was both a product of the party apparatus and a well-read party intellectual, embarked on radical reform with the support of a small minority of *apparatchiki* and of a much more substantial proportion of the party intelligentsia.[19]

The changes in the broader society are also, of course, an essential part of the context in which perestroika must be understood. On the eve of perestroika, the percentage of the population with higher education was approximately four times greater than it had been at the time of Stalin's death thirty-two years earlier. The general level of education, in spite of an excess of rote learning, was also high. It is partly on the basis of the reasonable claim that at the beginning of perestroika Soviet citizens were 'among the best educated in the world' that Gorbachev rejects the view that 'the people were unready for freedom of expression'.[20] The society had changed greatly over the previous three decades. Although knowledge of the outside world was not at the launch of perestroika comparable with that in Western Europe or in parts of East-Central Europe—Poles and Hungarians had much more contact with their diasporas than had Russians—it was vastly in excess of what it had been in 1953. Moreover, as I noted especially in Chapter 6, there were thousands of

---

[17] See interview with Gorbachev by Yuriy Shchekochikin in *Literaturnaya gazeta*, 4 December 1991, p. 3.

[18] Another name for the people of this political generation was *deti dvadtsatogo s''ezda* or children of the Twentieth Congress. These were people in their twenties and thirties in the mid-1950s (young enough to reassess some of their previous deep convictions) and thus in their fifties and sixties by the mid-1980s. It was precisely this generation—not a younger one—which did most to produce the changes that bear the name of perestroika. That was partly a matter of institutional seniority. Given the extent to which this was a revolution from above, not many people whose early adult political socialization took place in the 1970s had reached positions of great influence by the time Gorbachev came to power. It would also, however, appear that more of the *shestideseyatniki* believed in the reformability of the Soviet system, and felt a moral imperative to undertake this task, than did their counterparts who reached adulthood in the Brezhnev years. Many of the latter combined conformism with cynicism. All such generalizations about generations have to come with a health-warning, inasmuch as there was a diversity of view within every age cohort, but the *shestidesyatniki* both recognized themselves as constituting a distinctive generational opinion grouping and were recognized as such by their opponents, whether those who thought of them as dangerous deviationists from Soviet orthodoxy or those who held that they were naive in holding to the idea of a more humane socialist society.

[19] Shakhnazarov observed: 'Trying to resolve the enigma of Gorbachev, one must not for a minute forget that two people in a paradoxical form joined together in Gorbachev: the party boss and the reformer-intellectual. Many times he said that "it is hard to break away from one's past"' (*Tsena svobody*, pp. 13–14).

[20] Gorbachev and Ikeda, *Moral Lessons of the Twentieth Century*, p. 44.

particularly well-informed people working in Soviet research institutes who were keenly aware of the gap between the Soviet Union and the West both in terms of personal freedom and economic well-being.

Gorbachev proceeded to use the highest office in the land to undermine the party structures in which he had made his career. In doing so, he ultimately undermined also his own power and authority. He played the key role in introducing political pluralism and a whole range of freedoms into a system whose longevity had depended on its vigilance in combating manifestations of group autonomy or of political, intellectual, artistic, and religious liberty. Gorbachev sometimes describes the pre-perestroika Soviet system as 'totalitarian', at other times as 'authoritarian'.[21] What it was not, he has argued in the post-Soviet period, was 'socialist', except in an extremely distorted sense. In his most recent book, Gorbachev writes: 'We came to the understanding that prolonging the existence of the system, we are defending not socialism, but that model which Stalin and his followers foisted on us. So is this socialism? Slogans, yes. Elements of socialism, indeed, but not more.'[22] Going beyond that, Gorbachev observed: 'The regime in which we were living on the eve of perestroika was a totalitarian regime.'[23] Although there was no repression of the type which had occurred under Stalin and there were 'democratic decorations', that 'did not alter the essence of totalitarian control by one party'.[24] Gorbachev makes a sharp distinction between such a regime and a pluralist system, but he is not particularly concerned with making fine distinctions between totalitarianism and authoritarianism. Thus, the Brezhnev regime, he contends, 'was neo-Stalinist, cleansed only of mass repression. An authoritarian regime, if we speak more mildly'.[25]

Perestroika started from above, Gorbachev observes in his memoirs, because it 'could not be otherwise in the conditions of totalitarianism'.[26] However, the reformers in the leadership realized that reform would fail unless it could gain mass support from below. Society had to be awoken from its lethargy and the people had to be involved in the process of change.[27] The conservatism of the *apparat* had defeated less radical reform in the past— Khrushchev's reorganizations and partial de-Stalinization and Kosygin's economic reform—but no previous leadership had taken the risk of empowering either the most educated stratum of the population or the people as a whole. But, Gorbachev notes, officialdom battled against systemic change to the end. Indeed, 'the system defended itself through the nomenklatura'.[28] Ultimately,

---

[21] See, for example, Mikhail Gorbachev, *Ponyat' perestroyku...pochemu eto vazhno seychas* (Al'pina Biznes Buks, Moscow, 2006), pp. 18 and 25.

[22] Ibid., p. 25.   [23] Ibid., p. 18.   [24] Ibid.   [25] Ibid., p. 25.

[26] Gorbachev, *Zhizn' i reformy*, Vol. 1, p. 281.   [27] Ibid.

[28] Gorbachev, *Ponyat' perestroyku*, p. 21.

this led a group of leading members of the nomenklatura to mount the putsch.[29] Gorbachev continues: 'Perestroika showed that change of the system, the path of profound reform of society was an extraordinarily difficult, dangerous and risky affair. But there are situations when this is what you have to do.'[30] A reform that 'was revolutionary in its essence' obviously required a radical approach as well as one that was evolutionary in its methods. The 'totalitarian character' of the system of power had to be 'gradually overcome and liquidated', leading to the removal from the system of those elements which suppressed freedom, making possible the development of democracy.[31] Given that the bureaucracy was adamantly opposed to fundamental political reform, there were only two ways of ensuring success, Gorbachev argues. One was to encourage 'powerful pressure from the part of the majority in the society' and the other was 'tactical manoeuvring to weaken the resistance of the top stratum' of officialdom. He is clearly right when he contends that 'the powerful bureaucracy' could never have been sidelined 'without political manoeuvring'.[32]

GORBACHEV, LENIN, AND LENINISM

Until very late, indeed, in the Soviet era, the way in which to legitimize concepts and policies was to invoke Lenin. By 1990–1 that was less effective. Yeltsin, during that period, had ceased to cite Lenin, and by then Gorbachev may have lost as much as he gained by continuing to do so. This is notwithstanding the fact that as late as December 1989, according to a VTsIOM survey, far more Soviet citizens (68 per cent) proposed Lenin than anyone else when asked to 'name the most outstanding people of all times and nations'.[33]

Gorbachev, after he became General Secretary, said much less about 'Marxism-Leninism' than had been traditional ever since the term was coined after Lenin's death. The reason is that Marxism-Leninism, from Stalin's time onwards, had been the ideological battering-ram used against any manifestation of independent thought. When Gorbachev does speak of Marxism-Leninism, it is often to chide those who use it as a cloak for their selfish interests. Thus, for example, in his unpublished book manuscript of 1989, he writes: 'How many mourners for socialism and for Marxism-Leninism have multiplied among us! And in fact . . . they are defending their own interests.

---

[29] Gorbachev, *Ponyat' perestroyku*, p. 21.   [30] Ibid.   [31] Ibid.   [32] Ibid., p. 180.
[33] *Obshchestvennoe mnenie v tsifrakh*, 2/9, January 1990 (VTsIOM, Moscow), p. 6.

And what they are weeping for is not socialism, it is a perverted representation of socialism.'[34]

Yet Gorbachev frequently cited Lenin. In his unpublished manuscript he said that if Marx and Lenin had seen the political and theoretical activity in Communist states (meaning pre-perestroika), they would have been horrified, which was doubtless true.[35] Gorbachev writes of 'returning to Lenin' but adds that 'now the country is different and democratization is proceeding in a different context'. He observes that 'the last works of Lenin were permeated by anxiety'.[36] In his unpublished book, Gorbachev makes a sustained attack on Stalin and Stalinism and refers to the Great Terror of 1936–8 not as the Yezhovshchina, the name it was given after Stalin's NKVD chief, Nikolay Yezhov (who was himself executed shortly thereafter), but as the Stalinshchina.[37] Gorbachev much more occasionally refers to Leninism than to Lenin, and his 'Leninism' is selective and used as an argument for changing the Soviet system. Thus, for example, he writes: 'I never cease to repeat: we are children of our time. And we need to overcome the past in ourselves, if we are to be party people, if we are to be Leninists.'[38]

In his unpublished book, Gorbachev is still defending a one-party pluralism rather than a competitive party system, which he had accepted by 1990. At this stage in his thinking Gorbachev presents the issue of one party or more than one as not a decisive criterion of democracy. There are, he says, multiparty countries which are not democracies and there is not a direct link between democracy and a multiparty system.[39] In principle, he argues in 1989, a one-party system may serve democracy and the harmonization of interests in society and be a guarantor of socialist pluralism. For that to happen, however, it is necessary to have 'glasnost, political culture,[40] and

---

[34] Gorbachev's unpublished 1989 book MS, 'Perestroyka—ispytanie zhizn'yu. Dnevnikovye zapisi', p. 20. Clearly, the notes of what Gorbachev said in the Politburo, in small group meetings and in conversations with Chernyaev were used in the compilation of this unpublished book. The passage quoted here follows practically verbatim the words used by Gorbachev in conversation with Chernyaev in early 1988. See 'Zapisi pomoshchnika general'nogo sekretarya TsK KPSS, Prezidenta SSSR, sdelannye na zasedaniyakh Politbyuro, drugikh razlichnykh soveshchaniyakh, uskikh i shirokikh, s uchastiem M.S. Gorbacheva, 1986–1990 gg.', Chernyaev notes of 11 February 1988, Gorbachev Foundation Archives.

[35] Gorbachev, 'Perestroyka—ispytanie zhizn'yu', p. 18.

[36] Ibid., pp. 24–6.   [37] Ibid., p. 56.   [38] Ibid., p. 48.   [39] Ibid., p. 397.

[40] In common with a number of Russian politicians, as distinct from political scientists, Gorbachev sometimes uses 'political culture' not as a neutral term for something whose content—in the sense of people's fundamental political beliefs, values, perceptions of history, and expectations—is a matter for empirical investigation, but rather as a synonym for political knowledge and understanding, i.e. 'being cultured politically'. Even Brezhnev on occasion used the term, but for him 'political culture' meant people thinking along the lines of *Pravda* editorials. At all stages in the development of his thinking during the perestroika years Gorbachev's notion of political culture went well beyond that.

a mechanism of control by the working people over all the processes under-way in the country'.[41]

Elsewhere, Gorbachev has said that, in essence, he had accepted the principle of a multiparty system by 1989 with the inauguration of the new legislature (even, indeed, by 1988 when the decision was taken to have competitive elections for an assembly with real power), since that was in the logic of its development.[42] It is impossible to say for sure whether his more cautious public defence as late as 1989 of a 'socialist pluralism', with the Communist Party holding the ring, was based on his true preference at the time or on a prudential need not to inflame the nomenklatura unduly. That it may well have been primarily the latter is suggested by his response to Aleksandr Yakovlev when Yakovlev proposed to Gorbachev as far back as 1985 that he divide the Communist Party to create two-party competition. Gorbachev accepted with equanimity this proposal, but said it was 'prema-ture'.[43] To call Yakovlev's suggestion 'revisionist' would be an understatement. However, as I have already noted in Chapter 7, to call it 'unrealistic' in the Soviet Union of 1985 would be entirely appropriate.

Although Gorbachev's 1989 book project was soon to be overtaken by the pressure of fast-moving events and the development of his own thinking—which is doubtless why he did not publish it—the manuscript already goes further than Gorbachev's earlier (1987) book, *Perestroika: New Thinking for our Country and the World*,[44] which is endlessly cited as if it were the definitive text on Gorbachev's ideas. Gorbachev is scathing in his March 1989 text about the practice hitherto in the rubber-stamp Supreme Soviet. He cites as a positive example the way in which in the US Congress presidential nominees are examined 'with a fine tooth comb'.[45] Gorbachev notes that there were attempted reforms under Khrushchev and Brezhnev, but that they failed 'because the structures of power remained untouched', and the reforms were smashed by 'group interests'. He also refers to the critical speech made at the Nineteenth Party Conference by the Director of the Institute of Economics of the Academy of Sciences, Leonid Abalkin, who had attacked the lack of progress in improving the economy. The speech had irritated Gorbachev at the time, and he still disagreed with its pessimism, but,

[41] Gorbachev, 'Perestroyka—itspitanie zhizn'yu', p. 397.

[42] For example, Gorbachev has written that the Inter-Regional Group of Deputies who emerged at the first Congress of People's Deputies (and were highly critical of the Communist Party leadership from a radical democrat standpoint) began to form an embryonic political party which would be in competition with the CPSU. See *Ponyat' perestroyku*, p. 182.

[43] Yakovlev, *Sumerki*, p. 383.

[44] Published by Collins, London, 1987. For the Russian original, see M.S. Gorbachev, *Perestroyka i novoe myshlenie dlya nashey strany i dlya vsego mira* (Politizdat, Moscow, 1987).

[45] Gorbachev manuscript, 'Perestroyka—ispitaniya zhizn'yu. Dnevnikovye zapisi', p. 94.

reflecting on that speech just a few months later, he praises Abalkin for his courage and openness and cites it as a good example of the new public pluralism of opinion.[46]

Gorbachev's frequent citations of Lenin were undoubtedly partly to legitimize innovation which was deviating sharply from past Soviet theory and practice. But they were more than that. Gorbachev believed that there were parallels between what he was doing and what Lenin was engaged in during the last years of his life, the period of concessions to private property, together with market reform, which characterized the NEP. He identified his own view of the need for fundamental reform of the Soviet system with what he took to be Lenin's second thoughts in his last years about what had been constructed in Russia during the period of 'war communism'. In 1987 Gorbachev could claim, whether or not he completely believed it, that the party leadership was united in its support for perestroika. To the extent that it *was*, this was because they meant different things by 'perestroika'. By 1989 the divisions had become impossible to overlook. A year earlier the conservative (indeed, reactionary) sentiments expressed in the Nina Andreeva letter had enjoyed the support of more than half the members of the Politburo until Gorbachev, with the strong backing of Yakovlev, in particular, mounted a counter-attack. Gorbachev had already described perestroika as a 'revolution' in his 1987 book,[47] and in his 1989 manuscript he observes that many had so regarded it from the outset. However, he argues, 1988 was the year in which the revolutionary character of the process underway was confirmed.[48] While still defending a 'socialist pluralism' (rather than 'political pluralism') in 1989, Gorbachev stressed that the Communist Party must be subject to the law and that it should be providing leadership rather than wielding executive power. The 'command-administrative system', he said, had 'strongly deformed the function of the party as a political force'.[49]

The adoption of the term, 'command-administrative system', was, as one of the most perceptive specialists on Soviet politics, T.H. Rigby, has argued, a departure from the past of some significance. Rigby writes:

The year 1988 saw the emergence of the phrase 'command-administrative *methods*', its speedy adoption by Gorbachev himself, and then its extension to characterise the whole traditional Soviet socio-political order as a 'command-administrative *system*'.... This pejorative labelling of the fundamental structuring principle of the existing order was the first unambiguous signal that Gorbachev was resolved to

---

[46] Ibid., p. 174.
[47] Gorbachev, *Perestroika: New Thinking for our Country and the World*, pp. 52 and 74.
[48] Gorbachev manuscript, 'Perestroyka—ispitanie zhizn'yu', p. 389.
[49] Ibid., p. 396.

move from restructuring *within* the system to restructuring *of* the system, and its implications struck at the hallowed 'leading and guiding' role of the Party.[50]

The archival evidence suggests, indeed, that Gorbachev may have been leading rather than following in this regard. In a small group discussion on 12 February 1988 of the ideas that should go into the theses being prepared for the forthcoming Nineteenth Party Conference, he remarked that 'almost everywhere we still feel the imprints of the administrative-command *system* and of stagnation' (italics added, AB).[51]

Alongside his frequent positive invocation of Lenin, Gorbachev, in the course of perestroika, embraced more and more ideas which would have been anathema to the Soviet Union's principal architect and first leader. These included Gorbachev's acceptance of the desirability of checks and balances within a political system (as noted in chapter four). He came also to believe that a social democratic conception of socialism provided the basis for a more just, more humane, and more economically efficient system than the political and economic model that had been adopted in the Soviet Union. The contested elections, held in the Spring of 1989, were both a reflection of Gorbachev's changing ideas and a stimulus to move further in the direction of social democracy. As he put it in conversation with Zdeněk Mlynář:

In 1989, after the elections, when we saw what attitude the people really had toward the CPSU and the *nomenklatura*, what it really thought, and what its attitude was toward democracy and glasnost, there began a period of accumulation of experience that brought us to the conclusion that it was necessary to arrive at a new conception of socialism. Since that time I have been occupied more and more with the question: What are the criteria for calling something socialist? It seemed to me that the main one had to do with: What is the position of the individual in society? From that moment on, you might say, the road I have taken has essentially been the Social Democratic conception of socialism.[52]

Increasingly, while continuing to cite Lenin with great respect, Gorbachev used 'Bolshevik' as in a 'Bolshevik approach' or 'Bolshevik tradition' as a term of reprobation. Thus, while Lenin is still cited in a favourable context even in a book which Gorbachev published in 2006, in that same volume, Gorbachev writes: 'We strove to be finished with the old Bolshevik tradition: to create an ideological construct and afterwards to strive to introduce it in the society,

---

[50] T.H. Rigby, 'Some Concluding Observations', in Archie Brown (ed.), *The Demise of Marxism-Leninism in Russia* (Palgrave Macmillan, Basingstoke, 2004), pp. 207–23, at p. 213.

[51] 'Razmyshleniya v uzkom krugu ob osnovnykh ideyakh tezisov k XIX partkonferentsii, 12 fevralya 1988 goda, Novo-Ogarevo', from 'Zapisi pomoshchnika general'nogo sekretarya...', Chernyaev notes, Gorbachev Foundation Archives. The key word, as Rigby observed, is 'system'. 'Command-administrative' and 'Administrative-command' were used interchangeably.

[52] Gorbachev and Mlynář, *Conversations with Gorbachev*, p. 79.

not taking into consideration the means or the opinion of the citizens.'[53] Yet Lenin had been the number one Bolshevik and contributed more than anyone else to Bolshevik doctrine and distinctive patterns of thought, including the way of thinking aptly rejected by Gorbachev. 'Perestroika', Gorbachev has written in that same book, 'began under the sign of the late Lenin.'[54] Whatever the limitations of that source of inspiration, and of the doubtful justification for differentiating Lenin from Bolshevism, it remains an important fact that an idealized view of Lenin helped both to inspire and to legitimize the break with six decades of Soviet history in the eyes of Gorbachev and of a number of the leading progenitors of perestroika. However, when perestroika ended, Gorbachev's political beliefs were closer to those of Eduard Bernstein (a point to which I shall return) or of a German social democrat of more recent vintage, Willy Brandt, than to those of the founder of the Soviet state.[55]

In his support for religious tolerance and respect for religious believers, for the idea that there were universal values and interests which transcended class interests, and in the high priority he came to place on political freedom, Gorbachev departed radically from the outlook of Lenin. If he had expressed the views he put forth after consolidating his position as General Secretary in the years *before* he became party leader, he would have been a prime candidate for expulsion from the CPSU as a 'deviationist', if not, indeed, imprisonment as a dissident. Indeed, at a meeting of the Secretariat of the Central Committee in April 1988, over which Gorbachev presided—normally it would have been chaired by Ligachev, but this was an especially important meeting to consider issues related to the upcoming Nineteenth Party Conference—Yakovlev remarked: 'Three years have passed since the April [1985] plenum. If we had spoken then as we have spoken today, we would have been considered dissidents.'[56] Among those who would have fallen into such a category on the basis of their contribution that day was Anatoliy Lukyanov. Notwithstanding his later alliance with the putschists, Lukyanov had

---

[53] Gorbachev, *Ponyat' perestroyku*, p. 27.

[54] Ibid., p. 16.

[55] As early as April 1988, indeed, Gorbachev gave an enthusiastic report to the Politburo of a meeting he had had with Brandt in the latter's capacity of chairman of the Socialist International, the organization of social democratic parties (including the German Social Democrats, the French Socialists, and the British Labour Party). Gorbachev told the Politburo that 120 million people voted for these parties in Western Europe. Their support for perestroika was, accordingly, important. See 'Politbyuro, 14 aprelya 1988 goda' in 'Zapisi pomoshchnika general'nogo sekretarya TsK KPSS...', Chernyaev notes, Gorbachev Foundation Archives.

[56] 'Sekretariat TsK, 23 aprelya 1988 goda (zapis' Medvedeva)' in 'Zapisi pomoshchnika general'nogo sekretarya TsK KPSS...', Gorbachev Foundation Archives. Although Vadim Medvedev was not an aide (*pomoshchnik*) of Gorbachev but, rather, a full member of the Politburo, his notes are included in this amalgamated archival collection, along with the more numerous notes of Chernyaev and some by Shakhnazarov who, like Chernyaev, was a Gorbachev aide.

pronounced himself in favour both of a 'separation of legislative, executive and judicial powers' and of the creation of 'a system of checks and balances'.[57]

From 1988 onwards, although neither his lifelong regard for Lenin nor political prudence allowed him to put it in such terms, Gorbachev had clearly rejected Lenin*ism*, and he had made a major contribution to creating a new political climate in which other members of the top leadership team felt free to depart from the verities of the previous seven decades. Chernyaev has written of Gorbachev and Lenin:

Lenin wasn't quite his icon, although he admired him greatly and said that he always 'consulted' with him. Gorbachev would make an example of his actions in 'analogous' situations arising during perestroika. But unlike Lenin apologists, he sought out in Lenin not what the others used to prop themselves up. For example, he valued highly Lenin's readiness to dispense with any dogmas if a real-life situation warranted it.[58]

We know that Gorbachev, from his university days, had taken Marxist and Leninist thought seriously. His friend Zdeněk Mlynář is a reliable witness to the fact that whereas other students engaged in rote learning of parts of the required texts, Gorbachev fully engaged with the arguments of Marx and Lenin. Indeed, reading their theories and their involvement in vigorous debate helped to free Gorbachev from the Stalinist dogma he had grown up with. As he put it in conversation with Mlynář:

Before the university I was trapped in my belief system in the sense that I accepted a great deal as given, as assumptions not to be questioned. At the university I began to think and reflect and to look at things differently. But of course that was only the beginning of a prolonged process.[59]

When Gorbachev saw for himself Western countries with their higher stand-ards of living and, to put it mildly, more democracy than existed in the Soviet Union, he could have given up both on the idea of socialism and his

[57] Ibid. Later, according to Georgiy Shakhnazarov, Lukyanov displayed scepticism about the principle of separation of powers. He considered that the presidency was not 'our way'. Shakhnazarov says that the Congress of People's Deputies—the outer body of the new legislature which began its existence in 1989—was Lukyanov's 'invention', adding: 'Lukyanov combines qualities of a professional jurist with revolutionary romanticism.' See the interview with Shakhnazarov by E.L. Kusnetsov in *Demokratizatsiya*, Vol. 2, No. 2, Spring 1994, pp. 228–33, at pp. 231–2.

[58] Anatoly Chernyaev, *My Six Years with Gorbachev*, translated and edited by Robert English and Elizabeth Tucker (Penn State University Press, University Park, PA, 2000), pp. 212–13.

[59] Gorbachev and Mlynář, *Conversations with Gorbachev*, p. 23. While Marx and Lenin were more intellectually rewarding than the crudities of Stalinism, also important was Gorbachev's introduction to a far wider variety of ways of looking at the world, especially in the lectures on the history of political and legal thought delivered by Professor S.F. Kechekyan, a favourite teacher of both Gorbachev and Mlynář, who had received his own university education in pre-revolutionary times.

admiration for Lenin, but he did not. For Boris Yeltsin it was enough to see an American supermarket for the first time to be converted to a belief in capitalism (although he fought shy of using the word). Aleksandr Yakovlev was different again. He continued to speak reverently of Lenin as late as 1989,[60] when, for example, he said: 'And though Lenin did not live long enough to work out all the conceptions of socialism that we need, we are returning to his basic perceptions. In this sense, Lenin is a living adviser in our analysis of present-day problems.'[61] However, the more Yakovlev learned in detail about the Soviet past, including the Lenin years, the more comprehensively he turned, internally, against Lenin. In his memoirs, Yakovlev describes Lenin 'as the most outstanding representative of the theory and practice of state terror of the twentieth century...' and goes on: 'In other words, Vladimir Ulyanov Lenin emerges as the initiator and organiser of mass terror in Russia [and] eternally indictable for crimes against humanity.'[62]

Gorbachev has never spoken of Lenin in remotely similar terms. However, one can hardly overstate just how different Gorbachev was from Lenin– tolerant where Lenin was intolerant; abhorrent of violence, in contrast with Lenin's readiness to use it ruthlessly; aware that the ends do not justify the means, whereas for Lenin the ends justified destroying all who barred the way of the Bolsheviks; seeking a reasonable middle-way solution in any major political impasse, whereas Lenin, though ready to make short-term tactical compromises, was implacable in the pursuit of his goals. Gorbachev was a reformer, whereas Lenin was a revolutionary. Gorbachev spoke of perestroika having a revolutionary character, but it was a 'revolution' to be achieved by evolutionary means. In terms of Soviet orthodoxy, it was, indeed, a 'counter-revolution', for it was a rejection not only of Stalinism but of the Leninist ideological foundations of the Soviet state. While convergence between the Soviet Union and the West was (very prematurely) said by some scholars to be taking place in the1960s, Gorbachev was ready to seek a real convergence, especially between the 'new thinking' and West European social democracy. The doctrine of *kto kogo* (who will crush whom) was being replaced by the goal of ever-closer East–West relations, in which both sides in the great divide would learn from the other and act cooperatively to tackle threats to the entire

[60] See, for example, Stephen F. Cohen and Katrina vanden Heuvel, *Voices of Glasnost: Interviews with Gorbachev's Reformers* (Norton, New York, 1989), esp. pp. 39–40.

[61] Ibid., p. 40.

[62] Yakovlev, *Sumerki*, p. 26. Yakovlev is here using Lenin's real surname 'Ulyanov' as if it were his middle name. What is surprising in the light of such a wholesale condemnation of Lenin is that one of Yakovlev's grievances against Gorbachev was that he never invited him to give the annual Lenin anniversary speech, an occasion when a celebration of Lenin's life and work was obligatory.

planet, whether that of nuclear war or environmental catastrophe. Putting the Lenin–Gorbachev comparison on a normative level, one can say that Gorbachev had little need to look up to Lenin, for his understanding of politics was both more humane and more enlightened.

There is, nevertheless, a paradox which has to be addressed. How do we account for Gorbachev's continuing high esteem for Lenin at the very time he was moving further and further away from anything remotely resembling Leninism? Gorbachev, after all, was embracing a form of socialism against which Lenin had waged ruthless ideological war, namely social democracy of the kind espoused by the German social democrat, Eduard Bernstein.[63] Bernstein's ideas, as summarized by Neil Harding, come close to those to which Gorbachev's thinking evolved:

Socialism, in Bernstein's account, came not to destroy, but to complete liberalism—to press it to the limits of its liberatory possibilities.... It had to be integrationist rather than separatist. It built upon what already existed rather than a nebulous and unknowable future. It was rational, pacific and developmental, rather than elemental, violent and abrupt.[64]

Clearly, Bernstein's thought had practically nothing in common with Lenin's.[65] For Lenin, indeed, it represented 'all that was rotten in European socialism'.[66]

Unlike many in the Soviet Communist Party, Gorbachev was not ready to abandon overnight either his heroes or his principles (even though his flexibility has often been misinterpreted as absence of principle). Thus, he remained loyal to socialism but only by redefining socialism fundamentally, so that it became different in kind from the practice of Brezhnev's Soviet Union, not to speak of Stalin's. He remained attached to Lenin by seeing in him what he wanted to see and projecting on to Lenin his own zeal for reform. This was Gorbachev's way of dealing with cognitive dissonance—the discomfort and potential stress involved in holding beliefs inconsistent with one another or inconsistent with the way one is behaving. He was able to move

[63] In his conversations with Zdeněk Mlynář, Gorbachev refers explicitly to Bernstein (a contemporary of Lenin), saying: 'We both should publicly acknowledge the great mistake we made when as supporters of Communist ideology we denounced Eduard Bernstein's famous dictum: "The movement is everything, the ultimate goal nothing". We called that a betrayal of socialism. But the essence of Bernstein's idea was that socialism could not be understood as a system that arises as a result of the inevitable downfall of capitalism, but that socialism is a gradual realization of the principle of equality and self-determination for the people who constitute a society, an economy, a country' (*Conversations with Gorbachev*, p. 167).

[64] Neil Harding, *Leninism* (Macmillan, London, 1996), p. 64.

[65] For the classic statement of Bernstein's views, see Eduard Bernstein, *Evolutionary Socialism: A Criticism and Affirmation* (Schocken, New York, 1961; the book was first published in 1899).

[66] Harding, *Leninism*, p. 59.

further away from Lenin while believing that he was moving closer. The vast literature on the theory of cognitive dissonance has shown that people have a tendency to screen out information that is not congruent with their existing beliefs and attitudes. Although Gorbachev had, in fact, changed his thinking on many matters—demonstrated, indeed, an unusually open mind—his degree of emotional attachment to, and identification with, Lenin meant that he dealt with cognitive dissonance by focusing not on Lenin's writings and actions which were at odds with his own values but on those which seemed to be offering a relevant, reformist example.

Lenin laid the foundations on which Stalin built, although he was a true believer in a future utopia involving a withering away of the state.[67] His character was very different from that of Stalin. As Adam Ulam wrote: 'We do not find in Lenin the sadism and personal vindictiveness characteristic of Stalin. But, as the aftermath of the Revolution was to show he was equally incapable of true generosity toward a defeated enemy, or of gestures of humanitarianism where no political gain was evident.'[68] And as Ulam also puts it: '[Lenin's] fury was aroused by any concept, any postulate, any phenomenon that in some circuitous way could reflect the mentality of the intelligentsia: liberalism, independence of the judiciary, parliamentarism.'[69] Although Lenin had studied law (of all Soviet leaders, only the first and the last had a legal education), he had an 'almost insane' hatred of lawyers.[70] While Lenin embarked on NEP in 1921, and made major overtures to the peasantry, he simultaneously cracked down on dissent and opposition, telling the Tenth Congress of the party in that year that it was necessary to 'put the lid on opposition'.[71] The very real limitations on Lenin's reformism in the last

[67] Although implacably opposed to political pluralism and liberal democracy, Lenin believed in an ultimate 'socialist democracy' in a way in which Stalin did not, although he adopted authoritarian means to reach the illusory utopian goal. In John Gooding's admirably concise summary: 'Lenin's adaptation [of Marxism] had substituted the party for the missing proletariat and the party elite for the inadequately prepared party masses. The effect was to place power at the outset in the hands of a small group; but Lenin's assumption was that, as socialist consciousness spread, so the bounds of the effective political nation would broaden until they embraced the whole population. For the time being, "democracy" would extend no further than the party elite—but at that level it would be, and was, real enough' (Gooding, *Socialism in Russia: Lenin and his Legacy, 1890–1991* (Palgrave Macmillan, London, 2002), p. 249).

[68] Adam Ulam, *Lenin and the Bolsheviks* (Collins Fontana edition, London, 1969), p. 274.

[69] Ibid., p. 275.   [70] Ibid.

[71] Leonard Schapiro, ' "Putting the Lid on Leninism": Opposition and dissent in the communist one-party states' in Schapiro (ed.), *Political Opposition in One-Party States* (Macmillan, London, 1972), pp. 32–57, at p. 32. As Schapiro observes (p. 37): '... it is arguable that, had the socialists been allowed full freedom of action during the tense and precarious years of 1921–2, the communist government would have been ousted by the force of popular discontent in favour of a socialist government—with, or more probably without, participation of the, by then, almost universally detested communists. As the self-appointed agents of the forces of history, the communists could hardly have been expected to face such a prospect with equanimity.'

years of his life are noted by Robert Service, the author of the most recent major biography of Lenin, when he writes that Lenin 'did not challenge his own political creation: the one-party state, the one-ideology state, the terrorist state, the state that sought to dominate all social life, economy and culture'.[72]

In contrast, Gorbachev was moving from 1988 onwards to make elections, rather than an ideologically ordained monopoly of power of the Communist Party, the basis of legitimacy of the Soviet system. To an audience likely to be far from receptive to such heretical thoughts, a gathering of obkom secretaries, Gorbachev said: 'The question is posed not only in the West: on what basis do twenty million [members of the CPSU] rule 200 million people? *We* awarded *ourselves* the right to govern the people!' (italics added, AB).[73] Gorbachev was preparing party officials for the first serious step of democratization—contested elections for a new legislature—and had moved away from the idea that Marx and Lenin had provided the theoretical equivalent of a divine right to rule for the Communist Party. Taken together with his radical rejection both in principle and in practice of many of the central tenets of Lenin's thinking, Gorbachev's frequent positive invocation of Lenin cannot, in common sense, be equated with fealty to Lenin*ism*. Part of the explanation of the apparent contradiction is political—Lenin remained the source of legitimacy for changes of policy within the CPSU. I have suggested, however, that for Gorbachev it also had a significant psychological component.

THE RESPONSE TO NATIONALISM AND SEPARATISM

From the time of the first Congress of People's Deputies in the spring of 1989 but, especially in the years 1990–1, Gorbachev was under fire from opposite directions. Although he was still the most popular politician in the country until May–June 1990 when Yeltsin overtook him, he was losing support among the most politically engaged sections of society. On the one side, there was increasing dissatisfaction from the Communist Party apparatus, the military, the KGB and the governmental bureaucracy. On the other side, nationalists— especially in the Baltic states and Georgia—were demanding greater autonomy and, ultimately, full independence. Above all, Boris Yeltsin had made himself the principal spokesman for a wide range of anti-establishment opinion

[72] Robert Service, *Lenin: A Biography* (Macmillan, London, 2000), p. 467.
[73] 'Vstrecha Gorbacheva s tret'ey gruppoy sekretarey obkomov, 18 aprelya 1988 goda' in 'Zapisi pomoshchnika general'nogo sekretarya TsK KPSS . . .', Gorbachev Foundation Archives.

in Russia. He won the support of several different constituencies. With his attacks on the privileges of the nomenklatura, Yeltsin appealed to those who sought a greater egalitarianism and social justice. With his effective use of the mechanism of competitive elections which Gorbachev's reforms had introduced, he attracted those who sought a faster transition to full democracy. And with his support for speeding up marketizing economic reform, Yeltsin appealed both to those who felt this was the only way to a more efficient economy and those whose ambitions were the more egocentric ones of converting as much state property as possible to their private ownership.

Much that happened during 1989 made the conservative majority among party and state officials anxious about the future, including their personal future. The advent of contested elections meant that in the last years of the Soviet Union there was a legislature possessing a real power to hold the executive to account. This had not happened in the Soviet Union in seventy years (and it did not take long in post-Soviet Russia for the executive to regain much of its traditional dominance). The achievement of independence by the East-Central European countries in the course of 1989 was seen by many within the elite as a blow to the prestige of the Soviet Union, even though it enhanced the country's standing in the outside world. Its chief unintended consequence, however, both for the Soviet state and for Gorbachev personally, was that it raised the expectations of the most disaffected nations within the USSR. They began to realize that greater autonomy within the Union might not be the limit of their possibilities but that, given the Soviet leadership's acquiescence with the developments in the Warsaw Pact countries, they might realistically aspire to full independence.

That was an unforeseen and unacceptable outcome, so far as Gorbachev was concerned. It was second nature for him to believe in a Soviet identity which transcended people's sense of belonging to particular nationalities. He himself—though his father was Russian and he had grown up, and worked, only in the Russian republic—was of Ukrainian descent on his mother's side. His wife, Raisa, was half-Ukrainian. For Gorbachev—as, indeed, for most Russians and for a majority of the population of Ukraine until well into 1991—the idea that Russia and Ukraine should become separate states was almost unimaginable. Gorbachev attempted to hold the Union together by a variety of means. The main approach was to seek a 'renewed Union', on the basis of a voluntarily agreed new Union Treaty. A referendum was held in March 1991, which six of the republics—the three Baltic states plus Armenia, Georgia and Moldova—refused to conduct. The question asked was: 'Do you believe it essential to preserve the USSR as a renewed federation of equal sovereign republics in which the rights and freedoms of a person of any nationality will be fully guaranteed?' Answers in the affirmative were above 70 per cent in all the republics (including Ukraine) in which the referendum was held, and 80 per cent of the total adult population of the Soviet Union voted. While the question was evidently designed with a view to securing a positive response, it remains a fact that a fissiparous descent into separate statehood was not the preferred option of a majority of Soviet citizens as late as March of the year in which the Soviet Union ceased to exist.

In the winter of 1990–1 Gorbachev came under immense pressure from conservative forces to crack down on separatist tendencies. The idea of creating a state of emergency was considered, and was strongly pressed on Gorbachev by those who hoped it would open the way for a comprehensive crushing of all separatists. But Gorbachev, having considered the option, never adopted it. When he was on vacation in Foros on the Crimean coast in August 1991, he wrote, with the help of Chernyaev, a long article which was intended to be a kind of philosophical justification of perestroika (in its radical transformative sense) and of the new relationship between the federal centre and the republics to be embodied in the Union Treaty, due for imminent signature. The issue of emergency powers is explicitly addressed:

The introduction of a state of emergency, in which even some supporters of *perestroika*, not to mention those who preach the ideology of dictatorship, see a way out of the crisis, would be a fatal move and the way to civil war. Frankly speaking, behind the appeals for a state of emergency, it is not difficult sometimes to detect a search for a return to the political system that existed in the pre-*perestroika* period.[74]

Gorbachev had earlier hoped that warning of the dire consequences of breaking up the existing political, economic, and military integration, combined with the promise of much greater autonomy within a genuine and quite loose federation, would be enough to keep all or most of the republics in the Union. He found himself, however, caught in the middle between, on the one side, ever more radical demands from the leaders of several republics and, on the other, the hard-line conservatives. The latter were looking for ways to turn the clock back. There were several occasions when blood was shed by Soviet forces under the command of people who were later to join the attempted putsch against Gorbachev. The first such tragedy occurred in Georgia in April 1989 and was followed by Azerbaijan in January 1990, Lithuania and Latvia in January 1991.[75] The only time the use of force was explicitly approved by

---

[74] Mikhail Gorbachev, *The August Coup: The Truth and the Lessons* (HarperCollins, London, 1991), p. 111.

[75] For a detailed account of the circumstances, see Archie Brown, *The Gorbachev Factor*, ch. 8, 'The National Question, the Coup, and the Collapse of the Soviet Union', pp. 252–305. Much earlier, in December 1986, there had been bloodshed in Kazakhstan, following the

Gorbachev was in Baku—in response to a pogrom of Armenians in Azerbai-jan. However, the implementation of the attempt to restore order was botched by the Soviet troops, and scores of Azeris were killed who had nothing to do with the deaths of over sixty Armenians some days earlier. In the aftermath of the earlier slaughter of peaceful young demonstrators in the Georgian capital, Tbilisi, Gorbachev told the Politburo in April 1989: 'I've long said—we must learn to work in conditions of democracy. Now look at how all that is being borne out. Our cadres regard political methods as a display of weakness. Force—that's the thing!'[76] The curfew and the resort to violence in Tbilisi, Gorbachev said, had been completely unnecessary. He instructed the Minister of Defence, Dmitriy Yazov, not to use the army in any such future stand-off without a decision by the Politburo.[77]

The counterproductive results of the use of force, when it was employed against nationalist demonstrators, strengthened Gorbachev in his view that while, in the last resort, force could sometimes be justified in order to save lives, generally it exacerbated national tensions and did nothing to resolve them. He came under attack, however, from liberals who argued that none of the crackdowns anywhere could have been carried out without his approval. The flaw in that argument is that they each took place on one night only and were halted the following day when Gorbachev was appraised of the full facts. Thus, the isolated use of force was never allowed to become a more general repression in any republic. Moreover, the people in charge of the troops on the ground included those who were part of the conspiracy against Gorbachev in August 1991. The idea that they were quite incapable of exceeding the wishes of the President of the USSR earlier in the year hardly corresponds with their willingness to put him under house arrest some months later. Aleksandr Yakovlev, who advances numerous criticisms of Gorbachev's leadership in his memoirs, comes to the following judgement on this issue:

The spilling of blood is attributed to [Gorbachev] in, for example, Baku, Vilnius, Alma-Ata and other places. I do not share that point of view. The former putschists introduce it into people's consciousness, trying to deflect the guilt from themselves for

removal of the Brezhnevite First Secretary of the Communist Party in that republic, Dinmu-khamed Kunaev, and his replacement by a Russian, Gennadiy Kolbin. Kunaev himself had recommended the appointment of a non-Kazakh, possibly in the hope of provoking public protests but mainly because he did not want the succession to go to his younger rival, Nursultan Nazarbaev. In fact, Nazarbaev succeeded Kolbin in June 1989 and, throughout the post-Soviet period, has been President of Kazakhstan.

[76] 'Politbyuro 13 aprelya 1989 goda', 'Zapisi pomoshchnika general'nogo sekretarya TsK KPSS . . .', Chernyaev notes, Gorbachev Foundation Archives.

[77] Ibid. This was at a time when the Politburo was still, in effect, the highest organ of state (as well as party) power. It was almost a year later that the executive presidency was created which signaled a breakthrough in terms of transfer of real power from the party to the state.

many provocations which ended with bloodshed. Gorbachev himself always said that national and other conflicts could not be resolved with force. But the *siloviki*[78] thirsted for blood, shed it, and afterwards announced that the use of force had been a responsive measure.[79]

If Gorbachev was blamed, wrongly, for instigating the killing of demonstrators, whether in Tbilisi or Vilnius, he was blamed by many more Russians both at the time and especially subsequently for not authorizing the use of *enough* force—coercion on a scale sufficient to prevent the breakup of the Soviet Union. During the perestroika period most of the republican leaders, including all the Central Asian party First Secretaries, were in favour of preserving the union, since they could not predict how well they would fare in an independent state. (In fact, such were their political resources and networks, they flourished in the post-Communist era. More than half of the early post-Soviet presidents of the successor states had been senior Communist Party officials in that republic. The political longevity of the First Secretaries-turned-Presidents in a majority of the Central Asian states has been especially striking.)

DILEMMAS OF INSTITUTION-BUILDING

In the winter of 1990–1 Gorbachev's position was weakened by a widening gulf between him and those who considered themselves to be more thorough-going democrats, many of whom had transferred their allegiance to Yeltsin. This emboldened the conservatives within the Soviet establishment to increase their pressure on Gorbachev and they regained at least some of their lost influence. Their criticisms often illustrated real dilemmas, focusing on issues that troubled Gorbachev as well. A legislature with significant powers was now in existence and an executive presidency had been created. Yet the Presidential Council—which had looked to be the new, state counterpart of the Politburo—was essentially an advisory body and it could not give instructions to anyone. There was no departmental or regional organization underpinning the presidency, capable of making sure that decisions taken at the top of the political hierarchy were implemented. The Communist Party had hitherto provided a vertical power structure, in which policy adopted

---

[78] People from the power ministries—the KGB, the Army, and the Ministry of Interior.

[79] Yakovlev, *Sumerki*, p. 520. Yakovlev added: 'Gorbachev has gone into history. He has no blood on his hands.' Baku, as already noted, is a partial qualification to Yakovlev's remark. Gorbachev did authorize the use of force there in order to put a stop to attacks on Armenians, but did not condone the indiscriminate response of the troop commanders on the ground.

centrally was implemented throughout the country. There was nothing democratic about this 'democratic centralism', as it was called in the jargon of Marxism-Leninism. It had more in common with a military chain of command, but it functioned effectively enough as a mechanism for maintaining central control.

The structures of the CPSU had constituted the higher authority within the special kind of dual executive which characterized Communist systems. There was a ministerial network as well as a network of party institutions, but the party bosses had the last word. When a minister became an especially powerful figure within the Soviet system—as, for example, Gromyko or Ustinov—this owed much to his membership of the highest party institution, the Politburo. Ministers who became Politburo members acquired enhanced influence over major policy as compared with the period when their ministerial rank was not accompanied by such high party office. The relationship between the party and the state (in conventional Soviet terms)[80] was a precursor of the semi-presidentialism which most of the post-Communist states have adopted, whereby there is a President and presidential apparatus sharing executive power with a Prime Minister and government.[81] Gorbachev, however, became weaker vis-à-vis the ministerial network, not stronger, after the creation of the executive presidency, for he could no longer use the panoply of institutional levers over the ministries which had been provided by the departments of the Central Committee. These had, indeed, already been significantly curtailed by the contraction in their number which Gorbachev's reform of the party organization in 1988 had produced. At the same time as the Presidential Council was created in March 1990, a Federation Council was also instituted. It was composed, however, of the heads of the fifteen union republics (the Chairmen of their Supreme Soviets) and so was hardly a substitute for an executive arm of the federal presidency.

Gorbachev's reforms had robbed the CPSU of its 'power vertical' not only by his party organizational reforms but, still more, by his introduction of real

[80] Terms that are somewhat misleading, given that in reality the highest party organs until the end of the 1980s were also de facto the highest organs of state power, even though the Soviet Constitution was, at best, ambiguous on the point. Such important institutions as the Politburo and the Secretariat of the Central Committee were not mentioned in the Constitution which described (Article 108) the Supreme Soviet as 'the highest body of state authority', even though that body was almost entirely decorative and wholly manipulated by the party leadership. The nearest the Constitution came to recognizing the real role of the Communist Party was in the vaguely worded Article 6 which, *inter alia*, described the CPSU as 'the leading and guiding force of Soviet society and the nucleus of its political system' (*Constitution [Fundamental Law] of the Union of Soviet Socialist Republics*, Novosti, Moscow, 1977, p. 16).
[81] See the valuable symposium, 'A Fresh Look at Semipresidentialism', with articles by Robert Elgie, 'Variations on a Theme', pp. 98–112, and Timothy J. Colton and Cindy Skach, 'The Russian Predicament', pp. 113–26, in *Journal of Democracy*, Vol. 16, No. 3, July 2005.

elections (as distinct from the pseudo-elections in the pre-perestroika Soviet Union) as the source of legitimacy and by the creation of numerous countervailing forces. All this, however, did not obviate the need for authoritative, as distinct from authoritarian, executive decision-making. Gorbachev was seriously interested in democratic institution-building, but the process proceeded on the basis of trial and error and in exceptionally difficult conditions. Any attempt to strengthen federal executive power could be interpreted as a threat to the developing autonomy of the union republics or as an attempt to re-establish the old order of Communist Party hegemony. In a memorandum to Gorbachev of 5 November 1989, Shakhnazarov said he shared the opinion of a number of deputies in the Supreme Soviet (including the prominent academic lawyer, Sergey Alekseev, the Director of the Sverdlovsk Juridical Institute) that a clearer division of executive and legislative functions was required. Shakhnazarov added that this would not be simple. Thought would have to be given to the tactical side of it since the Inter-Regional Group of Deputies (the radical democrats) would make a great noise about 'dictatorial tendencies'.[82] Some who urged a strengthening of the powers of the federal presidency, up to and including the declaration of a state of emergency, were, indeed, eager to return to the *status quo ante*. That did nothing to facilitate the task of those such as Shakhnazarov—and Gorbachev himself—who wished to combine a strong and effective federal presidency with further democratization on the basis of a genuine federalism, with very substantial rights accorded to the republican participants in the federation.

The advice of Shakhnazarov was predicated on the assumption that a strengthening of the presidential structures was a necessary element in enhancing the chances of the Soviet Union completing a successful transition to democracy.[83] Some of the pressure Gorbachev came under in the Politburo and Secretariat of the Central Committee, especially in the winter of 1990–1, was based on very different assumptions and desiderata. Criticism of Gorbachev, both implied and direct, surfaced strongly at a Politburo meeting held on 16 November 1990. Early in the proceedings, Gorbachev said that his

[82] Shakhnazarov, *Tsena svobody*, p. 431. Later in the month Shakhnazarov, in a memorandum to Gorbachev, advocated the creation of a Presidency, with the Chairmanship of the Supreme Soviet going to someone else. Gorbachev, he said, had been, in effect, the Speaker of that body and now needed stronger executive power. The post should be elective by the whole people but in the present time of turmoil, it would be better if the President were elected for a first term by the Congress of People's Deputies (ibid., pp. 441–3).

[83] Shakhnazarov, earlier than Gorbachev, realized that the Baltic states would never be likely to remain, voluntarily, as part of even a renewed Union. By the spring of 1991 Gorbachev had also tacitly accepted that Estonia, Latvia, and Lithuania would in due course go their separate ways.

idea was to form a 'democratic coalition'.[84] The response of Stanislav Gurenko, at that time First Secretary of the Central Committee of the Communist Party in Ukraine, was to say that the CPSU was still a ruling party. Coalitions were formed when a party did not have a majority. So long as the party had its majority, then nothing was owed to the 'pretensions of some extremists'.[85]

Several Politburo members objected to the composition of the Presidential Council (chosen by Gorbachev)—not only the presence of writers such as Aitmatov but the membership of Aleksandr Yakovlev. Oleg Shenin, who had become a Politburo member in July 1990 and was in charge of the party organization, was among those present who called for the introduction of 'presidential rule', a synonym for a state of emergency, and added: 'I support Comrade Gurenko: are we a ruling party or not?'[86] For Shenin, who less than a year later was one of the organizers of the putsch against Gorbachev, this was very much a rhetorical question. The Armenian Party First Secretary, Vladimir Movisyan, expressed similar sentiments, saying: 'It's necessary to decide: if we are an opposition party, then we have to act in a different way. And if we are a ruling party, then let us act correspondingly.'[87] Movisyan also complained that, speaking on the anniversary of the October Revolution in Red Square, Gorbachev had said nothing about the party. Gorbachev told him: 'You read badly. I said that perestroika was developed on the initiative of the Communist Party...'. This was not, of course, what Movisyan or most of his colleagues wanted to hear. They were more concerned with saving themselves from the consequences of perestroika than in taking collective credit for its initiation. It is characteristic that Movisyan's response to Gorbachev's remark about the launch of perestroika was to deplore the fact that the First Secretary of the Communist Party of the Russian Federation (CPRF)—Ivan Polozkov, a conservative Communist who had been elected to that recently created post—had not been able to obtain an apartment in Moscow![88]

At that same Politburo meeting, Polozkov told Gorbachev: 'Your guilt lies in the fact that now you do not operate through the party.'[89] Gorbachev agreed that he did not, but added that his problem was that he did not have the presidential structures that would take the party's place.[90] The tone in which Politburo members now addressed Gorbachev was very different from that of the earlier years of his leadership. Meetings of the Politburo were now held monthly instead of weekly and Gorbachev told the meeting on 16 November that he did not think it essential that he preside over every session

---

[84] 'Zasedanie Politbyuro TsK KPSS ot 16 noyabrya 1990 goda', HIA, Fond 89, 1.003, opis 42, file 30, p. 6.

[85] Ibid., p. 8. [86] Ibid., p. 11. [87] Ibid., p. 17.

[88] Ibid. [89] Ibid., p. 25. [90] Ibid.

of that body.[91] Rather than causing delight among Politburo members who would theoretically be freer to come to different decisions, this served instead as a reminder that real power had moved elsewhere. Far from all of it, however, had gone to the federal presidency. Much had been seized by the republican leaders. At the 16 November Politburo meeting, Ayaz Mutalibov, the hard-line First Secretary of the Communist Party in Azerbaijan, went so far as to say that the impression had been created that 'you ask permission from Yeltsin' in coming to an appraisal of something.[92]

Oleg Baklanov, the Central Committee Secretary responsible for the military-industrial complex—and a future putschist—lamented the abolition of the Administrative Organs Department of the Central Committee he had formerly headed and which had supervised the Ministry of Justice, the Supreme Court, the procuracy, the Ministry of Interior, the KGB, and the armed forces. Now the activity of those organs was hampered for lack of 'the major work of coordination' which the department (abolished by Gorbachev in 1988) had carried out.[93] Yuriy Prokofyev, the Moscow Party First Secretary, announced that he had no faith in either the Presidential Council or the Council of Ministers. Gorbachev agreed that it was time to abolish the Presidential Council, though the Federation Council should be kept, since it was an organ which united the leaders of the republics.[94] Even the Politburo moderate, Nursultan Nazarbaev, the First Secretary of the Communist Party of Kazakhstan, told Gorbachev that it was 'necessary to liquidate' the Presidential Council. Instead, he should appoint state counsellors, but he should keep the Federation Council.

The superfluousness of the Presidential Council was something on which there was broad agreement in the Politburo. Gorbachev, however, explicitly rejects the suggestion that 'the Politburo coerced' him into making the changes he was to announce the following day.[95] The Politburo by that time was, indeed, in no position to 'coerce' him to do anything he did not wish to do, but the meeting is likely to have been one of a number of factors affecting his decision to announce significant institutional changes to the Supreme Soviet the next morning. Gorbachev notes in his memoirs that after a stormy session of the Supreme Soviet earlier on 16 November, he spoke with a number of republican leaders, including Nazarbaev. He does not refer to the particular Politburo meeting held later in the same day, but mentions that he sat up until four o'clock in the morning preparing the speech he delivered just a few hours later.[96] In that address he called for an enhanced power of presidential decree; the abolition of the Presidential Council; the

    [91] 'Zasedanie Politbyuro TsK KPSS ot 16 noyabrya 1990 goda', HIA, Fond 89, 1.003, opis 42, file 30, p. 8.
    [92] Ibid., p. 19.   [93] Ibid., p. 14.   [94] Ibid., p. 15.
    [95] Gorbachev, *Zhizn' i reformy*, vol. 1, p. 585.   [96] Ibid.

replacement of the Council of Ministers by a Cabinet of Ministers which would be headed by a prime minister subordinate to the President; the strengthening of the Federation Council; and the creation of a Security Council. While he did not give way to the hard-liners on the essentials—such as the demand of Shenin and others that he assume emergency powers—it seems likely that he was influenced to some degree by the Politburo discussion. As Gordon Hahn has observed: 'Tactically, Gorbachev appears to have been responding to the more moderate republic leaders in the Politburo and moving in the direction of hardline Politburo members [only] where these two groups agreed: eliminating the Presidential Council and strengthening the presidency and the *siloviki*.'[97] (The creation of the Security Council was a concession to the last-named.)[98]

Gorbachev was engaged in a tactical retreat during the last three months of 1990 and the first quarter of 1991. Two bad appointments in December 1990 were examples of this. Boris Pugo (who subsequently participated in the attempted coup against Gorbachev and committed suicide on its failure) replaced the liberal Vadim Bakatin as Minister of Internal Affairs, and the colourless conservative, Gennadiy Yanaev (another future putschist), was appointed to the new post of Vice-President.[99] Gorbachev was further weakened in the eyes of his former democratic supporters by the deaths in Vilnius and Riga in January 1991. Thirteen demonstrators were killed and 165 wounded when KGB special forces stormed the Lithuanian television tower which was surrounded by peaceful demonstrators, attempting by their presence to protect it.[100] A week later Ministry of Interior special forces, OMON,

[97] Gordon M. Hahn, *1985–2000. Russia's Revolution from Above: Reform, Transition, and Revolution in the Fall of the Soviet Communist Regime* (Transaction Publishers, New Brunswick, NJ, 2002). In general, this Politburo meeting—a significant manifestation of the pressure that Gorbachev was under from conservative and hard-line forces—is ignored (along with much else of value in the archives) in the academic literature on perestroika. Hahn is an exception to that rule. He devotes nine pages to it (ibid., pp. 292–300).

[98] Those appointed to the Security Council were Vadim Bakatin; Shevardnadze's successor as Foreign Minister, Aleksandr Bessmertnykh; KGB Chairman Kryuchkov; Valentin Pavlov, who was to become prime minister; Minister of Internal Affairs Pugo; Yevgeniy Primakov; Minister of Defence Yazov; and Gennadiy Yanaev. Of these nine people, six were active participants in the August 1991 coup against Gorbachev. The three exceptions were Bakatin and Primakov, who took an active part in the opposition to the attempted putsch, and Bessmertnykh who more passively dissented. Gorbachev had also proposed Boldin as a member of the Security Council, but the Supreme Soviet of the USSR had the good sense to reject that nomination.

[99] For Vadim Bakatin's account of his appointment and removal as Minister of Internal Affairs, see Bakatin, *Doroga v proshedshem vremeni* (Dom, Moscow, 1999), pp. 133 and 227–8.

[100] Mark R. Beissinger, *Nationalist Mobilization and the Collapse of the Soviet State* (Cambridge University Press, Cambridge, 2002, pp. 378–9; and Anatol Lieven, *The Baltic Revolution: Estonia, Latvia, Lithuania and the Path to Independence* (Yale University Press, New Haven, CT, and London, 2nd edn., 1994), pp. 250–1.

killed four people in the Latvian capital, Riga.[101] These events were meant to set in motion a process of repressing separatist movements which would put an end to the 'new thinking' tendency within the Communist Party which Gorbachev had encouraged and led. If Gorbachev had gone along with it, he would have been replaced by a hard-liner before long, since he was the one, in the eyes of conservative Communists and the leading figures in the power ministries, who had got the Soviet Union into its current predicament in the first place.

From the other side, Gorbachev was coming under mounting pressure from the leaders of the most separatist-minded republics and from miners' strikes in Russia and large demonstrations in Moscow. An umbrella movement, 'Democratic Russia', had been formed with the purpose of bringing together a wide array of groups and new political parties.[102] As Steven Fish has observed, it was principally 'a coalition of groups' and it was made up of 'self-avowed democrats'.[103] Yeltsin, fleetingly, suggested that it might become a 'super-party', but that proposal 'was immediately quashed' by the group's other leaders.[104] By the summer of 1991 'Democratic Russia' was playing an important political role, working for Yeltsin's victory in the Russian presidential election. Already by the end of the winter of 1990–1 Yeltsin had become substantially more popular than Gorbachev in Russia.[105]

THE STRUGGLE FOR A 'RENEWED UNION'

Gorbachev took two important steps to break free from the cross-pressures. The first of these was to hold the March 1991 referendum on a 'renewed Union'. As noted earlier, this was answered overwhelmingly in the affirmative in all the republics which conducted the referendum, including both Russia and Ukraine. Gorbachev, accordingly, succeeded temporarily in tilting the balance back towards preservation of a Union of some sort. That success, however, was to be short-lived. Several republics added questions of their own to the main one about preserving, through renewing, the Union. Of huge

---

[101] On the activities of OMON see Lieven, *The Baltic Revolution*, pp. 254–5.

[102] M. Steven Fish, *Democracy from Scratch: Opposition and Regime in the New Russian Revolution* (Princeton University Press, Princeton, NJ, 1995), pp. 109–13.

[103] Ibid., pp. 109–10.   [104] Ibid., p. 111.

[105] By March 1991 Yeltsin enjoyed over 60 per cent popularity as compared with a little over 30 per cent for Gorbachev. A year earlier Gorbachev had still been the more popular of the two. The data are from the most reliable survey researchers at that time. See 'Reytingi Boris Yel'tsina i Mikhaila Gorbacheva po 10-bal'noy shkale' (VTsIOM, Moscow, 1993), for a copy of which I am grateful to Professor Yuriy Levada.

significance was the question which Boris Yeltsin and his advisers decided to add to the referendum within the Russian republic. Voters were asked whether they wanted direct elections for a new post of President of Russia. If the answer were positive, that contest would take place just three months later—in June 1991.Yeltsin had since May 1990 been Chairman of the Supreme Soviet of the Russian Federation, elected by members of the Congress of Peoples Deputies of the RSFSR. He was aware, however, that election by the people as a whole would increase his authority, not least in his struggle for power with Gorbachev. Almost 70 per cent of voters in the referendum supported direct election and Yeltsin's subsequent electoral victory added greatly to his democratic legitimacy.

The second important initiative taken by Gorbachev at the end of the winter of 1990–1, marking the end of what had been a tactical retreat to a centrist position, was his launch of 'the Novo-Ogarevo process'. There had already been more than one draft of a new Union Treaty.[106] However, Gorbachev realized that if he were to have any chance of reversing the fissiparous tendencies in the Soviet Union without resorting to the show of force being urged upon him by the hard-liners in the CPSU Central Committee and the power ministries, there had to be genuine negotiations with the leaders of all those republics ready to move towards a new and voluntary Union. Thus, without seeking the approval of the Communist Party hierarchy, Gorbachev initiated the Novo-Ogarevo process in April 1991, variously known also as the 1 + 9 (Gorbachev's favoured variant) or the 9 + 1 talks, in which a new draft treaty was negotiated between the federal centre (the one) and the nine republics which were prepared, in principle, to belong to a renewed Union.[107]

After hard bargaining over several months, in which the main struggle was between Gorbachev's team, who were ready to make concessions but determined to maintain a viable federal authority within the 'renewed Union', and Yeltsin's team who wished to maximize the powers of the Russian and other republics at the expense of the all-Union political institutions, a text was finally accepted that was to be initialled by five of the parties to the agreement at a ceremony in the Kremlin on 20 August 1991. The expectation was that others would sign later, though Ukraine had not yet agreed to it and, in the absence of the coup, much would have depended on its participation if

---

[106] See Jeffrey Kahn, *Federalism, Democratization, and the Rule of Law in Russia* (Oxford University Press, Oxford, 2002), esp. ch. 4, 'Gorbachev's Federalism Problem', pp. 83–101.

[107] Novo-Ogarevo was a country house, built in Khrushchev's time in the style of the home of a nineteenth-century Russian landowner. On the process, see Shakhnazarov, *Tsena svobody*, pp. 221–39.

a Union were to be preserved.[108] The Union Treaty, which a majority of Soviet republics seemed likely, nevertheless, to sign up to, was a radical departure from past Soviet theory and practice. The USSR was to keep its initials, but the Union of Soviet Socialist Republics was in future to be the Union of Soviet Sovereign Republics. So much power was being devolved to the republics that the new arrangements hovered between a loose federation and a confederation. Whether such a Union would have survived, without the intervention of the putschists which accelerated the collapse of the Soviet state, must remain a very open question. The imminent signing of the Union Treaty, however, was the last straw for those who mounted the coup against Gorbachev and it was to prevent this occurring that they put Gorbachev and his family under house arrest on 18 August 1991 and the whole country in a state of emergency the following morning.

ABANDONING THE PARTY'S LEADING ROLE

The importance of the Nineteenth Party Conference in 1988—and of the first competitive elections at the all-Union level in 1989 which resulted from it—has been emphasized already. Earlier in this chapter I have shown how far Gorbachev had by that time moved away from Leninist orthodoxy. It is important also, however, to pay attention briefly to the further developments in his thinking in the last two years of the Soviet Union's existence. These involved an ever more public embrace of the principles of social democracy, though, with the growing polarization of Soviet politics, the impact of fundamentally new pronouncements from Central Committee plenums or even Party Congresses was far less than it would have been in the past. Yet, when attention is paid to the platform presented to the 28th Party Congress in the summer of 1990 and to the draft Party Programme a year later, it can be seen how absurd are the all-too-common assertions that Gorbachev's political thinking did not change.

There were not only significant differences between what Gorbachev wrote in his 1987 book, *Perestroika*, and what he said in his report to the Nineteenth Party Conference in 1988 and in his unpublished book manuscript in 1989. There was also a substantial difference again to be found in his statements in 1990 and 1991. At a meeting of the Central Committee in February 1990

---

[108] See the very thorough study by Mark R. Beissinger, *Nationalist Mobilization and the Collapse of the Soviet State* (Cambridge University Press, Cambridge, 2002); on the Novo-Ogarevo process specifically, see pp. 422–5.

he went beyond 'socialist pluralism' and embraced 'political pluralism', accepting in principle that there could be more than one party competing within the political system.[109] He persuaded this same plenary session that it was time to give up on the existing Article 6 of the Soviet Constitution, thus paving the way for the Congress of People's deputies, meeting the following month, to remove the guaranteed 'leading and guiding role' of the Communist Party from the country's fundamental law.[110] In the liberal outlets of the mass media there had already in 1989 been calls for the removal of Article 6 of the Constitution which accorded the Communist Party its privileged place. There were, however, very few members of the Central Committee of the CPSU who were ready to abandon the party's monopoly of power. One who showed more foresight than the vast majority was Vadim Bakatin. Speaking at a Central Committee plenum on 9 December 1989, shortly before the second Congress of People's Deputies was held, Bakatin argued for the removal of this article and supported the principle of a multiparty system in which the CPSU would compete with others. He also held that, strategically, it would be much better for the Communist Party to take the lead in recognizing this principle than to be seen to be rescinding Article 6 only under pressure.[111]

Whether Gorbachev could at that point have persuaded the Central Committee to abandon the assurance of power offered by Article 6, even though by this time it was a very dubious guarantee of anything, must remain uncertain. He did not, however, try to do so until two months after Bakatin had received a rough reception from Central Committee members for making the same proposal. Gorbachev had internally accepted that a multiparty system was a logical and desirable development, but had hoped to retain control over the speed at which it came into being. The abolition of Article 6 became a more salient issue later in December not only because it had been pressed vigorously by Academician Andrey Sakharov at the Congress of People's Deputies in the middle of that month—and resisted at the time by Gorbachev—but also because Sakharov died of a heart attack on the evening of 14 December, on the eve of another session of the Congress. The death of Sakharov added extra emotional force to the pressure for the removal of the Communist Party's monopoly of power from the Constitution. Indeed, willingness to remove Article 6 became a test of commitment to democratization, and Gorbachev embraced that position just two months after he had resisted it in December.

This change was an essential part of making state institutions rather than party bodies the locus of political authority within the state, a process on

---

[109] *Pravda*, 6 February 1990, pp. 1–2.   [110] Ibid.
[111] Bakatin, *Doroga v proshedshem vremeni*, pp. 207–10.

which Gorbachev had already embarked. He believed, however, that it was not enough to transfer all party power to the legislature without having appropriate state executive organs in place, given the number of problems—from the condition of the economy to growing separatist demands—that required a strong executive. In principle, Gorbachev says in his memoirs, the decision to give up the Communist Party's monopoly of power was taken at the Nineteenth Party Conference, but finding the optimal moment to complete the shift was, he argues, difficult and exacerbated by the 'revolutionary impatience' of the radical democrats who made the abolition of Article 6 the 'first major political act of the rising opposition'.[112] Gorbachev says that the Politburo discussed at length the place of the CPSU in the political system and the possibility of abolishing or amending Article 6 as early as June 1989. They split into three groups, with only Vadim Medvedev, Eduard Shevardnadze, and Aleksandr Yakovlev emerging as 'active proponents of reform'.[113] Gorbachev's own position then evidently remained cautious. The new Article 6, approved in March 1990, continued to mention the Communist Party, but said that 'other political parties' as well as trade unions, youth organizations, other social organizations and mass movements, through their elected representatives, participate in 'establishing the policy of the Soviet state and in the administration of state and societal affairs'.[114] Gorbachev, in his memoirs, admits that this was in some ways a half-measure, given that the Communist Party was still mentioned in the first place, but he observes that 'it was none the less revolutionary' inasmuch as it opened the way for the legal creation of other parties.[115]

By the time of the 28th Party Congress in the summer of 1990, Gorbachev's acceptance of other political parties was unequivocal. In a televised speech on 2 July he said: 'In place of the Stalinist model of socialism we are coming to a citizen's society of free people. The political system is being transformed radically, genuine democracy with free elections, the existence of many parties and human rights is becoming established and real people's power is being revived.'[116] Later in the same speech Gorbachev addressed demands that the party return to 'the Leninist understanding of the party as society's vanguard

[112] Gorbachev, *Zhizn' i reformy*, vol. 1, pp. 478–83.

[113] Ibid., p. 482.

[114] Gorbachev, *Zhizn' i reformy*, vol. 1, p. 483.

[115] Ibid. A less cumbersome formulation, and one that was still more of a radical break with the past, was proposed to Gorbachev by Shakhnazarov but evidently watered down in the Politburo. See Shakhnazarov's memorandum to Gorbachev of 20 February 1990, published in *Tsena svobody*, pp. 458–9.

[116] The 28th Party Congress, text of Gorbachev's televised speech, BBC SWB, SU/0807, C1/1–C1/18, at p. C1/1.

force' which, he says, was prompting the question whether they were merely changing the term 'leading role' to 'vanguard'.[117] He continued:

There must be clarity on this: we believe that one cannot foist a vanguard role on society, it can only be won by an active struggle for the interests of the working people, by practical deeds and by our whole political and moral image. The party will pursue its policy and fight to maintain its mandate as the ruling party within the framework of the democratic process and elections to the central and local bodies. In this respect it is acting as a parliamentary party.[118]

This, again, was a dramatic break with the past, although it remained more important in principle than in practice. That was partly because, while a real battle was still taking place *within* the Communist Party with conservative forces attempting to wrest control from Gorbachev and the reformers, the main opposition forces had adopted an increasingly comprehensive anti-Communist standpoint and disdained to pay much attention to changes in the official platform of the CPSU. Although the formation of other political parties became legal, following the Third Congress of People's Deputies in March 1990, 'Democratic Russia', as already noted, did not become a political party after its establishment as a socio-political organization in October of that year. The many new parties which emerged in the Soviet Union during 1990–1 did not, *qua* party, become major political players. Indeed, even in post-Soviet Russia political parties have remained weak—with the exception for most of the Yeltsin years of the Communist Party of the Russian Federation.[119]

THE PROCESS OF SOCIAL DEMOCRATIZATION

By the summer of 1991 Gorbachev had continued to prevail over his enemies within the CPSU to the extent that the draft party programme published in July had much more in common with social democracy than with anything remotely like traditional Soviet Communism. The enunciated principles of the party now included 'the affirmation of freedom in all its diverse manifestations—social and personal, economic and political, intellectual and spiritual', and 'the affirmation of consistent internationalism, and the free development of peoples—large and small—and the renewal of the union as a voluntary federal association of sovereign republics'.[120] The programme

---

[117] Ibid., p. C1/14.   [118] Ibid.

[119] With the exception, however, of the brief prime ministership of Yevgeniy Primakov in 1998–9, the Communist Party of the Russian Federation was never offered any ministerial posts.

[120] Draft CPSU Programme, *Nezavisimaya gazeta*, 23 July 1991, and BBC SWB SU/1134, C1/1-C1/7, at p. C1/1.

speaks about the 'establishment of a totalitarian system' under Stalin and 'unreservedly condemns the crimes' of the Stalin period. The political system must, says the document, consist of a 'democratic federation of sovereign republics', a state based upon the rule of law and on the basis of a separation of powers—legislative, executive, and judicial. The draft programme favours 'transition to a mixed economy and recognition of the diversity and equality of different forms of ownership—state and private, joint-stock and co-operative'.[121] The party's basic principle is stated to be 'the idea of humane, democratic socialism'.[122] For any student of Soviet ideology, this was another manifestation of conceptual revolution. Throughout almost the entire Soviet period an intense propaganda war had been waged against democratic socialist parties in the West. 'Democratic socialism' was synonymous with social democracy, and Soviet ideologists claimed that this could be nothing but pseudo-socialism. The term, they said, did not even make any sense, since socialism was, by its very nature, democratic. The approved term for the Soviet system throughout the post-war era was 'socialist democracy', always to be distinguished—until the Gorbachev era—from 'democratic socialism'!

Gorbachev, in his speech to a plenary session of the Central Committee on 25 July 1991, commending the draft party programme to them, went further in turning Marxism-Leninism on its head. The 'previous theoretical and practical model of socialism' had proved to be bankrupt. Socialism and the market were 'not only compatible but indivisible in essence'![123] On the 'ideological basis' of the CPSU, he declared:

In the past the party recognized only Marxism-Leninism as the source of its inspiration, whilst this doctrine itself was distorted to the extreme to suit the pragmatic purposes of the day and was turned into a kind of collection of canonical texts. Now it is necessary to include in our ideological arsenal all the riches of our and the world's socialist and democratic thought. Such an approach is dictated by the fact that the realization of the socialist idea and movement along the path of economic, social and spiritual progress can be successfully implemented today only in the channel of the common development of civilization.[124]

Gorbachev openly addressed the accusation by 'representatives, I would say, of communist fundamentalism' concerning the 'social-democratization of the CPSU'. This was evoking some fears, he acknowledged, but they were based on ideological differences that belonged to the years of the revolution and civil war when Communists and social democrats found themselves on opposite sides of the barricades. These were now a matter for historians, for the 'criteria

---

121   Ibid., C1/3.   122   Ibid., C1/6.
123   BBC SWB SU/1135, C1/1–C1/7, at C1/1–C1/2.   124   Ibid., C1/4.

of the confrontation which appeared at that time—the attitudes they adopted towards violence, towards the dictatorship of the proletariat and democracy, and the role of socialist consciousness and political van- guard—have lost their former meaning'.[125] Gorbachev also raised, and accepted, the possibility that the party might in the future be in opposition. It was necessary to use political methods, to persuade people to vote for the party's representatives, and 'where this is unsuccessful, to make up a constructive opposition, supporting the authorities' sensible measures and opposing them when this is necessary for the defence of the interests of the working people'.[126]

This was a far cry from even the 'new thinking' of Gorbachev's 1987 book, *Perestroika*. Indeed, the sentiments expressed in that July 1991 speech would have been perfectly acceptable to the leadership of the British Labour Party, the German Social Democrats, or the French or Spanish Socialists. Yet they no longer made a great impact on Soviet society. The party was now speaking with many voices and a majority of the apparatchiki in Gorbachev's audience had no intention of following social democratic precepts. Some of them were already thinking about ways to remove him from office. The polarization in the society was increasingly that of a nationalist-separatist character against the federal authorities, accompanied by a growing anti-Communism whose adherents made little or no distinction between Communism and a variety of socialisms. They had, after all, spent decades being told that the system (now being so thoroughly castigated by Gorbachev) in which they had lived their lives was socialist.

Thus, Gorbachev's use of the term, 'democratic socialist', was better under- stood in Western Europe than in the Soviet Union or, for that matter, Eastern Europe or the United States. Governments led by Clement Attlee in Britain, Willy Brandt in West Germany, François Mitterrand in France, or Felipe González in Spain, had nothing in common with those led in the Soviet Union by any of Gorbachev's predecessors. Given the very different experience of Russians and the other nations which made up the Soviet Union, it may be that the evolution of Gorbachev's ideas of socialism was doomed to be misunderstood. One phrase he used, which was legitimately open to objec- tion, was his quite frequent references to the 'socialist choice' made by the Soviet people. From Lenin onwards, they had been given no choice in that matter, and the phrase also blurs the distinction between Communism and the socialism of a social democratic type which Gorbachev by the last years of the Soviet Union had embraced. Of relevance here are the reflections of Vadim

---

[125] Ibid., C1/5.   [126] Ibid., C1/7.

Bakatin, a former Communist Party official whose own evolution (like that of Aleksandr Yakovlev)[127] had made him a liberal rather than social democrat by the time perestroika came to an end.[128] He wrote:

I was convinced that Gorbachev sincerely and deeply understood the necessity and inescapability of a fundamental transformation of the country—its economy and political system. I liked his inner democratic spirit, gentleness, and humaneness. At the same time it is hard to believe that the greatest reformer of the century suffered from a peculiar dogmatism. A blind, some kind of fatal devotion to the 'socialist' choice greatly hampered him.[129]

Bakatin goes on to say that Gorbachev should have embraced the market economy far earlier than he did, adding: 'I did not understand democracy without a market, a market without private property, private property without "exploitation" and in that I was closer to the "democrats" than was the general secretary.'[130] One could argue that, given Gorbachev's changed understanding of what was meant by socialism, of the two words, 'socialist choice', it was the second that was the more objectionable in the context of Soviet history. However, it is certainly true that Gorbachev moved quicker to embrace democratization than the market, and this was an area in which the fault of which he is often accused, indecisiveness (though it is easy to find many examples of him acting decisively, especially in the breakthrough year of 1988), did manifest itself. In the end, as his speech commending the party programme to a sceptical Central Committee in July 1991 illustrated, Gorbachev embraced the market, albeit one operating in a mixed ownership economy, regulated in the way it would be by a West European socialist government.

GORBACHEV AND YELTSIN—DEMOCRATIZATION AND DISSOLUTION

The relationship between Gorbachev and Yeltsin as politicians, their influence over democratization, and the responsibility of each of them for the

---

[127] Yakovlev writes in his memoirs: 'Mikhail Gorbachev genuinely believed in the conception of democratic socialism' (*Sumerki*, p. 468). Yakovlev, latterly, evidently did not.

[128] As already noted, Bakatin was a remarkably liberal Minister of Interior from 1988 until, following hard-line pressure, he lost that job in late 1990. However, Gorbachev and Yeltsin jointly agreed that he was the right person to become Chairman of the KGB after the defeat of the August coup. He did his best to conduct a democratic purge of that organization and divided it into two, separating its domestic arm from the foreign intelligence service.

[129] Bakatin, *Doroga v proshedshem vremeni*, pp. 231–2.

[130] Ibid., p. 232.

dissolution of the Soviet state are all controversial issues.[131] As I have already argued in Chapter 7, Gorbachev played the more crucial role in the democratization of the Soviet Union and Yeltsin the more decisive role in its dissolution. That bald statement, however, needs further elaboration. The first point should be incontrovertible. Yeltsin was not part of the team which developed the new thinking and put democratization on the political agenda. Indeed, only a general secretary, given the nature of the Soviet system, could do so. Gorbachev—as much of the evidence already deployed in this volume affirms—played the principal role in legitimating ideas that broke with Soviet Marxism-Leninism and in promoting democratization both in theory and practice. Yeltsin's positive contribution to the democratization process came after the key decisions that produced the breakthrough had already been taken in the run-up to the Nineteenth Party Conference. When Yeltsin spoke critically at a Central Committee plenum in late 1987, he had not yet formulated any coherent thoughts about democracy. His intervention, though bold, was more a result of personal pique that he was still only a candidate member, not a full member, of the Politburo.[132] When, however, from the Nineteenth Party Conference onwards, he criticized in public some of the country's leaders—at first, Ligachev, and later Gorbachev—he enlarged the political significance of the developing freedom of speech. When he stood for election against candidates favoured by the party hierarchy in 1989, 1990, and 1991—and won—he gave greater substance to the practice of democracy. Only, though, the introduction of competitive elections—the most important institutional step on the path of democratization—permitted Yeltsin to make a political comeback, and it was Gorbachev, not Yeltsin, who initiated that break with the past.

Yeltsin, like Gorbachev, had many of the characteristics of a charismatic leader. He has said that as a boy, 'from first grade to last', he was invariably

---

[131] For a perceptive and judicious study, see George Breslauer, *Gorbachev and Yeltsin as Leaders* (Cambridge University Press, Cambridge, 2002).

[132] When Yeltsin was first offered as early as April 1985 the post of head of the department of the Central Committee responsible for the construction industry, he refused the offer, saying that he preferred to stay as first secretary of the Sverdlovsk obkom. He was irritated, as he admits in his first volume of memoirs, that the offer was not accompanied by a Secretaryship of the Central Committee. He was very conscious that previous Sverdlovsk first secretaries had become Secretaries when they were similarly promoted. Yeltsin only took the post when his sponsor, Ligachev, called him and told him that the Politburo had already decided, and party discipline meant that he had no choice in the matter. Yeltsin also mentions that when Gorbachev was brought to Moscow from his provincial post 'and from a region, what's more, which in economic potential was considerably inferior to the Sverdlovsk region . . . *he* had been promoted to the rank of secretary of the central committee'. Yeltsin did not, in fact, have long to wait for his further party promotion. In June 1985 he became a secretary of the Central Committee which he regarded as a 'natural progression'. See Boris Yeltsin, *Against the Grain: An Autobiography* (Jonathan Cape, London, 1990), pp. 72–3, 76, and 82.

'elected class-leader', even though he went to several different schools.[133] To anyone who ever met him, it was immediately clear that Yeltsin was not one of nature's subordinates. Indeed, in his earliest volume of memoirs Yeltsin mentions that it had been his 'fortune in life' that until he went to work in the Central Committee of the CPSU he had 'practically never had to work as a subordinate, had never been anyone's deputy', adding: 'Never having been a "number two", I was consequently used to taking decisions without shifting the ultimate responsibility on to someone else.'[134] Like Gorbachev, especially in the early years of their leadership in both cases, he evoked a warm response from crowds. Yeltsin had a commanding presence and, whatever his other failings, never lacked courage. He was decisive to a fault—a decisiveness that often turned into impulsiveness. Like Gorbachev, he was a workaholic, but— unlike Gorbachev—his bursts of frenetic activity were followed by lengthy periods of lassitude.[135]

Yeltsin's electoral activity in the last years of the Soviet Union both exem- plified and promoted the cause of democratization. However, his political behaviour as President of post-Soviet Russia, although beyond the scope of this volume, requires brief attention, for it throws light on the limitations of Yeltsin the 'democrat'. Throughout the 1990s Yeltsin displayed more interest in wielding personal, often arbitrary, power than in democratic institution- building. He took a distant and disdainful view of political parties, and refused to join one, and he failed to work constructively either with the legislature which had chosen him to be Chairman of the Russian Supreme Soviet or with its successor, the State Duma and Federation Council, created by the new Russian Constitution of December 1993. Yeltsin's failure to maintain support in the legislature which had supported him in 1990–1 was so great in the following two years that, when faced by revolt from a large number of deputies who asserted the authority of the Supreme Soviet over that of the Presidency, Yeltsin closed down the legislature in September 1993. The following month he ordered the shelling of the Russian White House in which the rebellious deputies were encamped.[136]

---

[133] Yeltsin, *Against the Grain*, p. 18.   [134] Ibid., p. 75.

[135] In post-Soviet Russia Yeltsin frequently disappeared from view, sometimes suffering from depression, sometimes from too much alcohol, but, as George Breslauer observes, 'after a period of either despondency or calculated personal absence', he would return to the Kremlin 'to re-seize the initiative' (*Gorbachev and Yeltsin as Leaders*, p. 222).

[136] On this, see Archie Brown, 'Political Leadership in Post-Soviet Russia', in Amin Saikal and William Maley (eds.), *Russia in Search of its Future* (Cambridge University Press, Cambridge, 1995), pp. 28–47; and Lilia Shevtsova, 'Russia's Post-Communist Politics: Revolution or Con- tinuity?', in Gail W. Lapidus (ed.), *The New Russia: Troubled Transformation* (Westview Press, Boulder, CO, 1995), pp. 5–36. In Shevtsova's words: 'Having adopted the principle that "the end justifies the means", Yeltsin had opened the door for an even more ruthless and cynical round of politics in Moscow. But the ideological contradictions between his goals and the use of means drawn from the traditional arsenal of communist politics were too great to bridge' (ibid., p. 23).

Yeltsin turned a blind eye to electoral malpractice which benefited him in the Duma election of 1993 and the presidential election of 1996, and came close to cancelling the latter.[137] He presided over the sell-off of Russia's natural resources to pre-selected purchasers at knockdown prices.[138] He showed none of Gorbachev's reluctance to use massive force to put down separatist movements. He launched two wars in Chechnya—in 1994 and again in 1999. Although Vladimir Putin is usually accorded responsibility for the second of these, he was at that time prime minister, while Yeltsin was President. Oddly, some of those who believed that no act of violence could be perpetrated by any branch of the *siloviki* in any part of the Soviet Union on one night without the prior knowledge of Gorbachev have absolved Yeltsin of any responsibility for the reinvasion of Chechnya and the prosecution of a war there between September and December 1999.[139] No one, however, could take away from Yeltsin political responsibility for the first Chechen war of his

[137] At one point, when he was convinced that he could not win the 1996 presidential election, Yeltsin told his staff to prepare decrees dissolving the State Duma, banning the Communist Party (the party with the strongest popular support at the time) and cancelling the presidential election. However, he was talked out of taking such blatantly undemocratic steps by, among others, his daughter, Tatyana, and by Anatoliy Chubais, who were convinced that—with vast sums of money put at the disposal of his campaign and the mass media mobilized behind him— he could defeat his Communist rival, Gennadiy Zyuganov. For Yeltsin's own account of this, see Boris Yeltsin, *Midnight Diaries* (Weidenfeld & Nicolson, London, 2000), pp. 20–7. A much less flattering account than Yeltsin's own mildly self-critical version of his plan to dispense with even a façade of constitutionalism and democracy is given in a careful study by Peter Reddaway and Dmitri Glinski. After the Minister of Internal Affairs, Anatoliy Kulikov, had been presented with Yeltsin's plans, he went 'to consult with Prosecutor General Yuri Skuratov and Constitutional Court Chairman Vladimir Tumanov about questions of legality. Tumanov quickly revealed Yeltsin's method: "The president told me that Kulikov had agreed, Barsukov [commandant of the Kremlin, with the rank of general] had agreed, and the prosecutor general had agreed. How could I tell him that his plan was impermissible?" Kulikov's comment: "It turned out, as was later confirmed, that everyone who saw the president was told by him that the others had agreed".' Kulikov, in Reddaway's and Glinski's account, then became the leader of the opposition within the administration to Yeltsin's plan. The episode, according to Reddaway and Glinski, was far from the only example of 'Yeltsin's capacity to tell big lies'. See Reddaway and Glinski, *The Tragedy of Russia's Reforms: Market Bolshevism Against Democracy* (United States Institute of Peace Press, Washington, DC, 2001), p. 513. See also Lilia Shevtsova, *Yeltsin's Russia: Myths and Reality* (Carnegie Endowment for International Peace, Washington, DC, 1999), p. 172.

[138] See, for example, Chrystia Freeland, *Sale of the Century: The Inside Story of the Second Russian Revolution* (Little, Brown, London, 2000); Thane Gustafson, *Capitalism Russian-Style* (Cambridge University Press, Cambridge, 1999); Yoshiko M. Herrera, 'Russian Economic Reform, 1991–1999', in Zoltan Barany and Robert G. Moser (eds.), *Russian Politics: Challenges of Democratization* (Cambridge University Press, Cambridge, 2001), pp. 135–73; David E. Hoffman, *The Oligarchs: Wealth and Power in the New Russia* (Public Affairs, New York, 2002); and Paul Klebnikov, *Godfather of the Kremlin: Boris Berezovsky and the Looting of Russia* (Harcourt, New York, 2000).

[139] Yeltsin's premature resignation from the presidency, to give his chosen successor, Vladimir Putin, the advantage of becoming acting president—and an election brought forward from June to March 2000—took place on 31 December 1999.

presidency, waged, with atrocities on both sides, between 1994 and 1996. The federal Russian forces, with their greater firepower and lack of discrimination between combatants and non-combatants, left the Chechen capital, Grozny, looking like Dresden or Stalingrad at the end of the Second World War.[140] Kulikov, Yeltsin's Minister of Internal Affairs, at the time of the first Chechen war,[141] has said that 'in the course of the two wars in Chechnya Russia ... lost as many men as the war in Afghanistan in 1979–1989'.[142] Scores of thousands more on the Chechen side were killed.[143] What should be absolutely clear is that post-Soviet Russia, during the presidency of Boris Yeltsin, was not the continuation of perestroika in a more democratic form, as some Western observers have imagined. Far from continuing an evolution in the direction of social democracy, it moved towards what Stefan Hedlund has called 'a bad case of predatory capitalism'.[144] Elections, even with the existence of a variety of political parties, have had less impact on public policy than in the years, 1989–91. The shelling of the parliament building in central Moscow in 1993 was unnecessary and war in Chechnya the following year could have been avoided. In both cases, patient political negotiations over the previous two years—of the kind Gorbachev attempted to practise—could have averted the crises and the subsequent resort to large-scale bloodshed.

The Mindset of the Russian 'Democrats'

Some of what has happened in post-Soviet Russia—in which a hybrid regime has been created, hovering between democracy and authoritarianism, without falling in the Yeltsin years into either category—is rendered more explicable when the ideas of the 'democratic' opposition to the federal authorities in the last years of the Soviet Union are examined more closely. Just as the views of the Soviet central authorities have to be disaggregated, given the differences, for example, between Gorbachev and Pavlov, Bakatin and Baklanov, Yakovlev and Kryuchkov, or Primakov and Pugo, so the ideas of the self-proclaimed 'democrats' cannot simply be taken at face value as democratic. Among the

---

[140] Or, as Mark Beissinger puts it: 'the Yeltsin government did not shrink from twice bombing the city of Groznyi to rubble for the sake of preserving the integrity of the Russian Federation' (Beissinger, *Nationalist Mobilization and the Collapse of the Soviet State*, p. 445).

[141] Ibid., p. 24.

[142] Lilia Shevtsova, *Putin's Russia* (Carnegie Endowment for International Peace, Washington, DC, revised and expanded edition, 2005), p. 251.

[143] See Anna Politkovskaya, *A Dirty War: A Russian Reporter in Chechnya* (Harvill Press, London, 1999).

[144] Stefan Hedlund, *Russia's 'Market' Economy: A Bad Case of Predatory Capitalism* (UCL Press, London, 1999).

democratic activists were many who pursued genuinely democratic goals, some of whom (though far from all) were aware that these would be affected by the means with which the struggle for democracy was waged. Many others were motivated by anti-Communism, without, apparently, noting the extent to which the principles of Communism had been discarded by Gorbachev. Admittedly, the danger of Communist norms being reasserted by another leader, and the power of the apparatus restored, were things that democrats had every right to be concerned about. Alexander Lukin (though he was himself a participant in the democratic movement of the last years of the Soviet Union) invariably puts the word 'democrat' in inverted commas, since his excellent study of the belief systems of the 'democratic' activists demonstrated just how heterogeneous their views were. Many of them made a poor ideational foundation for democracy. Emphasizing how a lot of self-proclaimed democrats were far more influenced by Soviet ideology than they realized, Lukin writes:

Many ideas borrowed from the West were reinterpreted within the framework of a belief system that saw democracy as an ideal society which could solve all of mankind's material and spiritual problems. The noble goal of achieving such a society made it acceptable to disregard 'formalities', including the laws of the existing 'totalitarian' society. The state was seen as the main obstacle to an ideal democracy, and the maximal weakening of the state was believed to be the most important condition for its creation. Finally, 'democratic' activists viewed democracy not as a system of compromises among various groups and interests, or as the separation of powers, but as the unlimited power of the 'democrats' replacing the unlimited power of the Communists. Naturally, people who shared these beliefs could hardly create a liberal democracy based on the rule of law, the separation of powers, an independent judiciary, and respect for individual initiative and human rights.[145]

Yeltsin himself became a genuine anti-Communist, but even with the Communist machine defeated, he combined a very partial acceptance of democratic values with the psychology of a Communist Party boss. He accepted the desirability of competitive elections (albeit with massive wavering in 1996) and of free mass media (although they were mobilized from above to provide overwhelming support for him in the 1996 election campaign). He did not concern himself with the building of such a key democratic institution as the rule of law, which would have meant embracing an independent judiciary. Indeed, when law officers reached a different conclusion from his own, his first thought was to fire them.

---

[145] Alexander Lukin, *The Political Culture of the Russian 'Democrats'* (Oxford University Press, Oxford, 2000), p. 298.

The Dissolution of the Soviet State

Yeltsin, as I have already argued, played at times a positive role in the democratization of the Soviet Union in its last years, but his contribution overall was, at best, ambivalent. Indeed, his determination to replace Gorbachev and reduce his power to a minimum weakened Gorbachev's attempts to create new federal state structures to replace the institutions of the Communist Party. This simultaneously undercut Gorbachev's efforts to reconstruct the Union on a new and voluntary basis. Yeltsin's enormous contribution to the dissolution of the Soviet Union (as distinct from the dismantling of the Soviet political system) was epitomized by his assertion of Russian law over Soviet law and his call, ultimately, for the independence of Russia from the Union. While paying lip-service to a desire to preserve a Union up to, and for a short time beyond, the August coup of 1991, Yeltsin consciously undermined it during the last two years of existence of the USSR. To weaken as comprehensively as possible the federal arm of the Soviet state was an integral part of his own struggle for supremacy over Gorbachev.

It would have been reasonable to expect a Russian leader to join forces with the Soviet president in the attempt to persuade as many republics as possible to join in a new and voluntary union, one which would embrace as much as was possible, given the new democratic constraints, of greater Russia. However, Yeltsin was ready to destroy Soviet statehood for the sake of personal ambition. Politicians are often assumed to be in the business of power-maximization. The generalization does not fit Gorbachev very well, for he had more power at the apex of the unreformed, highly authoritarian Soviet system than he had after introducing pluralizing reforms. It fits Yeltsin much better. Some of those who worked with him have said 'Power is Yeltsin's ideology'. One who worked with Gorbachev, rather than Yeltsin, made the same point more charitably: 'Yeltsin's main political strength is his unfailing instinct for power.'[146]

While Yeltsin, for reasons of maximization of his individual power, acted in ways that made the disintegration of the Soviet state much more likely, Gorbachev played an unintended role in the process. It is highly unlikely that the Soviet state would have broken apart if (*a*) the liberalization and democratization of the system had *not* been undertaken; (*b*) the countries of Eastern Europe had *not* been allowed to gain their independence; and (*c*) if the use of a high level of sustained force against any secession-seeking republic had *not* been eschewed, although in the absence of (*a*) and (*b*) it is unlikely

---

[146] Pavel Palazchenko, *My Years with Gorbachev and Shevardnadze* (Pennsylvania State University Press, University Park, PA, 1997), p. 372.

that (c) would even have needed to be put into effect. It would have been well understood, as it was from Khrushchev's time to Chernenko's (not to speak of the Stalin era), that open nationalism would mean arrest and imprisonment, or worse. The readiness of all Soviet leaders before Gorbachev to use whatever level of force might be necessary to combat any manifestation of separatist sentiments had been enough to ensure that expectations of change were not aroused. Those, however, who wish to blame Gorbachev for the breakup of the Soviet Union should be clear what they are blaming him for: it is for embarking on the liberalization and subsequent democratization of the system and for eschewing bloodshed either in Eastern Europe or in the Soviet Union itself.

THE AUGUST 1991 COUP

The attempted coup began for Gorbachev and his family on the afternoon of 18 August 1991. Some of his staff, including Chernyaev, were also kept in isolation for the duration of the attempted putsch. The delegation from the self-styled State Committee for the State of Emergency which flew to the Crimea and Gorbachev's holiday home at Foros consisted of Politburo member Oleg Shenin; Secretary of the Central Committee Oleg Baklanov; presidential chief of staff Valeriy Boldin; Army General Valentin Varennikov; and KGB General Yuriy Plekhanov. They had counted on being able to persuade Gorbachev to hand over his powers—'temporarily', they told him—to Vice-President Gennadiy Yanaev and the 'committee'. Gorbachev told them where to go, 'using the strongest language that the Russians always use in such circumstances'.[147] Varennikov, who had been in charge of the troops in Vilnius during the killings there in January 1991, later complained to the legal investigators of his case that Gorbachev's vocabulary when addressing him and other members of the delegation had included 'unparliamentary expressions'.[148]

As Gorbachev was in isolation in Foros from 18 August until the coup ended, when its organizers lost the will to continue, on 21 August, the focus of world attention was on Moscow and the building of the Russian parliament

[147] Gorbachev, *The August Coup*, p. 23.
[148] V. Stepankov and E. Lisov, *Kremlevskiy zagovor: versiya sledstviya* (Ogonek, Moscow, 1992), p. 14. Valentin Stepankov was at the time the Procurator General of Russia and Yevgeniy Lisov the Deputy Procurator General. They conducted the investigation into the coup and use many of the materials they gathered in the course of their inquiries, including the answers to questions of both the perpetrators and victims of the attempted putsch.

(at that time), the Moscow White House. At the centre of the resistance was Boris Yeltsin whose communications with the outside world had not been cut off, and Yeltsin's determination and courage in those days served him and his country well. He emerged from the putsch immensely strengthened. Gorbachev's resistance to the putschists was also crucial, for if the President of the USSR had endorsed the declaration of a state of emergency, the army and KGB might have been less divided than they were. Gorbachev's refusal to cooperate with the putschists did not, however, prevent these August days becoming almost the final nail in his political coffin. It was widely recognized—and, in retrospect, by Gorbachev himself—that he had made some very bad appointments. A majority of the leading figures in the putsch had been nominated to their posts by him.

Against that, it can be said that Gorbachev also made a number of very good appointments and that, so far as the positions of Minister of Defence and Chairmanship of the KGB were concerned, he would have found it difficult to appoint a liberal or radical reformer. That became easy only after the failure of the coup when, as already noted, Vadim Bakatin became the new (and last) head of the KGB. Indeed, if one looks not at the personalities of the putschists but at the institutional interests they represented, there is a logic to their participation in an attempt to turn the clock back. One of the main participants in the putsch was Oleg Shenin, the Politburo member in charge of the Communist Party apparatus. That apparatus had already lost much, and stood to lose more, from the process of democratization and, the apparatchiki assumed, from marketization (although, as it turned out, many party officials proved adept at gaining ownership of the state assets they formerly controlled). The coup plotters were aware, however, that by August 1991 the CPSU had become sufficiently unpopular that it was better if neither Shenin nor anyone else with a high Communist Party profile were to be an overt member of the 'State Committee'. Indeed, all the utterances of the putschists were couched in terms of patriotism and saving the Soviet state from the disintegration which, in fact, their actions helped to accelerate. Not a word was spoken about Marxism-Leninism.

The extent to which those who mounted the coup were leading representatives of threatened interests suggests that, even with different people at the head of those organizations, a similar attempt to wrest control from Gorbachev might have occurred. All the 'power ministers'—the people who felt that their hands had been tied in fighting nationalists, separatists, and radical democrats—took part in the coup. Among the members of the State Committee for the State of Emergency were the Minister of Defence, Yazov; the Minister of Internal Affairs, Pugo; the Chairman of the KGB, Kryuchkov; the head of the military-industrial complex, Baklanov; and another leading figure from military industry, Aleksandr Tizyakov. They represented interests which had been subordinated to a foreign and domestic policy that removed their privileged status within the Soviet system. The Prime Minister, Pavlov, was a member of the Committee, as was the Vice-President, Yanaev. The latter, since the putschists had announced to the world that Gorbachev (who was in robust health at the time) was too ill to carry on his duties, became acting president. Yanaev was far from being a leading member of the team, but Soviet society had changed to such a degree that some attention was paid to providing a fig leaf of constitutionalism. According to the Constitution, the Vice-President assumed the powers of the presidency when the president was incapacitated.

Notwithstanding the fact that, in many ways, it was one of Gorbachev's greatest achievements that he succeeded in staving off a coup attempt until the political system had changed sufficiently for it to be resisted and defeated, the coup meant that from that time on he and the federal centre were fatally weakened. Not only had Yeltsin become the national and international symbol of resistance to the putschists while Gorbachev was under house arrest, but immediately on his return from isolation Gorbachev misjudged the changed mood in the country. On 22 August Gorbachev, not realizing the extent to which most of the Central Committee of the CPSU had thoroughly compromised themselves during the days of the coup, unwisely mounted a defence of the party at a press conference and continued to speak of reforming it. Pavel Palazchenko, who was interpreting the press conference for the English-speaking world, thought to himself: 'This will cost him dearly.' Earlier the same day Palazchenko had said to an English-speaking colleague 'The Party is over.'[149]

Power within the space of a few days had moved to those in Russia who had taken up strong anti-Communist positions. It had also shifted still further to the republics, even though the majority of republican leaders had been prepared to knuckle down under the regime of the 'State Committee' if it had succeeded in establishing itself. In Ukraine, Leonid Kravchuk, unlike Yeltsin, had promptly caved in to the putschists and announced on television on 19 August that he was 'ready to respect and cooperate with the new "central authorities"', adding that 'What had to happen has now happened'.[150] Within a few days, however, Kravchuk was busy reinventing himself as a nationally minded 'democrat'.

Gorbachev had stood up to the pressures and strain of isolation in Foros remarkably well. His wife, Raisa, in contrast, when she heard from the BBC on

[149] Palazchenko, *My Years with Gorbachev and Shevardnadze*, p. 326.
[150] Ibid., p. 314.

their Sony transistor radio, that a delegation from the State Committee was on its way to Foros, feared that, having said that Gorbachev was seriously ill and incapacitated, they were going to turn the lie into reality. She suffered what appeared to be a stroke which caused paralysis in one arm, and for the next two years her health was impaired. In fact, the putschists, having themselves decided against using the level of violence that would permit them to prevail (at least in the short term), realized that the game was up. Kryuchkov wrote a letter to Gorbachev on 22 August begging for the putschists not to be imprisoned in view of their age and health. Could they not have a lesser penalty—for example, 'strict house arrest'? Kryuchkov says that he had heard the previous day Gorbachev's interview and asks, rhetorically, whether Gorbachev's condemnation of them was deserved. Kryuchkov underlines his next short sentence which reads: 'Unfortunately, deserved.'[151] In that same letter Kryuchkov writes: 'In general, I am very ashamed' and he finishes up by offering Gorbachev, 'as in the past' his 'deep respect'.[152]

Later all the putschists were to change their tune, and on their release from prison—they were amnestied by the State Duma in February 1994—they defended their actions and even came up with the absurd concoction that Gorbachev had not really been under house arrest at all, but was free to leave Foros at any time. A number of Gorbachev's enemies within Russia have attempted to suggest that Gorbachev was complicit in the coup. A few Western scholars, with an inclination for conspiracy theory and a reluctance to see the wood for the trees, have also preferred the testimony of proven liars to that of Gorbachev and his family and of Anatoliy Chernyaev who was at Gorbachev's side when he was held captive.[153] Boris Yeltsin added to the

---

[151] I am indebted to Mikhail Gorbachev for granting permission to me to receive a copy of the full text of Kryuchkov's letter. The original of the handwritten letter is in the Exhibition Hall of the Gorbachev Foundation. Gorbachev himself cites the most salient passages from the letter in his book, *Ponyat' perestroyku*, p. 331. The only detail omitted there is Kryuchkov's underlining.

[152] Gorbachev, *Ponyat' perestroyku*, p. 331.

[153] In an Afterward to the American edition of his book, *My Six Years with Gorbachev and Shevardnadze* (pp. 401–23), Chernyaev adds further detail to his earlier account of what happened in Foros during the coup and specifically replies to insinuations that Gorbachev might have been a participant in the conspiracy. He addresses his criticisms specifically to two authors, John B. Dunlop (and his book, *The Rise of Russia and the Fall of the Soviet Empire*, Princeton University Press, Princeton, NJ, 1993) and Amy Knight (author of *Spies without Cloaks: the KGB's Successors*, Princeton University Press, Princeton, NJ, 1996). Although Chernyaev says that the way the events of the coup are depicted in these books 'doesn't deserve serious discussion', he nevertheless answers them so effectively that one would have expected Dunlop and Knight to take note. It is surprising, then, to find these scholars making the same allegations three years after Chernyaev, the principal eyewitness to what happened at Foros (other than Gorbachev and his family), had convincingly rebutted their speculations. They make no reference to Chernyaev's response, published in the United States in 2000, in their latest articles relating to the coup. For the latter, see Amy Knight, 'The KGB, Perestroika, and the Collapse of the Soviet

speculation, celebrating his seventy-fifth birthday in February 2006—one month before Gorbachev reached the same age—by suggesting that Gorbachev knew about the preparation of the putsch. If Yeltsin had possessed such information, or if the investigation into the plot had uncovered it, one can be quite certain that he would have deployed it against Gorbachev years earlier.[154]

Chernyaev has, indeed, provided the most authoritative reply to those who have chosen to believe the revised versions of the putschists' stories.[155] He explains in detail how impossible it was for Gorbachev—or for him—to leave Foros and answers those who have given credence to the absurdity that Gorbachev was complicit with the coup plotters. Rather than waste time pondering minor inconsistencies in the recollections of those who lived out those traumatic days in August 1991, it may be more useful to address seven broader questions to those tempted to believe the later attempts at exculpation by the putschists, however little these corresponded with what they said to the prosecutors when they were interviewed individually soon after the events:

1. Throughout the spring and summer of 1991 Gorbachev devoted more time trying to reach the point at which a new Union Treaty could be signed than he did to any other issue. Why should he connive in a madcap plan to have himself reinstated as President following a pretend-coup in order to scupper the signing of that very pact between the all-Union centre and five of the republics (with others expected to sign later)?

2. If Gorbachev had wanted to declare a state of emergency in the country— it had long been urged on him, he had considered it, but always in the end rejected it—would it not have been much safer to do so while he was in full control of the federal executive in Moscow? Why would he wish to do it in such a roundabout way that he put himself at the mercy of those colleagues who blamed him for getting the country into what they regarded as a parlous condition?

3. Gorbachev had made his reputation at home and abroad as a liberalizer, a democratizer, and a peacemaker. Why should he turn his back on the most meaningful work of his life by cooperating in an action which would destroy that legacy and his honoured place in history?

Union' (pp. 67–93) and John B. Dunlop, 'The August 1991 Coup and its Impact on Soviet Politics' (pp. 94–127) of *Journal of Cold War Studies*, Vol. 5, No. 1, Winter 2003.

[154] When Yeltsin's new assertion was put to Gorbachev in an interview he gave to the newspaper, *Komsomol'skaya pravda*, Gorbachev's response was: '[He's a] liar. Write it down. A liar' (2–9 March 2006, pp. 4–5, at p. 4).

[155] *My Six Years with Gorbachev*, pp. 401–23.

4. If the premise that Gorbachev is not stupid is accepted (and it is generally agreed he is highly intelligent), could he have given credence to the notion that he would be allowed to continue as President of the Soviet Union for any longer than it took for him to be utterly discredited in the eyes of democrats in his own country and in the Western world? Could anyone reasonably believe that the majority in the Communist Party apparatus, the KGB and the military—whose dislike for Gorbachev's policies had grown into hatred as they witnessed the dismantling of the Communist system and what they perceived as the impending destruction of the Soviet state—would be happy to sustain in power the man whom they held to be, above all others, responsible for such catastrophes?

5. Given Gorbachev's utter devotion to his wife, Raisa—with whom he discussed everything that mattered to him—is it conceivable that, by play-acting, he would put her health in serious jeopardy, while permitting her to worry that his own health might be reduced to the condition the putschists said it was in?

6. Does it make sense to believe the coup plotters' retrospective stories that Gorbachev was not under house arrest but was free to return to Moscow at any time? Since they had announced to the world that he was too ill to perform his duties—and had made it clear that there would be no signing of a Union Treaty—would they have been perfectly content for Gorbachev to turn up in Moscow the next day and thus provide evidence that they were fools and liars?

7. If the putschists had believed their own later fabrications that Gorbachev was not really being held under duress on the Crimean coast, why did they not say so at the time? Why did Pugo commit suicide and Kryuchkov write a grovelling letter to Gorbachev? Given that it was already evident that the principal winner of their botched coup was Boris Yeltsin, why did they not ingratiate themselves with Yeltsin by announcing instantly that Gorbachev had been their accomplice?

Chernyaev is right that the idea that Gorbachev was complicit in the coup is too nonsensical to be taken seriously, but even the silliest of allegations can acquire a life of their own if they are not confronted.[156]

---

[156] In one respect the putschists have benefited from the passing of time. There has been in Russia a growing apathy concerning the coup and its outcome. A survey conducted by the Levada Centre in August 2006, and published on the eve of the fifteenth anniversary of the coup, found only 12 per cent of Russian citizens saying that they would now support resistance to the so-called State Committee for the State of Emergency; 13 per cent expressed support for their attempt to seize power. The majority of respondents—52 per cent—would consciously not take sides, while 23 per cent were 'don't knows'. See Oksana Yablokova, '15 Years On, Coup is a Dim Memory', *Moscow Times*, 18 August 2006.

GORBACHEV AND PERESTROIKA IN RETROSPECTIVE

Gorbachev's place in history will depend on where it is written, when it is written, and who writes it. The extent to which he is regarded as a success or a failure will long remain a matter of controversy. There seems no doubt, though, that both in Russia and outside he will be regarded as a figure of decisive importance, regardless of whether his activities are viewed positively or highly negatively. Even those who have most scathingly condemned him in Russia accord huge significance to the personal role he played. Thus, the former KGB Chairman Kryuchkov has said that Gorbachev's 'secret striving to destroy the Communist Party of the Soviet Union was crowned with success because at the head of the party stood a traitor and, along with him, a row of his associates who were engaged in that treacherous cause'.[157] Those who mounted the August coup, in their subsequent recollections, hold Gorbachev—much more than anyone else—responsible for the dismantling of the Soviet system and the disintegration of the Soviet state. They generally fail to distinguish clearly between the one and the other.

Russian and Western Public Opinion

In Russia the evaluation of Gorbachev has changed greatly over time. In a survey conducted by the most professional public opinion poll organization in the Soviet Union in December 1989, when respondents were asked to name the ten greatest people of all times and nations, Gorbachev (proposed by 22.6 per cent) came as high as fourth in this ranking of the 'all-time greats'. Above him were only Lenin (68 per cent), Karl Marx (36 per cent) and Peter the Great (just under 32 per cent).[158] Gorbachev's stock fell rapidly in the tumultuous years of 1990–1 and further in the post-Soviet period when the Yeltsin regime's unpopularity harmed the reputation also of the initiator of perestroika. People's satisfaction or dissatisfaction with their current state of affairs colours their assessments of the past. For example, the Brezhnev era, which was held in low esteem during the perestroika years, had by early in the new millennium become the period of twentieth-century Russian history viewed more favourably than any other.[159] Between 1994 and 1999 the proportion of Russian citizens positively assessing the Stalin era rose from

[157] Vladimir Kryuchkov, *Lichnoe delo* (Olimp, Moscow, 1996), vol. 2, p. 360.

[158] *Obshchestvennoe mnenie v tsifrakh* (VTsIOM, Moscow), No. 2 (9), January 1990, p. 6.

[159] Boris Dubin, 'Litso epokhi: Brezhnevskiy period v stolknovenii razlichnykh otsenok', in *Monitoring obshchestvennogo mneniya*, No. 3 (65), May–June 2003, pp. 25–32, at p. 25.

18 per cent to 26 per cent, while positive evaluations of the perestroika period fell from 16 per cent to 9 per cent.[160] This reflected growing disillusionment with what had happened in post-Soviet Russia—with perestroika taking the blame for setting that process in motion—rather than any startlingly new revelations about either the Stalin or Gorbachev eras.

In the year 2000, the VTsIOM asked a representative sample of citizens of Russia the question: 'Which politician, of all who have led our state in the 20th century, would you name as the most outstanding?' Although a number of surveys suggest that a majority of Russians prefer, in principle, democratic to authoritarian rule,[161] the answers to this question sit rather oddly with that preference. The first five preferred leaders in the list were authoritarian or (in *at least* the case of Stalin) totalitarian. Stalin topped the poll (with 19 per cent), followed by Lenin (16 per cent). Gorbachev was in sixth place, with 7 per cent of the population naming him as the most outstanding of the twentieth-century leaders of Russia.[162] (However, among respondents with higher education, Gorbachev's support equals Stalin's and is only one percentage point behind Lenin.[163]) To the extent that the results of this survey indicate, to say the least, an ambivalent attitude to democracy, that should *not* be interpreted—as such data sometimes are—in terms of an innate authoritarianism of Russians, but rather as a reflection of the fact that political cultures are the product of concrete historical experience. Democratic values become strongly internalized through successful experience of democratic political systems.[164] Russia has never had a fully fledged democracy and the Yeltsin regime which claimed to be democratic (and was misleadingly endorsed as such by many Western governments, scholars and journalists) was a bitter

[160] Dubin, 'Stalin i drugie. Figury vysshey vlasti v obshchestvennom mnenii sovremennoy Rossii', *Monitoring obshchestvennogo mneniya*, No. 1 (63), January–February 2003, pp. 13–25, at p. 21.

[161] See, for example, Timothy J. Colton and Michael McFaul, 'Are Russians Undemocratic?', *Post-Soviet Affairs*, Vol. 18, No. 2, April–June 2002, pp. 91–121.

[162] Boris Dubin, 'Stalin i drugie. Figury vyshchey vlasti v obshchestvennom mnenii sovremennoy Rossii', *Monitoring obshchestvennogo mneniya*, No. 2 (64), March–April 2003, pp. 26–40, at p. 34. In third place was Andropov (11 per cent) with Nicholas II and Brezhnev tying for fourth spot (9 per cent). Trailing behind Gorbachev were Yeltsin (4 per cent) and Khrushchev (3 per cent).

[163] Ibid. 15 per cent of respondents with higher education chose Lenin as the most outstanding leader of the century, 14 per cent each named Gorbachev and Stalin. Higher education was also a positive factor for Yeltsin, raising his support from 4 to 7 per cent.

[164] There is a vast literature on this topic. On Russian political culture, see Archie Brown, 'Cultural Change and Continuity in the Transition from Communism: The Russian Case', in Lawrence E. Harrison and Peter L. Berger (eds.), *Developing Cultures: Case Studies* (Routledge, New York, 2006), pp. 387–405; Stephen Whitefield (ed.), *Political Culture and Post-Communism* (Palgrave Macmillan, Basingstoke, 2005); and Lukin, *The Political Culture of the Russian 'Democrats'*.

disappointment to the majority of those who in 1991 had voted for Boris Yeltsin, making him the first popularly elected leader in Russian history. A VTsIOM survey of 1999 found only 9 per cent of respondents in Russia naming the perestroika period as more good than bad and 61 per cent saying the opposite. The Yeltsin period, however, fared worse—5 per cent positive and 72 per cent negative.[165]

Many surveys have suggested that Gorbachev and perestroika are blamed, above all, for the breakup of the Soviet Union.[166] As recently as 2005 a professionally conducted poll found that 66 per cent of Russians regretted the dissolution of the USSR, as against 23 per cent with no regrets. On the question as to whether the breakup was inevitable or could have been avoided, 34 per cent held it to be ineluctable and 57 per cent thought it was avoidable.[167]

As the serious survey data show, Gorbachev's standing with the people of his country was high throughout the greater part of his time in power. It has fallen drastically since then, but is by no means so negligible as is often suggested. In the West Gorbachev's standing remains extremely high. A Harris poll in 2006 found that '59 per cent of respondents in the European Union still consider Mikhail Gorbachev the best Soviet/Russian leader in the past 20 years'. Doubtless, the answer would have been no less positive had the question referred to the last hundred years, but the comparison was confined to Gorbachev, Yeltsin (named by 4 per cent of respondents) and Putin (12 per cent).[168] It remains to be seen whether Gorbachev's reputation will ever reach the heights in Russia that it retains in the rest of Europe and beyond. However, it is likely that it will, at any rate, rise in the Russia of future

---

[165] Dubin, 'Stalin i drugie', No. 1 (63), January–February 2003, pp. 13–25, at p. 21. The Brezhnev years topped the poll, with 51 per cent saying they were more good than bad and only 10 per cent saying more bad than good.

[166] Moreover, in a VTsIOM survey of May 2002, when respondents were asked to say when 'Russia lost its role as a great power', 51 per cent named the Gorbachev era and 32 per cent the Yeltsin years. (The Brezhnev era was named in this context by 5 per cent of respondents.) See Boris Dubin, 'Stalin i drugie', *Monitoring obshchestvennogo mneniya*, No. 2 (64), March–April 2003, pp. 26–40, at p. 26.

[167] VTsIOM Press-vypusk No. 363, Moscow, 21 December 2005, pp. 1–2. Only in the youngest age group was there a statistically insignificant majority who did not regret the breakup of the Soviet Union (39 per cent as against 38 per cent of 18- to 24-year-olds), although the most opposed (80 per cent of the 60 and over) were also the most fatalistic. Whereas a majority of the youngest group (57 per cent) believed that it had been possible to avoid the dissolution of the Soviet Union, 70 per cent of the oldest age group, though they regretted the outcome most, regarded it as inevitable. It should be noted that VTsIOM since 2003 has no longer been headed by Yuriy Levada, the doyen of Russian opinion-pollsters. He now has his own (still highly professional) Levada Analytical Centre.

[168] www.wps.ru, 18 August 2006 (reported in Johnson's Russia List, 2006, No. 187, 18 August 2006).

generations. Whether or not Russia develops into a stable democracy or reverts to authoritarian rule—and I am optimistic enough to believe that the former is more likely in the medium term—perestroika should emerge more clearly from the shadow of the decade which followed.

A SUMMING-UP

How, then, should we sum up Gorbachev's successes and failures? Not making the transition from a command economy to an essentially market economy was a major failure. There were many extenuating circumstances and cross-pressures, but this must count as the main strategic deficiency of perestroika. It was an area which Gorbachev left for much of the time primarily in the hands of the Chairman of the Council of Ministers, Nikolay Ryzhkov, but bolder marketizing reform was required (though not the sell-off of Russia's natural resources to predetermined buyers which followed in the Yeltsin era). Gorbachev was as unlucky as Vladimir Putin has been lucky with the price of oil. The price was falling during the second half of the 1980s, in sharp contrast with what has happened since 2000. But that was only a relatively small part of the problem. As I noted in Chapter 7, much more fundamental was the contradiction and tension between trying to get the existing economic system to work better and moving to a system based on different principles.

The second major failure was Gorbachev's inability to stem the separatist tide. In many ways, the dissolution of the USSR was a logical outcome of Gorbachev's break with the past in allowing the countries of Eastern Europe to become free and independent. And for thwarting his efforts to hold together a smaller Union on a voluntary basis, Boris Yeltsin bears a large responsibility. The Russian writer, Vladimir Voynovich, wrote in 2006: 'Gorbachev is a historic individual. He played an enormous role. It is said that he destroyed the Soviet Union. For that I am personally prepared to put up a statue to him.'[169] If the word 'system' had been substituted for 'Union', Gorbachev would, doubtless, have been happy to accept the compliment. But in Gorbachev's own terms, the breakup of the Soviet Union represented a failure.

Other tactical, rather than strategic, failures have been discussed in detail in this volume. They included the making of bad appointments (as well as some good ones) to senior positions, the decision to take the short-cut to the Presidency of the Soviet Union offered by election through the Congress of

---

[169] *Nezavisimaya gazeta*, 2 March 2006, Ex Libris section, p. 1.

People's Deputies rather than by the people as a whole, and the failure to take the chance of overtly splitting the Communist Party. To have done so would have been risky, but the potential rewards were great. In particular, such a move would surely have had two very beneficial results. It would have given birth to a serious and competitive party system, the weakness of which has continued to be one of the great obstacles to further democratization in post-Soviet Russia. It would also have made clearer to a Russian public the distinction between 'democratic socialism' of the social democratic type and the 'socialism' of unreconstructed Communists. In the absence of the creation of a social democratic party, socialism in the consciousness of Soviet (and many post-Soviet) citizens continued to be associated with dogma, the diktat of party bosses, and queues.

Gorbachev's achievements—in the face of far stronger conservative counter-pressures than are sufficiently appreciated—have already been noted in some detail. In retrospect, as at the time, it seems to me that his substantive successes overwhelmingly dwarf the failures, though such a judgement clearly depends, in considerable measure, on the values of the observer. I conclude simply by listing ten major achievements of Gorbachev and of perestroika, as he came to understand that concept by the end of the 1980s:

- The introduction of glasnost and its development into freedom of speech and publication
- The release of dissidents from prison and exile and the resumption of rehabilitations of those unjustly repressed in the past
- Freedom of religious observation and the end of persecution of the churches
- Freedom of communication across frontiers, including freedom to travel and an end to the jamming of foreign broadcasts
- The introduction of competitive elections for a legislature with real power
- The development of civil society—a result of perestroika, *not* a precursor of it
- Progress toward a rule of law, subjecting the Communist Party to the law and moving supreme power from party to state institutions
- Replacing Leninism and dogma with a commitment to pluralism and free intellectual inquiry
- Allowing the East European countries to become independent and non-Communist
- Withdrawing Soviet troops from Afghanistan and playing a more decisive role than any other individual on either side in ending the Cold War

There was even a success amidst a failure: the dissolution of the Soviet state at the end of the perestroika period was not accompanied by civil war as in Yugoslavia. Gorbachev refused to use the kind of force that would have been necessary to restore 'order' of the sort that was being urged upon him by many in the party hierarchy, the KGB and the military.

Gorbachev sacrificed the boundless authority, the unquestioning obedience, the orchestrated public adulation, and the growing power over time which each General Secretary could rely on securing as he placed more and more of *his* people in key positions. For what? For the creation of a better society and system than that which he inherited. The democratic shortcomings of post-Soviet Russia notwithstanding, the country Gorbachev bequeathed to his successors was freer than at any time in Russian history. Even today it remains incomparably freer than Brezhnev's Soviet Union, in spite of the nostalgia of many Russian citizens for that epoch, to which distance has lent increasing enchantment. The seven years of perestroika did change the world, and for the better, although the use that has been made of the opportunities it offered falls far short of the vision of a peaceful and more equitable world of those who attempted to reconstruct the Soviet system and the international system on new foundations.

Index

Index